CONCENTRATIONARY
IMAGINARIES

New Encounters

Arts, Cultures, Concepts

Series Editor: Griselda Pollock

Conceptual Odysseys: Passages to Cultural Analysis
Ed. Griselda Pollock, 2007

The Sacred and the Feminine: Imagination and Sexual Difference
Ed. Griselda Pollock and Victoria Turvey Sauron, 2007

Bluebeard's Legacy: Death and Secrets from Bartók to Hitchcock
Ed. Griselda Pollock and Victoria Anderson, 2009

Digital and Other Virtualities: Renegotiating the Image
Ed. Antony Bryant and Griselda Pollock, 2010

Visual Politics of Psychoanalysis: Art and the Image in Post-Traumatic Cultures
Ed. Griselda Pollock, 2013

Visioning Israel-Palestine: Encounters at the Cultural Boundaries of Conflict
Ed. Gil Pasternak, 2020

New Encounters Monographs

Helen Frankenthaler: Painting History, Writing Painting
Alison Rowley, 2007

Eva Hesse: Longing, Belonging and Displacement
Vanessa Corby, 2010

Auschwitz and Afterimages: Abjection, Witnessing and Representation
Nicholas Chare, 2011

Crossmappings: On Visual Culture
Elisabeth Bronfen, 2018

Post-Traumatic Art in the City: Between War and Cultural Memory in Sarajevo and Beirut
Isabelle de le Court, 2020

Concentrationary Memories: The Politics of Representations

Concentrationary Memories: Totalitarian Terror and Cultural Resistance
Edited by Griselda Pollock and Max Silverman, 2012

Concentrationary Imaginaries: Tracing Totalitarian Violence in Popular Culture
Edited by Griselda Pollock and Max Silverman, 2015

Forthcoming

Between Holocaust Memory and Racism: Belonging and Culture in Germany
Annette Seidel-Arpachi

Voices of Art, Belonging and Resistance: In Conversation with Sutapa Biswas, Sonia Boyce, Lubaina Himid, Claudette Johnson and Ingrid Pollard
Ella S. Mills

CONCENTRATIONARY IMAGINARIES
Tracing Totalitarian Violence in Popular Culture

EDITED BY

GRISELDA POLLOCK
and
MAX SILVERMAN

BLOOMSBURY VISUAL ARTS
LONDON · NEW YORK · OXFORD · NEW DELHI · SYDNEY

BLOOMSBURY VISUAL ARTS
Bloomsbury Publishing Plc
50 Bedford Square, London, WC1B 3DP, UK
1385 Broadway, New York, NY 10018, USA
29 Earlsfort Terrace, Dublin 2, Ireland

BLOOMSBURY, BLOOMSBURY VISUAL ARTS and the Diana logo
are trademarks of Bloomsbury Publishing Plc

First published in hardback in Great Britain by I.B. Tauris 2015
This paperback edition published by Bloomsbury Visual Arts 2021

Copyright selection and editorial matter © 2015 Griselda Pollock and Max Silverman
Copyright individual chapters © 2015 Adriana Cavarero, Olivia Guaraldo, Benjamin Hannavy Cousen, Brenda Hollweg, Ian James, Aaron Kerner, Griselda Pollock, Max Silverman

Griselda Pollock and Max Silverman have asserted their right under the Copyright, Designs and Patents Act, 1988, to be identified as Editors of this work.

For legal purposes the Acknowledgements on p. xi constitute
an extension of this copyright page.

Cover design: Simon Goggin
Cover image © Alex Santos

All rights reserved. No part of this publication may be reproduced or transmitted in any form or by any means, electronic or mechanical, including photocopying, recording, or any information storage or retrieval system, without prior permission in writing from the publishers.

Bloomsbury Publishing Plc does not have any control over, or responsibility for, any third-party websites referred to or in this book. All internet addresses given in this book were correct at the time of going to press. The author and publisher regret any inconvenience caused if addresses have changed or sites have ceased to exist, but can accept no responsibility for any such changes.

A catalogue record for this book is available from the British Library.

A catalog record for this book is available from Library of Congress.

ISBN: HB: 978-1-7845-3409-7
PB: 978-1-3502-2955-6
ePDF: 978-0-8577-2544-8
eBook: 978-0-8577-3908-7

Series: New Encounters: Arts, Cultures, Contexts

Printed and bound in Great Britain

To find out more about our authors and books visit
www.bloomsbury.com and sign up for our newsletters.

CONTENTS

List of Illustrations   vii
Acknowledgements   xi

Series Editor's Preface – New Encounters: Arts, Cultures,
Concepts   xiii
   Griselda Pollock

Mini-Series Preface – Concentrationary Memories: The Politics
of Representation   xvii
   Griselda Pollock and Max Silverman

Introduction – A Concentrationary Imaginary?   1
   Griselda Pollock

PART 1: THINKING

1. Framing Horror   47
   Adriana Cavarero

2. Between Realism and Fiction: Arendt and Levi on
   Concentrationary Imaginaries   59
   Olivia Guaraldo

3. Totality, Convergence, Synchronization   81
   Ian James

PART 2: DESIRE

4. Wrap me up in Sadist Knots: Representations of Sadism – From Naziploitation to Torture Porn — 99
   Aaron Kerner

5. Redemption or Transformation: Blasphemy and the Concentrationary Imaginary in Liliana Cavani's *The Night Porter* (1974) — 121
   Griselda Pollock

PART 3: CAMP

6. Seep and Creep: The Concentrationary Imaginary in Martin Scorsese's *Shutter Island* (2010) — 163
   Benjamin Hannavy Cousen

7. Haneke and the Camps — 187
   Max Silverman

8. Spec(tac)ularizing 'Campness': *Nikita* and *La Femme Nikita* the Series — 203
   Brenda Hollweg

Notes	233
Bibliography	269
Filmography	282
Contributors	283
Index	287

LIST OF ILLUSTRATIONS

Chapter 4: Wrap me up in Sadist Knots
4.1 *Ilsa, She Wolf of the SS* (Don Edmonds, 1975). 104
4.2 Top row: *Roma, città aperta [Rome, Open City]* (Roberto Rossellini, 1945).
Middle row: *Marathon Man* (John Schlesinger, 1976).
Bottom row: *Hostel* (Eli Roth, 2005). 114

Chapter 5: Redemption or Transformation
5.1 *The Night Porter* (Cavani, 1974): The final scene – car on the bridge. 122
5.2 *The Night Porter* (Cavani, 1974): The final scene – walking on the bridge. 122
5.3 *The Night Porter* (Cavani, 1974): The final scene – dead bodies on the bridge. 122
5.4 *The Night Porter* (Cavani, 1974): Costume test of Charlotte Rampling and Dirk Bogarde in the final scene. 123
5.5 *The Night Porter* (Cavani, 1974): Vienna, 1957. 127
5.6–5.8 Liliana Cavani Interview. DVD, Anchor Bay Entertainment, 2006. 133
5.9 *The Night Porter* (Cavani, 1974): Lucia sings in the camp cabaret – the iconic image. 140
5.10 *The Night Porter* (Cavani, 1974): Max tells the Countess of 'the Biblical scene' in the camp. 140
5.11 *The Night Porter* (Cavani, 1974): Max's memory: Lucia ends her song... *Trauerigsein*. 140

5.12	*The Night Porter* (Cavani, 1974): Max's memory: Lucia anticipates her gift.	140
5.13	*The Night Porter* (Cavani, 1974): Max's memory: Lucia recoils with the decapitated head exposed between Lucia and Max.	140
5.14	*The Night Porter* (Cavani, 1974): At the opera: Max's flashback to the camp – Sexual initiation into sadomasochism: Lucia in the camp watching.	145
5.15	*The Night Porter* (Cavani, 1974): At the opera: Max's flashback to the camp – Sexual initiation into sadomasochism: Max chooses Lucia for his sex 'play'.	146
5.16	*The Night Porter* (Cavani, 1974): At the opera: Lucia at the Opera.	156
5.17	*The Night Porter* (Cavani, 1974): At the opera: Lucia becomes aware of Max and turns.	156
5.18	*The Night Porter* (Cavani, 1974): At the opera: Max stares at Lucia intently.	156
5.19	*The Night Porter* (Cavani, 1974): At the opera: Max looks on.	156
5.20	*The Night Porter* (Cavani, 1974): At the opera: Lucia rings her hands in anguish.	156
5.21	*The Night Porter* (Cavani, 1974): At the opera: Lucia's hands are bound in the camp.	156
5.22	*The Night Porter* (Cavani, 1974): At the opera: Max's flashback: Max puts his fingers into Lucia's mouth.	156

Chapter 6: Seep and Creep

6.1	*Shutter Island* (Scorsese, 2011): Flashback of Dachau using the *Arbeit Macht Frei* Gate from Auschwitz.	174
6.2	*Arbeit Macht Frei* Gate at Dachau concentration camp, photograph (Arbeit Macht Frei Dachau 8235).	176
6.3	*Shutter Island* (Scorsese, 2011): Flashbacks of prisoners at Dachau camp.	176
6.4	Margaret Bourke-White, *Survivors at Buchenwald, April 1945* (Getty Images).	177
6.5	*Schindler's List* (Spielberg, 1993): Auschwitz-Birkenau shower scene.	181
6.6	*Shutter Island* (Scorsese, 2011): Shower.	182

Chapter 7: Haneke and the Camps

7.1	*Funny Games* (Michael Haneke, 2007): Sitting room as torture chamber.	191
7.2	*Funny Games* (Michael Haneke, 2007): Camp gates.	192
7.3	*The White Ribbon* (Michael Haneke, 2009): Innocence and hell.	197
7.4	*The White Ribbon* (Michael Haneke, 2009): Even a peaceful countryside...	198

Chapter 8: Spec(tac)ularizing 'Campness': *Nikita* and *La Femme Nikita* the Series

8.1	George Stevens, *A Cattle Truck with Corpses at Dachau Concentration Camp, 2 May 1945*. George Stevens Collection, Library of Congress, Washington DC.	210
8.2	*Nikita* (Luc Besson, 1990): First day at The Centre, medium-long shot of Nikita's (Anne Parillaud) legs.	211
8.3	*Night and Fog* (*Nuit et Brouillard*, Alain Resnais, 1955): A typical Kapo room at the camp.	212
8.4	*Nikita* (Luc Besson, 1990): Nikita's recruitment room at The Centre.	212
8.5	'Disposal: two former guards placing corpses in a mass grave'. *The Liberation of Bergen-Belsen Concentration Camp, April 1945* (BU 4031). War Office Second World War Official Collection No. 5 Army and Photographic Unit, Sgt. H. Sykes. Courtesy of the Imperial War Museum.	215
8.6–8.8	*Nikita* (Luc Besson, 1990): Disposal of human bodies after failed mission.	216
8.9	*Night and Fog* (*Nuit et Brouillard*, Alain Resnais, 1955): The survivors look on.	217
8.10	*Nikita* (Luc Besson, 1990): Dead bodies in the bathtub, the agents look on.	217
8.11	John Heartfield, *As in the Middle Ages... /... so in the Third Reich* [*Wie im Mittelalter... /... so im Dritten Reich*] 1934, photo-lithograph, 1957. Courtesy of Gallery of Modern Art, Queensland and DACS.	218
8.12	*Kapò* (Gilles Pontecorvo, 1958): Last gesture of human vulnerability.	219

8.13 *La Femme Nikita* (TV series, Canadian Fireworks/
       Warner Brothers, 1997–2000): Peta Wilson as 'Nikita'.   222
8.14 *La Femme Nikita* (TV series, Canadian Fireworks/
       Warner Brothers, 1997–2000): Operations (Eugene
       Robert Glazer) overlooks Section One from The Perch.   223
8.15 *La Femme Nikita* (TV series, Canadian Fireworks/
       Warner Brothers, 1997–2000): Torture in the White
       Room.   225

ACKNOWLEDGEMENTS

This book is the product of a four-year research project, *Concentrationary Memories: The Politics of Representation* (2007–11), funded by the Arts and Humanities Research Council of England. We gratefully acknowledge its financial support for this research. We would like to thank Francesco Ventrella for unstinting administrative support during the project. We are also grateful to the many students and participants in the seminars through which this book was developed.

SERIES EDITOR'S PREFACE

NEW ENCOUNTERS

Arts, Cultures, Concepts

Griselda Pollock

How do we think about visual art these days? What is happening to art history? Is visual culture taking its place? What is the status of Cultural Studies, in itself or in relation to its possible neighbours – art, art history, visual studies? What is going on? What are the new directions? To what should we remain loyal?

NEW ENCOUNTERS: Arts, Cultures, Concepts proposes some possible ways of thinking through these questions. Firstly, the series introduces and works with the concept of the *transdisciplinary initiative*. This is not a synonym for the interdisciplinary combination that has become *de rigueur*. It is related to a second concept: research as *encounter*. Conjoined, *transdisciplinary* and *encounter* mark the interaction between ways of thinking, doing and making in the arts and humanities. Each of these modes retains distinctive features associated with their own disciplinary practices and objects: art, history, culture, film, photography and practice. Yet new knowledge is produced when these different ways of doing, making and thinking encounter each other across – and this is the third intervention – *concepts*. Concepts circulate between different intellectual or aesthetic discourses and cultures, inflecting them, sharing common questions but approaching them in distinctively articulated practices. The aim is to place these different practices in productive relation to each other, mediated by the circulation of concepts.

We stand at several crossroads at the moment in relation to the visual arts and cultures, historical and contemporary, and to theories and methods of analysis. The Centre for Cultural Analysis, Theory and History (CentreCATH) was founded as one experiment in thinking about how to maintain the momentum of the intellectual cultural revolution in the arts and humanities that characterized the last quarter of the twentieth century while adjusting to the different field of analysis created by it. We were also responding to the constantly shifting economic, political and social ground on which we precariously stand in conditions of globalization and liquid modernity dominated by neoliberal reason.

In the 1970s–90s, the necessity, or the intrusion, according to your position, was Theory: a mythic concept with a capital T that homogenized vastly different intellectual undertakings. Over those decades, research and practice in the arts and humanities were undoubtedly reconfigured by the engagement with structuralist and poststructuralist theories of the sign, the social, the text, the letter, the image, the subject, the postcolonial and, above all, difference. Old disciplines were deeply challenged and new interdisciplines – called studies – emerged to contest the long-established academic divisions of knowledge production. These changes were wrought through specific engagements with Marxist, feminist, deconstructionist, psychoanalytical, queer and postcolonial theory. Texts and authors were branded according to their theoretical alignments. Mapping produced divisions between the proliferating models. Could one be a Marxist and a feminist while drawing on psychoanalysis queerly?

A deeper split, however, emerged between those who, in general, were theoretically oriented and those who apparently did without theory: a position that the theoretically minded easily critiqued. Being positivist is, of course, also a theoretical position. It simply did not carry a novel identity associated with the intellectual shifts of the post-1968 university.

The impact of 'the theoretical turn' was creative; it has radically reshaped work in the arts and humanities in terms of what is studied (content, topics, groups, questions) and also how it is studied (theories and methods). Yet some scholars came to argue that work done under such overt theoretical rubrics was becoming tired; theory constrained the creativity of the new generation of scholars familiar, perhaps too familiar, with the legacies of the preceding intellectual revolution that can too easily be reduced to Theory 101 slogans (the author is dead, the gaze is male, the subject is split, there is nothing but text, etc.). The enormity of the initial struggles – the paradigm shifting – to be able to speak of sexual difference, subjectivity, the image, representation, sexuality, power, the gaze, postcoloniality, textuality, difference and queerness fades before a new phase of normalization in which every student seems to bandy around terms that were once, and in fact still are, challengingly difficult and provocative. Or worse. It is clear that bandying indicated that at least something of this intellectual and theoretical revolution was still – even in an etiolated form – part of public discourse.

Recent events have shown how the terms of critical thinking from feminist to postcolonial theory are not part of general discussion, even as they reappear on the media stage in the wake of new scandals or sexism and racism. Outrageous acts of sexual harassment and abuse are greeted, however, not with knowing acknowledgement of their structural place in a patriarchal culture of asymmetrical power relations but as the signs of a surprising number of 'badly behaved' individual men. Where is the sense that facing revelations of such an order necessitated a political-critical analysis rather than surprise and celebrity 'outing'?

Theory, of course, just means thinking about things, puzzling over what is going on, reflecting on the process of that puzzling and thinking. A reactive turn away from active engagement with theoretical enquiries in the arts and humanities is increasingly evident in our area of academe. It is, however, dangerous and misleading to talk of a post-theory moment, as if we can relax after so much intellectual gymnastics and once again become unthinking couch potatoes. The job of *thinking critically* is even more urgent as the issues we confront are so complex, and we now have extended means of analysis that make us appreciate even more the complexity of language, subjectivity, symbolic practices, affects and aesthetics. So how to continue the creative and critical enterprise fostered by the theoretical turn of the late twentieth century beyond the initial engagement determined by specific theoretical paradigms? How does it translate into *a practice of analysis that can be constantly productive and critically self-reflexive?*

The *New Encounters* series proposes a way to go forward with, and even beyond, the distinct theoretical paradigms by means of creating *transdisciplinary encounters* that work with *travellling concepts*. The notion of 'travelling concepts' was proposed by Mieke Bal, the leading feminist narratologist and semiotician, who launched an inclusive, interdisciplinary project of cultural analysis in the 1990s with the books *The Point of Theory: Practices of Cultural Analysis* (Amsterdam and New York: University of Amsterdam Press, 1994) and *The Practice of Cultural Analysis: Exposing Interdisciplinary Interpretation* (Stanford, CA: Stanford University Press, 1999). In founding the Amsterdam School of Cultural Analysis (ASCA), Bal turned the focus from our accumulating theoretical resources to the work – *the practice of interpretation* – we do on cultural practices, informed not only by major bodies of theory (that we still need to study and extend) but also by the concepts generated within those theories that now travel across disciplines, creating an extended field of contemporary cultural thinking. Cultural analysis is theoretically informed, critically situated, ethically oriented to 'cultural memory in the present' (Bal, 1999: 1). Cultural analysis thus works with 'travelling concepts' to produce new readings of images, texts, objects, buildings, practices, gestures and actions. This book and its companion form a mini-series within the *New Encounters* series by elaborating the political and aesthetic significance of the concept: *the concentrationary.*

MINI-SERIES PREFACE

CONCENTRATIONARY MEMORIES

The Politics of Representation

Griselda Pollock and Max Silverman

Taking a term first proposed by returning French political prisoners from the concentration camps of the Second World War, we developed the concept of *the concentrationary* in four books that we published between 2011 and 2019. For David Rousset in *L'Univers concentrationnaire* (1946) and Jean Cayrol in *Lazare parmi nous* (1950), *the concentrationary* is a way of alerting us to a critical and dangerous legacy of events and anti-political, anti-democratic processes – totalitarianism – that had such devastating effects during the twentieth century. Following the logic of these texts, we argue that, while Stalin's and Hitler's empires and the dictatorships in Latin America and apartheid South Africa may well be historical relics of the past, *the concentrationary*, with its deeper roots in colonial imperialism in Cuba and South Africa, remains a constant menace to our polities, lives and lifeworlds in the present as it lives on in 'everyday life'. While an actual physical camp can be visible (or could be, were it not placed in hidden or out-of-the-way places), *the concentrationary* points to what is not always physically visible but is nevertheless present, and whose corrosive effects are embedded within our daily lives and normal social processes. Concentrationary memory, therefore, alerts us to the way we can be stripped of our humanity not only by the inhuman practices carried out in concentration camps but also through the familiar practices and structures that exist within and undermine 'democratic society'. We therefore need to see beyond the surface to perceive horror in the everyday and to recognize and challenge *the concentrationary* today.

The overarching project *Concentrationary Memories and the Politics of Representation* has two parts. First, as a research project, it contributes to cultural memory studies by identifying a specific configuration of threats that are not confined to their historical time and place of origin and continuously stalk our uncertain struggles to sustain and realize full democracy. Second, the term invokes an aesthetic of resistance. Concentrationary art, whether it be in the form of artworks, films or texts, both testify to the terror of *the concentrationary* and strive to warn us of its continuous presence through what Benjamin Hannavy Cousen, one of the authors of the texts in these edited collections, defines as a contamination, seeping and creeping into popular culture in ways that accommodate us to its ethos without our fully recognizing its presence. Thus, concentrationary memory is not a reflective memory. It is, instead, an active call to become conscious of the manner in which the assault on the human condition that was experimentally realized in the totalitarianisms of the twentieth century have infiltrated our imaginations and our political and cultural practices. But why this term, and what makes it distinct from Holocaust memory?

Holocaust memory and the concentrationary universe

Only by the beginning of the twenty-first century had the Holocaust been firmly established in cultural memory with both national and international memorial days, dedicated memorial museums, explorations in art, literature and cinema and a place, if fragile, in education. We felt, however, that 'the Holocaust' had become an overarching term for different, though interconnected, histories. Hence, one of the major aims of our *Concentrationary Memories* project was to disentangle certain aspects of the dire histories of the twentieth century that had been folded into the Holocaust. Let us clarify this statement.

The commemoration of state-sponsored, industrial murder and the intended annihilation of two European minorities, the Jewish and Roma communities, must, of course, never be forgotten and the losses and suffering should be perpetually mourned. Initially, mass murder was carried out by shooting the inhabitants of the small villages and towns with Jewish populations in those parts of the Soviet Union invaded and controlled by the army of the Third Reich, until the Battle of Stalingrad turned the tide and the Red Army drove the invaders back. A total of 1.5 million Jewish men, women and children were shot in these horrifying massacres. Mass murder was industrialized in December 1941, initially in Chelmno with the use of carbon monoxide poisoning of Jewish populations in occupied Poland. Three other small and dedicated extermination sites were specially constructed in 1942: Sobibor, Belzec and Treblinka. These were hardly camps at all since almost no one survived more than a few hours after their arrival, save a few selected and forced to assist in the preparation and clearing up of the killing process carried out exclusively by the SS. The victims of these three *Operation Reinhard* installations were the Polish Jewish communities that had been initially ghettoized in major cities and towns. These camps were secret and, once the Russians began to drive the German army back, they were dismantled and all evidence of their existence was effaced where possible by the end of 1943. Only a handful of witnesses – participants in Jewish uprisings at these sites or those who miraculously survived the executions by the SS when the camps were dismantled – survived to testify to what happened in these places. Madjanek, a forced labour camp, was added to the killing centres in March 1942, specifically to destroy the Jewish populations of the cities of Lvov, Krakow, Warsaw and Zamosc.

In the summer of 1942, Himmler oversaw the building of gas chambers and crematoria on a massive scale at a site 3.5 kilometres from the barrack camp at Auschwitz 1. Auschwitz 2 at Birkenau then became the major mass killing centre for European Jewish communities deported from Western Europe – Germany, France, Belgium and Greece. As late as spring 1944, 450,000 Jewish people from Hungary were murdered there in two months. Auschwitz 2-Birkenau was largely destroyed by the retreating Germans, and it was the Red Army that entered Auschwitz 1 and 3 (Monowitz) in January 1945 to find 7,500 abandoned and starving prisoners, many of whom, like Primo Levi, had been selected for forced labour at Auschwitz Monowitz, a rubber factory.

This detailed historical information about the process of racial extermination allows us to distinguish the genocidal project of the Holocaust more clearly from the concentrationary universe, whose real actualization ran across Germany and sites in its occupied territories such as France and the Netherlands. Few Western Europeans or their troops ever set foot in Poland, and none witnessed these killing centres at Auschwitz or the abandoned Operation Reinhard extermination camps. The horrific images that circulated in the Western press and in specially created films made by British and American troops recorded not the genocidal project but the vast network of concentration camps, created as a structural instrument of the totalitarian system that the Third Reich installed in Germany and its huge territorial empire. The images of staggering prisoners in tattered rags and striped jackets, emaciated and often desperately ill with typhus and other diseases, barely alive in unspeakable conditions of dirt and lice-carried infection, are images of *the concentrationary*, not the exterminatory.

The majority of the inmates of these concentration camps, either disowned by or who resisted the Third Reich domestically or in occupied territories, were political resistance fighters. In late 1944 and early 1945 some Jewish prisoners in Auschwitz and its 140 sub-labour camps were force marched from Poland to the huge concentration camps in Germany that had been established in the 1930s for dissidents, communists, queer people, Jehovah's Witnesses and the political resistance fighters from conquered lands. Although people died in numbers from the harsh and brutal conditions of the SS-run concentration camps, they were not there to die but to suffer and live as long as their bodies and minds could endure the conditions maliciously inflicted on them. Systematic cruelty and physical pain were at the core of this regime, which also used, and sold, these prisoners for slave labour to major industrial operations. By 1945, there were over ten thousand major concentration and slave labour camps across Germany, visibly present to, and serviced by, the towns outside of which they were located, for example, Dora Mittlebau and Buchenwald near Weimar, Dachau, a suburb of Munich; Sachsenhausen and Ravensbrück near Berlin; Bergen-Belsen north of Hanover; Neuengamme near Hamburg; and Mauthausen 12 kilometres east of the Austrian city of Linz. These are the names that evoked horror amongst the British and American Allies because these were the camps they saw as they liberated Western Europe. Researchers now believe that, between 1933 and 1945, there were a total of 42,500 camps, including at least 980 concentration camps, as well as their sub-camps, brothels, prisoner of war camps and over 30,000 slave labour camps.

In these concentration camps, human life was eviscerated from the living human being. Here, victims were systematically dehumanized, not exterminated (even though many would die). By folding *the concentrationary* into the Holocaust, however, we render ourselves less alert to the potential recurrence of similar dehumanizing practices, let alone the persistence of the concentrationary plague and the totalitarian threat.

Concentrationary memories and imaginaries

The project *Concentrationary Memories and the Politics of Representation* originated as a collaborative research project in transdisciplinary cultural analysis, funded by the Arts and Humanities Research Council of England. The two volumes that make up this *New Encounters* (Bloomsbury) mini-series – *Concentrationary Memories* and *Concentrationary Imaginaries* – are complemented by two other volumes, *Concentrationary Cinema* (Berghahn, 2011) and *Concentrationary Art* (Berghahn, 2019). The aim of the quartet is to re-engage with the relations between aesthetics and politics in the aftermath of the Second World War when the images of the opened concentration camps of Germany and the testimony of their largely political prisoner survivors dominated the world's horrified responses to what were then termed 'Nazi atrocities' but which were limited to the concentrationary system.

As we mention above, the term *concentrationary* was coined by the writer David Rousset, a French political deportee who survived imprisonment in Neuengamme and Buchenwald. On his return, Rousset wrote a 'political' analysis of, and a novel about, the world of 'the concentrationary universe', a term adopted by the French Surrealist poet and resistance fighter Jean Cayrol, another returning deportee from Mauthausen. After 1945, political theorist Hannah Arendt drew on Rousset and other political analyses of the nature and effects of the concentration camp as a systematic use of terror that not only dehumanized its inmates but also infected and politically eviscerated the entire society in which it operated. In 1951, Arendt published her compendious analysis of the historical conditions for, and the anatomy of the 'evil' enacted in, the concentrationary universe. Her book was not an ethical project but a political analysis of what she defined as the pursuit of total domination – totalitarianism. For Arendt, totalitarianism has its roots in colonialism and imperialism and their racisms. Totalitarianism had taken form in both Nazi Germany and Stalin's Soviet Union and of which the concentration camps were the core institution of terror. At this time the political rather than the racial deportee was the major symbol of victimhood, and Buchenwald was more infamous than Auschwitz. Arendt suggested that this moment marked a turning point in history as it unleashed the novel reality of total domination and ushered in the epoch in which, in Rousset's words subsequently adopted by Arendt, 'everything is possible'.[1]

By returning to this moment and these analyses, we wanted to bring back into focus a process that we felt had been eclipsed with the later, and vitally important, recognition of the racially targeted genocide at the heart of Nazism's atrocities that we know as the Holocaust. Our re-engagement with *the concentrationary* serves as a prism through which to examine both the relations between the politics of total domination and its systematic destruction of the human and the history of aesthetic practices as a mode of resistance, warning and refashioned anti-totalitarian hope.

Our aim has been to consider cultural responses not, then, to the specific event we now know as the Holocaust but to the larger context within which the genocide occurred, namely totalitarian terror. We also wanted to track the initial forms of response to the system of terror of which the camp was the primary instrument, both for its inmates and for the surrounding society its existence terrorized. In the first part of our project, we devoted eighteen months to the study of one film, *Night and Fog* (*Nuit et brouillard*), made in France in 1955 by Alain Resnais in collaboration with Jean Cayrol, French poet and novelist, and the German socialist composer Hanns Eisler.[2] This film was made specifically as a commemorative study of the experience of political deportation and internment in concentration camps in Germany. In the process of research for the film, however, a greater appreciation of the interweaving of political terror (*the concentrationary* – *Konzentrationslager*) and racialized genocide (the exterminatory – *Vernichtungslager*) emerged to produce a work that has since been criticized for insufficiently exposing the genocide of the Jewish and Romany peoples. Our argument resists this simplification and seeks to read its aesthetic structure as the attempt to produce a different kind of memory, one whose purpose is to agitate the present and warn us of the continuing threat – not of genocide, but of the totalitarian.

The concept of *the concentrationary*, as we have formulated it, has four aspects. The first is the **concentrationary universe** itself, that is, Rousset's understanding of the political/industrial/military complex which underpins totalitarian rule and situates those inside and beyond the camp in a concentrationary condition. The second, **concentrationary art**, is the term created by Cayrol to define art that will register the novelty of the concentrationary-infected world and the changed condition of the human subject in the wake of the camps and the system they represented. This new art will be equipped to perceive and challenge the continued presence of *the concentrationary* and its reappearance in the future in our everyday world, whose normality has been reconfigured by the concentrationary event. The third term, **concentrationary memories**, extends Resnais and Cayrol's understanding of the persistence of the concentrationary universe in post-war everyday life and registers the imperative for cultural responses to its continued threat in different contexts. The fourth term, **concentrationary imaginaries**, is the verso of this active vigilance. It refers to the presence of unprocessed and unacknowledged seepage of aspects of the concentrationary universe and totalitarian mentality into everyday popular culture where, unnoticed, these forms have become normalized.

Concentrationary Memories extends the enquiry into art's response to the concentrationary universe. It assumes that what Cayrol termed 'the concentrationary disease' ('la peste concentrationnaire'), which is mentioned at the end of *Night and Fog*, was not simply confined to Nazi Germany and destroyed along with the fall of the Third Reich. It infects and embraces other sites and times, colonialism and Stalinism being perhaps the two most obvious examples but also liberal, capitalist, Western democratic society more generally. It also assumes that, like Resnais and Cayrol in *Night and Fog*, other artists have created forms of concentrationary art by locating and resisting radical terror. In contrast to the ethical imperative of testimonial works on the Holocaust and related questions of the representability of the event, we argue that concentrationary art and concentrationary memory are more concerned with a political aesthetic of both representing – critically making it discernible and knowable – and resisting the radical presence in our midst of the concentrationary universe and its system of total domination, as well as its less obvious manifestations.

By seeking to conjugate the diagnosis of the 'evil' of totalitarianism with modes of critical-aesthetic resistance, *Concentrationary Memories* has to negotiate Theodor Adorno's paradoxical proposition that, although it is barbarity to offer the solace of any aesthetic artefacts to the cultures that 'beat people until the bones break in their bodies' (here Adorno is quoting Sartre), it is nevertheless only in art that the enormity of such suffering can find any voice. Our book seeks to supplement Adorno's perspective with a specific focus on the politics of representational practices. It includes chapters which, first, re-examine the responses by writers, poets, filmmakers and others involved in the cultural production of memories of the horror of totalitarianism and, second, analyse the works of those who sought to find forms/languages/image systems through which to make sense of and resist this new state in which 'human beings as human beings become superfluous'.[3] It is a transdisciplinary collection bringing together studies by philosophers, political theorists, literary critics, art historians, film historians and analysts, cultural theorists and artists engaged in research in the field of terror and resistance.

The partner book in this mini-series, *Concentrationary Imaginaries*, is based on the fourth aspect of the concept of *the concentrationary*. A concentrationary imaginary is the possible realization of Resnais and Cayrol's worst fear, namely that instead of being able to recognize, challenge and resist the continued presence of the concentrationary universe in our midst, our culture has become saturated with its devices and strategies to such an extent that we are largely unaware and ignorant of its presence. In *Concentrationary Imaginaries* we are, therefore, asking whether a failure of *concentrationary memory* to agitate the present (which it achieved by making us aware of a past that has never passed) could produce an insinuation of the totalitarian in the realm of the cultural imaginary where it continues to shape us and our imaginations in its violent, violating image.

Thus, *Concentrationary Imaginaries* asks: can a concentrationary legacy (revealed and resisted by *Concentrationary Memories*) be located in postmodern popular culture in the form of an unconscious and politically unprocessed *concentrationary imaginary*? Informed by but extending the work of Giorgio Agamben and Paul Virilio, who suggest that the camp and war are now the matrices of post-war society, the book considers the cultural forms and subjectivities that are symptomatic of a concentrationary imaginary. What would be its indices, locations, tropes and affects? How shall we know it given its slow erosion of our defences by familiarization and its entertaining and often spectacular manifestations? The use of the term 'imaginary' in the cultural field refers to two elements. The first is a repertoire of images, tropes and formulae that are, often unconsciously or spontaneously, drawn upon in representation. The second is the manner in which a cultural apparatus, relying on processes of identification and misrecognition to lure us as participant spectators and ideologically interpellated readers, structures subjectivity through the iterative operation of fantasy.

Refashioned by changing times, is *the concentrationary* now an unmarked presence of an egregious historical event that we should remember to condemn, not use to entertain? Has *the concentrationary* seeped from the political real into culture, from politics to entertainment? Unhinged from its specific historical origins in Nazi camps and Stalinist gulags, does *the concentrationary* shape the contemporary cultural imaginary like a political unconscious, normalizing narratives of military superpowers enslaving and annihilating their subjected and dispensable others, and accustoming us to unspeakable violence and suffering where arbitrary extinction is no longer murder but wasting, or, worse, just business? Is our cinematic culture of spectacular violence the iterating imprint on our cultural unconscious of what we were once shown in order to shock and warn us that this must never happen again? Is there a 'concentrationary imaginary' in popular cultural forms which exhibits an unconscious assimilation of totalitarian modes of violence that deprive us of our humanity by desensitizing us to violence itself and to the casual killing of others? Does this imaginary operate through fantasies of total domination via our specular identification as consumers of films, games and other cultural practices?

These are difficult questions that we wish to raise as a way of plotting a speculative field of enquiry which has no clear signposts. As an imaginary, *the concentrationary* does not announce itself as such but, nevertheless, may inhabit other spaces. Is it, though, too labile and non-specific? Does the concept merely colonize other existing sites such as critiques of colonialism and racism? How is it different from, yet related to, the colonial imaginary, the imaginaries of current urban cultures, of crime and the city, or political wars on terror, and so forth? What are the signs of 'concentrationariness' that probably piggyback on other formations for which we already have names and critiques? The book addresses these questions by exploring the *concentrationary imaginary* within the wider representation of violence, terror, criminality and dehumanization. It asks whether a cultural politics of resistance to this imaginary is possible. Is the very act of identifying such a possibility as the *concentrationary imaginary* already a resistance that may reveal contradictions within it? Both books investigate the legacies of *the concentrationary* in diverse forms of contemporary culture, from literature to cinema and video games, and explore the notion of cultural resistance to the threat they present.

New concentrationary forms

These books were conceived and written after 9/11 when a range of new threats and uncertainties in the world, newly identified forms of do-it-yourself totalitarianism, were doing the twenty-first-century job of the twentieth-century forms of *concentrationary* practice. For these new concentrationary forms have not been undertaken by an imperial state apparatus such as Stalin's Soviet Union or Hitler's Third Reich. Rogue militia groups leading popular movements, equally fired with the ambition to change entire worlds in the name of the religious-political ideologies they proclaimed as universally applicable, took on their 'enemies' and even established briefly a 'state' in Syria/Iraq before being militarily defeated. They are biding their time now for another attempt.

We have heard about new 'education' camps for the one million Uyghur Muslims in Xinjiang province. We have watched the aggressive policies of the Trump administration (2016–20) against immigrants from Latin America which created camps in which children, separated from their parents, were incarcerated, many left isolated because their parents were deported. Documentation on their identities and relations are missing. We have witnessed resistance movements in defence of legal agreements and have seen even limited democratic rights being violently repressed. After the election of President Trump in 2016 and the dawning realization of the nature of his populist movement, people anxiously began to read Hannah Arendt's *The Origins of Totalitarianism* once again (or, indeed, for the first time). It even raced to the top of the bestseller list. Other articles and books also appeared, warning us of the fragility of democracy. Economic forces of neoliberal capitalism traverse the world without political regulation or any form of existing democratic oversight capable of matching its electronic reach and real global scale. Some writers argued that democracy is being eroded from within. In a thoughtful article published on 1 December 2016 in the *London Review of Books*, political theorist David Runciman looked back to the 1920s and 1930s to examine the question on everyone's mind in that year: 'Is this how democracy ends?' He even asked if we might have to consider the United States a failed state:

> They want to know what happens when authoritarians win elections and democracy morphs into something else. The demagogue who promised to kill terrorists along with their families is moving his own family into the presidential palace. Even before he has taken up occupation his children are being seeded into positions of power. There he is on television, shiny and golden, his wife beside him and three of his children lined up behind, ready to take up what daddy has to offer. Here he is back on Twitter, unshackled by victory, rounding on his opponents in

the free press. His ten-year-old son is still too young to join in, but he was by his father's side on election night, looking hardly less bemused than the rest of us, as Trump delivered his notably conciliatory victory speech. Words of conciliation followed by the ruthless personal appropriation of the machinery of government, children in tow. Isn't this how democracy ends?[4]

After reviewing the histories of authoritarian revolutions during the twentieth century, Runciman concludes that we must not immediately compare events in Europe (Brexit and populist and right-wing movements) and Trump's election with the historical past. We should, however, be anxious because of what we know and what is new:

> Under these conditions, the likeliest response is for the grown-ups in the room to hunker down, waiting for the storm to pass. While they do, politics atrophies and necessary change is put off by the overriding imperative of avoiding systemic collapse. The understandable desire to keep the tanks off the streets and the cashpoints open gets in the way of tackling the long-term threats we face. Fake disruption followed by institutional paralysis, and all the while the real dangers continue to mount. Ultimately, that is how democracy ends.[5]

Early in 2018, political journalists Steven Levitsky and Daniel Ziblatt published a bestseller titled *How Democracies Die*. They argue that the passage from democracy to dictatorship does not happen today by military coups, martial law or suspended constitutions. The principal instrument that once ensured democracy – the ballot box – can also be the location. The imperceptible but dangerous erosion of the democratic through populist incitements over social media is happening, according to these authors, through the processes that reverse the underlying safeguards of traditionally understood democratic political space. We witness extreme polarization of political positions, ever more widespread financial instrumentalization of the political parties by powerful and narrow economic interests, and intentional aggravation of existing divisions, conflicts and inequalities through demagoguery, or more subtle processes of algorithmic manipulation of social media feeds and false news or misuse of executive power to stack the benches of the courts. For Levitsky and Ziblatt, these amount to the erosion of what they name the 'guard rails' of a democratic system: the independence of the judiciary, the critical responsibility and freedom of a reliable press, and the mutual acceptance of and respect for the legitimacy of the opposition's political and other opinions. These form procedural processes that are being replaced by a vicious antagonism between opposing parties and their supporters beyond party affiliation, seeking at any cost to ensure their own control of, or access to, power. This involves delegitimization of opposing versions of reality as untrue as opposed to being respected as differently conceived political options.

The authors argue that we have seen and know well how democracy can be overthrown by coups, wars and forced regime change. But, they ask, is democracy today dying by stealth, even though the apparent institutions of democracy – elections, the courts, the free press – if not acting in egalitarian and respectful forbearance of difference, are all in place:

> The electoral road to breakdown is dangerously deceptive. With a classic coup d'état, as in Pinochet's Chile, the death of a democracy is immediate and evident to all. The presidential palace burns. The president is killed, imprisoned, or shipped off into exile. The constitution is suspended or scrapped. On the electoral road, none of these things happen. There are no tanks in the streets. Constitutions and other nominally democratic institutions remain in place. People still vote. Elected autocrats maintain a veneer of democracy while eviscerating its substance.

Reading these books and articles, heavy with anxious warnings about real and present dangers to democracies, those of us involved in the historical study of *the concentrationary* through the prism of Arendt's postwar political theses and the warnings by Rousset, Cayrol and others of the persistence of the *concentrationary plague* in unlikely places, continuously scan current cultural forms to identify the concentrationary imaginary in fostering and normalizing this destruction of democracy from within. Popular culture is, at times, the site of shifting alerts as events are rapidly registered in our political dramas and series. For instance, the writers of *Homeland* 8, who had clearly anticipated a Hillary Clinton victory in 2016, had to rapidly rewrite their forthcoming episodes, with a woman president challenged by a populist demagogue with a huge social media following, using an independent media channel and funding a conspiratorial use of bots to shape hearts and minds in an alliance with armed militias, and an attempted assassination conceived by members of the opposing political establishment. Following the November 2020 election in the United States, we have witnessed a peaceful transfer of power to a Democrat president. This election has, however, left almost half the US population disaffected, some of whom mounted a paramilitary assault on the Capitol Building on 6 January 2020 in order to stop the ratification of the recent election. It is as yet unclear how this will play out while we watch and wonder across many parts of the world.

There are, indeed, real camps, in our own countries, containing refugees and asylum seekers across many parts of Europe. Although the conditions in these camps may not be as ghastly as the terrorizing concentration camps of the Third Reich in Europe between 1933 and 1945, or the gulags of the Soviet Union after 1931, or other concentrationary sites, such as the stadia or secret prison camps in which young Chileans and Argentinians were casually murdered by their own government in the so-called dirty war or under Pinochet's regime, nevertheless they too deprive desperate people of their right to live in safety and even their right to have rights. Judicial process still remains and many dedicated civil rights workers seek to defend these cases. The effect of these processes on our society is, however, a corruption in the very terms *the concentrationary* was invented to identify. While what takes place in these camps is almost beyond the law and removes the basic dignities of civil society and personhood, this realm is not another kingdom but a part of our society and eviscerates our democracy from within.

However, as the post-war thinkers of *the concentrationary* taught us, you do not even need camps to strip people of their humanity. It can be done, indeed is being done, in the name of economic rationality, progress, democracy, freedom, choice, efficiency and many other admirable terms. It piggybacks on what we take to be normality. This is, perhaps, what is truly terrifying – the fact that the forms of dehumanization have changed but our awareness has not necessarily kept pace, so we are more and more cut off from the reality of how this is happening in plain sight. And, just as terrifying, it often seems that we do not have the necessary tools to identify and resist the forms that dehumanization takes today, tools that would reveal to us the matrix-like cocoon in which we live.

Our recuperation and reanimation in these books of the concept of *the concentrationary* and the aesthetic response to it is offered here, therefore, with a view to providing us with those necessary tools to understand the transformed world in which we live. The need for a 'concentrationary art', and the Brechtian ideas of defamiliarization that inform it, has certainly not gone away. In fact, it has become even more pressing as the normalization of horror, the disfigurement of everyday lives and the erosion of democracy from within have new electronic means, new discourses, new forms at their disposal today to do their work. In *Night and Fog* concentration camps are shown to come in all sorts of commonplace architectural styles, torture is carried out in what appear to be hospitals, gas chambers masquerade as showers, the entrance to the inferno at Auschwitz proclaims, 'Work makes you free.' The narrator says at one point, 'We can but show you the shell, the surface, the decor.' But we must know how to see beyond the decor, to understand today, seventy-five years later, how evil can take on the most banal of forms, how human life can be disfigured, simply and efficiently, in the name of something else.

Leeds, 2021

INTRODUCTION

A CONCENTRATIONARY IMAGINARY?

Griselda Pollock

At the Fourteenth International Congress of the International Psychoanalytical Association (IPA), held on 2–8 August 1936 in the Bohemian spa town of Marienbad, a young French analyst gave a paper. The only trace is its title – 'The Looking-Glass Phase' – and its author – J. Lacan (Paris) – appearing in the conference proceedings summarized in the *International Journal of Psychoanalysis*.[1] Overstepping his allocated time, J. Lacan was rudely interrupted by his session's chair, Ernest Jones. Lacan promptly left the conference, taking the opportunity to visit the infamous Berlin Olympic Games (1 16 August), held under the auspices of the Third Reich and turned into one of the most notorious works of fascist cinema by Leni Riefenstahl's *Olympiad* (1936).

On 17 July 1949, the Sixteenth International Congress of the IPA assembled in Zurich. Now better-known, Lacan delivered another 'version' of the earlier paper. Published in the *Revue française de psychanalyse* 4 (1949), it has become the classic articulation of the Lacanian notion of the Imaginary: 'Le Stade du miroir'. Despite its aim to posit a Kleinian *position* (that remains operative throughout psychological life) rather than a Freudian *phase* (through which the subject should pass successively), the French *stade* (stage) has been translated as 'The Mirror Phase'.[2]

Towards the end of the 1949 text – and I am quoting the 1977 English translation – Lacan writes:

At the culmination of the historical effort of a society to refuse to recognize that it has any function other than the utilitarian one, and in the anxiety of the individual confronting the *'concentrational'* form of the social bond that seems to arise to crown this effort, existentialism must be judged by the explanations it gives of the subjective impasses that have indeed resulted from it: a freedom that is never more authentic than when it is within the walls of a prison; a demand for commitment, expressing the impotence of a pure consciousness to master any situation; a voyeuristic sadistic idealization of the sexual relation; a personality that realizes itself only in suicide; a consciousness of the other that can be satisfied only by Hegelian murder.[3] (my emphasis)

In the French original, the key adjective is *concentrationnaire*: 'Au bout de l'entreprise historique d'une société pour ne plus se reconnaître d'autre fonction qu'utilitaire, et dans l'angoisse de l'individu devant la forme *concentrationnaire* du lien...'[4] In translating this passage for the English publication of Lacan's selected writings in 1977, Alan Sheridan knew of no English equivalent for the French adjective *concentrationnaire*. He created 'concentrational', leaving it uneasily in quotation marks. Sheridan does acknowledge, however, in a translator's footnote: '"*Concentrationnaire*", an adjective coined after World War II... to describe the life of the concentration camp [sic]. In the hands of certain writers it became, by extension, applicable to many aspects of "modern" life.'[5]

There it was, all the time, a thesis about the concentrationary and the Imaginary. This book takes up such a thesis to offer some preliminary explorations of a concentrationary imaginary.

The historical brackets of Lacan's interventions – 1936 and 1949 – are significant as they straddle the emergence and the defeat of the Third Reich after a devastating world war and industrial genocide. They also confirm the post-war literary and political dissemination of the term *concentrationnaire* in France.

In his critique of Existentialism's failing to grasp the 'subjective impasses' created by the totalitarian legacy in modern society, Lacan identifies as a *concentrationary* social nexus the effects of an entire society dominated by only utilitarian purposes. He is not recalling the actual experiences the prisoners reported, but rather pointing to what is happening outside or beyond the camp at the level of the social system.

Lacan thus designates a contemporary bond(age) in which people live in anguish, feeling themselves reduced to being mere cogs in an economic machine or mere functions in a political regime, there only to be used, and used up, by the indifferent calculus of both capitalist or socialist systems. It is this widespread, atomizing, de-socializing nexus that Lacan chooses to characterize as *concentrationary*.[6] Occurring in a psychoanalytical text, Lacan asserts that this plays out in psychological – imaginary – dispositions that structure potential narratives mirroring these 'subjective impasses':

> A freedom that is never more authentic than when it is within the walls of a prison; a demand for commitment, expressing the impotence of a pure consciousness to master any situation; a voyeuristic sadistic idealization of the sexual relation; a personality that realizes itself only in suicide; a consciousness of the other that can be satisfied only by Hegelian murder.

Coined by French political prisoners who returned to France from their ordeal in such German concentration camps as Buchenwald, Dachau, Mauthausen and Ravensbrück, whither they had been sent for their *political* resistance to the Nazi occupation of France after 1940, the adjective *concentrationnaire* was introduced by Trotskyist writer and political deportee to Buchenwald David Rousset (1912–97) in the title of his book *L'Univers concentrationnaire* (1946) – 'the concentrationary universe'. Using his own blend of surrealism and bitter political irony, Rousset uncovered the *logic* of the concentration camps by producing a political anatomy of the camps as a system that not only operated inside the barbed wire but also eviscerated the political culture of the surrounding society that used the camps as their instrument. Rousset thus identified the system as the novel and terrifying *anti-political* political experiment in the total destruction of humanity in which the unimaginable became the fact that 'everything is possible'.[7] Obviously the inmates of such camps were defenceless; but Rousset is also arguing that their existence is part of a wider effect before which all become defenceless against the system.

In the research project *Concentrationary Memory: The Politics of Representation*, of which this book is the third publication, Max Silverman and I are translating *concentrationnaire* as 'concentrationary', following the rule by which Lacan's *l'Imaginaire* becomes 'the Imaginary'.[8] Benjamin Hannavy Cousen, one of the authors writing in this book (see Chapter 6), first drew my attention to the term *concentrationary* in Lacan's text on the mirror phase that I had formerly read only for its psychoanalytical theory of the Imaginary. In the most speculative strand of this project, Benjamin Hannavy Cousen and I set out into uncharted waters to test a hypothesis that recovers the implied connection in Lacan's text by posing this question: Is there a *concentrationary imaginary* in contemporary culture? I shall return to Lacan and the Imaginary (capitalized) at the end of this introduction. Initially, I need to unpack the concept of the *concentrationary*.[9]

Chance beginnings at the movies

The original question arose while I was watching a movie of which I did not know the title or the plot. There was a scene of prisoners of some kind, living in some extra-legal space outside normal society, who were controlled and manipulated by a group clearly acting outside the law or beyond it while officially endorsed to do so. It was a world apart, yet embedded in a system. The lead character was a former drug addict sentenced to death for killing a police officer. She was to die by lethal injection. Her death was, however, faked. When she awoke, appalled at having been tricked, she was offered a deal. She could die for real or agree to train as a secret assassin. For this she would learn to be able to kill without feeling. She would be refashioned to be able to pass as a sophisticated and attractive professional woman keeping secret her real job.

The film turned out to be *Point of No Return* (1993, John Badham), also known as *The Assassin*, an American remake of Luc Besson's action thriller *Nikita*, also known as *La Femme Nikita* (1990). In the final chapter of this book Brenda Hollweg develops a 'concentrationary' reading of the films and their various TV spinoffs, elaborating a critical apparatus for this genre of political thriller and its gender politics.

Both Besson's and Badham's films are thrillers about turning a violent miscreant and condemned murderer into a secret, trained, extra-legal government killer who will in turn be liquidated once any signs of resistance or any feelings emerge. Nothing overtly links this plot to the historical site of SS-run concentration camps. Yet it was from watching this film that I began to wonder how many elements, or rather the logics of possibilities beyond normal limits, which had originated in that historical experiment and its terror, wander and return, disguised through a variety of genres and narratives. What would be the implications of such recyclings? How many movies, having no intention to invoke a historical reference or to make a representation of the historical actuality, have as their premise an echo or trace of the logic of 'the concentrationary universe' where, as Rousset remarked, 'everything is possible' and, as Hannah Arendt would argue (see below), the human *qua* human is superfluous? What is happening to us if a specific and abhorrent historical event has generated its own place in the cultural imaginary as an unmarked resource for cinema or video games that 'imaginatively' play out as thrillers, science fiction or futuristic scenarios what was once a dire political reality?

The possibility of a *concentrationary imaginary* – the 'concentrationary social nexus' and its subjective impasses finding expression in cultural modes, images, narratives as a logic at work in contemporary cultural forms reshaping if not deforming our subjectivities as social and political beings – thus generates a raft of questions. Are we to understand that 'the concentrationary universe' has seeped beyond its historical confines into the cultural imaginary, shaping the repertory of images, self-understanding and cultural representations that we encounter through cinema or video games? Does a totalitarian mindset inform contemporary cultural forms without being acknowledged as such, thus not warning us, but entertaining and enthralling us? Have aspects of a political experiment in absolute domination been normalized into narratives, plots, styles, iconographies, attitudes or tropes and assimilated into conventional repertoires so that we no longer revolt against their representation of the world? Can aspects of the increasing obsessions with and spectacular rep resentations of violence and killing, with war as the norm, in media culture be related to an unacknowledged concentrationary legacy that redefines core issues such as death and dying, human value and valuelessness?

A once political reality has morphed into imaginative scenarios, generating newly compelling, or recycling borrowed iconographies. It may be, as Hannavy Cousen argues in this volume, that a concentrationary imaginary is identifiable primarily *in the negative*. That is to say, the lack of conscious memory combined with borrowed signs that might continuously warn of its menace mark the danger. In its imaginary form, Hannavy Cousen finds the *concentrationary* inhabiting, unannounced, many spaces appearing in several guises. In the theorization of the concentrationary imaginary across a range of films – here the example he studies is Martin Scorsese's film *Shutter Island* (2010) – he has produced a taxonomy of differing images – indexical, citational, amnesiac – and different modalities – seep and creep – by which traces of a concentrationary archive are mobilized, surface or inform, each with distinctive narrative and ideological effects as well as affects. Hannavy Cousen's work is the most systematic and insightful work on the concentrationary imaginary in post-war cinema to date.[10]

In addition to acknowledging that there are still instances of the concentrationary in changing political realizations, it is now crucial to recognize its virtual work in imagination and in imaginary forms that anaesthetize us to its presence while shaping our subjectivities in its image. Unhinged from the space and time of its historical origins in Hitler's camps and Stalin's Gulags, the concentrationary may have infiltrated its logics into cultural fantasy, becoming a sort of *apolitical* unconscious – the reference here is to Fredric Jameson's notion of a political unconscious – normalizing narratives of militarized superpowers enslaving or 'erasing' subjected peoples and dispensable others, accustoming us to unspeakable violence towards and the suffering of any given underclass, race or gender, where arbitrary disposal is no longer murder, but erasing, wasting, business.[11] At times, as we shall also show, the concentrationary imaginary may dress itself up in kitsch glamour distorting our responses to death and dying, borrowed from the unexpected return and fetishized recasting of icons and styles of what Susan Sontag denounced in 1975 as 'fascinating fascism'.[12]

The concentrationary universe

Three key points can be identified in the political, philosophical and sociological literature on the concentrationary: the destruction of the political community, the logic of dehumanization, and the creation of an order of terror that functions as a space-time of a new kind of power.

Drawing on Rousset's literary political text in her magisterial study *The Origins of Totalitarianism*, published in 1951, Hannah Arendt outlines her classic argument that the camp is a key instrument in the practice of total domination:

> The concentration and extermination camps of totalitarian regimes serve as the laboratories in which the fundamental belief that

everything is possible is being verified. Total domination which strives to organize the infinite plurality and differentiation of human beings as if all humanity were just one individual is only possible if each and every person is reduced to a never changing identity of reactions so that each of these bundles of reactions can be exchanged at random for any other. The problem is to fabricate something that does not exist, namely as a kind of human species resembling other animal species whose only 'freedom' would consist in 'preserving the species'. Totalitarian domination attempts to achieve this through . . . absolute terror in the camps.[13]

The concentrationary universe is thus an experimental, if ultimately defeated but never erased, locus for an anti-political project to destroy the political, of which genocide is but one of its extreme faces. The political is linked for Arendt to the quality of action: agency and choice: 'The camps are meant not only to exterminate people and degrade human beings, but they also serve the ghastly experiment of eliminating under scientifically controlled conditions, spontaneity itself as an expression of human behaviour and transforming human personality into a mere thing, something that even animals are not.'[14] If we are to seek signs of the concentrationary in our cultural imaginary, it will be at this level of any normalization of this depoliticized, dehumanizing vision of a de-socialized world.

Writing in the 1990s, Italian philosopher Giorgio Agamben identified the juridical-political structure that made the concentrationary universe possible. He argues that the historical camps were symptoms and a realization of a *logic* that is to be understood as a *nomos* – model – of all modernity, which also involves an assault on the human condition:

> The camp is merely the place in which the most absolute *conditio inhumana* [inhuman/nonhuman condition] that has ever existed on earth was realized: this is what counts in the last analysis, for the victims as for those who come after. Here we will deliberately follow an inverse line of enquiry. Instead of deducing the definition of the camp from the events that took place, we will ask: What is a camp, what is its juridico-political structure, that such events could take place there? This will lead us to regard the camp not as an historical fact and an anomaly belonging to the past (even if still verifiable)

but in some way as the hidden matrix and *nomos* of the political space in which we are still living.[15]

From another angle, that of the political sociologist, the key issue is that of the camp *qua* camp as 'universe of power'. In his aptly named book, *The Order of Terror*, however, Wolfgang Sofsky reminds us that:

> [A]bsolute power should not be confused with either asymmetrical relations of exchange or with punitive power. Nor should it be confused with modern disciplinary power or with relations founded on obedience. It is not based on exploitation, sanction or legitimacy but on terror, organization and excessive violence.[16]

Understanding the camp structurally as a system of terror, Sofsky argues, furthermore, that the concentrationary operates as both a separated *space* of boundaries, zones, hierarchies and as 'a structuring of *time* and a reconfiguration of sociality *in the negative* all structured through the power to kill'.[17] (my emphasis)

Then Sofsky adds three key factors. The concentrationary order of terror cannot be explained by the motivations or rationales of the perpetrators and thus explained away with their demise or defeat. It is also a closed system: a colony of terror at the far end of the social world. Finally, organized terror takes place in situations of action and suffering:

> It targets social situations in which human beings live and function. Here, it breaks their resistance, herds them together and shreds social ties; it dissolves action; it devastates life. Any investigation of the camps is short-sighted and flawed if it fails to include the power *that micrologically invades the structures of space and time, sociality and identity*.[18] (my emphasis)

Thus Sofsky concludes his 'thick description' of the order of terror:

> The destruction of sociality entails the negation of the human relation to the self. In the concentration camp, the social process of individuation is reversed. The regime of violence and misery obliterates individual space, ravages the sense of time and casts

the human being into a permanent condition of dying. Organized terror reduces social life, the foundation of any self humanhood, below the animal minimum... It seizes hold of bodies – not to turn gesture and movement into a blind automaton, but gradually to extinguish all manifestations of life.[19]

From his analysis of the architecture of totalitarian militarism – the bunker in particular – cultural philosopher and film theorist Paul Virilio has suggested that totalitarianism extends beyond the camp. The form it inhabits is war, which is now one of the other matrices of contemporary society.[20] In Chapter 3 in this volume, Ian James explains this supplementary logic in the post-war thinking of Paul Virilio as part of the extended exploration of the effects of the militarization of culture and reminds us, therefore, of the wide range of post-war thinkers alert to the signs of new logics of social and political life in the wake of the totalitarian experiments.

Such theorizations of the concentrationary as experiment in absolute domination, as matrix of our present social order, and as a spatialization/temporalization of an order of terror, all aimed at the destruction of the social, political, moral and embodied subject, identify signposts for an analysis of the concentrationary as it becomes an imaginary informing and shaping narratives, images, cultural horizons. It is to systems and logics on the one hand, and to subjective effects on the other, that we look in order to discern the tracing of the concentrationary universe into images, narratives, scenarios, situations and genres that performatively install a concentrationary imaginary without the outward and visible signs of a once-historical realization.

Imaginary conflation

At this point, we need to make some distinctions and clarify several confusions. The concentrationary defines the particularity of the system of concentration camps. It is not a synonym for what is now conflated under the overly broad understanding of the term 'the Holocaust'. Emerging as a necessary linguistic label that would make visible the specificity of racialized genocide – initially obscured by being overlaid by the many persecutions and atrocities performed by the Third Reich – the term Holocaust now falls into the opposite abyss of covering every terror and horror of that regime, including the persecution of the mentally and physically disabled, the religiously dissident, the socially undesirable, and the sexually diverse.[21]

The Holocaust thus becomes identified with images of what was actually the *concentrationary* universe. This is a result of the fluke of history, namely which armies liberated which sites. In 1945, the Allies discovered and liberated German concentration camps such as Bergen-Belsen, Dachau, Ravensbrück, Mauthausen and thousands of others. They made films that aimed to shock and circulated horrific photographs to indict the SS and Nazism. These images, these place names, became notorious in the Anglo-American and Western European world. They were far better known than the actual sites of racialized mass murder of European Jewry that took place at specially designed and short-lived death factories, such as Treblinka, Sobibor, Chełmno, Bełżec, Auschwitz-Birkenau, and briefly Majdanek – all in Poland. The first four sites were built in 1941–2 as dedicated extermination camps under *Operation Reinhard* following the Wannsee Conference (20 January 1942) that minuted the Final Solution, namely the proposed mass destruction of 11 million Jewish people throughout Europe. These Reinhard death camps were, however, destroyed in 1943 as the tide of the war turned against Germany after the defeat at Stalingrad (2 February 1943) and the Red Army began its advance into Poland and Germany from the East.[22] Until Claude Lanzmann's film *Shoah* (1985) cinematically retraced the journey to these now forested, farmed over, almost obliterated sites, and tracked down the handful of survivors of the death camps, and interviewed the bystanders, the understanding of the Holocaust was often projected onto the images made by the Allies in 1945 from a different set of places that at least has a visible record: the concentration camps of Germany.[23]

In contrast to the four dedicated and two other death factories, hidden in Poland, there were by 1945 over 10,000 concentration camps in Germany alone. Initiated at the very beginning of the Third Reich in 1933 – Dachau was the first to be built – these camps were the foundational instrument of the system of dominative domestic and imperializing terror although their death toll was only 1.2 million (out of the 1.8 million sent to concentration camps between 1933 and 1945) compared to 3 million killed in the death camps, while 3 to 4 million Jews and Romanies (Roma) died by direct killing by shooting during the invasion of the Soviet territories in June 1941 or in the ghettoes of disease and starvation.

At the level of the cultural imaginary – what we remember and carry in our heads – there is thus a conflation of the genocidal Final Solution targeting Jewish and Romany populations in Europe enacted in a few, short-lived and largely obliterated sites of mass murder in Poland, with this vast network of concentration camps across Germany. This is in part the result of the powerful effect of the photographic and cinematic documentation by the liberating Allies through which 'the concentration camp' (fences, barbed wire, watch towers, shaven prisoners in striped uniforms, unburied and emaciated corpses) has, therefore, become the iconic signifier of both general Nazi atrocity and its racialized genocide despite the fact that the sites of the two are distinct. Named the *Holocaust* (translating from the Greek as 'burnt whole'), or, in the Jewish world, as *Ha'Shoah* (the destruction), the historical event of an industrialized and racialized genocide has been increasingly misrepresented through images of concentration camps from all across Germany and its occupied zones. This conflation is so widespread that it has produced a distorting identification of the concentration camp and Jewish experience under Nazism. Two anecdotes will underline this tendency in the cultural imaginary that effectively makes it less likely for us to discern the specificity of the concentrationary *per se* that we need to recognize in order to analyse its potential dissemination into popular culture.[24]

In an article about Peter Weiss (1916–82), the German-born Swedish painter, filmmaker and playwright known for his monumental novel *Die Ästhetik des Widerstands* (*The Aesthetics of Resistance*, 1975–81) and his play *Die Ermittlung* (*The Investigation*, 1965) about the Auschwitz Trials in Frankfurt in 1964, I read that in his autobiographical novel *Der Fluchtpunkt* (*The Vanishing Point*, 1961), Weiss writes of the epiphanic moment at the cinema for him as a German-born Jewish artist who escaped the destiny he suddenly confronts in images on the screen. Weiss records that he watched a screening of the infamous footage made by the British army of the liberation of the concentration camp at Bergen-Belsen in April 1945. The footage horrifically shows bulldozers driving piles of already disintegrating corpses into mass graves.

What have scenes of this concentration camp in Germany, filmed by the Allies in the aftermath of liberation to shock the German people about the vileness of their former regime, to do with the racist genocide of European Jewry in the East that Weiss escaped by getting to Sweden, which he was now confronting by attending the first trials in Germany?[25] The answer to the questions is not quite 'nothing'. The widely distributed and remembered *images* of one site of Nazi terror – the concentration camps of Germany – have come to stand in visually for what they do not in fact show, causing a double disfiguration of both the concentrationary and the exterminatory.

In the spring of 2011, *The Promise*, a four-part drama by British writer Peter Kosminsky, was screened on British television (Channel 4). The premise is that a young disgruntled British student visits her alienated, silent and now dying grandfather in Leeds. During a bout of clearing out his house, the student comes across his wartime diary that she takes with her on a trip to spend the summer with a university friend going back to Israel to do her military service. On the plane she begins to read the diary and the film slips us through its pages to her grandfather's young self and his experiences in April–May 1945 in Germany and then in the British Mandate of Palestine. Thus, after the horrific experience of participating in the liberation of Bergen-Belsen in 1945, her grandfather, a British soldier, is sent to the British Mandate of Palestine to maintain peace between the Jews and the Arabs: that's the line he is given by his commanding officer. Carrying the memory of the atrocities he had witnessed at Bergen-Belsen in his mind as if these are the signs and sites of Jewish suffering, the soldier is initially inclined to sympathize with the Jewish struggle against the British and for an independent state because of what happened back in Europe. What he witnesses, however, of the Jewish armed struggle during the last days of the British Mandate, turns his sympathy towards the victimized Palestinian Arabs, one of whom works at the army base. The soldier befriends him and his family and is given the key to the house he must flee when the State of Israel is declared and war breaks out. For this act of solidarity, the soldier is court martialled, falling into the silent depression that had alienated his uncomprehending granddaughter who herself takes up the Palestinian cause once exposed to contemporary Israel and the Occupation in the West Bank and Gaza, where she traces the refugee descendants of the family whose house key her grandfather was given in 1948.

Early on, therefore, as the diary fades and the past emerges from its pages into images, we see a scene of the young Tommy writing his diary in post-liberation Bergen-Belsen, a scene which comes to stand in the narrative of *The Promise* for 'what was done to the Jews in Europe under the Nazis'. *The Promise* uses the Allied footage of British bulldozers clearing masses of unburied corpses to induce horror in the contemporary viewers but now, unlike 1945, it is conflated with what was not knowable to the Allied soldiers in 1945 at Bergen-Belsen, namely the extermination programme directed at two peoples of Europe that no army liberated or documented at the time of operation.

Thus 'campness' – emaciation and abjection of human beings in horrible and prolonged deaths from starvation and disease – has become a trope. The trope is misleadingly mobilized in this film to signify 'the persecution of the Jews of Europe' in one historical moment so as to function narratively as the dark mirror of what the newly formed Jewish State itself then did, and does, namely to discriminate against, drive out, and effectively but not purposely encamp the Palestinian Arabs. This equation, with its additional risk of accusing the Jewish State of attempted genocide rather than of settler colonization, depends upon the paradox of the *visibility* of the concentration camp in images and the *invisibility* of the extermination sites whose secret was preserved by the SS to the extent that almost no images of the process exist at all.[26]

What is used in *The Promise* is the same footage that Peter Weiss saw. Bergen-Belsen's ambulant or abandoned corpses are not evidence of the affliction of the Jews of Europe, but signs of the Nazi policies towards its various populations, domestic and foreign, for a variety of what the Third Reich classed as anti-social crimes and for any act of political or ethical resistance. These images furthermore expose *the concentrationary universe* in its dying days in 1945. As the Allies advanced the SS effectively abandoned the prisoners in the concentration camps to starvation and disease, aggravating the already horrific regime of malnutrition and affliction. When the British liberated Bergen-Belsen on 14 April 1945, 60,000 prisoners were found amidst 13,000 unburied corpses in a camp to which food had ceased to be supplied for three weeks and where typhus was rampant.

The emaciated, staggering men and women and the piles of unburied corpses that still so horrify anyone watching this footage do not, however, represent the Nazis' attempted Final Solution of the Jewish Question. Yet, as an effect of the imaginary, that genocide is represented by circulated images of places such as Bergen-Belsen as if this is what the daily destruction over months and years of millions of people looks like.[27] It does not. Mass destruction of lives by gassing in vans and chambers, the burning of bodies, the grinding up of bones and dispersing ashes in secret places where those who are forced to undertake this work are themselves regularly destroyed; this produces almost nothing. What remains are very few images and a handful of survivors who revolted, or escaped the final executions when camps were closed down.

Does it matter that the concentrationary is often used in cultural forms to signify *what these images do not represent*? Does it matter that we thus mistake the face of totalitarianism? My point is not, however, just irritable precision. It concerns the politics of cultural memory and the role of images in fostering an imaginary conflation that obstructs our understanding of the implications of the specificities of, and relations between, the concentrationary and the exterminatory. What people have in their mind's eye as the images of abject suffering that can be historically placed as the exceptional horror of genocide are in fact the signs of a novel and potentially recurring system of terror that is not more terrible than the racially targeted genocide. It is important to be precise because of what Arendt identified as that concentrationary system's core 'research question': the destruction of the human being *qua* human being. It is that system which produced the concentration camp as its instrument that we must understand if we are to be able to trace its dissemination into a cultural imaginary playing out across our contemporary media.

The time-space of death in life in the concentrationary universe

Both the death and the concentration camps were linked by virtue of the distinctiveness of the overall *concentrationary* system, developed and run by the SS. The concentrationary system is, however, also to be found in Stalin's Gulags and the camps of societies under dictatorships, or even across the entire society in some totalitarian regimes. The concentrationary represents an untrammelled experiment in the enactment of total power that does include systemic destruction of life. The concentration camps were, however, significantly different from the death camps in terms of space, time, and social experience, in ways we need to grasp if we are to track the concentrationary in our cultural imaginary and its many manifestations.

Firstly, prisoners entered the concentration camp and lived there. They were brutally deposited in a space apart – Sofsky's second principle: 'at the end of the world' – where many were 'disappeared' into a place to which no one could trace them. Political resistance in the Occupied Zones was punished specifically by a sentence of effective living disappearance called '*Nacht und Nebel*' or 'Night and Fog'.[28] Concentrationees lived, and many died, in this other planet. This is in contrast to the fact that almost no one *lived* in a death camp. The extermination camp has no population. Death is inflicted within hours of arrival in a constant production system of destruction serviced by selected and then replaced victims from the transports.

Concentrationees were intended to *live* for some time at least; some lived for 12 years in camps. They were to witness and experience their own systematic human destruction by torture, terror, starvation, overwork and exhaustion as well as by destruction of the fabric sustaining not only social but individual moral, affective and intellectual being that is synonymous with *human* life. Survival often meant radical compromise of former social and ethical norms. The SS camp system worked to obliterate the inherent particularity of each person whose sense of identity as social, cultural, juridical, moral and self-aware persons would be systematically destroyed before their probable, but not inevitable, physical death: they would *live* agonizingly to experience themselves and also to witness in others the daily, progressive evisceration of their socially founded humanity (family, language, cultural identity, ethical personhood). They also had to witness the desperate acts to which they were driven by the physical struggle of trying to stay alive in such conditions. They lived out the appalling paradox of becoming, in that desperation, the lesser 'thing' to which their political oppressors sought to reduce them by the destruction of their *human* being, given that we are humanized by complex social structures and subjective formations, practices and cultures of which this system systematically and programmatically deprived them. They would also witness the extremity of living death, namely the 'walking corpses', a condition created by prolonged starvation in which the body is forced to consume its own organs. This condition was known in the Auschwitz camps by the cruel misnomer, *Muselmann*. These atrocious sufferings were to work upon those whose condition as human was systematically eroded in a range of endlessly invented forms of torture.

Total domination required the complete evacuation of the conditions of the political, which Hannah Arendt would come to realize in her retrospective analysis of the concentrationary system were identical with the human. For Arendt, the human is not a pre-social essence, inserted into the social bond. The human is a truly unnatural creation that is the product of people collectively associating themselves to act on the world, creating thereby a *polis*. Thus, our human safety and dignity will depend precisely upon the political systems we create to protect what Arendt named the right to have rights.[29]

Political philosopher Dana Villa summarizes it thus: 'Made concrete by the camps, the pure form of anti-politics not only determined the nature and scope of *Origins of Totalitarianism* but also forced Arendt to rethink the nature of authentic political action and public freedom – tasks she took up in *The Human Condition* and *On Violence*.'[30]

In total contrast to Adorno and Horkheimer's understanding of the relations of reason and nature, Arendt, according to Villa, made a very different argument about the human as primarily a creation of the political:

> For her, freedom – like rights and human dignity – is, and always will be a function of the artificial world of laws and institutions that make up our public reality. It is the public realm that provides us, potentially, with a home in the world. This home protects us from nature and from the temptation to submit to pseudonatural forces in the quest for some imagined state of originary integrity, immediacy and authenticity.[31]

Villa continues: 'Nothing marks the separation between Arendt and Adorno more than her appreciation of the role public institutions and legal structures play in creating *human* life.'[32]

Arendt's book *The Human Condition* (1958) may be considered the counter-image of what she discovered through her genealogical analysis of the *Origins of Totalitarianism*. The latter revealed the destruction of, and the former asserted the conditions necessary for sustaining, a condition that is human because of the political sphere of common action.

What Arendt makes visible in both books are the forces that exist to undo the fragile creation of a political sphere, and hence its condition as the human condition. Separated from the *oikos*, the home economy of the production of daily life, the polis, the sphere of political action of the assembled group has been threatened by the developments of modern social and economic organizations, left and right, in which the economic (the realm of necessity) colonizes, hence privatizes, all forms of political life so that everything becomes subject to the rule of the economy or the law of the market or the logic of profit: Lacan's society of total utility. If fascism and communism eroded the political by subjecting everything to the unboundaried forces of Nature (expressed through racial discourse in the case of Nazism) or History (the Bolshevik view), our survival as people, our existence as the political human in Arendt's terms, requires the profound appreciation of what structures we must continually create to protect ourselves from these fantastical forces of absolutely determining Nature or History. In neoliberal capitalism we live under the ideological tyranny of the Market, the blind forces of pure economic necessity against which any notion of what constitutes human life is calculated and found too expensive; even basic life becomes dispensable.[33]

Far from being contained as a one off, geopolitically confined event, Arendt argued that the Nazi-created concentrationary system (with its horrific extension, the exterminationary factory) initiated a political novelty whose innovation was the erosion of the political, hence the sociality of human life depending on acting together with others for its realization. Totalitarianism – the ambition to exercise total domination – was, in Arendt's analysis, to be understood not only as an anti-political political experiment. As a result of tracing its calculated destruction in the regimes of overwork, malnutrition, untreated disease, consistent torture and arbitrary violence that characterize the concentrationary universe, Arendt drew out more clearly the two core qualities of the human that underpinned our potential for political human being. These qualities are spontaneity (the ability to act, and to make choices ethically, and with regard to others, politically) and plurality (the endless renovation of humankind through the coming of the new and the doing of the unforeseen and, hence, the spontaneous).

Not confined to the Third Reich, Arendt identified the concentrationary also as a feature of Stalin's Soviet Union and its satellite communist regimes. Unlike the Holocaust, which is defined by the uniqueness of state-sponsored, industrialized and systematic racially targeted mass murder, the concentrationary as a kind of logic, and not just as an image of its effects, can also be discerned in differing guises in totalitarian and racist societies such as Apartheid South Africa and under new dictatorships such as those of the later twentieth century in several Latin American countries, and in countries and regimes where there is state terror which may, or may not, use special camps into which its opponents are 'disappeared'. The specific instruments such as camps or special operations are but symptoms of the logic of the regime as concentrationary.

Arendt's argument is that the home for each of us in our plurality and spontaneity – the grounds of freedom – is built by the artifice of political life and political space. The camp space-time was the epitome of the anti-political space in the service of a regime driven by an imaginary dedication to the supra-political forces of Nature and History that were, for the Nazis, expressed through race. Under the Third Reich, the Jews were not a troublesome minority but the very epitome of an anti-race defined in paranoid imaginary ways as the obstacle to the absolute happiness of the tribal, pan-movement of the fictive Aryan.[34]

It is, therefore, in the name of the political rather than the memorial that this project to think about the concentrationary has sought to re-examine the historical and other conditions for the possibility of total domination which – far from being exceptional, aberrant, regressive or particular – lay underdetermined in all the major forms of modernity: economic, political, and cultural. Thus colonialism, imperialism, capitalism, the bourgeoisie, Romanticism, all contributed to the very possibility of conceiving of operations in which 'everything was possible' and humans become superfluous in their humanity. Enslavement or eradication were equally conceivable if logics of accumulation were released from the temporary housing of national states and boundaries within which, regardless of identity, citizens might be considered at home and protected. Villa makes clear in his analysis that Arendt was never a determinist. Nothing made totalitarianism inevitable. Nothing except action, therefore, prevents it from happening again.

Far from being destroyed or being safely in the past, the concentrationary has not only entered into the world as a repeatable political possibility. We are arguing that it also stalks our world imaginatively, in a form characterized as a menacing, (anti)political response to the complexity of democracy and difference. Its endless variations in stories, narratives, scenarios, situations and plots, effectively work to annul democracy by playing with total domination and avoiding the complexities of our human plurality that we need to face together. The concentrationary destroys democracy by extirpating difference, by destroying, dehumanizing and finally annihilating representatives of difference: both political opponents and racially and physically defined others. Both projects attack spontaneity and plurality as dynamics of human social and political living together.

Drawing on but going beyond these specific theorizations, we want to enquire into cultural forms and subjectivities that may be being reshaped through unremembered but assimilated legacies of the concentrationary. As a phantom of the imaginary, the concentrationary may be identified as a dimension of heightened violence, of fantasies of the apocalyptic, end of time confrontations, of the manner in which 'others' are projected as both fascinating and deadly, easily disposed of, erased, and unmourned. On the other hand, it might also manifest itself in thoughtlessness and amnesia about the past. It could be eroticized and stylized via fascist kitsch. It may have found a home and sometimes a counter-imaginary in science fiction. The concentrationary may appear in images of pestilence, viral contamination, or deadly epidemics let loose by uncontrolled scientists and their political masters seeking final domination. It plays through tropes of spaces of secret experimentation where scientists appropriate the right to life and death, and manipulate bodies of those rendered socially vulnerable in the name of a politically ordained 'power'. It normalizes war – on drugs, on terror, on crime – as the permanent condition.

If the concentrationary infuses our cultural imaginary in so many potential forms, we would need to discover methods for resisting its continuing seepage and, worse, its normalization; that is, our accommodation to its perversion of political, ethical and human co-existence. It may continuously play a role in the erosion of the political as our collective space of social realization and change. The political lessons of the concentrationary universe of mid-twentieth century Europe led Hannah Arendt to argue that we shall have to reground a basis for social and political life in what she felt obliged to re-theorize as *the human condition*. In that light, we are asking if the untracked dissemination across cultural forms of a concentrationary imaginary is continuing to put humanity, that is, our shared and living *humanity*, at risk? Thus the analysis of the cultural sites of the dissemination of the concentrationary becomes part of a political gesture to reclaim, in Arendtian terms, the space of the political.

Our project here is, therefore, about a politics of representation: it involves an understanding and analysis of the nature and effects of representation in literature, cinema, historical writing, and visual culture in general. But it is a *political* understanding and analysis, motivated by a sense of more than cultural significance and ethical responsibility to the dead and their suffering, and to the many victims of the concentrationary universes the world over.

Fascism, Nazism and the Imaginary

At the end of the war, Nazism was the damned part of Western civilization, the symbol of evil. Everything the Nazis had done was condemned, whatever they touched defiled: a seemingly indelible stain darkened the German past while preceding centuries were scrutinized for the origins of this monstrous development... By the end of the sixties, however, the Nazi image in the West had begun to change.[35]

This is a statement by the historian Saul Friedländer in his book *Reflets du nazisme* (1982) translated as *Reflections of Nazism: An Essay on Kitsch and Death* in 1984. An analyst of cultural memory, Friedländer analysed the cultural, or rather imaginary, re-appearance of Nazism, not as a political reality, but 'as a free *game of phantasms*'[36] (my emphasis). Friedländer notes that this new discourse on Nazism traverses left and right, while there is also 'an aesthetic elaboration that goes beyond ideology'. Dismissing the adequacy of available Marxist and other explanations of Fascism, Nazism and totalitarianism and their politico-economic preconditions as no longer present to explain this resurgence, Friedländer turns to the psychological and cultural: 'the power of images, emotions, and phantasms'. He continues: 'I shall trace associations of imagery, because I believe that these works, among others, carry within them a latent discourse ruled by a profound logic that needs to be clarified.'[37] Friedländer thus offers us two key terms: a discourse; that is, a pattern of statements, images, dispositions of its subjects and objects, and an organizing logic. We are not looking for content, or content alone. We are not looking for style. It is the rule of a logic by which elements come to be combined that leads to the identification of a specific imaginary constellation.

Thus a second distinction needs to be drawn out, at the level of the cultural imaginary rather than the level of political or social theory of the concentrationary itself. How is the *concentrationary* imaginary different from or indebted to a *fascist* imaginary, which, horrifyingly, resurfaced to infest certain cultural forms in the post-war period. Those who analyse the latter can help us methodologically in understanding the signs for which we must look to figure out the former.

Friedländer argues that the second coming of Nazism *in the form of images* contributes to our better understanding of the historical past. 'Thanks to their reflections in the present, some aspects that a direct approach has not clarified up to now, are revealed, *not so much by what this or that director or writer has intended to say, but by what they say unwittingly, even what is said despite them.*'[38] This indicates the need for a method of reading against the grain or against overt content. He then argues: 'In effect, by granting a certain freedom to what is imagined, by accentuating the selection that is exercised by memory, a contemporary re-elaboration presents the reality of the past in a way that sometimes reveals previously unsuspected aspects.'[39] There is a relay between the past and the present, played out across works that build up a repeating fascination:

> As a result of this kind of analysis, themes become visible, roads open up. The focus shifts from the new discourse on Nazism, to Nazism itself, and from Nazism back to the new discourse, allowing us to grasp some hidden forms of past and present imagination.[40]

Friedländer traces the entwining, in Nazism (as ideology and system) and in what is imaginarily recycled as the logic of the new discourse of Nazism, of what should be an impossible juxtaposition – kitsch and death. Kitsch is fabricated sentimentality, picture postcard lovers, cheesy poses and so forth. Death, which can, of course, be reduced to kitsch 'creates an authentic feeling of loneliness and dread' and hence 'at the level of individual experience kitsch and death remain incompatible'.[41] Friedländer explains the 'appeal' of the fascist aesthetic solutions to existential and also socio-political complexities of the modern world: 'Nazi power, in the duality we have tried to analyse (kitsch and death) was the expression, singular up to now, of a flow of ideas, emotions, and phantasms that are kept separate in all other modern western society.'[42] He continues in a vein that also resonates with Lacan's diagnosis:

> Now this fusion [of opposites] is only the expression of a kind of malaise in civilization, linked to the acceptance of civilization,

but also to its fundamental rejection. Modern society and the bourgeois order are perceived both as an accomplishment and as an unbearable yoke. Hence the constant coming and going between the need for submission and reveries of total destruction, between love and harmony and the phantasms of apocalypse, between the enchantment of Good Friday and the twilight of the gods. Submission nourishes fury; fury clears its conscience in the submission. To these opposing needs, Nazism – in the constant duality of its representations – offers an outlet. In fact Nazism found itself to be the expression of these opposing needs. *Today these aspirations are still there, and their reflections in the imaginary as well.* But this duality is grafted onto a much more profound contradiction made up of a dream of all powerfulness and the accepted risk of annihilation.[43] (my emphasis)

While such tensions resonate from the romantic tradition to Marxism, they are also a sign of 'the profound conflict of man facing modernity' which hides a 'fundamental temptation: the aspiration for total power, which is by definition the supreme transgression, the ultimate challenge, the superhuman combat that can be settled only by death'.[44] Friedländer's analytical reflections on the cinematic reflections of Nazism surfacing culturally and aesthetically long after the historical system was destroyed not only lend their force to the question of other 'reflections' at the imaginary level. They also point to the need to identify their specific configurations, and to understand that, although historically these took one form in a political actuality such as Nazism, they have their deeper roots in modernity itself, and weave themselves across societies that have taken different forms, liberal democracies as much as communist states.

In studying this imaginary of total power and apocalyptic transgression that reaches back to the modernity of Frankenstein but also to the culture of the machine and war, we encounter a militaristic vision, an ecstatic masculinist vision of violence, a deep culture of death. This resonates with Susan Sontag's reflections on the post-war work of Hitler's favoured filmmaker Leni Riefenstahl (1902–2003) in which Sontag identified continuities across her Nazi-commissioned films and post-war photographic studies of the Nuba people of the Sudan. Riefenstahl's gaze replays the fascist ideal of physical courage and victory of the strong over the weak played out, of course, in a society in which women are treated as 'merely breeders and helpers, excluded from all ceremonial functions and represent a threat to the integrity and strength of men...contact with women is profane'.[45] Sontag identified fascist aesthetics with 'a preoccupation with situations of control, submissive behaviour, extravagant effort and endurance of pain; they endorse two seemingly opposite states, egomania and servitude'. In Riefenstahl's work, Sontag identifies an aesthetic whose resonances we might well recognize in so many CGI apocalyptic blockbusters from *Star Wars* to *Lord of the Rings*,

> The relations of domination and enslavement take the characteristic form of pageantry: the massing of groups of people; the turning of people into things; the multiplication and replication of things; the grouping of people/things around an all powerful, hypnotic leader figure or force. The fascist dramaturgy centres on orgiastic transactions between mighty forces and their puppets, uniformly garbed and shown in ever swelling numbers. Its choreography alternates between ceaseless motion and a congealed, static, 'virile' posing. Fascism glorifies surrender, it exalts mindlessness, it glamourizes death.[46]

It is more than tempting to trace the lineaments of this analysis of fascist aesthetics, dramaturgy and choreography into aspects of contemporary cinematic and gaming culture which undoubtedly are part of the new discourse on fascism and the continuing potency of fascist aesthetics. What is specifically associated with the styles and aesthetics of Nazi fascism is not identical with the concentrationary imaginary. They overlap, but we need also to keep hold of the structuring habits or tropes that the earlier analyses of the concentrationary system and order of terror outlined.

Nonetheless, it is in these senses that we can pose the question: Is the cinematic culture of spectacular violence – as opposed to political critiques of violence – the iterating imprint on our cultural imaginary of what we were once shown in order to shock and warn us that something like this should never happen again? Are we becoming accustomed to situations of total domination and the rendering of humanness superfluous in an instrumentalized economy via the identification structures at work in our consumption of films, games and other cultural practices, facilitated by the distancing and thus fake intimacy of social media?

The concentrationary universe in *Blade Runner*

A film that hardly made the movie headlines when it first came out in 1984 has since become not only a cult classic for movie lovers but also an object of considerable academic reflection.[47] Indeed, for Marxist cultural theorist Fredric Jameson, the film was the emblematic movie of the emergence of the postmodern.[48] Dubbed the initiator of a new genre of *future noir*, the film was a seductive mix of pastiche and dystopia. It was both disorienting and spectacular. The film in question is *Blade Runner* directed by British filmmaker Ridley Scott, starring Harrison Ford. It offers itself, however, to a concentrationary reading.

As a constellation of themes that range from colonialism to racism, from urbanism to science fiction, from technophobia to subjectivity, from robotics to questions about the nature of the human, *Blade Runner* rewards probing cultural analysis.

The film allows us to dig deeply into the cultural imaginary of modernity since it touches on a core question: What makes the human *human*?

The Enlightenment challenged the authoritarianism of a predominantly theological definition of reality, in which the human is defined in distinction from the divine above and is determined by the presence of a soul. This conception was altered by the emergence of a scientific model that draws the distinction of the human from the animal below by virtue of humanity's use of language and development of a moral sense, moving towards a technocratic definition which has to establish a distinction between the human and the machine, also creating and often politically appropriating the hybrid figure of the cyborg as either a menacing chimera or a transgressive utopian possibility. The study of the human/animal distinction includes reference to Revolutionary French eighteenth-century scientist Jean Itard's experimental education of the wild child, Victor of Aveyron, discovered in 1800 in France, aged 12, naked, unclothed and abandoned in the woods, as well as to early twentieth-century colonialist American novelist Rice Burroughs' *Tarzan* (1912) or Rudyard Kipling's Mowgli in *Jungle Book* (1894). The animal/machine opposition takes us through Fritz Lang's silent film *Metropolis* (1927) to feminist philosopher of science Donna Haraway's feminist manifesto on the cyborg as anti-patriarchal allegory (1983).⁴⁹ Then comes *Blade Runner*.

In what way does the analysis of a concentrationary imaginary intersect with this genealogy?

The plot of *Blade Runner* is as follows. A nuclear war has brought perpetual night and constant rain to a Los Angeles that has become a virtual extension of Asia: a disorienting world of neon signs, flying cars and grounded desolation in which archaism mixes with advanced technology like a Tokyo night market. Off-world colonies have been built to restart human life free from progressively fatal nuclear contamination of the Earth. The ethnically mixed and rejected remnants of humanity on Earth eke out an existence in ruined buildings dominated by one vast corporation whose architecture combines the effect of a giant microchip with the shape of an Aztec Temple. This corporation manufactures advanced robots to service life on the new off-world colonies. Engineered to near-perfect mimesis of the human but with advanced strength and superhuman endurance of cold, these robots are, nonetheless, destructible. To foster their adjustment to this near-human replication, the latest models have been given a cushion of implanted memories upon which to rest the emotions that appear to evolve within them. The replicants are, however, forbidden to leave the off-world colonies. If they escape and come to Earth, they have to be 'retired' by special units trained to detect and destroy the machinic human doubles. These operatives are named *blade runners*.

How can blade runners distinguish the human from the non-human? Their specially designed test does not oppose animality to language use. What marks the replicants as different is their inability to feel empathy for living creatures, notably animals.

The film opens with news of a violent rebellion and breakout on the colonies. A team of replicants has come to Earth. Rick Deckard is required to return to his foresworn profession as a blade runner/bounty hunter and to seek out and destroy four robots. Why have they come? They have come to seek out their maker/father and to request the prolongation of their lives. As a fail-safe device these near-perfect replications who are becoming human through inserted memories have an inbuilt terminus date: they will 'close down' after four years. Yet they want more life. The pathos of the film hangs on the final confrontation between the easily overpowered Deckard and the technically super-powered Roy Batty, the leader of the renegade replicant band, whose final act is to save Deckard from falling off the building in which they have their final fight, and tell him poetically of all that will be lost of what he has seen in the universe with this premature and brutal cessation of his amazing being.

Feminist film theorist Kaja Silverman has pointed to two notable features of this film. Firstly, in the notable absence of any representations of African Americans within an American future, Batty represents the black 'other' of the racist colonial imaginary; but a blond, blue eyed, white German actor, Rutger Hauer, acts this other:

> Because Batty is the leader and presumably the instigator of the Nexus 6 Expedition, which is quite literally an uprising of slaves against their unjust masters, he is the figure who most fully represents 'blackness' in the film. It may seem at first glance deeply problematical that this category should be embodied by a figure who is physically the very embodiment of the Aryan ideal. However, it is precisely through this character's hyperbolic 'whiteness' that *Blade Runner* most dramatically denaturalizes the category of the slave – the category which our culture still manages in an attenuated way to rhyme with negritude. By putting Batty in the position classically occupied by those with dark skin, the film obliges the white spectator to understand the relation between that position and those who are slotted into it as absolutely arbitrary and absolutely brutal.[50]

Secondly, Silverman suggests that far from sustaining the unqualified difference between the human and the replicant, the film demonstrates that replicants with their implanted memories vividly represent the nature of constructed human subjectivity and its formations around the cultural scripts implanted through Imaginary specularity and symbolic interpellations. The replicant becomes an image of the Lacanian thesis by which subjectivity is formed through a series of identifications and the importation of organizing structures from the Symbolic realm of the Other via the Imaginary. As Deckard finally admits, the questions the replicants pose – where do I come from? where am I going? and how will I end? – are the ones 'we are all asking'.

Beyond these main lines of analysis, however, I think we can discern another imaginary, in which the threads of racism, colonialism, the manipulated definition of the human and the extra-legal right to determine life and death – be that the scientist or the bounty hunter authorized by an invisible regime – can be registered: the concentrationary imaginary.

The effects of absolute war and its resulting destruction of the Earth, the creation of colonies serviced by a fabricated 'race' of enslaved workers who look like humans but are divided from them by the lack of a natural life span and absolute subjection to a mode of destruction euphemistically called 'retirement'; these and many other elements seem to draw, unconsciously, on what we have come to understand about the totalitarian experiments undertaken in the twentieth century by regimes of left and right. The ultimate emblem of those regimes is the 'concentrationary universe' created within camps that actually existed for historical periods. The 'concentrationary universe' also extends beyond these limits in time and space in the now-embedded visions of mass enslavement, imperial expansion and total power whose ultimate exercise is the eradication of the human and the *production* of that which ceased to have the rights associated with human life but none the less suffered the experience of being dispossessed of them.

The film was based on a novel by a cult science fiction writer belatedly admitted into the canon of American literature, Philip K. Dick, *Do Androids Dream of Electric Sheep?* (1968). This novel has very different narrative and thematic concerns from Ridley Scott's amalgam of the Dickian oeuvre – including references to his other novel *Man in the High Castle* (1962). That novel imagines a world in which Imperial Japan and Nazi Germany had won World War II. They divided the US between them, rendering Americana an arcane commodity collected by Japanese or German elites in a manner comparable to Hitler's ambition to turn Jewish Europe into a merely musealized remnant. That novel's engagement with Japanese imperial conquest of the United States is referenced in Ridley Scott's dystopic setting of his version of *Do Androids Dream of Electric Sheep?* in a Los Angeles that is more or less entirely inhabited by Japanese and Chinese.

What was Dick's purpose, however, in writing his novels? At the time of writing *Man in the High Castle*, Dick was absorbed by reading British historian Alan Bullock's *Hitler: A Study in Tyranny* (1952) and William L. Shirer's *Rise and Fall of the Third Reich* (1960). In a rare interview about *Do Androids Dream of Electric Sheep?*, Dick spoke of his response to the Eichmann Trial in 1961 and referenced the impact of Hannah Arendt's book *Eichmann in Jerusalem: an Essay on the Banality of Evil*, initially published as articles in *The New Yorker* in 1963.[51]

Dick's conceit is not that replicants are other to the human as robotic creations, or as a newly created enslaved population, the new Jews and new Blacks. That would make the film part of the colonial imaginary. In direct contrast to this typical othering, for Dick the replicants function *politically*; they represent the fascist or the totalitarian perversion of humanity by fascism. They are representations of a politically crafted type, the perpetrators, the Eichmanns and the Hitlers of the world, the men without affect, without empathy, the truly inhuman because they are human but lack the necessary condition for human co-existence: the mutual recognition of shared humanity that is experienced not merely as a cognitive act, but as a capacity to feel with and for an other in her or his vulnerability – a theme taken up by Adriana Cavarero in Chapter 1.

Dick's novel is also about a new religion in the destroyed world. This is based on a machine that enables the participant to merge with a character called Wilbur Mercer, a strange Christological figure, who impersonates the suffering servant from the prophetic book of Isaiah. Mercer struggles up an endless hill receiving not the slings and arrows of outrageous fate but, via virtual reality, actual rocks hurled to wound and impede his perpetual struggle to ascend. At times he ascends far enough to fall into a tomb world, a Biblical world drawn from Ezekiel's vision of the valley of dry bones that is also an image from recent history showing the terrible conditions in camps such as Bergen-Belsen where 13,000 corpses lay unburied. Eventually, in the novel, Deckard finds himself on this very mountain and merges entirely rather than virtually with Mercer, becoming Wilbur Mercer to the extent that he is finally able to empathize with the *electronic replicant* toad he finds on the mountainside, his whole being having longed to have a real animal to care for. When, earlier in the book, Deckard's wife Iran discovers the lid of Deckard's pet toad's hidden electronic heart – revealing the robotic animal's secreted control panel – Deckard is at first crestfallen because he is forced to recognize he does not own a real but an electronic animal. But then – and this marks the change in him – he declares: 'The electrical things have their lives too. Paltry as those lives are.' As he sleeps, his wife phones the electrical animal store and orders the artificial flies needed to feed the toad. The assistant suggests a regular tongue replacement. 'Fine', says Iran, 'I want it to work perfectly. My husband is devoted to it.' In this final recognition that the nature of the thing matters less than the act of caring for wellbeing that itself constitutes the *humanizing* of the subject, irrespective of the humanness of the other, I would identify a total reversal of the concentrationary and its totalitarian master script that is the critical object of Dick's writing.

It is not the *what* of the other that determines the manner in which it may be addressed or treated. It is that in *being other*, even radically so, it calls forth from the feeling subject the capacity to act towards its needs for care, thus inciting precisely the human inclination towards an other and the humanizing gesture of creating a commonality. Thus Dick read in the historical legacy of the perpetration of the concentrationary exterminatory complex the ultimate perversion of the human when people could act without humanity, when what appeared to be people could become like machines: military, bureaucratic and ultimately willing agents of a search for total power that turned death dealing into the euphemism 'retiring'.[52] Thus Dick's novel further creates two worlds. Side by side with Deckard's world in which he longs to care for a real animal, is another one that represents the reversed mirror image. This parallel universe is run entirely by replicants. The Blade Runner Deckard there becomes the hunted victim rather than the bounty hunter.

Blade Runner the film, however, is less astute. In effect, I would argue that it reverses Dick's critical gesture that produced a fiction as a counter-concentrationary statement. Ridley undoes Dick's gesture so precisely by failing to read the politics of interrogative resistance to the concentrationary that underlies the original Dickian text. Translating Dick's political allegory of the play of human and robotic into the classic opposition between the threatened masculine and the excessively empowered other: robot, alien, black, or woman, the film is remade precisely as a fascist drama of the journey to restore the destabilized masculine subject to himself through overcoming the other in whose distorting mirror he cannot bear to see himself.

There is ambiguity, however, at the end of Scott's film. The final scene exists in several versions, some created to meet and others to resist the force of the production company's demands for the profitable ending. In one, Deckard falls for the replicant Rachel, failing to 'retire' her. The novel's discovery of empathy for the electric toad is translated into heterosexual desire for the machine woman. The suspicion hovers, however, over the entire film that, in order to be a bounty hunter/blade runner, Deckard himself is probably a replicant: in Dick's sense of a perverted human capable of coldblooded killing as a business, rather than in the film's deeper sense of the dangerous machinic other.[53]

Re-read in relation to the original novel, *Blade Runner* is but one case where I suggest we can begin to use the *concentrationary imaginary* to interrogate not the iconography or even the overt narratives we find in popular culture, but the ways in which a certain *habitus* of the concentrationary informs this cinematic recasting of a historically self-conscious fictional response to knowledge of the actual concentrationary universe and its fascist origins. At the same time, we can see the film emplotting older, conventional or generic stories that distract us from seeing the deadly legacy of what was introduced into political, social and imaginative possibility after 1933 by the historical totalitarian experiments that initiated new potentialities into human history. Finally, in comparing film version to original novel, we see the imprint of the concentrationary imaginary in its failure of the imagination, in the film's betrayal of the political warning the novel sought to effect in fictional form. It is only in Batty's final gesture and dying speech that the film glimpses its own betrayal, risking a moment of redemptive sentimentality in place of the horrific sadness that should be felt before this mechanical switching off. The mixing of kitsch and death identified by Friedländer flashes up here, stayed by the actor's delivery, even while the film has made us know that he must die and Deckard must live. That cinematic move by which we do not feel utterly appalled in the face of death, but accept its inevitability in the plotting of the hierarchy of life across the film, is the sign of the concentrationary norm.

It is in the analytical work between what is shown, often misused, and what is not seen, or noticed, often disguised, that the trace of the concentrationary imaginary can be deciphered for the purposes of alerting us to what we might be coming to accept: a concentrationary social nexus that we take as the normality of a world engineering us for its own profit at the price of our humanness as social and, above all, political beings. The dehumanization of death is the most obvious and now almost unremarked legacy of the concentrationary nexus that is not a matter of seepage so much as pervasion.

What would it mean to find, in an American science fiction film made by a British director trained in advertising, not images from the totalitarian experiment represented by the concentration camp, but thematic traces of what political theorists identify as the structural properties and anti-political innovation of the concentrationary universe? Is it evidence of what we are seeking to identify as the concentrationary imaginary that subtends contemporary popular culture without any overt reference to historical actuality, and which, therefore, bypasses the work of memory and representation in order to create a specular, fictive space in which the abhorred past is, none the less, translated into displaced contemporary retellings that, however dystopic, entertain and enthral and hence ideologically refashion our sense of what we can accept as possible?

The concentrationary imaginary/Imaginary

Whether we imagine it seeping from the anti-political real into *culture* or always already waiting to infuse it with renewed doses, the concentrationary works through a cultural reservoir of images that are no longer documentary of a specific historical event. These images then become mythic signifiers that can be recycled in other narratives that insinuate the concentrationary. Not by overt indoctrination and propaganda but by spectacle and entertainment, we are being groomed to accept a profound compromise of the human – in Arendt's terms – that prepares us to accept who can be 'wasted' without cost because they are positioned as being beyond the call of shared citizenship: humanness. The very dream of democracy, so unstable and fragile, is being fatally wounded as globalizing forces breach the localities of defence. Why does this work on us?

We need to return to where we began, with Lacan's introduction of the concept of the *Imaginary*, which has both general and technical meanings. We need to consider both the specificity of cinema as a machine of the Imaginary (capitalized to refer specifically to Lacan's psychoanalytical formulation) and how that apparatus replays to us the specular or Imaginary formation of our subjectivity.

So far in this introduction the phrasing, *concentrationary* imaginary, refers to such an imaginary framework of images, ideas, beliefs, tropes, myths, and stereotypes, within which the historical concentrationary universe was conceived and enacted. Beyond the historical analyses of socio-economic and historical conditions and causes, there lies a question about what made it possible for such a terror to be enacted by men and women who became its perpetrators, giving themselves over to its spectacular representation of a terrible historical necessity to rule and to kill.[54] This would reveal the power of the representations made to those inducted to serve in the concentrationary such that their encounters with the 'others' they were entitled to brutalize, torture and kill were deflected from involving shared human recognition and identification by means of racialization, even of political opponents, to a level of severing any human connection. There are speeches, documents, manuals, training processes as well as the imaginative production of films, images, exhibitions, rituals, parades, spectacles by means of which we can trace the component elements, predominant images and stock of ever more rigidly marked differentiations, exclusions and discourses on danger, purity, unity and the role of the One, the embodying leader.

The *concentrationary* imaginary is also the stock of images to which the actualized concentrationary universe gave rise as it was turned into representation by photography, film and other reports. Mostly created by the victors in order to shock, produced as evidence in post-war trials for war crimes, becoming historical documents of atrocity to be used in education and commemoration, images of the camps generated a selective and emotive iconography of horror which has an imaginary function insofar as the images fix a limited and incomplete knowledge to a selective repertoire of signs and images that can fail to make known the real as deeply as they become iconic. Barbed wire, staggering emaciated people in dirty uniforms, shaved heads, piles of naked dead bodies, barking officers in shiny uniforms are just some of these extracted tropes that become signifiers. What makes the move from the image to the imaginary is the sedimentation of certain images into an iconic landscape that can then be pillaged for representations of horror or terror that may or may not wish to activate the historical reference, but certainly are prepared to use the connotational freight for purposes other than generating political anxiety about a past historical event. The cultural practices may precisely use this repertoire to celebrate violence, to render it spectacular and entertaining, or as a means of creating commodities for profit and to normalize a Manichean universe of good and evil. The *concentrationary* imaginary is not a matter of films or fictions about concentration camps and their specific populations from *Kapò* (1959) to the *Boy in the Striped Pyjamas* (2008, Mark Herman, based on the novel by John Boyne). As prism, the *concentrationary* imaginary becomes analytically useful precisely when we can use it to unearth an unexpected relay between the historical concentrationary and its founding imaginary and what would appear to be entirely non-concentrationary situations that none the less reassert aspects of the apoliticizing logic and dehumanizing effects beyond the limits or the zone of the camp through imaginary forms such as cinema, games, or images.

Lacan offers a psychoanalytical theory of this field. His intervention focuses on the formations of subjectivity that make us susceptible to the imaginary (imagination and imaginarium) at a level where our encounter with images lures us into identification; allows us to be formed in their image. This brings us finally to a concentrationary *Imaginary*.

Jacques Lacan (1901–81) displaced Freud's tripartite, drive-based model of stages of psychic development – oral, anal and phallic – with his model of three registers on which subjectivity operates: the Real, the Imaginary and the Symbolic. The Imaginary is the register of making sense of the world through images and fantasies while the Symbolic is the register of words and thoughts that use symbolic language (namely that the real of the world is only knowable and is spoken/written through symbols: words and signs).

All three registers operate in an intertwining that Lacan later imagined as a plait of three strands in order to locate subjectivity as operating always across, and dependent upon, the knotting of these three co-existent registers. In this speculative formation, the Imaginary is a mode of apprehending the world and the infant's place in it primarily through fantasy; it is an image-based mode allegorized by the notion of the mirror which also gives prominence to mimicry of an imago projected to the child and thus imported from culture around which it shapes its own becoming self.

Several implications can be derived for cultural analysis from Lacan's original and (later radically revised) formulation of the mirror phase that relate specifically to the psychoanalytical contribution to a thesis on the concentrationary *Imaginary*. Firstly, by means of this allegory, subjectivity has a specular dimension. Thus the self – ego or 'I' – arises as an 'image of a self' and is, as a result, a fundamental *alienation* into an image. But the image is borrowed from the mirror, which operates as a cultural screen projecting its image onto the as yet un-selfed infant. On this screen the infant (meaning without language) sees but *misrecognizes* itself as image in the field of the Other (Culture). In contrast to the infant's own sense of helpless immobility, the image of what a human being is (upright, coordinated, territorialized within the space of the body and the skin) supports a fantasy of wholeness not yet experienced by the still incapacitated, dis-coordinated and dependent child. This child takes on/in this image as an *imago*, a coherent, seemingly self-sufficient container for the flow of sensations that play across its not yet cohering corporality. The mirror phase process thus territorializes – gives it a discrete location separate from the world and the mother's body – the beginnings of a sense of self, that is, however, borrowed from the outside, and then located inside an imaginary whole by a process of identification. The imago thus operates as an interiorizable, semi-orthopaedic architecture, around which to organize a chaotic bundle of sensations and psychically invested locations on the infant's body into a boundaried whole that can be imagined as the support for the projection of an 'I' that can then situate itself in the pronouns offered by language; in the pronouns by which a self or 'I' comes to be spoken.

It is equally important to grasp that there is a counter-pressure to this imaginary unified self formed by the bounding image – an outer limit – and an interior orthopaedic armature – an inner structuring. This counter-pressure is a fantasy of falling 'back' into bits and pieces. The assumption of the imaginary image of wholeness generates, retrospectively, like the negative of a positive photographic image, a shadowing fantasy of a 'former' state of fragmentation, engendering a perpetual anxiety around disintegration. Thus in the Imaginary, the binary pair wholeness/disintegration become a foundational and oppositional structuring fantasy of the ego as it forms by taking inside an image from the external screen/mirror of culture.

Since the Imaginary, initially a stage of formation, then becomes the fantasmatic lining of the Symbolic, always in converse with it, we can track the political or cultural mobilization of this double fantasy of wholeness versus fragmentation and dissolution into bits and pieces. We can recognize its work in fascist discourse and politics that foster a paranoid vision of the threat of the fragmentation and destruction of a mythic unity of a whole people, attributed to an other, which easily becomes a targeted scapegoat. The fascist and racist rather than nationalist fiction of the unified Aryan people, which is in turn fantasmatically represented as the ego ideal of the whole, embodied in the One, the Führer, was represented as being eternally and fatally menaced by a disease (threatening the whole and healthy social body) or an infestation (threatening the security of the home space) projected onto the abnormally feared but equally abjected other. Jews rule the world and Jews are sub- or non-human, to be killed like vermin, for instance. What is not incorporated into the ideal One becomes the image of a destructive threat, hence the power of the imaginary projection onto 'the Jew' of a crazy mixture of dirt, mobility, unfixity, infestation, infinite power, cunning and so forth.

This primary assumption of what is in effect an alien other (the imago) that will become the locus for the emerging ego is thus a primary act of misrecognition that paves the way for the very complex psychological operation named identification: taking on (dressing in) or taking in (introjecting) identifications with image others who are indicated by culture to be 'like' the 'me' that will emerge as the becoming I is constituted through them and partially builds itself upon these idealized forms. Its negative is the rejection of identification with what is presented as being unlike me because it threatens the misrecognized and idealized integrity. Racism and its normalized extensions of exclusivity operate here with the production of counter-images of non-identification, what is not me, making impossible the sharing of recognition, creating abjected exclusions from the ego ideal, from a shared human identity mobilized by a deadly fear of the disintegration of the ego itself.

This leads to the third important effect, which we need for the analysis of the role of the Imaginary in culture, which is described succinctly by Fredric Jameson:

> The mirror phase, which is the condition for primary narcissism, is also, owing to the equally irreducible gap it opens between the infant and its fellows, the very source of human *aggressivity*; and indeed, one of the original features of Lacan's early teaching is its insistence on the inextricable association of these two drives.[55] (my emphasis)

Misrecognition, identification (with the ideal Ego) and aggressivity (against the same) and fear of fragmentation form the Imaginary complex.

Lacan's speculations on the mirror phase and the Imaginary have become a foundational theoretical formulation for certain psychoanalytical explorations of the cinema that has been defined as the paradox of 'the imaginary signifier'.[56] Cinema is at once a system of semiotically produced meanings that work on us through words and narratives and a spectacle that operates through entrancing us and luring us in through specular fascination. Cinema reactivates and replays to us the psychic operations of identification, dis-identification and aggressivity typical of the Imaginary register. Linking the concentrationary to this sense of the Imaginary, we analyse the processes of identification, projection, introjection, and the relations to specular others, egos formed and deformed, and phantasies premised on the oscillation between desired and fantasized wholeness and its catastrophic collapse as well as phantasies of omnipotent vision and self-exhibition.

Critically, therefore, the Imaginary operates a primarily binary structure (in distinction from the triangulation which becomes the agony of the Oedipal moment wherein the binary structure of the Imaginary cannot resolve the question of sexual difference and cultural positioning under the law of the Father). Fredric Jameson argues that the Imaginary tends, therefore, towards a Manichean vision of the world, divided into good and bad, self and other, identification and rejection.

> The Imaginary may thus be described as a peculiar spatial configuration, whose bodies primarily entertain relations of inside/outside with one another, which is then traversed and reorganized by that primordial rivalry and transitive substitution of imagoes, that indistinction of narcissism and aggressivity, from which later conceptions of good and evil derive. The stage is already an alienation – the subject having been captured by his or her specular image – but in Hegelian fashion it is the kind of alienation from which a more positive evolution is indistinguishable and without which the latter is inconceivable.[57]

The Imaginary, therefore, positions the subject spectator or viewer or reader in relation to actual or imagined imagoes of others in whom the subject recognizes or misrecognizes him or herself while at the same time this activity generates a kind of primordial and simplified system of inside/outside, I/other, good/bad, endowing situations I may rationally and consciously encounter with a supercharge of polarizing phantasy.

Cinema, and cinematic derivatives such as TV or video games, with its unique combination of image – the specular – ordered symbolically by narrative which confines or limits the space of the specular image within some closure or ending, is a particularly powerful apparatus where the Imaginary and the Symbolic come into play. They do not, however, play out as binary pair. They are triangulated by the Real, which Jameson defines as History, as that which is substantively real in historical material terms but which cannot be confined within or exhausted by our representations, Imaginary or Symbolic. The Imaginary functions, however, culturally to forestall the challenge of the Real (History) on the Symbolic (Thought) to shift and accommodate it. The Imaginary is thus safe from History, becoming a safe haven from complexity, as well as being the always powerful realm of violence and aggression characterized by adamant identification and equally powerful rejection.

The Imaginary thus already echoes aspects of the concentrationary *per se*. Indeed I would argue that, structurally as well as historically, the concentrationary represents a form of regression to or reactivation of the Imaginary whose binary dispositions are released from socio-cultural policing by the Symbolic. A system or space that lets the Imaginary out to untrammelled play might then be experienced as a psychic liberation of the binary mode of the Imaginary from the rule of Law represented by the Symbolic, the imposition of a social law, the authority of the Father that prohibits jouissance and denies the subject what it wants. The Symbolic is instituted by a triangulated rather than binary system (child and sexually differentiated parents of the Oedipal triad) that rewrites the fantasies of the dyadic Imaginary ego (self/other). As a space outside the Law where the infinitely creative work of pure sadism and creative violence was encouraged and made into the new *ab*norm*ality*, the concentrationary universe became a playground based on the absolute alienation of each perpetrating subject from human intersubjectivity with what was constructed as the abjected other. Law was 'officially' suspended, fostering absolute identification with the fascist imago, called the ego ideal, that like me which I want to become, whose aggressivity was, however, directed in an equally absolute sense towards a racialized or political other, who was to be expelled absolutely, by indoctrination and propaganda, and by actual degradation in actual camps, from all possibility of identification, and in some camps at the very terminus of this horrifyingly realized Imaginary world, from life itself. The prisoner, the Jew, the victim, the disabled, the Roma, the queer – all were rendered the very principle of a repulsive, menacing, even non-human otherness. Such otherness had, however, to be creatively produced. It required the systematic erasure of all that might make the socially, politically, sexually or ethnically *different* person function as the specular *other*; that is, a source of identification. Both horrifying representations (propaganda and ideology) and the work of actual torture and social abjection productively erased from those the Nazi machine denied as fellow beings any trace of a shared human imago.

Once, however, we think about the Imaginary as being restaged and replayed through cultural apparatuses such as the cinematic, we do not need to expect the *mise-en-scène* of the historical camps in order to discern the *concentrationary Imaginary* (sic) at work. But I must qualify this. As I have shown, there is no single, homogeneous concentrationary imaginary. What we are tracking are the component elements that might surface within a larger cultural reservoir of images and scenarios, indicating the pressure or trace of this novel potentiality in culture, creating new constellations.

One such trace might be the extraordinary, even exponential, increase in cultural representation of cruelty, torture, violence, othering and the altered forms in which human dying takes place. One extreme case we might look at is video games in which a certain kind of play space is established, different from the cinematic experience of passive viewing, because it is interactive. It functions precisely as an Imaginary operation because it involves a certain kind of physical and motor activity relating to a screen mirror in which the will of the player is set in motion in relation to a Manichean scenario of me or them, me against them, in which all interactions involve a simplified choice through the exercise of an omnipotent phantasy that exercises an absolute power of killing or being killed and in which the other is never going to function as the big Other, the otherness that sets the limits to or confines the grandiosity of the ego. The games are played precisely as a space, and space is critical to the theories of the imaginary, which is a set of spatial coordinates. All choices in video games have no consequences and incite no responsibilities for indeed everything is possible since everything within this game space corresponds to a passage through or a blockage that must be overcome where the player makes decisions on this basis alone. The end is to win and all means are at the player's disposal.

It could be argued that because it is a game and known as such and played as such, there is no confusion between what is permitted in its space and the ordinary daily life in which such things are not allowed. But one of the aspects consistently identified in the documentaries that return us to the historical site of the reality of the concentration camps is not merely the terrifying proximity of horror and the everyday, but also the co-existence in the lives of the perpetrators between worlds in which they operated. The perpetrators and their lackeys lived one way with their peers and colleagues, family or friends and quite otherwise on duty within the camp. Such divisions are not the markers of real and fantasy but the potential splitting which the Imaginary makes possible. Reality is imposed as a system by either the Symbolic as law or the Real as History. But in the imaginary space of the Imaginary at play, we are in the zone of the game and the dream. Arendt writes:

> It is not so much the barbed wire as the skilfully manufactured unreality of those whom it fences in that provokes such enormous cruelties and ultimately makes extermination look like a perfectly normal measure. *Everything that was done in the camps is known to us from the world of perverse, malignant fantasies.* The difficult thing to understand is that, like such fantasies, these gruesome crimes took place in a phantom world, which, however, has materialized, as it were, into a world which is complete with all sensual data of reality *but lacks the structure of consequence and responsibility without which reality remains for us a mass of incomprehensible data.* The result is that a place has been established where men can be tortured and slaughtered, yet neither the tormentors nor the tormented, and least of all the outside, can be aware that what is happening is anything *more than a cruel game of an absurd dream.*[58] (my emphasis)

Conclusion

I am suggesting that we can find the trace or shadow of a historically created logic, system and space-time, what we are calling the *concentrationary*, in contemporary popular culture, not only at the level of iconography, although images will surface, and not as conscious narrative, although elements can be identified. It is precisely because images and elements unloosed from their historical or political moorings enter into circulation as part of a stock of images or even plot lines that we can invoke the concept of an imaginary, in the general sense of the term. Not as structural as Fredric Jameson's political unconscious, the concentrationary Imaginary, in Lacanian terms, is here proposed as an extended prism for critical work on the politics of representation by making visible the traces, whose otherwise unnoticed circulation has, we suggest, real, if not dire, effects on our subjective formations in relation to the sustaining of democracy and our political humanity. If the totalitarian as experimentally pursued in the singular time-space of the concentration camp is both a historical event and reflects, in its structure, the ultimate modern, anti-political zone, the graveyard of democratic aspiration, it behoves us to notice and critique the cultural assimilation of its fundamental properties rather than its appearance. As a result of our consumption, via the Imaginary fantasies offered in popular culture, of this aesthetically and fascinatingly packaged fictive world, we, in our humanity, are being refashioned in its image and, as its creatures, suffer the anguish of momentary recognition of this fact, as Lacan suggested. Camps do not exist any more in precisely this form, although forms of them are still present in all our societies. But campness was never confined within the actual barbed wired enclosures. If it has become image and is one that normalizes the conditions of destroyed political sociality and glories in excessive violence and indifference to human dying, are we, through the work of I(i)maginary capture, being reformed in our newly precarious humanity according to scripts that we would consciously abhor?

In the chapters that follow, this book plots out the theoretical and philosophical arguments for and against the idea that our culture is infused with traces of the concentrationary. They also reveal the complexity of any reading of or for the elements of a concentrationary imaginary as a force at work in popular culture, but always alongside and amongst other factors, sometimes even counter-forces. This introduction has made the larger case for asking the question. The substance of the book demonstrates and critiques the insights gained by the opening postulation.

The first section, titled *Thinking*, in honour of Hannah Arendt's argument that the banality of evil lies in thoughtlessness, probes the philosophical underpinnings of the project. Feminist philosopher Adriana Cavarero draws on Hannah Arendt's primary characterization of the concentrationary experiment in totalitarianism as an assault on the human condition in order to name an ontological crime against humanity. Identifying a new form of contemporary violence, which is inflicted above all on non-combatants, on civilians, on those most nakedly exposed in their humanity, Cavarero coins the neologism *horrorism* to define this ontological violence against the helpless: the most succinct position of the human condition.

In the following chapter, Olivia Guaraldo pits Arendt's post-totalitarian political theory of human plurality, spontaneity and contingency against the inherent totalizing characteristic of deterministic Hegelian theories of history. She thus draws out more clearly the significance of Arendt's anti-Hegelian theory of political agency in *The Human Condition*. She addresses Arendt's resistance to historicizing accounts, and their fetishized realism that destroys the human as political. She also explains the vital and political role of storytelling – fiction and the use of creative imagination and poetic language – that reveals more of the contingency and the agency of politico-human action than the preset frames of treacherously totalizing theories of History (Communism) or Nature (Nazism). Guaraldo explores the role of the imagination and of fiction in the work of survivor/witness to the concentrationary universe, Primo Levi, as he struggles to convey the unimaginable nature of the camp experience in language that must, however, yield to the unspeakable. As the opposite of the political effectivity of the creative imagination, Guaraldo proposes a reading of the concentrationary imaginary at work in the forms of contemporary entertainment, at whose extreme end is the Reality Show, flattening, eroding temporality and dulling the capacity to imagine change and futures with its insistence on the ever present and the banality of a consumed and timeless 'real'.

In his analysis of contribution of four thinkers, Jean-Luc Nancy and Philippe Lacoue-Labarthe, Paul Virilio and Bernard Stiegler, Ian James examines their arguments for identifying a totalitarian logic articulated in specific symbolic forms that both pre-existed and persist beyond specific historical incarnations. These thinkers define and then trace certain distinctive features at play in contemporary liberal democracies and, specifically, in the processes and effects of their communication and media systems. The purpose of the analysis is not to make equations between historical realizations of the totalitarian and contemporary social systems and media cultures. Using the insights of these four analysts of the symbolic, of myth, and of subjectivities, James argues that we can use their analytical prisms to hold up a mirror to contemporary liberal democracies and their consumer and media cultures in order to make visible the darker structures in which we are enthralled. Thus James focuses on the ideological and technological processes of totalization (linking back to Guaraldo's reading of Arendt), convergence and synchronization that, he argues, threaten democracy, which itself can only function through 'the ongoing and multiple process of singularization, divergence and de synchronization', thus echoing both Hannah Arendt's stress on plurality and spontaneity, and iterating Guaraldo's argument about dead time.

In the second section, *Desire*, two authors take up the challenge of reading some texts in a cinematic archive that overtly references, iconographically, the concentrationary universe and Nazism, and recycles its visible signs as the allegory of sadism, sexual perversity and cruelty. Aaron Kerner contrasts the obvious 'dressing up in fascist costume' of existing tropes of the genre of the sexploitation film in order to expose a deeper concentrationary logic at work in another recent genre of films that appear to have no historical reference, namely Torture Porn. In my own chapter, I study Liliana Cavani's *The Night Porter* (1974), which has been read/misread as part of the resurgence of Nazism as exploitation and entertainment, often in bad faith. I argue that Cavani's film performs an attentive and thoughtful feminist exposé of the persistence of the concentrationary imaginary precisely through daring to restage it in a fiction, and in so doing poetically and politically to track both its infestation of still-extant fascist secret societies and officially bourgeois high culture, and thus to identify blasphemous gestures, however futile, of resistance to it.

In the final section, *Camp*, three chapters subject the idea of the concentrationary imaginary to probing analysis through the reading of mainstream European and North American film and television. Benjamin Hannavy Cousen analyses the significance of the re-appearance of images of the liberation of Dachau in Scorsese's psychological thriller *Shutter Island* (2010), which demonstrates both a seepage of the image of the concentration camp into a narrative set on a prison island for the criminally insane, and also what Hannavy Cousen additionally identifies as 'creep', which operates by the deadening of the historical referent of an image such as those of Dachau so that the concentrationary becomes, explicitly and often only inferentially, an open or mobile signifier detached from historical connotation.

Max Silverman addresses a post-war debate in France in film criticism that concerned cinema's diminishing ability to critique and to refute concentrationary legacies and to resist submission to entertainment alone.

Silverman then offers a reading of the politico-aesthetic strategies of Austrian director Michael Haneke's film *Funny Games*, initially made in German in 1997 and then completely remade in English for the North American market in 2007 at whose television game culture it was aimed, and of his later film *The White Ribbon* (2009), in order to argue that Haneke seeks to interrupt the loss of the critical potential in cinema by exposing the viewers, by means of his cinematic process, to the insinuation of evil in the everyday and to the familiarization of camp-like logic and structures into the cultural imaginary. The concentrationary imaginary operates as that which the film's aesthetics seek to dislodge through exposing the spectator to the shock of recognition of the proximity of the concentrationary in the banal forms of everyday life, the family, and entertainment.

In her chapter Brenda Hollweg demonstrates the necessity for close readings of the characters, plots, and scenarios of the multiple manifestations of the character Nikita in European and American film and in the TV series that was, by chance, one of my own starting points for this speculation about seepage and persistence of the concentrationary. Working through the generic tropes of *film noir* political thriller, Hollweg's detailed visual and narratological analysis of the translation of Besson's heroine-focused cinema film to a multi-season TV series identifies the latter's refocus on the logic of the secret government agency that commissions its trained assassins, a shift she argues can be read through the lens of the concentrationary imaginary. Hollweg's careful scrutiny of this TV series' normalization of violence, cruelty and affectless killing as entertainment resonates, in the negative as it were, with what Silverman argues is the politico-aesthetic intervention Haneke has attempted.

The overall purpose of this collection is exploratory, speculative and analytical. In tracing through the imaginary of culture the lineaments of the concentrationary as the logic and system that political theorists rather than the historians have defined as its terrifying novelty for us, we are offering a prism for the analysis of undercurrents, tendencies, and tropings that suggest that we need to examine our popular culture politically for conscious and unconscious complicity with a perversion of human life that was experimentally initiated in actual camps but which is not at all confined to their time or their space, not marked by barbed wire fences and iron gates, not safely in the past at all.

PART 1

THINKING

1

FRAMING HORROR

Adriana Cavarero

A decade and a half ago, at the incipit of the new millennium, what we could call the 'Spirit of the time' manifested its violent core by shocking the entire world with the spectacular magnitude of the Twin Towers collapse. 'This catastrophic event changes the way we think and act, moment to moment, week to week, for unknown weeks and months to come, and steely years', Don DeLillo wrote in the *Guardian* on 22 December 2001.[1] In the same vein, Derrida claimed that 'what is terrible about September 11, what remains "infinite" in this wound, is that we do not know what it is and so do not know how to describe, identify, or even name it', for our understanding or imagination, it is hard 'to meaningfully attach any concept'.[2] Many years have passed, Ground Zero has become a symbolic place for mourning and commemoration, but the two sentences are still worth quoting not only because of their ability to express the feeling of inexplicability that, at the time, was perceived by ordinary people and many intellectuals, but also because they hint at an issue which is still crucial for political theory. To put it simply, the 9/11 catastrophe revealed the ineptitude of Western political vocabulary to conceptualize the distinctive form of human destruction spectacularly exhibited by the event, a form of radical violence, capable of breaking our frames of intelligibility, that cannot therefore be enlisted under the categories of terrorism and war. Yet, as is well known, the linguistic reaction of politics and the media took exactly this uncritical direction and spoke immediately of terrorism and war, either specifying the first as jihad terrorism and hyperterrorism, or denoting the second as war on terror and preventive war. This misleading nomenclature and its material consequences – thousands of civilians killed in various zones of the planet – could not, however, hide the real thing we were confronted with by the Twin Towers massacre and all of the carnages that followed; namely, the phenomenon of unilateral violence on defenceless people struck *en masse* and at random.

Speaking in terms of political theory, is it a new and unheard of phenomenon? Indeed, providing a straight answer to this question is not only very problematic but it also engages, directly, with the axiom of inexplicability, which the question itself presupposes. Yet, at least under Western eyes and in spite of the epochal specificity on which it is worth insisting, the phenomenon looks not completely new. In the Western tradition, notoriously, violence against the defenceless has a wide and atrocious gallery. Auschwitz, tortures, pogroms, genocides and other aberrations fit in the picture. Symptomatically, whatever their historical and geopolitical location might be, all of these infamous theatres of human destruction share a trait of perversion that escapes the political lexicon centred on the categories of 'terror' or 'war'. Moreover, they threaten intelligibility as such. The question, in fact, far from simply regarding a problem of terminology, touches unsuspected chords. Namely, it interrogates ontology.

Speculating on this issue, in a book published after 9/11, I coined the term 'horrorism'.[3] Rooted in horror rather than terror, the term aims primarily at providing a conceptual framework for historical scenarios where unilateral violence is inflicted on defenceless victims. As a matter of fact, inasmuch as massacres of defenceless people, no matter if more or less intense depending on the diverse areas of the planet, are today a global phenomenon, they hint at an urgent need to reconceptualize our language, if not our imaginary, in order to name a modality of destruction which targets the human as human. As is worth repeating, to verbalize it in terms of war and terrorism is useless, equivocal and misleading. Instead of describing the atrocious reality of facts, the obsolete lexicon of modernity ends up in justifying/producing the carnage as an immanent mode of its functioning and engenders linguistic confusion. This confusion, to put it simply, grows essentially out of a basic mistake: war and terrorism, faithful to traditional nomenclature, persist in observing the scene of destruction from the perspective of the regular or irregular warrior. The scene we are now focusing on, however, is different. On the stage of human destruction, warriors are today even invisible. Defenceless victims, vulnerable people, civilians butchered at random are the ordinary protagonists here. If the new era demands that meaning and the semantic continuity of traditional frames of intelligibility ought to be abandoned, the perspective of the defenceless looks, thus, much more plausible than that of the warrior.

A brief focus on some significant data of the last century could be useful to focus attention on the issue. The First World War (1914–18) inaugurated the model of Total War, characterized by 'the placing of civilians on the same level as military personnel, and the propensity to exterminate them without hesitation'.[4] Among the victims of World War II (1939–45), civilians formed a substantial majority. The proportion of civilians killed in wars or conflict during the last decades of the twentieth century exceeded 90 per cent. As for the first decade of the new millennium, which 9/11 2001 symbolically inaugurated, the percentage was even higher. For example, in Afghanistan, where the so-called 'terrorist attacks' were reaching an average of 14 a day and killed more than thousands a year, the victims were prevalently civilians. Somewhere – perhaps too far from the Western door of perception – the massacre of the defenceless goes on, just now, on a regular basis. As for the past century, at which Western eyes can now look from a distance, according to scholars, 'it has been calculated that, in round figures, those killed during the twentieth century in acts of mass violence numbered of two hundred millions'.[5] The million Armenian citizens deported to their deaths in the desert deserve special mention, as do the almost 6 million dead among Jews in camps, ghettos and through direct shooting, as do the uncalculated millions of persons swallowed by the Stalinist gulags. One could add the victims of Pol Pot's Cambodian killing fields and other numerous cases. On the other hand, it would be unreasonable to close the list without pronouncing names of sites such as Guernica, Coventry, Dresden, Hamburg and, obviously, Hiroshima and Nagasaki. Moreover, do not the 3 million dead in the Vietnam War, the majority of them defenceless victims of napalm bombing, deserve a mention too? The list is, indeed, tragically infinite, and obviously it cannot but be arbitrary and incomplete.

It is not just a question of providing complete data and exact figures. The figures serve merely to emphasize how, in recent times, butchery and carnage are mainly directed at the civilian population. Intra-specific human violence, in late modernity and even more in the last few years, consists predominantly in the murder, unilateral and sometimes planned, of the defenceless. What is at stake, here, is not simply war and terror but the human condition of vulnerability perverted by the work of horror.

The term 'horror', on which the neologism *horrorism* is, of course, constructed, has a very interesting etymology. Derived from the Greek verb *phrisso* and the Latin *horreo* – both alluding to the phenomenon of 'goose flesh' or, more literally, of hair standing on end – it hints at the corporeal manifestation of repugnance for the dismembering of the human body. The mythical Medusa, the Gorgon, represents it powerfully. There is a freezing and paralyzing effect, in horror, which does not depend on the natural fear of death – as in the case of trembling in the experience of terror – but rather on disgust for an ontological crime that outrages the human condition of vulnerability. Disfigured by a violence that aims to undo the incarnate embodied uniqueness of every human being, the vulnerable is here on stage as an exemplary icon of the helpless victim. What I designate with the term *horrorism* has to do precisely with the undoing of this uniqueness. It consists in an ontological injury that turns unique beings into a mass of superfluous creatures whose 'murder is as impersonal as the squashing of a gnat'.[6] This sentence, formulated by Hannah Arendt, refers to the inhuman condition experienced by the victims of the Nazi camp machine. As Arendt acutely underlines, in her seminal work on *The Origins of Totalitarianism*, in the concentration-extermination camp system, 'suffering, of which there has always been too much on earth, is not the issue, nor is the number of victims. Human nature as such is at stake.'[7] The scenario of the *Lager* is, in fact, characterized by an 'unpunishable, unforgivable absolute evil which could no longer be understood and explained by the evil motives of self-interest, greed, resentment, lust for power and cowardice'.[8] It is 'human nature' itself, in other words, under attack. This is why horror comes dramatically to the fore and prevails over terror.

By working on this issue, Arendt makes clear the distinction, but also the perverse connection, between terror and horror by introducing the category of *total terror*. Terror, she notices, 'as a means of frightening people into submission can appear in an extraordinary variety of forms and can be closely linked with a large number of political and party systems that have become familiar to us'.[9] Terror, in brief, is a well-known political instrument employed by institutional regimes, revolutionary movements, small groups of conspirators and other agencies of power for purposes of intimidation. Political terror belongs, therefore, to the logic of means with respect to ends. It is execrable, but not incomprehensible. Yet, in totalitarian violence, this very logic is extraordinarily absent. Real totalitarian terror, Arendt writes, begins when ordinary violence is left behind and the system turns to a 'terror [that] has lost its "purpose"'; that is, a terror which is 'no longer the means to frighten people'.[10] Arendt calls it *total terror*, a terror that is no longer strategic, because it has departed from the logic of means and ends, and appears, therefore, inexplicable. The inexplicable nestled in the ultimate nucleus of extreme horror comes thus to the fore. It is, in fact, precisely this surfacing of inexplicability that attests that the performance of totalitarian violence has already shifted from terror to horror. Although she is aware that the inexplicable cannot be resolved into any simple explanation, in order to 'fac[e] up to... reality – whatever it may be', Arendt tries to 'comprehend' the phenomenon by providing historical accounts and conceptual frames apt to describe it.[11]

In so doing, she ponders, first of all, on the cases that exemplify the principle that 'everything is permitted'. Arendt mentions wars of aggression, 'massacre of hostile populations', 'extermination of native peoples',[12] and the concentration camps – but not the death camps – the invention of which precedes the advent of totalitarianism. The task of comprehending total terror needs, however, a further step, a step that symptomatically compels Arendt to focus definitely on the concept of horror. In the totalitarian machine of extermination the principle that 'everything is permitted' is in fact substituted by the unprecedented principle that 'everything is possible'. That it was possible to manipulate human nature, reducing men to absolutely superfluous beings, was something that only the infernal laboratory of the *Lager* could conceive of and execute. And it was precisely in that inferno that total terror – intended as terror that has lost its purpose – finally came to coincide with the extreme form of horror. Life in the camps was such, Arendt writes, that 'its horror can never be fully embraced by the imagination for the very reason that it stands outside of life and death'.[13] By erasing the essential discrimination between living and dying, horror breaks the border of ordinary violence and renders it inexplicable.

The topic of the 'living dead' is notoriously central in the immense literature on the concentration camps; it has become a tragic icon of the Auschwitz imaginary. Arendt remains, however, an original scholar in framing the topic from the point of view of ontology. Horror, for her, as it is worth repeating, has to do with the human condition as such. It consists in the perversion of a living and a dying that, in the *Lager*, are no longer such, because the product of this perversion is 'a specimen of the animal-species man'[14] in which the uniqueness of every human being – and hence the necessarily individual dimension of a life that concludes with death – has been annihilated. The destruction of uniqueness, she writes, 'creates a horror that vastly overshadows the outrage of the juridical-political person and the despair of the moral person'.[15] In the meticulous annihilating process, 'many were the methods of dealing with this uniqueness of the human person',[16] Arendt notes. At the end, all that remained were 'ghastly marionettes with human faces',[17] that, like the 'miserable and sordid puppets' described by Levi, had nothing more of the human about them.

The topic of the human and the not-human is a very delicate and complicated one on which to speculate. Moreover, to dwell on the scenario of concentrationary imaginary in order to 'comprehend' the horror displayed by the Twin Tower collapse and its violent aftermath is quite a risky move. What is here at stake, however, rather than the concentrationary imaginary as such, is the recent impact of an 'excessive' form of human destruction that, again, challenges our imagination. From this perspective, within the horizon of political theory, the phenomenon looks, therefore, old and new. On the one hand, to quote Arendt's sentence again, it recalls the fact of an ontological injury that turns unique beings into a mass of superfluous creatures whose 'murder is as impersonal as the squashing of a gnat'.[18] Yet, on the other hand, some crucial aspects of the violence of our time make it different. Namely, even if Arendt's and Levi's works on the Nazi *Lager* are extremely important in the effort to conceptualize the inexplicable nestled in horror, political theory is nowadays presented with task of framing horror within the specificity of its current and determinate manifestations.

There is a peculiar aspect, in the *horrorism* of our time, which is, in fact, worth stressing. In the theatre of contemporary violence it is above all randomness that fuels the mechanism of horror production. It is *chance* itself, in other words, which produces the impersonal status of the victim. After the Madrid train bombings on 11 March 2004, in which 192 people were killed and 1,800 wounded, an anonymous commuter wrote on the wall: '*Todos ibamos en ese tren.*' Simple as it seems, the line has the merit of capturing the atrocious logic of the massacre: 'all of us took that train', it says – meaning: each of us, indifferently and casually, could be killed or wounded. This meaning, however, is not that simple or, at least, it uncovers the speculative urgency of two questions. On the one hand, it claims that the shocking impact of this kind of event cannot but turn the perception of our singular vulnerability into the awareness of a constitutive and shared human condition. By focusing precisely on this topic, Judith Butler, in her seminal book written after 9/11, *Precarious Life*, engages with the important task of 'reimagining the possibility of community on the basis of vulnerability and loss'.[19] Thus, as Butler's position and other similar speculations attest, there is a way to react to the outrage to human vulnerability which does not consist of retaliation, violent revenge and war. On the other hand, the line on the Madrid station wall also testifies to the fact that it is not simply the vulnerable but rather the defenceless without qualities, interchangeable and random, who take the centre of the stage where the current specialists in unilateral violence perform. From this point of view, the English word 'casualties' fits the script perfectly. The term applies to various contexts, from tsunami to bombing, and it evokes a violence without specific targets, whose victims turn out to be, precisely, casual. The term 'casual' derives from the Latin 'casus', 'case', which hints at chance and randomness. In a hurricane, some die and some survive, randomly. Significantly enough, however, it is contemporary *horrorism* that makes the term 'casualties' correspond to its etymologically exact meaning. In this case, in fact, more than their death, 'casual' is what really gives the victims their paradigmatic status. Struck just because they are casual, the victims' only value lies in this casualty, which makes them interchangeable and exemplary.

In this sense, if we persist in utilizing the old nomenclature of the warrior, although dripping with horror (indeed being its most notorious theatre), war can still count on a certain distinction from pure horrorism. Its casual victims, all the helpless ones it slaughters and enlists under the infamous rubric of 'collateral damage', are difficult to fit into an explicit framework in which their casualty rises to exemplary status. Differently told, war still does not look at the casualty of the victims in terms of a perfect theoretical coherence. On the other hand, given its propensity to technologize massacre, war has no horrorist competitor at the level of the butchery. Precisely because of the technological stamp – from intelligent bombs to weapons of mass destruction – there is, nevertheless, a certain crucial difference between the various scenarios that go today under the name of war and that of terrorism. In fact, more than to advanced technology, contemporary 'terrorists', in several cases, tend to entrust the task of dismembering bodies directly to bodies. As the scene of suicide bombing attests, the butchery is substantially an operation of bodies that blow themselves up so as to undo other bodies. The human embodied condition of vulnerability is, indeed here, at the centre of the scene: we are surrounded by an enterprise of degradation of the human as human which, perhaps, rivals anything of which the history of destruction was capable.

In *The Drowned and the Saved*, recounting his internment in the concentration camp at Monowitz-Auschwitz, Primo Levi declares that, as a survivor and one of the 'saved', he cannot be one of the true witnesses of the reality of the *Lager*, because he did not touch its depths. The only real witness, whom Levi calls the 'integral witness', is the drowned who has gone to the heart of the horror of the *Lager*. But 'those who did so, those who saw the Gorgon, have not returned to tell about it or have returned mute'.[20] Classical icon of horror, the Gorgon Medusa paralyzes those who are compelled to look at her face and renders them mute. She does not symbolize death alone. She alludes to an ontological injury to the human that finds many ways for manifesting its repugnant work of destruction: slow and meticulous annihilation, as in case of the concentration camps or the Armenian genocide, gigantic and sudden explosion, as in the case of Hiroshima and Nagasaki, and various other performances, including the recent ones that invest in the degrading effects of randomness and succeed in turning human vulnerability into a deadly resource.

Levi did not look at the face of the Gorgon, but, by writing about the ones who did, he provided a vocabulary, a new set of verbs and nouns ('the saved', 'the drowned', 'the grey zone' and others) for naming the inexplicable horror of the *Lager*. The great interest that philosophers and political theorists continue to manifest in Levi's works has probably to do with this linguistic challenge: inexplicability – all the more when what is at stake is real and crude violence – cannot result in ineffability. Derrida was right in claiming that it is hard meaningfully to attach any concept to a modality of destruction that breaks our frames of intelligibility. Nevertheless, we need names, perhaps old names relocated in different speculative contexts and new narrative. Words like 'casualties' and 'vulnerability', and even a disputable neologism like 'horrorism', aim precisely to respond to this thirst for names. Each of them has, of course, a story more or less interesting to tell and an etymology more or less suggestive to count on.

Significantly enough, with the crucial exception of Emmanuel Levinas, in the history of philosophy the word 'vulnerability' is virtually absent. The attention to the vulnerable is only a recent acquisition. Symptomatically, it has become the centre of a new radical interrogation on the human in the wake of events like 9/11 and its violent aftermath. Judith Butler's book *Precarious Life*, and its influence on contemporary political theory is, in this sense, exemplary. The term itself, like the case of the noun 'horror', has a very interesting etymology.[21] The word 'vulnerability' comes from the Latin *vulnus*, wound. It pertains to the domain of skin, at least according to two meanings that are, to a certain extent, similar, but fundamentally different. The primary meaning describes the traumatic rupture of the skin. In its textual context, it is related to violence and mostly to the theatre of war, armed conflict or violent death. It is usually the warriors who wound each other, dealing lethal blows. This primal meaning generates the semantic range that in the modern languages include 'wound' in English, *Wunde* in German, the Italian verb *ferire* and the Spanish *herir*, both contractions of the Latin locution *vulnus inferre* (to deal the blow that wounds). All in all, the *vulnus* is the result of a violent blow, dealt from the outside with a cutting weapon that tears the skin. Although the wound can penetrate deeper tissues and be lethal – or better – although the wound is essentially thematized as lethal, the tearing pertains primarily the skin, the bodily boundary, the enveloping barrier, but also the surface through which the body itself meets the outside, and is, therefore, exposed.

Crucially, the essential relationship between skin and *vulnus* lends itself to a secondary but very important etymological speculation. According to this etymology, the meaning of *vulnus*, located in the root *vel**, alludes to hairless and smooth skin, to skin which is most exposed. Words like 'avulsion' or 'avulsed' are part of this family. The two etymologies, although framed by different imaginaries, are not totally in contrast: they both deal with skin. By avoiding the figure of the warrior, the second etymology, however, stresses the valence of the skin as the site of radical, immediate, hairless and unprotected exposure. Vulnerable is here, in fact, the human body in its absolute nakedness, emphasized by the absence of hair, cover, or protection. If imagined in the totality of the exposed skin, as hairless as children and sometimes old people are, the 'vulnerable' by definition becomes, thus, the 'defenceless'. The etymological imagery shifts from the archetype of the bleeding warrior to that of the totally exposed child.

Not by chance, one of the most effective figures of Primo Levi's narrative on the unimaginable reality of the *Lager* is a child: little Hurbinek, about three years old, who survived few days after the camp's liberation, and could only articulate incomprehensible syllables in search of meaning. 'The speech he lacked', Levi writes, 'which no one had bothered to teach him, the need of speech charged his stare with explosive urgency' in the will 'to break his muteness'.[22] If it is true, as Olivia Guaraldo argues by commenting on Arendt, that *literary fiction* offers a special way of coming to terms with the inexplicable and unforgivable, the true story of little Hurbinek can perhaps be paralleled to that of little Useppe, a touching character of Elsa Morante's novel entitled *History*. Written in 1974, the novel takes place in Rome during World War II; its principal theme concerns the suffering of the innocent and the defenceless, the exemplary vulnerable whose singular stories are destroyed by the senseless turmoil of history. The protagonist of the novel, a woman and a mother, Ida, herself Jewish, witnesses the spectacle of the train cars filled with human beings at Tiburtina station, and ready for deportation to Germany and the camps. Unnoticed, she enters the station with her son Useppe, a child whose absolute vulnerability makes him the anti-hero of the novel. A joyful and innocent creature born from Ida's rape by a German soldier, Useppe is affected by epilepsy and he is gifted with a particular sensibility for the fragile expressions of life and the inexplicability of evil. At Tiburtina station, he is eventually confronted with the paralyzing effect of the Gorgon.

> The child was quiet, huddled in her arms, his left side against her breast; but he held his head turned to look at the train. In reality, he hadn't moved from that position since the first moment. And as she peered around to examine him, she saw him still staring at the train, his face motionless, his mouth half-open, his eyes wide in an indescribable gaze of horror.
> Useppe – she called him, in a low voice.
> Useppe turned, at her summons; the same stare, however, remained in his eyes, which, even as they encountered hers, asked her no

question. There was, in the endless horror of his gaze, also a fear, or rather a dazed stupor; but it was a stupor that demanded no explanation.[23]

In the novel history goes on, war come to its end, but the Gorgon finds a further occasion for freezing little Useppe with her horrible gaze and thus accelerating the final devastation to which, as absolutely vulnerable, he is destined. The second encounter between the Gorgon and the child takes place in Ida's kitchen, where Useppe happens to observe some photographs on a newspaper. The pictures show:

> Some little skeletal human shapes, staring behind a fence, wearing striped tunics, loose and sagging, which make them look like puppets. Some of them have bare, shaven heads; others wear caps; and their faces show an agonizing smile, a wretched, definitive depravity.[24]

It will be forever impossible to know what poor illiterate Useppe may have understood of those meaningless photographs, writes Elsa Morante. Anyhow, she adds, Ida 'recognized in his pupils the same horror she had seen there that noon at the Tiburtina station, about twenty months earlier. At his mother's approach, he raised his eyes to her, drained and discoloured, like a little blind child's.'[25] As expected, the further experience of the Gorgon results in a final breakdown of Useppe's paradigmatic vulnerability and, eventually, kills him. He is defeated by history's darkest face, but most of all, he is destroyed by the image of the unimaginable which renders him speechless and blind; that is, by an ontological injury whose inexplicability is so clearly mirrored in his staring eyes that he succumbs to it without asking for an explanation.

2

BETWEEN REALISM AND FICTION
Arendt and Levi on Concentrationary Imaginaries

Olivia Guaraldo

> There are crimes of passion and there are crimes of logic.
> Albert Camus, *The Rebel*[1]

Whatever is, is right

In 1734, in his famous poem *An Essay on Man*, Alexander Pope wrote: 'Whatever is, is right.'[2] Welcomed and admired by a generation of Enlightenment philosophers throughout Europe, Pope's poem was a celebration of his times, an artistic expression of Leibniz's idea that we live in 'the best of all possible worlds', an enchanted version of the optimistic *esprit* of the era. Yet a few years after Pope's poem, the Lisbon earthquake (1755) and its apocalyptic magnitude confronted a whole generation of confident intellectuals with the baffling issue of nature's cruel meaninglessness, and with the moral and cognitive question of attributing a place and a sense to evil. After the Lisbon earthquake, Voltaire, one of the first enthusiastic admirers of Pope, revisited his optimistic faith in 'the best of all possible worlds' by parodying theodicy and intellectual optimism in his famous *Candide*. Yet, modern philosophy, in its highest expression, did not, in spite of the trauma of the Lisbon earthquake, and in spite of Voltaire's irony, renounce its optimism. Indeed, one could even argue that in the simple yet eloquent sentence pronounced by Pope a century before, are already present the seeds of Hegelian philosophy, expressed in the famous motto '*Was wirklich ist, das ist vernünftig*' ('Whatever is real is rational').[3]

The reality of Reason has for Hegel a *universal necessity and a universal scope*: everything that can be comprehended and reduced to a rational process, therefore can always be comprehended by the mind of the philosopher. Conversely, whatever is irrational cannot have a conscious certainty of its own reality. In fact, the senselessness of nature notwithstanding, Hegel affirmed that man could always retrace the path of his development towards rationality by conceiving of human history as a process. Hegel's titanic enterprise is characterized by a philosophical attempt to include human affairs, the chaotic realm of *praxis*, into the realm of rationality. Philosophy is able to account for the contingent inasmuch as this realm – the realm of human affairs – also can become an object of science. 'To think is to act': with this statement Hegel performs a radical shift as regards the preceding philosophical tradition, rarely interested in taking seriously the sphere of the *vita activa*. Hegel's philosophy, on the contrary, embarks on the ambitious task of mobilizing thinking and consciousness, by rendering them subject to a temporal transformation: to think does not mean simply to possess clear and distinct concepts (Descartes), neither does it mean to purify the activity of thinking itself in order to provide it with the accuracy of science (Kant). To think, for Hegel, means to possess the key to the understanding of history and politics, to dwell in the chaotic realm of change and conflict in order to reconcile reality and reason. Hegel indeed succeeds in transforming reality into a product of thinking, some sort of cognitive artefact that the mind alone can make and consequently know. Reality can be embraced – or entrapped – in a totalizing system, which develops dialectically; through contradictions and their 'solution' it moves to further contradictions and further 'conciliations'. Hegel's system offers the ultimate speculative solution to the philosopher, namely the possibility of coming to terms with reality and its apparently insoluble dilemmas through the powerful means of dialectical thinking. Totality is its aim, insofar as reality can be rightly comprehended – can become '*rational*', '*vernünftig*' – only as a 'whole', as an entirety where particulars can be fitted into a general (and mental) scheme. Even human actions and historical events acquire, within the system and its totalizing intent, the impalpable yet necessary nature of thought products.

According to Hannah Arendt's critical reading of idealist philosophy, Hegel's system is essentially the dogmatic transformation of the mere, common-to-all activity of thinking into a cognitive structure able to grant solidity to the frailty of the invisible mental process. The activity of thinking – turned dogmatic and systematic in the titanic effort of transforming philosophy into the universal, omnipervasive tool to uncovering the hidden laws of reality – acquires, within the system, a more solid status. Thanks to the system, in other words, the philosopher can be certain that 'whatever is real is rational'.

Yet, continues Arendt, the totality according to which the system seems to function is nothing more than a hypothesis, a mental frame aimed at maximizing the speculative capability of comprehension. As Arendt points out, when discussing Hegel's philosophy of history,

> this whole, scientifically speaking, can never be more than a plausible hypothesis, which by integrating every particular into an all-comprehensive thought transforms them all into thought things and thus eliminates their most scandalous property, their realness, together with their contingency.[4]

In other words, the indisputable optimism of Pope's sentence, reinforced a century later by Hegelian philosophy of history, testifies to a great confidence in the human capacity to come to terms with 'what is', as the result of a process, of ' what has come to be'. This human talent for comprehending, rendering rational what appeared as virtually incomprehensible depends, says Arendt, on the interiorization or mentalization of facts into products of consciousness. According to her, one of the most significant effects of the justification of 'what is' according to a philosophical speculative perspective is the transformation of contingency and facts into necessary stages of the development of human rationality (Spirit). To her mind, this transformation of the contingent (typical of the political realm, or the 'sphere of human affairs') into the necessary, or the modern invention of a philosophy of history, entails a *neutralization of politics*.

As is well known, Arendt strongly opposes this transformation of the political into the historical (or, better put, the historically inevitable), since it is the typically modern notion of historical necessity or historical inevitability which she finds destructive to politics:

Before the backward-directed glance of thought, everything that had been political – acts, and words, and events – became historical, with the result that the new world which was ushered by the eighteenth century revolutions did not receive, as Tocqueville still claimed, a 'new science of politics,' but a philosophy of history.[5]

In the words of Jacques Taminiaux, 'In Hegel action is hypostatized into the chronological efficacy of the World Spirit, and the thinker remembering it is merely its witness.'[6] That the movement of history is dialectical and driven by necessity, as Hegel strenuously emphasizes in his *Phenomenology of Spirit*, is, for Arendt, 'perhaps the most terrible and, humanly speaking, least bearable paradox in the whole body of modern thought'.[7] The conceptualization of contingency through its absorption into the speculative system eventually works in Hegel as a theoretical annihilation of politics.

This neutralization of the past, of what has happened, its transformation into a philosophy of history, has important consequences also for the way in which we can think of, or imagine, the future. In fact, the transformation of history into a speculative realm, in which rationality comes to terms only with itself, annihilates newness in favour of conciliation, the famous Hegelian *Versöhnung*, between thought and reality. A reasonable need for comprehending and making sense of what has happened is transformed into a universal law of movement under which every expression of human freedom is subsumed; the unpredictable human capacity for action – for Arendt the most human of all activities – is 'downsized', deprived of its novelty, inserted in the developing rationality of the Spirit and thereby eventually obliterated. The temporality of the developing Spirit of Reason forces novelty and unpredictability to be eliminated, by trapping them into the overarching speculative frame of thought, which transforms contingency into necessity and reality into a thought process.

Hannah Arendt develops instead a notion of both history and historiography which retains very little of the modern conceptualization of temporality. She writes: 'Newness is the realm of the historian, who – unlike the natural scientist who is concerned with ever-recurring happenings – deals with events which always occur only once.'[8] The Hegelian notion of history, she writes, 'with its unparalleled emphasis on history as a process, has many origins and among them especially the earlier modern concept of nature as a process'.⁹ History is conceived as a necessary process that, similarly to the cyclical process of Nature, unfolds according to necessary laws, so that the realm of human affairs, *ta ton anthropon pragmata* – according to Aristotle the sphere where things could be otherwise – is now understood as the sphere of necessity, where things simply cannot be otherwise. Just as Reason dictates, they are the necessary unfolding of the speculative comprehending that process demands. For Hegel the same inexorable chain of developmental consequences which rules organic nature from germ to fruit, in which one phase always negates and cancels out the earlier one, rules the undoing of the mind's thinking process, except that the latter, since it is 'mediated through consciousness and will' through mental activities, can be seen as 'making itself'.¹⁰ As with natural processes, history is necessity-driven, and even if it is conceived as rectilinear, its trajectory is already designed.

Storytelling versus the philosophy of history

This brief reconstruction of Arendt's critique of Hegel's notion of history is central to the understanding of how Arendt tried to elaborate a different notion of history (and politics) as the realm of the new, the unexpected, and the unpredictable. According to Arendt, in fact, in both acts, that of understanding the past and that of imagining the future, we must get rid of the philosophical attitude of conceptualizing reality as a process that can be intellectualized, transformed into a thought-process and, therefore, justified. To her, the sentence by Pope, 'whatever is, is right', would be profoundly a-political, if not totalitarian. In fact, Arendt did try to elaborate, in her main works, both a different notion of historical knowledge and a new, unprecedented notion of political action. Both terms cannot be separated, according to Arendt, and it is not by chance that she opposes free human action to historical necessity, and storytelling to philosophy of history.

In order to *imagine* a different notion of politics after the deadening experiences of totalitarianism, Arendt seems to claim that we must finally get rid of the notion of historical necessity. Even in her controversial essay *On Violence*, when trying to give a political interpretation of the students' movements of 1968, Arendt criticizes the reliance of most of them on the notion of history as a process, the old *adagio* of nineteenth-century philosophy of history, and the consequential emphasis on violence as the *natural* force that inevitably accompanies all historical changes. In that essay, Arendt criticizes the equation of change with necessity, of violence with action, of history with nature. What she strongly resists is the role of historically inevitable processes in understanding political change, and the corollary of an indispensable role of violence in them.[11]

Yet Arendt also proposes a different notion of politics as the realm of unexpected human actions that disclose themselves in a public space. This well-known – but often difficult to grasp – Arendtian notion of politics is, in a way, her attempt to respond, *imaginatively*, to the deadening effects of totalitarianism. To my mind *The Human Condition* is indeed a work of political imagination, where what is at stake is the courage to speak the political through different words and different categories. Needless to say, this imaginative effort takes its bearings from the sheer fact of extermination under totalitarian rule, seen by Arendt as the systematic project of annihilation of human plurality.

It is perhaps redundant to remark that she was among the first intellectuals to emphasize the centrality of *l'univers concentrationnaire* for the totalitarian regimes. The *Lager* or camp was, according to Arendt, the core of the totalitarian experiment, the practical attempt to carry out the ontological modification of the human condition, by eliminating human spontaneity and reducing individuals to 'ghastly marionettes with human faces'.[12] Against that background Arendt embarks on the difficult yet indispensable task of imagining a politics based on the human condition of plurality and spontaneity, on the sheer fact that 'men and not Man inhabit the world'. It is not by chance that the Arendtian notion of political action – imaginatively constructed through a daring yet efficacious interpretation of the Greek polis – strongly relies on storytelling, on the immortalizing function of poetry and literature, in order to be represented and remembered.[13] For Arendt only storytelling – a narrative recount of what has taken place in the public sphere, as ancient epics and historiography used to do – is able to preserve, represent, understand the volatile and contingent realm of politics and human plurality without committing the error of transforming it into the material indispensable to the revelation of historical necessity. Storytelling does not reduce contingency to necessity, nor does it transform history into a philosophy of history. Storytelling helps the spectator in understanding political phenomena in their contingency, without subsuming them under the 'whole' typical of philosophical speculation and later adopted by social sciences in the guise of statistical trends. In *The Human Condition* Arendt writes:

The justification of statistics is that deeds and events are rare occurrences in everyday life and history. Yet the meaningfulness of everyday relationships is disclosed not in everyday life but in rare deeds, just as the significance of a historical period shows itself only in the few events that illuminate it. The application of the law of large numbers and long periods to politics or history signifies nothing less than the wilful obliteration of their very subject matter, and it is a hopeless enterprise to search for meaning in politics or significance in history when everything that is not everyday behaviour or automatic trends has been ruled out as immaterial.[14]

Not only does Arendt revert to storytelling in order to frame the possibility for politics to become comprehensible and representable, she also relies concretely on narrative accounts of the past in order to frame the history of totalitarianism in a non-speculative way – and this is why her book on totalitarianism is full of literary accounts of history and society. From Proust to Conrad, from Zola to Céline, from Kipling to Chesterton, she makes extensive use of literature, as if convinced that *fiction*, poetic reconfiguration of reality in the form of novels, could best explore the way in which history and politics converged in a new way, and an unprecedented amalgam of phenomena gave rise to anti-Semitism, imperialism, totalitarianism.

Arendt seemed to be convinced that in order to clarify historical phenomena history alone, the sheer recount of facts could not render the complex and unprecedented nature of the political phenomena she wanted to explain and understand. She was well aware of the difficulty of making a historical reconstruction of how totalitarianism came to be: the difficulty was both ethical and epistemological. She claimed that she wanted to understand without justifying, avoiding all the neutralizing effects a traditionally historical account might produce. Yet, in spite of her need to understand, she was aware of the unheard-of nature of the political phenomena that combined, contingently, to produce the totalitarian phenomenon. How could the impasse be faced? For her to recur to literature was not simply a question of taste, or refinement, but it was a way of responding to that ethical and epistemological impasse.

The book on totalitarianism is the attempt to contaminate history with stories, in order to give a fair account of what had happened without inserting it into the tranquil flow of historical continuity: this is why she turns to *fiction* in order to understand reality, and this is why she needs imaginative accounts of events in order to understand the unimaginable. Literature installs in history the bewildering element of mystery and poetry, provides us with the symbolic awareness we need in order to make sense of unprecedented phenomena that are, as Arendt put it, incomprehensible and unforgivable. *Fiction*, as a way of emplotting events in order to make them understandable but not justifiable, provided her with a useful epistemological tool to overcome the ethical dilemma of understanding unprecedented phenomena such as imperialism and modern anti-Semitism without falling prey to the dogma of historical necessity. It is as if she perceived that *literary fiction* offered a way of coming to terms with what had happened that differed consistently from the 'Whatever is, is right' approach of philosophical thinking. As she briefly mentions in her essay *On Humanity in Dark Times*, no past can be properly 'mastered', and certainly not the past of Hitler's Germany. What we can do with the past is try to 'know what has happened' and 'wait and see what comes of knowing and enduring'.[15] Yet the form our 'knowing' of the past takes is that of 'narration', which 'does not master anything once and for all', but reveals the human need for poetry, a 'human potentiality' we constantly expect 'to erupt in some human being'.[16] What Arendt has in mind, when she speaks of 'narration', is exactly the poetic configuration of events as it reveals itself in literature. To be able to understand the past does not equate to mastering it. On the contrary, it means being able to listen to meaningful stories of what has happened. Yet the ability to 'set the process of narration into motion' and share it with the world is the task of storytellers *and* poets, who can configure the past into a meaningful whole: 'No philosophy, no analysis, no aphorism, be it ever so profound, can compare in intensity and richness of meaning with a properly narrated story.'[17]

Ideology and terror

The crucial political role of imaginative works of literature becomes even more interesting when Arendt famously discusses what she considers the innovative combination, in totalitarianism, of ideology and terror.

As is by now very well acknowledged, Arendt refers to totalitarianism as a method of government based on what she calls 'the law of movement', where what is at stake is not the content of the law – which in the case of Nazism was 'Nature' (the ideological centrality of the purity of the 'race'), and in the case of Stalinism was 'History' (the ideological centrality of the fulfilment of history in communism) – but the sheer process, and the law becomes simply that of totalitarian movement. One of the political novelties of totalitarianism was the obsessive yet successful adjustment of reality in its entirety to the law of movement propounded by ideology. The main feature of totalitarian regimes was their capacity to abolish all kinds of resistance and reaction since they abolished the human capacity to act, to start something new, thereby substituting it with the predictable and controllable dimension of behaviour. According to totalitarian ideology, human beings in their uniqueness and plurality are sacrificed to the fulfilment of the ideological aim. Nature must be realized by exterminating unfit races; History must be completed by eliminating the decadent classes, and so on.

Crucially, Arendt notes that the novelty of totalitarianism is the fact that once the idea that needs to be implemented in reality is established through a purely ideological gesture, power resorts to terror in order to accelerate the historical process, to make the prophecy come true. What totalitarianism pursues is essentially the fulfilment of a philosophy of history, perverse as it might be, but essentially conceived as the realization in history of an idea, in order to be able to say, in the form of a collective slogan, 'whatever is, is right'.

Instead of acting politically, thereby exercising their innate 'freedom', individuals under totalitarianism become indistinguishable parts of the mass, which must follow a historically inevitable process, shaped by ideology and implemented through propaganda and terror, but essentially legitimized as the 'natural' development of humanity. Arendt notes that in the massive effort of adapting reality to the dictates of ideology, to shape humanity according to the laws of biological purity purported by Nazism, or the realization of a classless society envisaged by Stalinist communism, the concentration and extermination camps became essential. As the 'core institutions' of Totalitarian regimes, camps had the crucial task of eliminating superfluous human beings, remnants of a humanity that could not fit into the new world ideated and implemented by ideology. Nonetheless, the concentrationary experience was not only a political instrument of repression but also an experiment in the possibility of transforming human nature.

This is what Arendt emphasizes in the paragraph of *The Origins of Totalitarianism* titled *Total domination*: at stake in the *Lager* was not simply the repression and killing of superfluous people, but also the experimentation of a new kind of living (human) being, artificially deprived of the features that qualified the human as such (spontaneity, freedom, relationality): 'The problem is to fabricate something that does not exist, namely, a kind of human species resembling other animal species whose only "freedom" would consist in "preserving the species".'[18]

The artificial, experimental production of 'bare life' is what the concentrationary is about, claims Arendt: human beings reduced to 'bundles of reactions', incapable of any response to the concentrationary reality, but, more importantly, deprived of the most human faculty, namely the ability to act, to start something new, to will as a way of imagining and acting for change. The zombies of the camp lived in an eternal present, deprived of both past and future, incapable of living and not yet dead:

> The camps are meant not only to exterminate people and degrade human beings, but also serve the ghastly experiment of eliminating, under scientifically controlled conditions, spontaneity itself as an expression of human behaviour and of transforming the human personality into a mere thing, into something that even animals are not.[19]

The transformation of human spontaneity into a 'bundle of reactions' similar to that of Pavlov's dog carried out in the concentration camp – continues Arendt – depended on 'sealing off the latter against the world of all others, the world of the living in general, even against the outside world of a country under totalitarian rule'. This is the reason why the experimental perversity of the camp more often than not made it difficult, if not impossible, to be recounted and understood: 'This isolation explains the peculiar unreality and lack of credibility that characterize all reports from the concentration camps and constitute one of the main difficulties for the true understanding of totalitarian domination.'[20] Arendt notes that the reports of those who survived record details and experiences but fail to communicate:

> None of these reports inspires those passions of outrage and sympathy through which men have always been mobilized for justice. On the contrary, anyone speaking or writing about concentration

camps is still regarded as suspect; and if the speaker has resolutely returned to the world of the living, he himself is often assailed by doubts with regard to his own truthfulness, as though he had mistaken a nightmare for reality.[21]

When dealing with the complex problem of understanding the perverted and unimaginable reality of the *Lager*, we are tempted to reduce the 'intrinsically incredible' to all kinds of rationalizations. The risk of explaining away the unimaginable experiment of fabricating a different human nature by means of simplifications, clichés, and comparison with other kinds of domination is strong, and politically devastating: similarly to the diabolic intent of Nazism – 'to treat people as if they had never existed and to make them disappear in the literal sense of the word' – this need for rationalization can obliterate the very novelty of the phenomenon, can make the crime disappear, because 'terror enforces oblivion'.[22]

Arendt notes that while it is important to know the details of the camps, to 'dwell on horrors' cannot automatically guarantee a significant understanding of totalitarian domination. The recollections of survivors, the eyewitness reports of horror, are not sufficient. Because of the 'abyss' that separates the world of the living from the world of the living dead, those reports 'cannot supply anything more than a series of remembered occurrences that must seem just as incredible to those who relate them as to their audience'.[23] Receptive as she was to the poetic and the literary element in human existence, Arendt almost parenthetically notes that only the 'fearful imagination' of those who have been 'aroused by such reports but have not actually been smitten in their own flesh, of those who are consequently free from the bestial, desperate terror [...] can afford thinking about horrors'.[24]

If, in other words, a sense can be conveyed of the nature of totalitarian domination as it happened in the central institution of totalitarianism, namely the *Lager*, it is a sense produced by imagination, by the imaginative effort of going beyond mere facts and figures in order to engage fearfully with 'what has been'. By contrast with the eyewitness reports or the mere recording of facts, imaginative endeavours at understanding the horror – the literary reconfiguration of the *Lager* experience by a limited set of survivors, among which she enlists David Rousset – can serve, if only, to modify the 'perception of political contexts and the mobilizations of political passions'.[25] Yet the most important task of the 'fearful imagination' is, according to Arendt, that of dissolving 'the sophistic dialectical interpretations of politics which are all based on the superstition that something good might result from evil'.[26] To strive, therefore, against the secular, sophistic and superstitional version of theodicy – that something good might result from evil, that 'whatever is, is right' – is the political task of imagination.

The totalitarian project of subsuming reality in its totality to ideology, the logic of an idea, and the horrific experiment on human nature in the camps, considered by Arendt 'the "theoretical" verification of the ideology', albeit not having reached 'total realization', dramatically altered the way in which history and politics converge. As Primo Levi has often reminded us, after Auschwitz we cannot avoid meditating that 'this has been', that something unimaginable has entered the sphere of the possible, and against this possible no conciliation, no rationalization can be of help.[27] The mind reflecting on the horror of the camps cannot reconcile itself with what has been, cannot produce a rational or dialectical account of it. It cannot, in other words, indulge in the sophistic transformation of evil in good.

The reality of the camps cannot undergo a process of rationalization, yet this does not mean that we must consign it to silence or ineffability. Imagination can help us where theory and reason cannot – perhaps also because of their very complacency with the totalitarian system.

'How is it that under the worst political and social conditions, during war and revolution, in jails and in concentration camps, most victims turn toward works of imagination?'[28] This question, posed by Iranian writer Azar Nafisi, reinforces the idea, perhaps the mystery, of the human need for imagination, and could even remain without a univocal answer. The question addresses, even if indirectly, a crucial issue Arendt and others faced, namely that of the political and ethical role of imagination (and its products; that is, literature and poetry) as a precious source of 'humanity' in situations of extreme oppression.

Primo Levi, the *Lager* and imagination

Italian writer Primo Levi seemed to have perceived the centrality of that issue, and experienced that same impasse Arendt experienced in relation to the difficulty of grasping the meaning of the unimaginable. More than Arendt, who observed the horror of the camps from the distanced perspective of the refugee, not of the prisoner, Levi experienced directly the concentrationary reality, and even if he considered himself an imperfect witness – he survived, whereas the perfect witness was the one who 'lived' to the terminus of the concentrationary experience – his life and works tell us even more about the importance of imagination and literary *fiction*.

Before his deportation, Auschwitz-Monowitz survivor Primo Levi, was a scientist, a chemist. After Auschwitz, symptomatically he became a writer. As a writer – and a man, oppressed and obsessed by the survivor's dilemma 'why am I alive?' – Levi strenuously fought to solve the paradox of the testimony of horror, namely the need to remember and the personal frustration inherent in experiencing the *impossibility* of recounting that same horror. Yet Levi, even if personally unsatisfied by his way of responding to that paradox, represents the most valuable example of how literature can be of immense help where history and theory simply fail. In his literary work, in fact, the memories of the witness are integrated with a certain degree of *fiction*. As a direct witness, he seemed unable to rely only on the sterility of information, on the realm of facts and figures. Since his writing is also a practice of understanding – and of self-understanding – pure scientific objectivity cannot be of help. Levi found himself unable, in other words, to convey the complexity of the *Lager* without using the means of *fiction*: poetizing, so to say, the horror, in order to understand it.[29] As literary theorist Hayden White has pointed out, by underlining the specific style of writing on the Holocaust, 'our notion of what constitutes realistic representation must be revised to take account of experiences that are unique to our century and for which the older modes of representation have proven to be inadequate'.[30] Significantly, he defines this new mode of representation as 'modernist' and enlists Primo Levi among the most effective modernist writers.

In his last work, *I sommersi e i salvati* (1986) [trans. *The Drowned and the Saved*], a sort of 'moral lexicon' of *l'univers concentrationnaire*, Levi analyses the epistemological and ethical impasses he found himself facing in both his lived experience and the narrativized retelling. In other words he dedicates his last work to the ethical and aesthetical dilemmas of the 'imperfect witness'.[31] In the preface, Levi warns against easy generalizations and glorification when dealing with the complex and multilayered reality of the concentrationary universe. The commemorative aspect of 'monumental history', the glorifying and celebratory role of ancient historiography, undergoes a radical change during the dark times of which Levi speaks. It might be true, he says, that monuments and sepulchres contribute to the improvement and enhancement of civil society, but one must also remain wary of engaging in over-simplifications. In other words, this specific past – the very past which, according to Levi, still represents a *unicum* in our world history – cannot undergo the usual standardization, namely the rhetorical process of either glorification or condemnation.

His works related to the phenomenon of the *Lager* belong to a genre we might call 'survivors' literature', vast and differentiated. Yet, Levi was more than a survivor, or not only a survivor. As I said, Levi was a scientist, and his prose bears the signs of the scientist's familiarity with transparent accounts. There are still traces in his recount of the *Lager* experience, of his former attitude toward reality and truth. The crystalline style of his prose is one of these traces. Levi himself is aware, however, of the impossibility of applying that clarity and transparency to the new political content of life and death in the *Lager*. His texts fascinate because of the apparently ice-cold attitude with which he poses tragic dilemmas and indecipherable stories. It is as if his aim was to explore the representative capacities of language and take them to their limit.

Levi forces the expressive boundaries of a rational, objective and rather abstract language in order to test how far it can go, how forcefully it can clash against the wall of an experience that, technically, cannot be referred to at all as an experience. The fragile position of his own 'character', which lies somewhere between the witness and the survivor, is the only stand he can take, the only one he feels legitimized to take, having survived to tell. This is why, in Levi's works – more intensely in his proper literary works, although very visibly, and perhaps more interestingly for our purpose, in his essayistic ones – the crystalline hope of attaining a transparent use of language becomes contaminated with traces of pain, of the unbearable incomprehensibility, of elegantly posed raw and hopeless half-sentences, broken images, unfinished reasoning. This could only be attained by means of a literary account: only within the free horizon of a poetic configuration of meaning – the fictive element being not that of 'inventing facts', but of rendering them through poetry – could the ethical difficulties of 'understanding without justifying' be solved.

Levi did not want to be an historian of the *Lager*. Both history and science seem to be inadequate in terms of his testimony. As Hayden

White put it: 'Like the historian, he wants to tell the truth, but as a participant in the events he reports, he knows that his memory of those events is likely to be coloured and deformed by psychic defences.'[32] At a certain point in the book, Levi warns his readers of the special nature of his recount.

> This book is drenched with memory, a far memory. It originates from a suspect source and it must be defended against itself. It contains more considerations than recollections, it prefers to linger on the present state of affairs than on retroactive chronicle.[33]

In this passage Levi once again underlines his distance from a mere record; his inability to be a historian is as vital a part of his writing as his paradoxical use of language. For him to refrain from being a historian does not mean to commit the sin of humility but, I suggest, to produce, in a modernist way, a new prose. Considerations are preferred over mere recollections (*ricordi*) not because they are less verifiable, but because the very objective verifiability of recorded events does not make any sense in this respect. Recollections, *ricordi*, can be either true or false, can be more or less precisely verified. *Considerazioni*, on the contrary – as the etymology of the word suggests – are products 'of an imaginative projection of figures onto a field of phenomena which lacking both a frame and outlines must be constituted by the observer on the basis of his own expectations and notions of possible worlds'.[34] According to Hayden White, Levi's considerations are a sort of grouping together of elements in order to constitute them as possible objects of understanding. Where a mere recollection of events has to do with whether they are true or false, the realm of 'considerazioni' does not explore the limits of verifiability or evidence, but the possibility of meaning. White affirms that by moving from recollection to consideration, Levi practises a work of imagination, therefore moving from 'history' to '*fiction*'.

This does not mean that by going from history to *fiction* Levi is moving from reality to illusion. On the contrary, by means of a fictionalization of history we can build configurations of meaning in which the problem is not exact knowledge nor truth, but understanding and reality. The problem for Levi was to establish, not only for his readers but also for himself, the 'reality' of that 'monstrous' world he experienced in the camps. This is much more the task of literature than it is of historiography, for it is literature that locates, probes, investigates and establishes the boundary between the real and the imaginary.[35] The ambiguous reality of the camps required in addition a special means of representation, because there was no clear line between victims and perpetrators. Reality in the camps was never entirely black and white but, rather, an ambiguous grey zone. This is probably why Levi, through his literature, seems to tell us that in order to understand what is complex, ambiguous and equivocal – but also what is new and monstrous – we need a certain degree of imaginative power, even if the reality of what has happened exceeds imagination.

Levi tells several controversial stories: from Chaim Rumkowski, the head of the Łódź ghetto, to the members of the *Sonderkommando*, and many others.[36] In one single chapter of his book of considerations – namely a book *not* conceived of as pure narrative – stories emerge as the recurring source of his considerations. Considerations can test the meaning of those stories, their force or inability to understand the *Lager* phenomenon. There, we are moving on the level of the imaginary, not because we want to suppress reality, but because that reality is in itself unimaginable. In order to establish a reality of that species one needs *fiction*: this is the inherent paradox of Levi's greatness, the precious source his literary work provides us, without pretending to be exhaustive and 'objective'.

Paradoxically then, one could argue following Levi that pure objective knowledge based on facts and figures is unable to recount the unimaginable character of the concentrationary universe, when not totalitarian in its pretence of being exhaustive. Differently put, and following Levi, in order to avoid the ever-present risk of rationalizing and neutralizing the impact of what had happened, of being content with the 'rightness' of what there is, the poetic configuration of meaning through a literary account becomes a valuable resource.

Levi, in fact, explains that one of the most haunting fears he and his inmates experienced in the *Lager* was a common recurrent dream. The dream was that they would return home and passionately tell the story of their suffering to a person close to them. The person would not believe such a story and would often turn around and walk away in silence.[37] It is precisely to the prescience of those dreams that Levi's literary art responds, from the position of the imperfect witness who is aware that a realistic account of what has happened would risk, as Arendt would say, to report without communicating, or worse, to consign the stories of the witness to incredulity and oblivion. To disrupt the enormity of that experience in order to be understood, or at least in order to be listened to, is to some extent the aim of Levi's writing, torn as it is between realism and imagination. Moreover, as Levi continuously underlines in his books, the need to convey a meaning for the *Lager* experience, and consequently to find a literary form that is able to represent it, does not only concern the past. It is a need that is future-oriented, a necessary act the survivor must perform in order for 'what has been' not to repeat itself in history.

The concentrationary imaginary and the reality show

In the light of this incursion into the ways in which two different witnesses of the totalitarian experience relate to the past and its 'unbearable reality', in their similar way of emphasizing the use of literary imagination, of *fiction* in order to understand the past and imagine the future, let us come to the concentrationary imaginary. Is there a link between the reality of the camp, as Levi reports it, and the 'reality' of today's societies? Are there 'remnants of Auschwitz', as Giorgio Agamben would say, in the way in which we today experience reality and the (im)possibility of its transformation?[38] What spectres of totalitarianism still haunt us?

As a famous Italian architect, Luca Zevi, has recently stated, 'on the ashes of the ideologies that animated and shredded the twentieth century, a unitary thinking aimed at the substantial acceptance of the present state of affairs seems to triumph'.[39] This acceptance of the present state of affairs, according to Zevi, coincides with the impossibility of imagining the future, with a lack of imaginative courage that should instead animate policy-makers, architects and urbanists alike. This sentence is important because it links the lack of imagination to the end of the ideological frame that structured the twentieth century. As if with the end of the ideological era only a prosaic and chaotic acceptance of the 'present state of affairs' would be possible; as if, in other words, all that remains of that great frame is the essentially concentrationary horizon of an immutable present.

Among the current tendencies of our Western societies there is, in fact, an obsession for reality, understood, however, as something banal, daily, intimate yet public and eventless: think of the proliferation, in TV broadcasts worldwide, of reality shows. It is as if contemporary culture – in both its popular and learned versions – were obsessed with the present, with the 'here and now' of a timeless present, forgetful of the past and uncertain of the future. We are all stuck, so to say, on the *Now*, forced to *enjoy* the present or, as Lacan would say, disciplined by an imperative to enjoyment.

Apart from being a trivial version of the ancient motto of 'carpe diem', adjusted to a consumer society and enhanced by the weakening of political imagination, this imperative is a totalitarian legacy. Built as it is on the immutability of a given situation, strengthened by individual impotence, lack of political relations and shared public experiences, the 'imperative of the Now' reinforces a concentrationary imaginary. This, in turn, is the imaginary that materially concretizes itself in reality shows: a closed place where an experiment on humans is taking place. It is not only entertainment-oriented programmes that deal today with the obsessive exploration of a day in the life of anonymous people; the documentary and informative programmes are also realized according to the logic of reality shows. I happened to watch a documentary on the independent channel Current TV about people seeking to clandestinely enter the USA. The protagonists are followed by a camera day and night, and report to the cameraman, moment by moment, the journey and their feelings. We spectators follow this trip toward freedom as if we were following the reality show *Survivor*.

Spectacularization of reality in its crudeness is what characterizes contemporary entertainment, but this aspect of our 'culture' is not as futile as it would seem at a first glance. In fact, pop-culture in a way mirrors the apparently univocal ideology of the West today: realism is its name. The realism of the economy – the 'real stuff' of money, commodities, national product, national debt and so on, are our daily companions – the realism of politics, the realism of war, the realism of migration, deportation, internment, all must be accepted because, as Pope would say, 'Whatever is, is right'. This is another way of saying we must reconcile ourselves with what is and be content with it.

Realism tyrannically governs our present in a twofold manner: on one side through the hegemony of scientific discourse and evidence (to which economic discourse belongs, together with 'rational choice' oriented social sciences) and on the other through the entertaining dimension of TV shows.[40] But what we call 'reality', in this present situation, is neither the ungovernable and unpredictable realm of human actions nor is it the realm of 'facts', as Arendt would put it. The reality of so-called 'realism' is simply a 'fetish' of reality, insofar as it is an immutable dimension of either truth (the scientific method approach in all spheres of human life) or entertainment. Entertainment, the other side of the coin of the seriousness of science, is both a relaxing and hypnotizing sphere, where what is exhibited is perceived as belonging to the eternal present of myth.

It is against the ideological predominance of this realism (both scientific and trivial) that critical thinking should militate, not in order to produce yet another critique of the present, but to liberate Western affluent societies from their lack of imagination, or what could be also called 'creative frigidity in political matters'.

'Whatever is, is right', we seem to repeat to ourselves, perhaps incapable of imagining a future that could be better than this apparently endless present, ruled exclusively by growth rates, balance between GDP and deficit (the raw reality of facts and figures, far from being 'realistic', is as unavoidable and unchangeable as fate was in Homeric culture) on one hand, and idiotic reality shows on the other. In Italy this is perhaps more visible than in other countries since the ideology of 'whatever is, is right', or 'We live in the best of all possible worlds' is not only broadcast by the media, but performed daily by one-time Italian prime minister Berlusconi, who incarnated at best this ideology. This is to say that the triumph of realism as ideology of the present – crude or visionary as it might be – has to do with our inability to use imagination, or, to put it more bluntly, our total reliance on reality – be it the banal, intimate and boring reality of reality shows, or the official, institutional, diplomatic realism of our policy-makers and decision-makers. Public opinion is hypnotized by TV entertainment – almost entirely conceived as reality shows – or, when needed, awakened to the fatal and unchangeable reality of figures, rates, and percentages. Caught in this double bind of the ideology of realism, we are incapable of exiting the concentrationary imaginary of this endless and immutable present. There is a nihilist nuance in this tyranny of realism: a nihilism that has lost its heroic features and has transformed into the banal, domestic surrogate and spectacularized reality of 'entertainment', where we are simply restrained from acting.[41]

'We want your dreams', a Tunisian migrant wrote on the fences of a detention centre in southern Italy: he surely could not imagine that 'our dreams' have already been taken away from us by the ideology of realism. Facts and figures, just like in Levi's account of the *Lager*, cannot be of help in understanding the unimaginable. In the same way, facts and figures, or the conviction that only realism can guide us in shaping our future, is a haunting presence, a curiously new kind of acquiescent version of the sentence 'whatever is, is right'. It is perhaps not a totalitarian spectre, but surely a spectre that has the strong capacity of rendering change, and resistance, and opposition – what, in short, Albert Camus called *révolte* – to this state of things difficult if not impossible.

We are stuck in the immaculate *Lager* of our wealth, unable to give up our petty worries even in front of entire populations seeking help and asylum: our inability to support the Arab peoples in their revolts[42] is reinforced by the brutality of our indifference toward the thousands of people who are now trying to enter Europe. Realism in this situation is another word for racism, and it is almost baffling the way in which the boat-people arriving at Lampedusa remind us of the millions of unwanted refugees that became the main problem for Europe at the end of the First World War. Those refugees were, and continue to be, as Arendt explains, the representatives of a 'superfluous humanity', a name and a phenomenon that contribute to install in our minds the idea that for some there is simply no space on earth. The idea that some humans were superfluous was, as Arendt remarks, the necessary precedent to the fact that one could also find a final solution to that humanity in excess.

Caught as we are in the hyperrealism of our present we refuse to think that there can be *other* 'possible worlds', as if we were incapable of imagining transformation and change. We seem to be deprived, so to say, of the most humane of our faculties: imagination. This is not only 'fantasy', or unrealism, but also, and most of all, the ability to perceive reality from a different point of view, above, so to say, the raw tyranny of the *Now*. As Iranian writer Azar Nafisi has written, by quoting Saul Bellow,

> a culture that has lost its poetry and its soul is a culture that faces death. And death does not always come in the image of totalitarian rulers who belong to distant countries; it lives among us, in different guises, not as enemy but as friend. To mistake sound bites for deep thought, politics for action, reality shows for creative entertainment; to forget the value of dreams; to lose the ability to imagine a violent death in Darfur, in Afghanistan, in Iraq; to look at this as passing news: Are these not indications that now – more than ever – we need the courage and integrity, the faith, the vision and dreams these books instilled in us?[43]

According to Nafisi through literature we can learn democratic practices, or better, we can all contribute to create what she calls 'the republic of the imagination', a way of exiting the totalitarian dimension of the passive acceptance of 'what there is', grounded in the imaginative potentialities of *fiction*.

> Too often we conclude that we are practical creatures, essentially political animals. But in us there is a far greater impulse – a longing for the universal, a desire for a shared humanity. It is in that leap toward middle ground that we move toward what truly binds us: toward culture, toward stories, toward language. And it is here, in the republic of the imagination, that we are most humane.[44]

To imagine is not the same as to create; to enjoy a work of literature or poetry does not equate to being an artist, but we can learn from literature the 'art of imagination', and perhaps abandon realism and its paralyzing effects, to dwell courageously in the world of *fiction* and learn how to desire a different future.

3

TOTALITY, CONVERGENCE, SYNCHRONIZATION

Ian James

Totality, convergence and synchronization; these three concepts or figures connect the work of a number of contemporary French thinkers who have warned against the persistence or possible return of a totalizing and homogenizing logic within contemporary technological society. Such a logic may be seen as a hidden legacy, as a repetition, a re-inscription or echo of the totalitarian ideologies of 1930s and 1940s such as they were theorized by Hannah Arendt in the immediate aftermath of World War II.[1] These thinkers, Paul Virilio, Bernard Stiegler, and the close collaborators Jean-Luc Nancy and Philippe Lacoue-Labarthe, have a broadly common understanding of what might be called a totalitarian logic. They do not understand this logic as being necessarily restricted to the existence of a specific regime type or a particular organization of state power. In different ways they all understand the totalitarian as being articulated in a specific symbolic form before it comes to be embodied in a particular type of political regime. In identifying a fundamental totalitarian logic which is not necessarily exclusive to a particular organization of state power, each of these thinkers wish to find a means of responding to the contemporary or possible future re-emergence of totalitarian tendencies in different and perhaps unrecognizable forms.

The figures of totality, convergence and synchronization will be used here in order to explore the ways in which Virilio and Stiegler, in particular, highlight what they perceive to be the totalizing and undemocratic character of contemporary communications and media technologies. These thinkers arguably allow questions to be posed about new media and systems of information technology and to question the impact they may have had upon social and political organization but also upon individual and collective experience more generally.

Totality

In the late 1950s Paul Virilio, urbanist, cultural theorist and thinker of speed, began to explore and photograph World War II bunker fortifications of the French Atlantic seaboard. The book which resulted from these explorations was his first major work *Bunker Archeology* and was originally published in French in 1975.[2] The book, which includes many of Virilio's own photographs of the fortifications themselves, is a meditation on the nature of war and of military space. As an archaeology, it is also an attempt to uncover a hidden aspect of the past through an encounter with its material remains. By the same token, as an archaeology, it is also an exploration of the way in which aspects of the past may remain hidden or clandestinely persist within the present. The bunkers, of course, were erected by the Third Reich between 1942 and 1944 and at the time of Virilio's encounter with them many were in various states of decay or ruin. His extensive wanderings amongst the often crumbling, and sometimes sinking, lopsided or overgrown remains inspires a meditation, at once historical, architectural and philosophical, on the nature and destiny of fortified frontiers in modern warfare, but a meditation also on the ideological imagination of Nazi Germany itself.

For Virilio, these fortifications are not simply or solely defensive structures, they also have a symbolic dimension and testify to the way which political space has been conceived or imagined. In fact he sees these concrete structures as monuments of the inner logic of the Third Reich, as icons which represent the mode of ideological organization proper to the Nazi regime. This leads him to make some perhaps surprising statements, for instance: 'the bunkers of the European littoral were from the start the funerary monuments of the German dream'.[3] Insofar as they mark the outer limit of the Third Reich's territorial domination of Western Europe, the bunkers, huge in number and protecting the Atlantic seaboard in a vast chain of concrete fortification, reveal that this was a dream constituted in a specific spatial imaginary. Virilio suggests that the dream the bunkers reveal is not, however, simply or solely one of territorial domination but is also a dream of a European space imagined as an entirely homogenized entity whose borders and inner organization would be subject to total control. This would be the total control of German state power certainly, but more than anything, it was the total control of military and state power wielded in the name of a specific German identity and on the basis of a total mobilization of society. It is only in such a context that Total War declared by Goebbels in February 1943 could be declared and waged. Virilio's insight is that the building of the concrete bunkers marked the limits of a political space imagined as being 'at last homogenized, absolute war had become a reality, and the monolith was its monument'.[4] For Virilio, then, the bunkers signify a desire to totalize the space of a continent in a manner which is as much symbolic or imaginary as it is actual and real. As he puts it: 'The immensity of the project is what defies common sense'; in the vast concrete fortifications of the Atlantic littoral the totalizing imaginary of the German dream and the Nazi regime's pursuit of 'Total War' was revealed 'in its mythic dimension'.[5]

In uncovering this mythic, symbolic, and imaginary dimension Virilio formulates the key insight of *Bunker Archeology*, namely that the essence of the German dream did not lie simply or solely in the military domination of territorial space. The essence of this dream can be found also, and perhaps firstly, in an imaginary projection, in the desired image of a totalized and homogenized figure. This is a spatial imaginary which dreams of total territorial control, certainly, but it is also an imaginary which dreams of a territorial control realized *in the name of* a particular homogenized subject and its production or fabrication. Developing this argument in broader terms it could be said that, before it is a specific arrangement of state power that might come to be characterized as a totalitarian regime, the essence of a certain totalitarian logic can likewise be located in the desire for an image of totality, in a totalizing mythic, symbolic or imaginary dimension. This, at least, is the insight of *Bunker Archeology*, an insight which, as will become clear, is developed in various ways in many of Virilio's subsequent works.

Of course, he is not by any means alone in taking this view. Most obviously the account given by Hannah Arendt of totalitarianism and ideology in *The Origins of Totalitarianism* resonates strongly, albeit with certain differences of emphasis, with Virilio's characterization of the German dream as a desire for homogeneity and totality. The collaborative work of Jean-Luc Nancy and Philippe Lacoue-Labarthe also resonates particularly forcefully with Virilio's invocation of a 'mythic dimension'. Like *Bunker Archeology*, Nancy's and Lacoue-Labarthe's book *The Nazi Myth* published originally in 1991 [as *Le Mythe nazi*], aims to think the fundamental character of German fascism in terms of something which is first represented, symbolized and imagined before it is made manifest in a specific apparatus of state power.[6]

In the preface to *The Nazi Myth,* Nancy and Lacoue-Labarthe discuss the question of a return of fascism and the fear that history might repeat itself. They suggest, however, that it is not in the reappearance of swastika flags or Roman salutes that such a return needs to be feared. Simple repetition, they warn, is rare or even inexistent in real history. What we need to concern ourselves with rather are other kinds of repetition, those which we cannot immediately recognize or discern, and which are perhaps more complex but no less dangerous.[7] Their comments here echo very strongly the warning David Rousset gives at the end of *L'univers concentrationnaire,* namely that effects analogous to those which were produced in Germany under the Third Reich may be produced once again in the future in, I quote, 'a new figuration'.[8] Likewise Arendt warned at the end of *The Origins of Totalitarianism* that 'totalitarian solutions may well survive the fall of totalitarian regimes'.[9] Nancy and Lacoue-Labarthe follow Rousset and Arendt in affirming that the demise of the specific very visible form of the totalitarian regime is not enough to guarantee that its inner tendencies will not assert themselves in different ways in the future.

Like Rousset, Arendt, and of course many others, Nancy and Lacoue-Labarthe also suggest that the inner logic of Nazism is not aberrant, exceptional, or restricted to the specific regime that came to embody it. The argument here is that well-springs of fascism lie not in a logic of national or political exceptionalism, but rather should be located in wider European culture and history, and more particularly within the interdependent economic, social and political realities of Modern Europe; that is to say capitalism, anti-Semitism and imperialism, but also within more abstract forms of knowledge and modes of representation. For their part Nancy and Lacoue-Labarthe very explicitly endorse Arendt's understanding of totalitarian ideology as a logic of total realization or accomplishment. Arendt's highly influential analysis is, of course, well known: the totalitarian form of thought, she argues, posits a specific idea as that which will necessarily be accomplished or realized in the totality of historical becoming. For totalitarian ideology a single idea or concept suffices to explain the entirety of all that can and does happen. It posits, therefore, the movement of history as a unique and coherent process and ignores, suppresses and excludes any and all empirical particularities that do not conform to this process. Of course, various practices of violence, terror, and even extermination can easily be seen to follow as a consequence of this ideological logic of total realization. To this extent such a logic of total accomplishment and, indeed, the figure of totality itself can be seen as a form of symbolic violence and as the symbolic condition of actual or empirical violence. Building on Arendt's understanding Nancy and Lacoue-Labarthe argue that what needs to be clearly shown or rigorously demonstrated is that the Total State which the ideology of German fascism produced was in fact a Subject-State, that is to say the assertion of state power and the organization of a state apparatus in the service of the production of a unique and homogeneous subject: the Aryan people.[10] Although quite a short work, *The Nazi Myth* aims at just such a clear and rigorous demonstration. So the unique and coherent process of historical movement that Arendt identifies, Nancy and Lacoue-Labarthe identify as the process by which a unique and monolithic subject would be produced as the destiny of a state and its people.

The implications of this for Nancy and Lacoue-Labarthe are wide-reaching. Their emphasis on the subject and on the ideologically desired creation of a Subject-State leads them to situate the genesis of German fascism not simply or solely in the wider economic, social and political forces of capitalism, anti-Semitism, and imperialism. Rather they emphasize the extent to which the ideology of the totalitarian Subject-State is entirely consistent with and, indeed, is a concrete instantiation of, the modern metaphysics of the subject as conceived within the broader European philosophical tradition. More precisely they want to argue that a certain logic is totalitarian or fascist and that this logic is in no way foreign to the more general logic and rationality of a distinctly European metaphysics of the subject.[11] This metaphysics of the subject could be characterized in broad terms as the understanding of being and becoming as grounded in a self-present, self-sufficient and autonomous instance which acts as the site and source of all certainty, representation and volition or agency. They even go so far as to make some bold and perhaps extreme claims; for instance, that fascism in its essence is 'the ideology of the subject'.[12] This may seem extreme, but it is worth bearing in mind that Nancy and Lacoue-Labarthe's emphasis is on an *ideological* moment and the way in which ideology desires that individual subjects be produced as a homogeneous collective subject. What counts, for Nancy and Lacoue-Labarthe, is the way in which the ideological desire for a homogeneous and totalized subject belongs, not just to the ideologies that produced totalitarian regimes, but more widely to a fundamental disposition of Western thought and culture.

Recognizing and acknowledging this does not mean that we may be justified in conflating different political forms or types of regime, or in claiming for instance that democracy as we think we know it is no better than the Total State of the Third Reich and that there is, therefore, little to choose between them. Rather than reducing our power to distinguish and differentiate, such a recognition and acknowledgement might arguably enhance possibilities of discernment and differentiated understanding. Nancy and Lacoue-Labarthe put this in the following terms: 'it is not possible' they write in relation to advent of Nazism, to:

> simply dismiss it as an aberration [n]or as an aberration which is simply in the past. Comfortable assurance in moral certitude and in democracy, not only does not guarantee anything, but exposes one to the risk of not seeing the coming or the return of that which was not simply a pure accident of history.[13]

It is in this context that Nancy and Lacoue-Labarthe's understanding of the mythical dimension of Nazism may be useful and instructive. For if Nazi ideology often appealed to certain forms of myth – that is, myths relating to the origin and the pure lineage of Germanic, Nordic and Aryan peoples – it did so arguably because any metaphysics of the subject always and necessarily appeals to some form of myth, fable or essentially fictional construct. This is an argument, at least, which is made at some length by both Nancy and Lacoue-Labarthe in their various joint and single-authored publications of the 1970s and early 1980s. A metaphysics of the subject, they argue, requires a mythical, fabulous or otherwise fictional figure in order to give form to the unified or coherent conception of the human that it presupposes as the self-evident, self-present, and autonomous ground of all being and becoming.[14]

Nancy and Lacoue-Labarthe's analysis in *The Nazi Myth* suggests that it is not the specific content of National Socialist mythology and ideology which may come to repeat itself in the present or the future. Nor is it the particular historical form of the totalitarian Subject-State of the Third Reich. The implication of their argument is that the 'ideology of the subject', a specific, dangerously totalizing logic which totalizes historical becoming and collective identity, has the potential to emerge within or from any apparatus of state power, however it may be organized, but also that it may not necessarily and exclusively be the sole preserve of the organs or technologies of the state. At the same time the 'ideology of the subject' may also, in the present or in the future, appeal to other different or unexpected mythical, fabulous or fictional figures of the human. It may then also come to assert its desire for the production of a homogenized subject and for the totalization of all that is or becomes in other forms of apparatus, and in other techniques or technologies. If, therefore, the totalitarian logic of the Nazi Subject-State was indeed an expression of a fundamentally totalizing disposition of Western thought and culture, then the real question to be posed is about the contemporary forms and possible future modes of expression of that disposition.

Convergence, synchronization

It is here that, under the motifs of convergence and synchronization, one can return to the bunker-inspired meditations of Paul Virilio. If, in *Bunker Archeology*, the concrete fortifications of the Atlantic seaboard revealed themselves as funerary monuments of the German dream, this was because they served as signifiers of an untrammelled desire for a homogeneous European space subjected to the total control of a supra national people. Yet, when viewed in the light of the outcome of World War II, what the bunkers ultimately also presage is the effective *redundancy* of fortified military frontiers. For Virilio Total War was most decisively waged from the sky: and, in particular, in the intensive area bombing of urban and civilian populations. In the context of such Total War the battle fronts of sea and land of course still have their very significant place but take on a very different status, since the successful penetration of sea and land space by military means is now underwritten by the force of airpower, air supremacy and aerial bombing. For Virilio then, the systematic opening up of the third front of the air as a means of waging Total War completely transforms the nature of frontiers themselves. Bunker fortifications, at first so essential to the Nazi conception and defence of Fortress Europe are made more essentially redundant, and appear *only* as monuments, and as mythical icons of an expired dream.[15]

More importantly still, this redundancy of the bunkers heralds a wider and more globally significant transformation of national frontiers in the wake of World War II. This is a transformation which results from the way in which the Total War of aerial bombing is brought to an end in Hiroshima and Nagasaki and inaugurates what Virilio dubs the Total Peace of nuclear deterrence and of the Cold War. For, in a world dominated by the threat of nuclear destruction fortified military frontiers have little real meaning.[16] Likewise the total control of space through the conquest of land shows itself to be a dream of a past era. In the books that follow *Bunker Archeology* Virilio explores the implications and consequences of this transformation in the nature of frontiers. Most strikingly and provocatively he argues that in the shift from the Total War of saturation bombing to the Total Peace of nuclear deterrence the logic of totalization and total control that characterized spatial imaginary of the Third Reich does not entirely disappear but rather is maintained and perpetuated, albeit in a different form.

He makes this argument in relation to a number of contexts and in a number of ways but often does so in a provocative or polemical manner. For instance, in his second work *Popular Defence and Ecological Struggles* published in 1978 he writes: 'in order to create a *totalitarian Lebensraum* today it is no longer necessary to resort to extraordinary invasions with the motorized vehicles, tanks and stukas, of lightning warfare, since one can use the *ordinary penetration* of the new media, the information blitz'.[17] And again in the same work:

> The suppression of national frontiers and the hypercommunicability of the world do not increase the space of liberty. They are, rather, a sign of its disappearance, its collapse, before the expansion of an all-too-tangible totalitarian power, a technological control of civilized societies that is growing ever more rapid and refined.[18]

Such statements may indeed appear to be provocative, polemical, extreme even. On the face of it Virilio appears, perhaps fancifully or bizarrely, to be directly comparing what he calls the new media, and nascent communications and information technologies more generally, to fascism, and to the totalitarian expansionism of the Third Reich. Yet if one looks beyond the polemical hyperbole a more serious argument can be discerned. Virilio is suggesting that the totalizing and homogenizing logic that characterized the German dream no longer manifests itself in a spatial dimension, nor in a broader geopolitical need for total territorial control. This logic, which may remain no less totalizing and homogenizing, now manifests itself, he argues, in a different dimension which is not primarily spatial. This different dimension is more temporal than it is spatial or territorial and the total control that the ordinary penetration of the new media may bring about is, for Virilio, a control of collective temporal experience rather than a national territorial domination.[19]

Firstly, Virilio is interested in the way in which, in the last decades of the twentieth century, diverse modes of communication and information technology converged to form a system or substructure which has come to underpin interrelated forms of contemporary social, political and economic life. This convergence can be discerned in the impact modern technologies have had upon the fundamental structuring of the site or place of politics. In the contemporary world, Virilio argues, it is the production in real time of quasi-instantaneous communications, exchanges and data transfer which makes the operation of electronic markets and the flow of global capital possible, and this in turn has come to shape the space or site of the polis; in this site or space the activity of politics itself has in turn come to be shaped by the necessities of markets, by global capital flows, and by the demands of economic growth that these dictate: politics therefore has become less a matter of reflection and thought, or of conflict and the struggle for emancipation, and more a question of calculated management. Most importantly, however, for Virilio, this new space or site of the polis is primarily one of temporal projection rather than one of spatial extension. If there is a temporal rather than a spatial imaginary at work here it is one which dreams of a collective homogeneous subject produced in and through the synchronization of collective consciousness which modern communications technologies make possible.

The politics or ideology that is produced from the convergence of diverse modern technologies is, therefore, concerned far more with the homogenization and control of a certain temporal becoming than it is with the space of national or territorial sovereignty. This is a chronopolitics of real-time information exchange. Resulting as it does from the convergence of communication and information technologies in the functioning of a global system of markets and capital flow, chronopolitics for Virilio is not in itself democratic. On the contrary he refers to the regime of 'real time' which governs the activity and becoming of chronopolitics as '*tyranny of real time*'.[20] His primary concern here is with the way in which the temporal dimension of instantaneity and intensivity proper to the high-speed transmission of information leads to a wasting of the political culture of democracy. This is because the instantaneity of 'real time' is not a temporality which is conducive to the processes of thought and reflection required by a properly democratic subjectivity. Virilio poses the question of whether whatever democracy we think we do have or have had, may 'disappear with the advent of a new tyranny, the *tyranny of real time* which would no longer permit democratic control, but only the conditioned reflex, *automatism*'.[21] He repeats this point in an interview with Philippe Petit published in 1996:

> The tyranny of real time is not very different from classical tyranny, because it tends to liquidate the reflective capacity of the citizen in favour of a reflex action. Democracy is about solidarity, not solitary experience, and humans need time to reflect before acting. Yet the real time and global present requires on the part of the telespectator a reflex response which is already of the order of manipulation.[22]

What is at stake here is, firstly, the convergence of technological structures or forms into a system which coordinates all aspects of political, social, and economic life according to its own unique logic and mode of necessity: that of economic production and consumption and of economic growth and the distribution of its benefits. Secondly the coordinated production of subjects and of subjectivity within a specific mode of temporal projection is also at stake. When Virilio talks about 'real time' as 'the new tyranny', and about the conditioning of reflex or automatic responses he is also talking about the way in which real-time media and information technologies seek to interpolate or produce subjectivities and do so *en masse* in a homogenized or more precisely a temporally synchronized manner.

In the intensive temporality of real time, subjectivity is conditioned as structure reflex reaction rather than one of reasoned reflection. In a recent text, *City of Panic* [*Ville panique*], Virilio expresses this in the following terms:

> We today face the threat, no longer simply of a democracy of opinion which would replace the representative democracy of political parties, but the excess of a veritable DEMOCRACY OF EMOTION; of a collective emotion, simultaneously synchronised and globalised whose model could well be that of *a post-political televangelism*.[23]

The risk here is one of a fatal convergence. On the one hand there is the convergence of the systems of communication and information technology that underpin the operation of markets, the flow of capital and necessities of economic growth. On the other hand the different modes of modern broadcast media converge to produce an 'era of synchronization' in which the temporal flux of subjective consciousness is coordinated *en masse* by an industrialized form of vision and perception which privileges a temporality of the instant, and of instant reflex response which is inimical to the kind of informed participation which is necessary to any properly democratic polity.

In this convergence of technologies of real-time communication, and in the propensity of contemporary mass media technologies to seek a synchronization of subjective experience a totalizing and homogenizing logic is, therefore, at work. This logic, for Virilio, is a legacy of the spatial logic that revealed itself in the bunkers of the Atlantic seaboard but which is now systematically articulated in a temporal dimension and in a desire for the total control of that temporal dimension and its present and future becoming. What he calls the 'tyranny of real time' in his later work is a development of the 'all-too-tangible totalitarian power, [the] technological control of civilized societies' that he identified in 1978. These formulations also resonate very clearly with Nancy and Lacoue-Labarthe's analysis of the 'ideology of the subject' in *The Nazi Myth*: the modes of convergence and synchronization Virilio identifies suggest that there is deep-seated structural tendency which underpins the workings of contemporary technological society. This is a tendency orientated towards the total penetration of historical becoming by a logic of economic exchange and production, the saturation of collective experience by that logic, and the production of subjects whose temporal experience is synchronized in a manner which accords with the exigencies of that logic.

This is an analysis that has been taken up and developed further over the last 15 years by the contemporary, and much younger, French philosopher Bernard Stiegler. Stiegler is, above all, a philosopher of time and of the technological rootedness of human temporal experience, on both a collective and historical, as well as on an individual and subjective, level. His philosophical work on the technological structuring of temporal and historical experience is accompanied by analysis of contemporary society and the impact of digital information technologies on individual and collective time perception. This is an analysis heavily influenced by Virilio's thinking in key respects. Across a number of different works published in the late 1990s and throughout the last decade, Stiegler develops a critique of contemporary technological systems, which, he argues, produce what he comes to call an industrialized synthesis of memory. In particular Stiegler is, like Virilio, interested in the way in which the diverse technologies which underpin both economic and cultural modes of production have converged in what he terms a 'functional integration'. This convergence constitutes a distinctive stage of industrialization to which he gives the name 'hyper-industrial'.[24] For Stiegler our epoch is not one of late or post-modernity but rather of an industrial society that has become a hyper-industrial society. He argues that the functional integration of hyper-industrial society is one in which all the technical systems of representation which constitute cultural life and support cultural memory converge with the material modes of production, consumption and economic exchange. The risk of this convergence of technical, economic and cultural production is that it subordinates the entirety of the social and cultural sphere to its own (principally economic) exigencies and necessities. It should be clear the extent to which this analysis of the hyper-industrial is extremely close to Virilio's analysis of the 'tyranny of real time'.

Yet Stiegler gives a much more developed account of synchronization and the production of subjectivity within the context of hyper-industrial society than does Virilio. What most concerns him is the question of individuation, the process through which individuals differentiate themselves and become more distinctively singular or unique within any mass or group of people. The problem, for Stiegler, is that the functional integration of hyper-industrial society orders the fundamental tendency of mass media to synchronize subjectivities. The risk is that this will lead to a generalized wasting of individuation. In the terms developed by Nancy and Lacoue-Labarthe the risk here is that this functional integration is operating systematically according to the 'ideology of the subject', that is to say the *desired* production of subjects as a homogeneous totality which is given a single and unique figure or form.

Stiegler puts this in the following terms: 'the functional integration of the information and culture industries makes possible a total control of markets, that is, collectivities consciousnesses whose temporal flux it is necessary to SYNCHRONIZE'.[25] Once again there is this key emphasis on total control. Without a strong orientation towards a totalizing synchronization of consciousness and experience mass markets and consumer culture cannot, Stiegler argues, function as such. It is a question of the flux of temporal experience being formed homogeneously *en masse* by information and media technology in the service of markets and economic productivity. In an industrial synthesis of time consciousness all those processes that would favour individuation are blocked in favour of those which promote homogenization.

It is important to note at this point that the manner in which the temporal flux of consciousness is coordinated *en masse* in hyper-industrial society is not, for Stiegler, a kind of brainwashing according to which our self-awareness is monolithically programmed or determined by technical systems and the representations they produce. Rather the synchronization of experience here is viewed more as a conditioning which ensures that, despite the processes of singularization and differentiation which may always inevitably be at play, enough people will nevertheless desire and consume in the same way such that mass markets will function. Stiegler makes it clear that: 'The coincidence of temporal flux does not mean that each consciousness sees and lives exactly the same thing.' He is not saying that the convergence of technical systems '"program" the time of consciousness in the sense that they determine it', but rather that 'it is a conditioning', and he argues that 'the efficiency of this conditioning is enormous'.[26] It is not a question of determinism, then, but more a question of the way in which the organizing processes of hyper-industrial society seek to synchronize consciousness. They necessarily do so on a huge scale and thereby tend towards totalization and homogenization rather than individuation, singularization, and differentiation. For all the talk of individual freedom, autonomy and choice in contemporary consumer societies, Stiegler argues that these societies are, in fact: 'profoundly hostile to the processes of individuation, to heterogeneity, to singularity and to the exception'.[27]

Now it would be very easy to be sceptical of Stiegler's claim that modern markets function according to a logic of total control, let alone a logic of total control that would be comparable to the kinds tyranny or totalitarian power analysed by Virilio or by Nancy and Lacoue-Labarthe. Many would believe that, in reality, markets are inherently unstable, unpredictable and uncontrollable, or at the very least a function of the rational autonomy of all those who participate in markets. On the other hand it might be said that what is significant in Stiegler's account is the argument that the convergence or 'functional integration' of technologies structurally tends towards a logic of, or a desire for, total control, for synchronization and homogeneity and that they necessarily synchronize and homogenize as a function of their successful operation. Stiegler is trying to understand the mechanisms by which hypermasses who consume industrially manufactured material and cultural products on a global scale and in global markets, can function successfully as such.

At the same time it might be very easy also to be sceptical of the account given by both Virilio and Stiegler of the general structure of technological modernity and of communication and information technologies in particular. The accounts of both stand in direct opposition to contemporary orthodoxies relating to digital media and communications technologies that proclaim their inherently democratizing power. These are discourses with which we will all be familiar and which are recycled relentlessly in media coverage, in political analysis of world events, but arguably also in marketing discourse and other forms of cultural production. Whether it be the democratizing power of the internet through open access to information, blogging, social networking, or other communications technologies, it is taken as axiomatic that the technological advances in this realm are a function of, but are also inherently able to promote, the historical progress of liberal democracy, and the freedom of choice and self-determination that necessarily go with it. To this extent Virilio and Stiegler could be said to be holding up a mirror to contemporary technological society in order to reflect back an unfamiliar or inverted image of what orthodoxy takes it to be.[28]

What should also be underlined, in this context, is the fact that neither Nancy and Lacoue-Labarthe, nor Virilio and Stiegler, are attempting to describe some monolithic process of ideological totalization, convergence, and synchronization, within which we might all be somehow fatalistically and inevitably caught up or entrapped. They are not offering grand narratives that describe the contemporaneous stage of an inevitable world-historical process of totalization. Rather they are describing more or less hidden ideological, technological, cultural and socio-economic, but ultimately *contingent*, processes, which, in their convergence and shared inner logic, *tend* towards totality, a violent totalization, and a totalitarian logic. Each of these thinkers attempts in different ways to show the ways in which these processes of totalization can be countered or opposed, or ways in which they might always ultimately and inevitably *fail*. This can be seen in Nancy's insistence in *The Inoperative Community* that any totalizing logic of shared or fusional national community is always suicidal and that by implication the Third Reich was necessarily a suicidal regime.[29] It can also be seen in Virilio's insistence that the Atlantic seaboard bunkers in their embodiment of a totalizing logic were: '*from the start* funerary monuments to the German dream'[30] (my emphasis). This also echoes Hannah Arendt's analysis in *The Origins of Totalitarianism* of the failure of the Third Reich. At the same time all of the thinkers discussed here aim to develop strategies or means by which the processes of totalization which they describe might be countered.

The importance and interest of Virilio's and Stiegler's analyses, therefore, lie in the way they allow questions to be posed in different terms so that we might be able to identify certain tendencies which we might otherwise ignore and, on this basis, locate strategies or resources to respond critically and politically to those tendencies. Their thinking directly calls into question the alliance of technocratic and democratic discourse which has arisen over the past two decades and which has shaped orthodoxies relating to technological modernity and historical progress in the wake of the Cold War. As Nancy and Lacoue-Labarthe said: 'Comfortable assurance in moral certitude and in democracy, not only does not guarantee anything, but exposes one to the risk of not seeing.'[31] Virilio and Stiegler allow us to see in a different way, to view things from a divergent perspective. Specifically the concepts of *totality*, *convergence*, and *synchronization* provide a means of interrogating different phenomena and of posing the question of what kind of logic is really at work in forms which we might unreflectively, ideologically, or otherwise consensually take to be inherently democratic.

In particular the thinking that has been exposed here tells us that it is not simply in political or governmental types, be they totalitarian or democratic in a very restricted sense, that we may need to perceive historical threats on the one hand and solutions on the other. Rather, for Virilio, Stiegler, Nancy and Lacoue-Labarthe, what we firstly need to *see* are structural processes and forms. We need to uncover the deep symbolic structure of cultural processes and ideological forms and to interrogate the technologies through which these processes and forms are realized or accomplished. What is most fundamentally at stake here is whether cultural and political forms, our own or those of the future, are in reality pluralizing or totalizing, whether they allow for genuine divergence and multiplicity or tend towards convergence and totality. It is a question of whether they foster a de-synchronization and therefore singular and plural becoming of subjectivity, or whether in actual fact they promote a synchronization and therefore a homogenization and monolithic becoming of subjectivity.

Ultimately, then, these thinkers may tell us that the constitutional mechanisms of the liberal democratic state and the values of consumer choice and economic freedom are not a sufficient means of guarding against the repetition of a totalizing and violent historical becoming. The motifs of totality, convergence and synchronization which connect the different arguments of these thinkers provide a conceptual framework which, I would argue, allows for a critical distance to be taken from any form of social or political organization which would seek to extend itself into every sphere of human action and interaction and thereby to prescribe a unique and coherent course of present and future historical becoming. In identifying both logical and technological structures of *totalization*, *convergence* and *synchronization*, these thinkers may, therefore, allow us to think democracy more properly, not as an already achieved state, but as an always ongoing and multiple process of *singularization*, *divergence*, and *de-synchronization*.

PART 2

DESIRE

4

WRAP ME UP IN SADIST KNOTS
Representations of Sadism – From Naziploitation to Torture Porn

Aaron Kerner

What is sadism?

The colloquial conception of 'sadism' – pleasure derived from the pain of others – does little justice to the complexity of the term. It does seem apt, though, when considering, for instance, the character of Amon Goeth in Steven Spielberg's *Schindler's List* (1993). Recall the image of Goeth perched in his palatial villa amusing himself by using concentration camp internees for target practice. Indeed, in some cases the victim–perpetrator relationship set within the concentration camp – be it in film or in life – merits this rather simple colloquial designation, and this colloquial conception of sadism undoubtedly fuels the popular imagination. At first glance what I intend to present here will appear utterly paradoxical, because the films that I have selected that explicitly trade in the imagery of the concentration camp shed little light on that historical space and the nature of sadism, while the films that only bear the faint traces of the event are potentially more productive – that is to say more nuanced in their representation of sadism and perhaps more insightful in the examination of the 'concentrationary imaginary'.

So what is it then? What is sadism? Just briefly, because others have explored this in detail, sadism is a disposition that evacuates ethics from the discourse of reason.[1] The term derives from the infamous French author, the Marquis de Sade, who wrote some of his most notorious works during the Reign of Terror. On the surface of things his literary work has the appearance of pornography, a veritable encyclopaedia of perversions, but read through an allegorical lens his stories offer a poignant social-political commentary. Specifically, Sade was critical of the implementation of Enlightenment ideals, which fanned the flames of the French Revolution. Philosophically speaking he was an advocate of progressive human values, but the problem that he saw (in vivid and gory details) was the implementation of these humanist ideas. He was utterly horrified by the mechanization of death – the guillotine – and noted that it is only 'by [a] dint of murders that France is free today'.[2]

The suggestion here is that Kant and Sade share certain affinities, and this parity is one of deep profundity and significance. 'A lot – everything, perhaps – is at stake here', Slavoj Žižek writes, and subsequently asks, 'is there a line from Kantian formalist ethics to the cold-blooded Auschwitz killing machine? Are concentration camps and killing as a neutral business the inherent outcome of the enlightenment insistence on the autonomy of Reason?'[3] Even matters regarding sex for the libertine are not premised on passion, but rather on duty, and strict adherence to a code of conduct. This might strike us as counterintuitive, and indeed it flies in the face of our commonly held conception of the sadist, because the libertine is not prone to 'raw, brutal, passionate satisfying animal sex, but, on the contrary', as Žižek observes, 'a fully regimented, intellectualized activity comparable to a well-planned sporting match'.[4] Indeed, and despite our preconceived notions otherwise, any inspection of the Sadean volume will reveal that the sexual acts, no matter how benign, or vicious, they may be, are all executed under strict guidelines, and within highly controlled environments. (These characteristics – calculated behaviour, strict guidelines, and a controlled environment – are important features in the Torture Porn genre, which I'll address later.) There is nothing capricious or spontaneous about the libertines, and their salacious encounters; that is to say, no action is perpetrated through love, or genuinely erotic feelings. The sadist when it comes right down to it is enslaved to reason; what gives the sadist pleasure is 'the activity of outstripping rational civilization by its own means'.[5] The thrust of this chapter, then, is to survey the ways in which sadism has been represented within the context of the concentrationary imaginary, while being mindful of the treatment of sadism.

Naziploitation

Filmmakers in the horror, pornographic, and exploitation genres tend to resort to tawdry fetishistic visions of sadism, where for instance Nazis (or their derivatives) are depicted administering painful punishments for the sheer fun of it. Victims are mere foils for the violent spectacles, and little regard is given to the character (or characters), be they victim or perpetrator; rather in these films the sadistic character tends to be a one-dimensional cookie-cutter image of pure evil, or easily dismissed as deranged. Victims, likewise, are little more than props on which the sadistic operation of power is exercised.

In the Naziploitation genre, for example, there is little regard for the industrialized nature of the extermination process and these films foist responsibility for abject crimes onto a 'sick' character, or a band of characters, as opposed to the very mundane realities of a bureaucratic system that assimilated ordinary men and women into the machinery of mass murder. Nevertheless, it is the more colloquial understanding of sadism that permeates our culture, and it comes as no surprise – because no film is ever made in a vacuum – that filmmakers draw on this commonly held understanding of sadism.

Ilse Koch and Josef Mengele serve as archetypes of the sadist, both in its more colloquial form and its more clinical manifestation. Popularly known as the Angel of Death, Mengele conducted medical experiments on Auschwitz internees. He had a particular interest in twins as they offered unique experimental potential. According to the popular imagination the infamous Ilse Koch was known for possessing a lamp fashioned from human bones, fitted with a lampshade made of human skin, as well as having a human skin handbag, and flaying people for their tattoos. She was popularly known in the press as 'Lampshade Ilse', 'the Bitch of Buchenwald', 'the Witch of Buchenwald', or 'the Beast of Buchenwald'. As the wife of the SS officer Karl Otto Koch, the commandant of Buchenwald, she exercised her privileged position with the utmost brutality. On the one hand she had all the privilege of an SS officer, but on the other hand she held no official office; effectively she wielded power and authority and yet answered to no one. This fact would prove problematic later when she was subject to prosecution, because she was not 'working' in any official capacity in Buchenwald. She was prosecuted not once, but three times, by the Nazi regime (for corruption – Karl Koch was convicted and executed, Ilse Koch was acquitted), the Allied war crimes tribunal, and the post-war German government. Among her acts of naked cruelty, for which she was tried as a war criminal, 'she allegedly had more than forty inmates killed for their tattooed skins. The report commissioned by the US Army immediately after the liberation of Buchenwald also documented the reign of terror of the "homosexual" commandant Karl Koch and his "nymphomaniac" wife Ilse.'[6] Naziploitation films have capitalized on the sensationalized accounts of Ilse Koch.

Cesare Canevari's *The Gestapo's Last Orgy* (1977), for instance, includes a female SS officer, Alma, who is clearly modelled after Koch. In one scene in particular all the popular tropes associated with Koch are on exhibit: Alma beckons an internee, Lise Cohen, to approach. Alma gently caresses the internee's face, then offers a backhanded compliment: 'Beautiful as a beast, you're like my Dobermans.' Alma then entreats Cohen to inspect a collection of things, 'Look, it's so silky. Isn't it? These panties are made with the most delicate fabric in the whole world', pressing them to Cohen's face, 'it wasn't very easy to match hairs one-by-one. We were forced to kill off quite a few girls to keep it right. You must see its beauty Lise.' Cohen asks what will become of her, but she's rebuked and again ordered to inspect other articles, 'Come here! Now! Do you see these gloves? Touch them.' Alma grabs Cohen's wrist placing her hand on the supple leather, 'They're made out of baby skin. There's nothing softer or more delicate than the skin of a newborn baby. But then the baby grows up, and its skin gets old – becomes ugly.' Alma turns and steps away, adding, 'So it's best to take it off right away.' Cohen is sickened by the parade of grisly items, rebuking, 'It's monstrous what you're doing.' Alma revels in the power she wields over Cohen, and the power exercised by the regime, as she presents a flagon full of urine-coloured liquid to Cohen, ordering her to 'Drink this!' As Cohen drinks excess liquid spills down her naked breasts, which Alma proceeds to massage while continuing to rant, 'We enjoy being able to do whatever we like to the world. Like I'm doing to you now. I feel that you're being broken-in.' In a series of quick flashbacks, a naked male internee echoes the unfolding events; he too drinks from a flagon while Alma massages him. Cutting back to Cohen, Alma orders, 'Now look', thrusting Cohen's face toward an adorned lampshade. 'Look at it,' Alma rails, 'that tattoo was too beautiful to die with a man. Look at it, look at it! We took it from him. But first we made him happy.' Flashing back to the sexual encounter between Alma and the male internee, she recounts, 'He must've had a beautiful last memory of life.' Again cutting back to the sexual encounter Alma is finally seen flaying the male internee alive to remove his tattoo. Without an ounce of subtlety (one would hardly expect anything less from an exploitation film), the character of Alma is clearly drawn from the popular vision of Koch.[7]

Don Edmonds' *Ilsa: She Wolf of the SS* (1975) is exemplary of the Naziploitation genre.[8] The primary character, Ilsa, is a composite character; drawing on Mengele, and her namesake. The iconography of Ilsa's character in Edmonds' cult film points back to the historical record. In her regalia Ilsa is typically seen wearing a white shirt – unbuttoned to emphasize her buxom cleavage, of course – black riding boots, riding pants, and riding-crop in hand. In addition to being accused of flaying internees for their tattoos, Koch was an avid horse-rider, and a special rink was constructed in the camp for her, using internees as labour. Numerous accounts recall her provocative attire and her pretension to whip internees with her riding-crop.

Ilsa: She Wolf of the SS trades heavily in the sadistic visual culture associated with the concentration camp. Ilsa is the commandant of Medical Camp 9, where she conducts medical experiments on internees. One of Ilsa's pet projects is to prove that a woman's pain threshold is higher than a man's, thus demonstrating that women can serve in military combat. Ilsa, like her historical counterpart, was interested in mastering the human race. Mengele's medical experiments were geared towards unlocking the secret of racial genetics and envisioned the potential of manufacturing Aryan traits – for instance he experimented with changing an individual's eye colour. Among the many gruesome experiments that Ilsa conducts on female internees is an experiment in rapid decompression (a medical experiment in fact conducted by Nazi doctors). A buxom female internee is bound inside a compression chamber. Watching through the portal in the compression chamber door, Ilsa commands her assistant to reduce the pressure dramatically, causing the female subject to writhe in agony as she haemorrhages, spitting up comic-book-red blood from her mouth (4.1). The portal is particularly interesting because it evokes the sadistic power associated with looking. Within conventional (cinematic) paradigms of power, women are not granted the 'right' to look, and when women do look, it is ascribed as exceptional and perverse.[9] There could hardly be a more explicit

4.1   *Ilsa, She Wolf of the SS* (Don Edmonds, 1975).

illustration of the sadistic gaze as illustrated in *Ilsa*, which so closely corresponds to feminist film theory, where 'pleasure' derives from the control, subjugation, and punishment of the female form. Moreover the perversion of the female gaze is amplified in its cohabitation with the Nazi gaze. The amplification of the upending of patriarchal paradigms is seen throughout the film. Ilsa conducts a number of other experiments, including administering electrical shocks to female internees with an electrified dildo: the literal materialization of the perversion of phallic power.

Truth be told though the film is more accurately a picture of male anxiety in the 1970s in the wake of the Women's Liberation movement, than it is a depiction of the historical horrors of the concentration camp. *Ilsa* is what (Western) patriarchal culture fears the most: a woman 'on top', authoritative, and an independent sexually active woman. It is fitting that the film opens with Ilsa having sex with one of the male internees, on top, astride him.

In the first scene there is nothing that contextualizes the sex act, and it stands in opposition to normative representations of feminine sexuality. In a conventional narrative the sexual act is located at the end of a protracted chase; a female character throughout a film might rebuff the overtures of a male character, before she finally accepts her male suitor. And in fact in many instances the sexual act effectively functions as a narrative resolution. Rather in *Ilsa* in the opening moments of the film we find the couple in the midst of the coital act with the woman on top – in control and enthralled with pleasure. Immediately, it is clear that the 'order of things' is not in line with the traditional patriarchal paradigm, or narrative traditions – there is nothing that precedes this encounter to allow for an investment in characters or to know their relations and motivations. In this opening scene, however, pleasure quickly turns to disappointment when Ilsa's male partner climaxes, despite her pleas to hold on, leaving the insatiable Ilsa unfulfilled. Sullenly she slumps down and rests upon her spent sexual partner admonishing under her breath, 'you should have waited'. Unsatisfied by her male partner Ilsa retreats to the shower where she pleasures *herself*. Returning to the bedside she orders two female associates to take the hapless man away; soon we find him in Ilsa's lab, naked and strapped to an examination table. Like the female praying mantis – which devours its mate – Ilsa and her two female accomplices castrate the internee and presumably allow him to bleed to death. The scene ends with blood pouring down a trough designed to capture and dispense with bodily fluids coming from the examination table.

The objective of Ilsa's medical experiments in the 1975 film is to prove that women have a higher pain threshold than men, and this resonates with the politics of the 1970s. In one such case, we see a woman harnessed to an examiner's chair; her right foot is in a vice bloody and mangled, as one of the commandant's female accomplices rips out the inmate's toenails – with the sound of torn-blood-soaked flesh and cracking toenails the sound design greatly enhances the visceral disgust of the scene. The camera tilts upward to reveal that the inmate's eyes have also been gouged out. As Ilsa's obedient guards continue with the gruesome experiment Ilsa bitterly declares, 'Berlin laughed at my theory. Soon I will give them documented proof, and they will laugh no more.' One of her minions retorts, 'They do not wish to believe it.' To which Ilsa responds, 'No, they are men; it is unthinkable to them that a carefully trained woman can withstand pain better than any man.' These arguments about a woman's equal capacity to serve in the military resonate with the struggle for women's rights in the 1970s. A rather primitive and naive psychiatric assessment of Ilse Koch in 1951 determined that 'the multiplicity of her loves is explained by a thirst for vengeance because of her resentment at not having been born a man'.[10] This diagnosis seems more symptomatic of a misogynistic culture than of Koch's actual violation (criminal inhumanity), but what this illustrates is how the figure of Ilse Koch – a perversion of 'proper' woman in the popular imagination – might easily serve as a model for Ilsa the she-wolf.

The misogyny of patriarchal culture is projected in reverse here, with highly embellished scenes of women perpetrating violence against and sexually exploiting men (and other women), rendering them as objects of satisfaction, and when finished casting them away like rubbish. Rather than a vision of a real Nazi (or the real Ilse Koch, or Mengele), Ilsa instead signifies the monstrous feminine (as Barbara Creed might say) and is figured as the epitome of evil: a woman with (sexual) agency.[11] The concentration camp, in this case, is merely a narrative device – or an excuse – on which contemporary social anxieties are projected.[12] The grotesque horror of the spectacle that we see on screen amounts to an articulation of male hysteria. The infamy of Ilse Koch, then, serves as a model for the negative stereotype of the 'liberated woman', a woman in a position of authority and in control of her own sexuality. Ilsa is not castrated as such, but a castrator. Edmonds renders the 'liberated woman' as the quintessence of Western evil – a Nazi.

Torture Porn

While the more 'explicit' representations of Nazi atrocities tend to reveal little about the clinical manifestation of sadism – such as found in *Ilsa* – in the genre of Torture Porn, the Holocaust manifests in more implicit ways. The term 'Torture Porn' was coined by film critic David Edelstein, who published an article, 'Now Playing at Your Local Multiplex: Torture Porn', in the 28 January 2006 issue of *New York* magazine. There are several distinct features of the genre. In Torture Porn victims are typically confined or imprisoned in some fashion. Whereas in Slasher films victims used to be dispatched with some sharp instrument – a knife, machete, chainsaw – penetrating or lacerating the victim to deal a lethal blow, in Torture Porn, on the other hand, victims are not just impaled or cut, they are frequently dismembered, or in some fashion mutilated, made to die a slow painful death. It almost goes without saying that in Torture Porn, victims are tortured. Victims are not, however, merely subjected to savage physical brutality; additionally, they are tormented emotionally and psychologically. On occasion victims are forced into situations where they are made to perpetrate acts of violence against others (in a bid to save their own lives), faced with some sort of grievous choice – usually involving bodily mutilation – or are simply allowed to languish in their own suffering knowing that they have little or no hope of surviving.

Victims suffer at the hands of sadistic characters, and they are usually sadistic in the clinical sense of the term. The perpetrators are usually very intelligent, cool, calm and collected. While malice might be a motivating factor, the perpetrator in Torture Porn usually remains composed. Perpetrators do not act capriciously, but rather meticulously execute their plans; everything is premeditated. And just as with Sade's libertines, perpetrators establish and are governed by a set of rules, frequently manifesting as some sort of game (however, rules might be amended to suit the perpetrator's best interest).

There tends to be no satisfactory resolution in a Torture Porn film. Quite different from the Slasher genre where the 'final girl' vanquishes the monster, her actions subsequently bringing about the restoration of proper order. In Torture Porn, on the other hand, the order of things does not change, and the villain might even walk away unscathed and unpunished. Where victims in Slasher films pay for some sort of moral transgression, in Torture Porn characters perceive themselves to be innocent, and may in fact be. Victims are generally ill-equipped and/or confounded by the situation that they find themselves in, and are incapable of processing what they did to deserve such a fate. Blissful ignorance might be transgression enough for a perpetrator to select a victim and to exact a punishment, and in one form or another victims frequently ask, 'Why are you doing this?' Efforts to save victims are either thwarted or useless. This is due in part to the representatives of authority – doctors, police, agents of the state apparatus – who are either ineffectual, or even at times complicit in the deadly game being played, creating an environment permeated by fear and hopelessness. At the conclusion of a Torture Porn film evil still exists in the world, and there is no overarching authority poised to set things right. Actually it is quite the opposite: spectators leave a Torture Porn film knowing that evil lurks 'out there', and could pounce at any moment.

Let me be abundantly clear here, I am in *no* way arguing that the genre of Torture Porn is directly related to the event we now name the Holocaust or to the terrors of the concentration camps. What it appears to be doing (intentionally or not) is to draw from the history of its *representation*. This recent advent in the horror genre does, then, share certain *affinities* with the discourse of the concentrationary imaginary, and there are certain repercussions as a result for the cinematic strategies of representing the Holocaust.[13]

To further detail the characteristics of this genre let's consider one of the progenitors of Torture Porn, James Wan's 2004 film *Saw*; at present the franchise now includes seven films. Torture Porn films, and especially the *Saw* series, are typically framed within the critical discourse of the post 9/11 era, or video games. As for this latter critical framing device, characters are required to solve riddles, to navigate through spaces, to follow a set of prescribed rules, characters plot against one another in a bid to survive (i.e., win);[14] failure to do these things usually has lethal consequences. Most explicitly the parlance of the films also evokes the discourse of video games. Jigsaw, the pro-antagonist of the *Saw* series, for instance, ends the first film by saying, 'Game over', before the screen fades to black. This becomes a catchphrase for the whole film series.

As I view it, there is much to gain by discussing the Torture Porn genre in relation to the discourse of video games. My subject here, however, is not gaming, but rather how this genre might inform the practice of making and viewing the sadistic character in the concentrationary imaginary; and subsequently, I do not intend to exhaust the gaming component of the genre. While it might not be productive to draw any direct correlation between the gaming elements of Torture Porn and the concentrationary, we can nevertheless read this trope next to it; the discourse of video games – with its set of rules, actions that typically unfold in a defined space, and codes – follows the contours of the sadist motif. In no small part the success of the *Saw* series is predicated on the elaborate traps that victims must extricate themselves from; audiences are lured to the films by the promise of intricate devices that exact grievous bodily harm (Jigsaw, the pro-antagonist of the film was an engineer). There are, though, clear examples where the *Saw* films draw on the visual culture of the Holocaust. In *Saw II* (Darren Lynn Bousman, 2005), for instance, one of the traps is set within a furnace designed to cremate bodies – echoing the crematoriums in Nazi death camps. A woman is frozen to death in a trap derived directly from István Szabó's 1999 Holocaust-related film *Sunshine* in *Saw III* (Darren Lynn Bousman, 2006).[15]

Where *Saw* most explicitly employs the discourse of video games, Eli Roth's 2005 film *Hostel* evokes the spectre of 9/11.[16] The Torture Porn genre continually invites comparisons to the brutalities perpetrated by Americans, whether it's the infamous photographs that came out of Abu Ghraib, or hooded detainees at Guantánamo Bay prison. As Kim Newman observes, 'In a world where foreigners worry about winding up at the mercy of Americans, *Hostel* is about Americans being terrified of the rest of the planet.'[17] And this fear that Americans sense is largely a product of our own doing, because of our general disregard for world affairs, made bitterly palpable in that question that was never fully addressed in the wake of the 9/11 attack: 'Why do they hate us so much?' Clearly the question has never been given much consideration precisely because of what the answers might reveal about our place in world affairs.

The two American male characters in *Hostel* – Josh and Paxton – are indicative of contemporary American attitudes. They are both 'book-smart', both are presumably off to graduate school in the near future; Paxton encourages his friend to be more adventurous because soon Josh will be 'writing his thesis', and he will be studying for the Bar Exam. On their European trip, sowing their wild oats before they embark on their imminent success, Josh and Paxton are the epitome of the American sense of entitlement; they are clearly privileged, arrogant, and believe the world is theirs to plunder (in this case specifically, European women are theirs to plunder). And yet despite their privilege, sense of self-assuredness, and their 'book-smarts' they are also incredibly ignorant of the world that they inhabit.

In the film *Elite Hunting*, a syndicate that caters to the sadistic tastes of rich patrons who pay thousands of dollars to do *anything* to another person, kidnaps young people from a Slovakian hostel.[18] Young men – like Josh and Paxton – are lured to Slovakia with the prospect of finding young attractive women who will do *anything*. An abandoned Slovakian factory is re-purposed as a complete in-house-torture facility, where the rich come to maim, dismember, and kill those unlucky souls ensnared by the syndicate.

'Why are you doing this?' is a question that is frequently asked during the course of a Torture Porn film. After being drugged Josh, for example, finds himself hooded and strapped to a chair in a dark and dank room equipped with a vast array of tools and surgical equipment. Once his torturer enters the room and unhoods him, he pleads for answers, 'Who are you?' and 'Where the fuck am I?' and then also, 'I didn't fucking do shit to you, what the fuck!' and 'Please, I didn't fucking do anything.'[19] Josh, the smart and 'responsible one', as Paxton refers to him, is utterly bewildered by his situation. All this pleading though distinctly resonates with that question: 'Why do they hate us so much?'

Perhaps owing to Eli Roth's own biography – descended from a European Jewish family – the *Hostel* films exhibit the most distinct residues of Holocaust representations. In *Hostel* the emblem of the torture syndicate is a bloodhound. All the torturers – and presumably all members of the syndicate – have the syndicate's emblem tattooed on their left arm (in *Hostel II* the tattoo is placed on the right arm, or the lower back). At first glance the moniker in itself is nothing special; however, this implicitly relates the members of the syndicate to the SS, many of which also had tattoos on their left underarm, indicating their affiliation with the Waffen-SS and the individual's blood-type. Adopting the *blood* hound as the tattooed emblem meets up with the tattooed *blood* type of the SS.

The torture chambers in *Hostel* are located in an abandon Slovakian factory. The factory is topped with a large smokestack, which echoes the profile of the concentration camp, where the crematoria smokestack – belching smoke and human ash – looms large. In addition, when the rich client is finished the Elite Hunting staff clean up. A large hunchbacked man hauls bodies (or just body parts) into a room where they are then butchered into smaller pieces, and finally tossed into a crematorium. The oven, the smokestack, and the piles of mutilated corpses are hard, if not impossible, to separate from the images that we associate with the concentration camp. These images are strikingly similar to Tim Blake Nelson's 2001 film *The Grey Zone*, which dramatizes the uprising of the Sonderkomando at Auschwitz. The furnace is precisely where Roth's 2007 film *Hostel: Part II* begins; an unseen undertaker rummages through a victim's belongings, setting aside valuables, and casting other personal possessions – clothing, a diary, photographs and postcards – into the flames. Sorting through the victims' belongings, and the discarding of personal effects, resonates with the Nazis plundering of loot collected from deportees.

Roth's films are an interesting confluence of cinematic history. The Japanese filmmaker Takashi Miike, an extreme filmmaker in his own right, makes a cameo appearance in *Hostel*. In *Hostel: Part II*, Ruggero Deodato appropriately plays an Italian cannibal; Deodato directed the infamous film *Cannibal Holocaust* (1980). Quentin Tarantino produced both *Hostel* films, and then also cast Roth as Sergeant Donny Donowitz, the Bear Jew, in *Inglourious Basterds*. Donowitz's weapon of choice is a baseball bat that he takes to the head of captured Nazis, bludgeoning them to death. The Nazis believe that Donowitz is a golem. The character biography, as stated on imdb.com, also observes that his 'wooden baseball bat, [is] signed by fellow members of his Boston Jewish community with names of their loved ones in Europe'.[20]

Roth's films specifically, and the genre of Torture Porn in general, also evoke an earlier film, John Schlesinger's 1976 film *Marathon Man*. The content and the *mise-en-scène* of his thriller set the stage for the Torture Porn genre some 30 years later. In the simplest of terms, and echoing the Torture Porn format, in this film an innocent character is pitted against a sadist. The primary male character, Babe (his name even connotes innocence), is a young graduate student in the History Department at Columbia University; he is writing his dissertation on tyranny. The antagonist of the film Christian Szell – who I'll speak of shortly – has amassed a huge collection of diamonds, confiscated from Jews during World War II, and Szell believes that Babe knows about it. Babe, then, functions much in the same way that the tortured characters in Torture Porn do, and figuratively speaking, Babe could have fathered either Josh or Paxton – they are cut from the same cloth. Like Josh and Paxton in *Hostel*, Babe is also book-smart – attending graduate school – though not especially worldly and somewhat naive.

In contrast to the figure of innocence is the sadistic antagonist Christian Szell, a Nazi war criminal. We learn during the course of the film that in Auschwitz he was known as Der Weisser Engel (the White Angel), on account of his stark white hair. Obviously trading in the currency of the historical figure of Doctor Josef Mengele, Szell ran an experimental camp at Auschwitz, and there are other comparisons to be made in their names as well – because of course Mengele was referred to as the Angel of Death. When his character is first introduced, the soft-focus camera tilts up to reveal a glass cabinet that contains human and animal skulls. In themselves the bones are not especially evocative; however, coupled with German newspapers, and other signifiers of 'German-ness' adorning his secret hideaway in South America, the cumulative connotative value meets up with the image of Ilse Koch, and her predilection for collecting body parts. In the popular conception of it, Szell's character is the 'perfect' Nazi sadist, in effect a composite of both Mengele and Koch.

Szell in his actions and disposition is a clinical sadist. A dentist by trade, he approaches his work dutifully, and with the utmost professionalism. In terms of narrative content and its form, this critical scene, where Szell employs his dental trade to torture Babe, establishes clear heredity between *Marathon Man* and the genre of Torture Porn. Szell believes that Babe knows something about his stash of diamonds, and so Szell's associates abduct the graduate student and take him to an undisclosed warehouse. Babe is strapped to a chair in a bare room. When Szell, with his two accomplices, finally enters the room where Babe is confined, he enters with purpose, opens his briefcase, and places his toolkit matter-of-factly on a worktable adjacent to Babe. Szell is clinical in manner and speech, never once losing his temper, or letting his emotions get the better of him. Dressed in a three-piece suit Szell retreats to the back corner of the room where there is a sink, removes his coat, and washes his hands as any doctor would.

Szell then asks, 'Is it safe?' Of course, Babe is completely ignorant of the saga unfolding all around him, and is confused by the question. Repeatedly Szell asks, 'Is it safe?' Babe searches for the answer that Szell wants to hear. Walking back over to the worktable, all the while calmly asking, 'Is it safe?' Szell unfurls his toolkit, revealing an assortment of dental tools. Picking up a pick and a dental mirror Szell proceeds to examine Babe's teeth, but not before some resistance and fidgeting from the reluctant patient. Poking about, Szell finally asks, 'That hurt?' Babe manages, 'Uh-huh.' 'I should think it would', Szell admonishes. 'You should take better care of your teeth. You have quite a cavity here.' And then abruptly Szell asks again, 'Is it safe?' Babe begins to utter a few words before Szell firmly launches into the cavity with his pick, causing Babe to lurch and scream in agony. Szell is convinced that Babe knows something. Szell calmly applies some clove oil to his little finger and administers the oil to Babe's tooth, 'Isn't that remarkable?' he says with a gentle smile. Babe feels instant relief. Szell steps back, holding the bottle of clove oil and the pick, he begins, 'Life can be that simple. Relief . . . discomfort. Now which of these I next apply, that decision is in your hands, so . . . take your time, and tell me . . . Is it safe?'

True to the sadist disposition, everything is meticulously planned. After this first round of dental procedures are over Babe is dragged off to another room where he is allowed to rest. One of Szell's accomplices nurses Babe, administering more clove oil to relieve the pain. A government agent, Janeway, surreptitiously enters the room, dispatching Szell's accomplice with a knife, gunning down the other, and springing Babe from the clutches of the former Nazi. In the getaway car in an overwrought tone Janeway reveals the plot – telling him about Szell's treasure, and that Doc (Babe's elder brother) worked as a courier – and asks if Doc said anything before he died. Still, of course, Babe is clueless; he knows nothing of this international intrigue. The whole escape however turns out to be a ruse; when the car comes to a stop, Babe finds himself exactly where he started, and back in the hands of Szell's accomplices, who are very much still alive. In the true meaning of sadism, which is more about power and intellectual mastery, even the escape was intended to pump Babe for information. Babe once again finds himself in Szell's makeshift dentist's chair. This time though Szell brings out an electric drill and purposefully drills into a healthy tooth to inflict intense pain; he is finally assured that Babe knew nothing. But as he now knows too much, Szell instructs his accomplices to 'get rid of him'.

At the beginning of the torture scene, Babe finds himself in a dark room, immobilized and confounded. Babe struggles to get his bearings; remarkably similar in many respects to Josh's predicament in the first *Hostel* film. The banality of the space, the decor, and the instruments displayed before the victim are charged with a wholly different character, rather nefarious in fact. The everydayness of the objects – a drill, a dentist's pick, a chair – recontextualized in the framework of torture become weapons; which is designed to evoke dread in the character subjected to torture and the spectator where the stability of the order of things is undone.[21] 'The appearance of these common domestic objects' in the discourse of torture, as Elaine Scarry observes, owes to the fact that 'much of our awareness of Germany in the 1940s is attached to the words "ovens," "showers," "lampshades," and "soap"'.[22] The figure of Mengele (and the characters that are derivatives of him, including Szell) then also corresponds to this, because here is a man of science, of medicine, whose pledge to 'do no harm' is radically turned on its head.[23] An earlier film that resonates with the tropes found in *Marathon Man* is

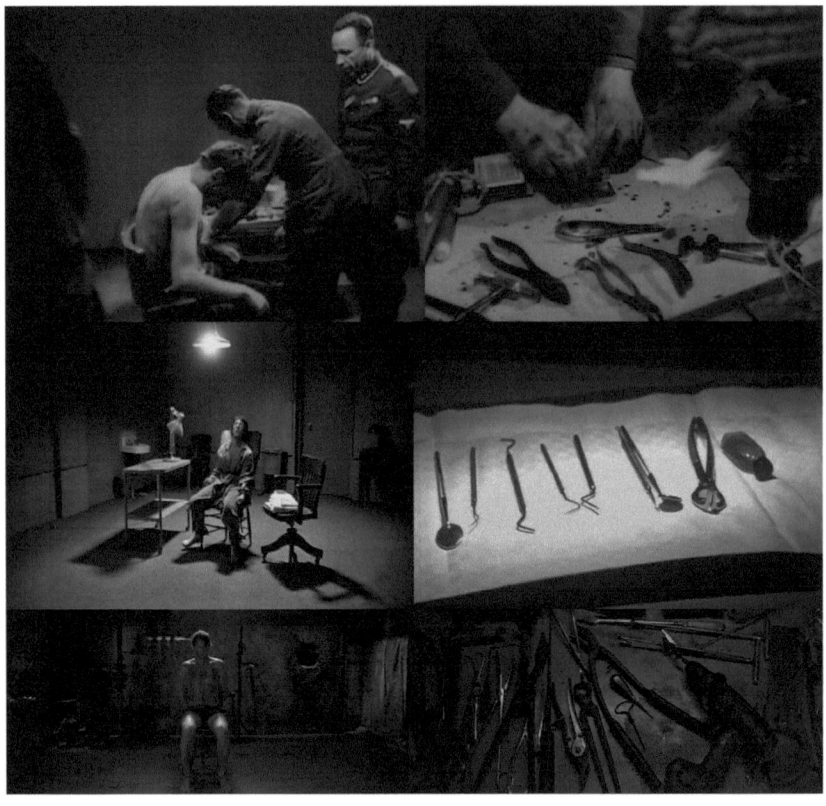

4.2 Top row: *Roma, città aperta [Rome, Open City]* (Roberto Rossellini, 1945).
Middle row: *Marathon Man* (John Schlesinger, 1976).
Bottom row: *Hostel* (Eli Roth, 2005).

Roberto Rossellini's 1945 film *Rome, Open City*, which exhibits many of the same characteristics: Nazis torturing righteous victims, sparse room, a tortured subject strapped to a chair, ordinary household tools transfigured into instruments of torture (4.2).

The signature enclosed space in Torture Porn films corresponds to the sadist's reliance on a hermitic universe, where within a strictly defined space nothing is abject.[24] (Perhaps locating affinities with Rousset's notion that 'everything is possible', as cited by Pollock in the introduction.)[25] And from this perspective it is possible to see how the torture chamber in Torture Porn films is an overdetermined site; alluding to the concentrationary imaginary, the libertine's hermetic spaces in Sade's novels, and Pier Paolo Pasolini's rendition of those in his 1975 film *Salò, or the 120 Days of Sodom*. The torture chamber in the Torture Porn genre though is frequently dank; dark damp spaces coloured in the various shades of faecal matter. And in the faecal palette the torture chamber in Torture Porn evokes the conceptualization of the concentration camp, which has been referred to as *anus mundi* – the asshole of the world.

Torture Porn films do not paint a neat Manichean worldview, victims are not always likable characters, and when given the chance the victims prove to be just as brutal as the perpetrators. And this is probably Torture Porn's most distinct characteristic relative to the tradition of Holocaust films; the latter is apt to construct more clear-cut narratives of good versus evil. The sadistic Nazi operates with absolute impunity and is discernibly deranged. Outside the confines of the hermetic space where torture takes place the perpetrator in Torture Porn conforms to conventional social mores. And this is what is so frightening in these films: the perpetrators are out there amongst us, and perhaps even more frightening still they are no different from us. And in this respect, perhaps the characters that administer torture in the genre might begin to enact the concentrationary imaginary.

Michael Haneke: the real sadist

In Michael Haneke films the clear division between good and evil dissolves; violence seems to well up from nowhere. Somewhat unfairly placed under the heading of Torture Porn, which properly speaking only emerges in the post-9/11 era, Haneke's work deals with the existence of violence (or perhaps evil) in the world, but its exact source is ethereal. Haneke's work is clearly on a different order, but some film critics hastily group his films together with the likes of *Hostel* simply because he engages with sadomasochistic themes. While I might be accused of doing precisely the same thing (too hastily characterizing Haneke's work as Torture Porn), I hope that I might differentiate Haneke's work by discussing his engagement with sadism with more regard.

Disorientation, riddles or games, are plot devices that are associated with the German/Austrian filmmaker's work. In *Funny Games*, as with most of Haneke's films, malevolence appears like a ghostly apparition. Haneke made essentially two identical versions of this film: first, a

German film in 1997, and then again ten years later in 2007 he made an American version. Two young men arrive at an exclusive summer vacation spot, a lake dotted with holiday homes; the pair skip from one house to another, and deride their heedless captive family, before finally savagely and coldly dispatching each one.²⁶

In an interview speaking about his 2005 film *Caché* [*Hidden*], Haneke says that the film is about guilt, 'how one lives with guilt'. Although the film deals with the post-colonial experience in France, he insists that this theme could be situated in any country or time, because as he says, 'In any country, one can find a secret hidden by the "common sense" of that country.' Casting off the yoke of memory (or history) is how we generally negotiate guilt, or actually more precisely responsibility for the past; the primary male character, Georges, for instance, abdicates his responsibility, 'I was only six, how am I supposed to remember?' Max Silverman argues that this denial of guilt, as expressed by Georges, in *Caché*, consciously or not allows Haneke to incorporate

> [the] iconography of the Holocaust to invade a narrative ostensibly about colonial and postcolonial relations between France and Algeria. The abduction of children, disappearance, and denials of guilt have become central elements in our cultural vocabulary of racialized violence and trauma and oblige us, even unconsciously, to view one event (colonialism) in the light of another (the Holocaust).²⁷

Perhaps more than any of the other filmmakers I have discussed here, Haneke's gamesmanship motif, which appears in many of his films, but is explicit in his *Funny Games*, follows the outline of clinical sadism. Throughout *Funny Games*, Paul, the angelic torturer peppers the Farber family with questions, riddles, and little games. At various points in the film, Paul directly addresses the audience, either with a 'nod and wink', or through explicit dialogue.

Paul propositions the Farber family with a bet, 'Okay we bet', turning to his accomplice Peter, 'What time is it?' Peter responds, 'Eight forty.' Paul continues, 'In, let's say 12 hours all three of you are going to be kaput. Okay?' Ann Farber, confounded, asks, 'What?' Paul clarifies, 'You bet that you'll be alive tomorrow at 9:00, and we bet that you'll be dead, okay?' Eventually Paul turns to us, the viewer, and asks, 'I mean, what do you think? You think they stand a chance? You're on their side, aren't you? Who are you betting on, hm?' Towards the conclusion of the film, after the film languishes in the suffering of the Farber family – including the execution of the Farber's young boy – Paul once again addresses the camera directly, 'Do you think it's enough? I mean, you want a real ending, right? With plausible plot development, don't you?' These digressions from the narrative diegesis bother some, and they are unquestionably didactic, but nevertheless the intention obviously is to call attention to our own expectations and desires; we *want*, we *crave* retribution, but Haneke refuses to give it to us.

In fact, during the latter part of the film Paul tauntingly asks Ann to play a game, if she wins then she gets to choose who will die first and by what device – a knife or a shotgun. The absolute callous cruelty exhibited by Peter and Paul elicits not only anger from the audience, but a desire for retribution. This desire is brought to a fevered pitch as Paul continues to taunt Ann. Frantically Ann reaches for the shotgun on the table and shoots Peter in the abdomen; the blast is so violent that it throws him up against the wall, spraying blood across the pristine white wall. And let there be no mistake: there is a definite sense of gratification at the sight of violent retribution, but this moment of *pleasure* is taken away from us. Paul, distressed, screams out, 'Where's the remote control?' Finding it he simply puts the scene in reverse, and restarts the scene at the point where Ann reaches for the shotgun; this time, Paul stops her. George is then summarily shot, as he lies prone on the floor – although this all takes place out of frame. What makes this scene stand out though, is not simply the cheeky cinematic conceit of rewinding the film as we watch the film unfold, but that whenever Peter or Paul kill it happens off-screen.

Aside from the anti-climatic pushing overboard of Ann, which comes casually without malice and almost accidentally, we never see Peter or Paul kill. There are traces – and audio cues – that tell us something of what has happened, or how someone has been dispatched, but we never see the gruesome details. And there is a strange morbid abject fascination, a desire to see. Has the Farber's child been shot in the head? In the chest? We have no idea, but we want to know. And this is essentially true of all the tortured victims; we want to know, and Haneke refuses to give it to us. And this denial once again points to the morbid connection between sadism and voyeurism, and while Haneke is *not* making a Holocaust film, perhaps this points to our continued fascination with its representation. We want to see, and we want to know how. But perhaps more to the point it also indicates the presence of the concentrationary imaginary.

In 'The *Sight and Sound* Top Ten Poll of 2002', Haneke ranks Pasolini's *Salò* fourth on his list of top films.[28] And this speaks to how Haneke handles historical violence. As in *Salò*, Haneke would never represent an historical event 'as it really was', for the medium of film inherently abstracts events – it is always already pure artifice. Haneke does not speak about the Holocaust; he speaks next to it (to borrow a phrase from Trinh T. Minh-ha).[29] In his discussion with Anthony Lane, Haneke does not want to specifically locate *The White Ribbon* (2009) as a Nazi film *per se*: 'I will not be happy if the film is seen as a film about a German problem, about the Nazi time.' Rather he says, 'It's a film about the roots of evil.'[30] Haneke embraces, rather than runs from the darker side of the human psyche, saying that, 'There is no crime I couldn't have committed. . . . It is so easy to say, "Oh no, I would never do that," but that's dishonest. We are capable of everything.'[31] As Lane correctly observes, Haneke does not want *The White Ribbon* 'or any of his other works, to be construed as a parable of Nazism. Nonetheless, it seems fair to say that without so drastic a template of savagery and amnesia his films would not be as ruthless as they are.'[32]

Contemplating the genre of Torture Porn, Edelstein asks: 'Fear supplants empathy and makes us all potential torturers, doesn't it?' The genre of Torture Porn upsets the conventional narrative constellation, and places us uncomfortably close to the agents of evil. Be they horror films or not, in Holocaust films Nazis are typically cast as the epitome of evil, and in the standard clear division of cosmic order, the victims of Nazi persecution are subsequently positioned on the side of utter goodness, and through an identification with these characters, we, the spectators are comfortably placed on the side of the righteous. Especially now, in our post-9/11 environment, and in the wake of Abu Ghraib, waterboarding, bound and hooded prisoners, Guantánamo Bay prison, the detention facility at Bagram Air Base, aligning spectator identification with righteousness seems laughably naive at best, and downright duplicitous at worst.[33] Our faith in the Manichean worldview has faltered, and the consequences of this perhaps necessitate a new critical viewing position of existing Holocaust films, and might require future films to reconsider the nuances of Holocaust narratives and characters, especially when rendering perpetrators; for if we take Haneke's word for it, we all have the capacity to wrap each other up in sadist knots.

5

REDEMPTION OR TRANSFORMATION
Blasphemy and the Concentrationary Imaginary in Liliana Cavani's *The Night Porter* (1974)

Griselda Pollock

Scene I: final scene

In the murky darkness of a wet city street at night, two figures stagger out of an apartment building towards a small car. One seems to be a young girl dressed in a pink party dress wearing long white socks and bar shoes. Unsteady on her feet, she is supported uncertainly by a man dressed in full SS uniform. They get into the car. It moves off. Another larger, black vehicle follows them. Close-ups of the pair in the first car reveal haggard and emaciated faces. Close-ups of the driver of the following car reveal a hard, determined face. Dawn breaks on a scene of the car now parked on an empty suspension bridge. The sound of the footsteps on the rain-washed pavement are tracked by the camera to reveal, on the other side of the bridge's heavy metal supports, walking along the pedestrian walkway, the two figures – girl-woman and uniformed man – swaying as they walk. They continue to stumble across the bridge. Gunshots are fired and both fall to the ground. The camera remains on this long shot for a moment before moving slowly into focus, ultimately remaining at some distance, on the tumbled corpses lying on the wet walkway of the bridge. The screen goes black. The credits roll. I (5.1–5.3)

5.1–5.3 *The Night Porter* (Cavani, 1974): (5.1) The final scene – car on the bridge; (5.2) walking on the bridge; (5.3) dead bodies on the bridge.

The scene I have just described closes Italian director Liliana Cavani's film *The Night Porter* released in 1974. The two figures we see being shot are Max (Dirk Bogarde), a former SS officer in a concentration camp where he played doctor and filmmaker, now the night porter of the film's title, and Lucia (Charlotte Rampling), a former inmate of the concentration camp overseen by Max, arrested as vulnerable teenager and sexually violated by Max, who re-encounters her former tormentor during a visit to Vienna when she has accompanied her husband who will conduct a performance of Mozart's opera *The Magic Flute*.

Why are Max and Lucia together, dressed like this (5.4)? Why do they have to be shot? What does it mean to end this film thus? These questions take us to the heart of the political aesthetics of the film and its singular relation to the concentrationary imaginary. That relation is paradoxical. Through the re-staged encounters created by the film through cinematic conventions such as flashback, we glimpse the initiating site of the meeting of Max and Lucia while also returning to the present which reveals the persistence of the concentrationary imaginary both as the prison house of the former SS men like Max and of its victims. In its highly considered cinematic play with past and present, the film critically exposes and finally contests that imaginary whose power resides in its possession of its subjects. Because of its political aesthetics, the film is

5.4 *The Night Porter* (Cavani, 1974): Costume test of Charlotte Rampling and Dirk Bogarde in the final scene.

adamantly not an instance of the unconscious or thoughtless repetition of the concentrationary imaginary. It fictionally represents its scenarios in order to counter their deadly politics. This claim requires a close reading of several key scenes in the film. In so doing, I aim to rescue the film from misplaced criticism that it is merely a malign instance of a thoughtless emergence in the 1960s–70s of another imaginary generating and generated by the inexplicable return of an aesthetics associated with Nazism – a fascist imaginary reinvesting the outward signs of Nazism as style or as scenario for pornographic or sadistic fantasy.

Imaginary: fascist or concentrationary?

In the initial stages of research into the possibility of a *concentrationary* imaginary pervading, or otherwise discernible within, popular culture, I came up against the question of distinguishing its specificity from a much more easily identifiable phenomenon: a *fascist* imaginary. In turn this phenomenon would also have to be identified as distinct from the recycling of fascist imagery in fashion, pornography or pseudo-historical film. This chapter seeks to address the structural relations and affective relays between the image of fascism, a fascist imaginary and a hypothesized concentrationary imaginary through a close reading of three scenes from the controversial film *The Night Porter*, directed in 1974 by Italian filmmaker Liliana Cavani, starring Charlotte Rampling (Lucia) as a young Jewish woman camp inmate and Dirk Bogarde as an SS officer (Max). Max and Lucia first encounter each other in the conditions of 'the concentrationary universe' and then meet again unexpectedly in post-war Vienna where he works as a night porter in the hotel to which she comes, now the glamorous wife of a famous American conductor.[1] At one level, the film demonstrates the slippage from the historical Real of the power and perversity of the camp to a haunting of two people by that experience that still enthralls its participants. The concentrationary universe functions as a past that is only temporarily suspended. It is still terrifying in its power to reclaim the couple who replay their past outside of time and history: the concentrationary has become a determining fantasy they cannot escape. It develops, however, into the imaginary grounds for their unwitting but, I shall argue, ultimately transformative re-enactment of its formative marks on their subjectivities. This is certainly one level at which this film serves to make visible the components of the concentrationary as an imaginary, in the sense closer to the psychoanalytical notion of phantasy and its role in the formation of subjectivity.

At the same time, I want to argue that Cavani's film is not a restaging alone. It is an investigation into a concentrationary imaginary, using cinema's specific capacity to address and critique our imaginary relations to screen and image. As such, the film articulates, in a counter direction, an aesthetics of resistance to the very force of that imaginary through the replay by the couple that, at first, seems to be the mere reclamation of its players. In this way, *The Night Porter* might well be aligned with those post-war films in which a critical use of aesthetics drew our attention to the persistence of totalitarianism and demanded a form of anxious and agitating memory to remain alert to such dangers. In a previous volume in this series, *Concentrationary Memories*, and in our study of Alain Resnais's film *Night and Fog* (*Nuit et Brouillard*) (1955), *Concentrationary Cinema*, a range of authors have identified a politics of representation in films that confronted the historical event of fascist regimes and their totalitarian anti-political experiments.[2] *The Night Porter* differs, however, in a crucial way from documentary films such as *Night and Fog* (*Nuit et Brouillard*) (1955) while also being distinct from films such as *Kapò* (Pontecorvo, 1960) that fictionally recreated a camp scenario to tell a fictional story about love and death in that universe.[3] Set in Vienna in the aftermath of the war when the fascist regime had been formally destroyed, the film focuses on the unexpected manner of the engraving of its affects on the psyches of both perpetrators and victims. It is in the film's exploration – and it is a radical one, I shall argue – of the fantasmatic *mise-en-scène* that links the past moment within a camp and a present moment outside the camp that Cavani's film can be said to trace the lineaments of a concentrationary imaginary.

Feminist film critics have interpreted Cavani's challenging film as a critical and thoughtful aesthetic resistance to the endemic fascism of post-war European culture.[4] It will be necessary to consider these interpretations. In placing this film in the frame of a concentrationary imaginary infusing contemporary culture, I am suggesting, however, that the signs, or rather the symptoms, of such an imaginary can only be approached obliquely by identifying the tropes and images through which it might appear. These tropes and images have representational 'content', as well as iconographies, and histories that overlap with the imagery of fascism and Nazism. The feminist critique gains its strength from identifying the elements of a fascist imaginary in the unmarked forms of bourgeois culture; already, therefore, showing a seepage or infiltration or even identity between the two.

The Night Porter plays with the image of fascism or, more precisely, with fascism having become an image, and its persistence beyond the official dates of historical defeats of Hitler's or Mussolini's different fascist regimes by 1945. Fascism is synonymous with neither the concentrationary nor the Third Reich as its instituting regime. The regime created by National Socialism in Germany was but one specific form of fascism, one amongst several apparitions. Its fascism was distinguished above all by its genocidal racism and its programme for industrialized mass murder. At the same time, and as the overall structure for conceiving and carrying out its assault on Jewish and Romany (Roma) Europeans, this fascist regime realized a system of total terror whose key laboratory for the destruction of the human *qua* human necessary for total domination was, as Hannah Arendt revealed in her post-war anatomy of totalitarianism, the concentration camp, of which there were by 1945 more than 10,000 sites in Germany alone.[5] Nazism's core racism produced an extreme form of that terror, a form that was specialized, short-lived and quickly obliterated, namely the extermination camp, of which there were only *four* dedicated sites operating between 1942 and 1943 with two additional death sites within existing concentration camps: Majdanek, and the most infamous Auschwitz-Birkenau (operating its gas chambers between spring 1942 and October 1944).[6]

The concentration camp system, whose total population we think was 1.8 million over 12 years, had been initiated in 1933. Its scale increased and declined through the 1930s in relation to moments of intense persecution of Nazism's political enemies in 1933 and the pogrom against German Jews in 1938. It then expanded again after the invasions and occupations by the Third Reich of several European countries. By 1945 there were thousands of such camps, used as political and prisoner of war camps, slave labour camps and sites of medical experimentation, while enforcing a regime of terror through starvation, overwork and arbitrary brutality. Run by the SS, the camp was also a space for forging the SS corps' coherence through shared, secret and self-witnessed transgression of legality and other taboos, often sexual and sadistic. Against the initial grain of the policy of genocide, some Jewish victims became prisoners in concentration camps either when selected from the death trains on the ramp at Auschwitz II (Birkenau) instead of immediately being gassed, or when distributed from Auschwitz (Poland) to slave labour camps, or, during the final months of the war, marched to concentration camps within Germany to escape the onslaught of the Red Army.

Thus disentangling a generic fascist from a specified concentrationary imaginary is hardly possible in terms of such historical overlay. What made 'the concentrationary universe' a distinctive novelty of twentieth-century politics has, however, been theorized politically, and under the rubric of 'Concentrationary Memory' it has also been culturally analysed, showing how critical aesthetic forms can generate vigilant anxiety in the face of the evidence of the totalitarian system. While drawing on the political theory of the meaning of the camp, and on the aesthetics of resistance to the ideology of the camp, I am arguing that *The Night Porter* is a distinct mode of investigation into the form in which the concentrationary persists beyond memory and politics: as an imaginary. As such, the working through or transformation of its grip on its subjects requires the strategic work of that which has itself been called the imaginary signifier: cinema. At the intersection, therefore, of cinema's imaginary structures and the imaginary as a structuring of subjectivity, *The Night Porter* stages a challenge to the deformations of a concentrationary imaginary which is, on one side, also embedded in a fascist imaginary, and which is shown to be in collusion with other structures of power outside the camp.

Vienna, 1957

The Night Porter opens in Vienna, 1957, (5.5) a dead city, a shell of emptiness and wet greyness. The action takes place just after the ending of the city's post-war division into four militarized zones each controlled by one of the Occupying powers: the Soviet Union, the United States, France and Great Britain. In homage perhaps to Carol Reed's atmospheric thriller about the Occupied era of the city and post-war corruption, *The Third Man* (1950) set in immediate post-war Vienna, Cavani's film opens with its central character walking through the rain-dampened streets of an uncannily empty city before arriving at the entrance to a scaffold-clad grand hotel, Hotel zür Oper: Hotel beside the Opera (5.5).

Just as Anton Karas's musical theme, played on the Austrian zither, became identified with Reed's *The Third Man*, so Cavani's opening shots are accompanied by Daniele Paris's recurring musical theme played on an

5.5   *The Night Porter* (Cavani, 1974): Vienna, 1957.

oboe. This music will play for the duration of the final scene I described above, forming a musical as well as a visual rhyme with the streets of Vienna, capital of Hitler's home country, Austria, embraced by and embracing the Third Reich in 1938, and being the site of Eichmann's first experimental 'processing' of the Jewish question. These ghosts clearly haunt the film; but they are not its subject.

The film plots the re-encounter of a former SS officer in an unnamed concentration camp, now working as a night porter in a hotel, and a former inmate of that same concentration camp but now the glamorous wife of an American opera conductor. Before any suggestion that these two facts, the camp and opera, represent barbarism versus civilization, let it be stated that Cavani's juxtaposition of these two worlds of political terror and cultural prestige will lose their clear demarcations through the film precisely as a working through of the idea that camp power structures are not confined to one time and one place, and are not unique to that exceptional time and place.

The immediate context of the unexpected re-encounter of Max and Lucia is, however, the practice of a secret group of Nazis who subject each other – its being Max's turn at this point – to a mock tribunal. Through diligent research in archives, they assemble all possible evidence of their crimes in the past only in order to 'free' themselves – not from guilt, and not for the purpose of personal expiation. Instead, using illegal means, they extract and erase from the archives the documentary traces of their activities during the war. Elimination of such evidence, however, also includes 'erasing' from life any living witnesses. Thus will they become 'free' not of history, but of any judgement that still stalks them in its name.

The sudden reappearance in Vienna of Lucia at this point, when the secret tribunal is about to be held to perform this ritual of 'liberation' of Max, therefore, threatens Max's freedom and continued invisibility in the new order which, by virtue of these Nazi men's continuing to function in contemporary Vienna, is shown to be incompletely cleansed of the old. They are not ghosts of the past, but its still vivid presence/present.

How will Lucia respond to meeting her former SS tormentor? Will she denounce him and thus derail the cleansing process? How will Max respond to meeting not only his former victim but also the one person in the present who could still expose him and destroy his new cover hidden in the darkness of his work as a night porter sleeping away the daylight? That the film ends in the summary execution of Max and Lucia, on the rain-drenched streets of Vienna as dawn breaks ending the dark night with their double 'erasure', means that the secret society has won. More living 'files' have been processed.

The shooting of Max and Lucia is, however, at the same time, shown to be a joint suicide. Coming out of hiding, to walk in public dressed once again in the uniforms of the roles they played out in the exceptional space of the camp, their deaths/suicides affirm that Lucia neither denounced Max, nor did Max destroy Lucia. She was not, in the parlance of the Nazi tribunal, 'filed away permanently' by Max. He has, however, been transformed and severed from his Nazi group of men by what happened to him when he re-encountered Lucia in the present, shaped by a past, interrupted by new disguises: night porter and glamorous wife that are revealed to be fragile shields against the past which now re-enters, reworks and is reworked by the present. Between ideas of memory as a haunting of the present, and the present as secretly storing its contamination by a past that is no such thing, the film uses the rhetoric of cinema itself to play off the agitations of concentrationary memory – anxiety and political resistance to the concentrationary – against the dissemination and omnipresence of the concentrationary imaginary – the altered conditions of human relations under a totalitarian logic enacted by the camp logic where 'everything is possible'.

It is this dialectic of the exposure of a concentrationary imaginary through a cinematic fashioning for the spectator of a position more akin to concentrationary memory that takes this film out of the debate about Nazi kitsch and porn, or the sexualization of fascism, of which the film has been accused, allowing it, instead, to perform a politics of representation through its cinematic investigation of the seepage of a concentrationary imaginary into the infected present.

Let me comment briefly on this choice of words. 'Seepage' suggests the escape of noxious substances from supposed confinement. It sets up an inside and outside across whose porous boundaries the substance has seeped. Historical thinking tends to set up boundaries for events, zones and times of happening. The war is over. Nazism was defeated. A new order has been installed. People, of course, have memories; others become amnesiac through trauma or guilt. But if a noxious substance, like a gas or an invisible agent like a virus, seeps and infects, we have entered a different metaphorical realm that suggests that once the extreme event has happened, it cannot be confined to a historical past or to an individual memory. If the noxious substance, like a virus, has become part of the structure of its host, bonded in and reforging the psychic structure of the exposed victim, it then becomes an active agent, carried beyond the limits of the historical camp of its inception and elaboration, into post-camp, post-war, everyday life. The concentrationary has no obvious outward signs, like fascist insignia, uniforms, and styles. It is the restructured formation of a personality, a psyche or, as we shall see, a social nexus. Cavani's purpose in *The Night Porter* is to explore the presence of this infection that now inhabits the current world, with some people actively secreting and fostering its original formation, while others are unaware they carry it, as some aspects fold into new, seemingly normal forms of life.

What plays out over the film is not the compulsion to repeat that binds the present to the past. Rather, the film performs a search for a way beyond that entrapment in the deadly embrace of a past that the Nazi men are preserving behind the secret doors of the hotel guarded by the nocturnal guardian of their secrets, Max. Meeting in that space of apparently free encounter which covertly hides and replays the camp in which these men are stalled, Max and Lucia are drawn back, initially violently, into an entanglement, which results, however, in a change in their presents. The outcome includes Max's loss of his masculine place in the order of men shaped fantasmatically by the frozen fascist imaginary of the Nazi group and Lucia's exile from the bourgeois world of decorative wifehood and numbingly dependent femininity that appeared to be her liberation and feminine destiny. What Max and Lucia play out *sexually* as a result of their mutually dangerous re-encounter is neither the perverted order of sexual difference of the camp nor the normalized heterosexual order of sexual difference of bourgeois marriage that both of their post-war scenarios enshrine. Rather what happens *between* and *to* them produces a transformation of the present by the resurgence of what they created, horrifically and in the Real of the camp. What happened in their past is shown to have remained merely dormant. Now violently reawakened, it has become expectant. What happens now? It thus becomes subject to a different reworking from that which the secret tribunal seeks to effect, which involves no real transformation at all, just more 'filing away'. Awaiting another site of enactment that neither redeems the past nor falls back into the past, Max and Lucia struggle, ultimately unsuccessfully, to find an escape through the very unexpected love that emerges now out of the ruins of what was originally both a perverse extremity and an abusive intimacy.

Such is the treacherous and easily misunderstood claim that I shall be attempting to substantiate in my reading of this film under the rubric of the concentrationary imaginary and its disruption by a work of critical cinema. Firstly, we need to understand something of Cavani's intellectual interests in making the film. Secondly, we shall have to distantiate the film from the disturbing cultural phenomenon of the 1960s and 1970s that the Chicago film critic, citing Susan Sontag, rightly condemned – the emergence of Nazism as kitsch in popular and even high culture.[7] Thirdly, I shall draw into the conversation a range of feminist writers who have read this film as a critical and thoughtful aesthetic resistance to the endemic patriarchalism and fascism of post-war European culture. To perform this analysis, I shall be juggling with the distinctions between fascism, Nazism and the concentrationary which, none the less, overlay each other at the level of the imaginary in ways that muddle our thinking while also indicating a genuine level of seepage and mutual contamination.

Cavani's approach to *The Night Porter*

In an interview included on the DVD edition of her film, Liliana Cavani discusses the encounters that initiated the main lines of the narratives that were transformed into the film. She had been interviewing women who had worked in the Italian resistance during World War II when, after the fall of Mussolini, the Germans invaded and occupied Italy. She met several women survivors of German concentration camps whose 'attachment' to these locations of torture and suffering initially perplexed her. One former political deportee, for instance, returned constantly to Dachau for her holidays, drawn back to the site of her terrible memories by a compulsion she could not explain. Something had happened there that, whatever its apparent complexion, was indelibly part of her and suspended the logic of there and then and now and here (5.6–5.8).

What happened there? What could bind a person, once liberated, to an experience the ordinary person might imagine they could only wish to flee and to obliterate from memory? Another woman was initially reticent, but once prompted poured forth an unstoppable flow of memories that she said few had ever wanted to hear. She had been encouraged to forget; but how could she forget such *intense* experiences irrespective of their complexion? A third woman explained that she could never forgive the Germans for making her discover things about herself she never wanted to know: capacities dictated by the naked urge to survive. Cavani was both troubled and intrigued by what these interviews revealed about being forced to breach human solidarity in the necessity of staying alive. Although not spoken aloud, these interviews hinted at the most troubling aspect of the extremes experienced in surviving the concentrationary universe: sexuality.

The film became a means of exploring with the utmost seriousness profound questions arising from Cavani's encounters with survivors who bore witness to the place of their historical experience in their own *imaginaries*. I use this term because it is not a matter of memories to which the survivors bear witness by testifying and bringing the unspoken into language. Nor is it exactly trauma in the sense of an inchoate and terrifying void seeking to be relieved by the covenant of dialogic speech. Cavani overheard a subjectively constitutive *attachment* to a set of experiences that theories of both trauma and witness seek to take the subject beyond

Redemption or Transformation 133

5.6–5.8 Liliana Cavani Interview. DVD, Anchor Bay Entertainment, 2006.

into 'memory' and narrative. This attachment may well be perverse, but it involves radical personal self-revelation that remains difficult to accommodate to the other world beyond the concentrationary universe. It becomes a concentrationary imaginary at the level of the imaginary nature of relations of the subject to her/his conditions of existence that bind subjects to systems.[8]

Thus, using flashbacks that punctuate and cut into the present, Cavani created, imaginatively, several scenes within her film that stage the interior of a 'camp': not any one specific historical place, not any documented event or practice. The film consciously creates a *mise-en-scène* to 'imagine' for us the unexpected, even inexplicable to the non-internee, psychological effect of this space of exception that cannot be escaped once it has reforged its subject through induction into its universe.

Cavani has not interviewed individual witnesses to find out the specifics of their experience. While the film is not at all testimonial, it does not, by using fiction, betray its ethical responsibility to the experience of survivors. Knowingly, Cavani creates and distils from a range of materials and memories, histories and images, a setting that can explore both the invasion of the imagination of those who created or inhabited the camp (both SS and prisoners) and, as importantly, the imaginary that itself underpinned that very creation. Furthermore, the films show how the concentrationary universe became for its perpetrators an imaginary space of seemingly infinite freedom, released from the authority of the Symbolic Law and from the monitoring by the internalized super-ego.

Let me clarify *creation*: the SS were alone responsible for establishing concentration camps and for creating the culture and logic of the camps. Those taken to them were innocent of everything save political resistance in the case of the political prisoners, or being themselves in the case of those persecuted for 'race', religion or sexuality. I am not in any way suggesting the complicity of the prisoners in their own suffering in the camps. This is not another study of the grey zone, as Primo Levi named the conditions often required for survival.[9] Logically, a camp can only be 'camp' with both its SS and its prisoners, however asymmetrical and horrific were the relations forced upon the prisoners. Cavani's daring contribution to thinking about the concentrationary imaginary is to create, through cinema – the 'imaginary signifier' according to Christian Metz – a retrospective analysis based on the discovery – so surprising to her – of the continuing potency of the 'camp' on former prisoners that was neither rational nor something that anyone could anticipate.[10]

Far from being a film about the camp's exploiting or performing its sadistic and perverse sexual abuse, the film, I suggest, can be read as an experimental investigation into the unspoken and even unspeakable legacy of the SS/prisoner logic. That logic may keep its participants locked into the positions and subjectivities the camp engendered. A transformative working through might refute it. It would be this resistance that men of the secret Nazi group who 'are' still bearers of camp logic, while now passing as rehabilitated civilians in post-war society, ultimately could not allow.

Reception of *The Night Porter*

The Night Porter has inspired very varied, and sometimes extreme, responses. In Paris, where it opened quietly, word of mouth soon made the film a *succès de scandale*, with lines forming around the block. When it was first screened in the United States, however, the film met with largely hostile criticism, being denounced as a work of depraved pornography and 'Nazi chic':

> *The Night Porter* is as nasty as it is lubricious, a despicable attempt to titillate us by exploiting memories of persecution and suffering. It is (I know how obscene this sounds) Nazi chic. It's been taken seriously in some circles, mostly by critics agile enough to stand on their heads while describing 180-degree turns, in order to interpret trash as 'really' meaningful.[11]

On the other hand, the distinguished film historian specializing in cinema and the Holocaust Annette Insdorf has written:

> *The Night Porter* is a provocative and problematic film. Made in 1974 by Italian director Liliana Cavani, it can be seen as an exercise in perversion and exploitation of the Holocaust for the sake of

sensationalism. On the other hand, a closer reading of this English-language psychological thriller suggests a dark vision of compelling characters doomed by their World War II past.

Insdorf argues that the re-encounter of Max and Lucia leads to a restaging, with a difference, of their violent and sadistic past which has now become an 'obsessive love' that opens onto both historical and psychological revelation:

> The obsessive love of Max and Lucia ultimately re-creates a concentration camp situation in which they are both victims. They experience paranoia because they are being pursued; they no longer go out; finally, hunger and lack of air make them regress to an animal level. The core of the film might be Max's confession that he works at night because during the day, in the light, he is ashamed. His repressed guilt is perhaps as great as his initially repressed lust, and Max's ultimate action is to turn himself into a physically degraded and emotionally shattered prisoner. *The Night Porter* depicts not only the political continuity between wartime Nazism and 1957 Austria, but also the psychological continuity of characters locked into compulsive repetition of the past.[12]

Furthermore, for those who admire the political aesthetics of the film, *The Night Porter* can be placed alongside Pier Paolo Pasolini's *Salò* (1975) as a critical and intelligent analysis of the intimacy between fascism, the bourgeois order and capitalism. The film has, however, also been acclaimed by feminist analysts for its deconstruction of phallic masculinity and a phallocentric ordering of sexual difference.[13]

I suggest that the film's capacity to provoke such disparate responses lies in its daring to explore questions of sexuality, desire and intensity through the prism of the concentrationary. Not being understood in its political and structural specificity, the concentrationary is often confused with what the umbrella concept 'Holocaust' has come to include: namely everything the Nazis did. By drawing on the theoretical distinction between 'the concentrationary universe' with its specific operations and effects on its inmates (prolonged exposure to degradation, dehumanization and torture) and racialized mass murder (immediate destruction) in the specialized extermination camps, the function of the 'camp' as a laboratory for the violent assault on the living human subject and hence on humanity itself becomes available for *political* analysis while its subjective effects on those exposed to its regime draw a different kind of understanding of what 'survival' implies: exposure to a world where 'everything is possible' from which, in the words of the French political deportee to the concentrationary universe Charlotte Delbo (1913–85), 'none [of us will] return'.[14]

Theorizing a concentrationary imaginary

The concentrationary imaginary can be understood in many ways. In this project exploring the potential significance of the concentrationary for cultural analysis, I am identifying the concentrationary imaginary at the level of culture in general as the seepage of elements of what happened in this out-of-time other space, 'the concentrationary universe', in terms of systematic dehumanization of human subjects. This opens onto economic and political normalization of using people as instruments and things in a pure economic calculus of profit, suggested by philosophers such as Giorgio Agamben in proposing that 'the camp' (the concentration camp system, not the extermination camp alone) has become the *nomos* (the codes, habits, norms or customs) of contemporary, post-war socialist and capitalist societies structurally afflicted with what actually occurred in these specific installations.[15] The term may also inform new horizons regularly used in cinema and video games to ground plots and narratives that do not represent any specific historical concentrationary site, but borrow and adapt what was experimentally enacted there, now re-presented as a form of play that engages the player in imaginary relations to these scenes which exhibit a camp logic: everything is possible and all life is expendable.

A different perspective leads us to what is projected onto the concentrationary in terms of fantasy that might, terrible to say, have been actualized in the camps themselves as sites for the untrammelled play of the Imaginary with its own Manichean features. In capitalizing the term, I am referring specifically to a major theorization of the Imaginary by Jacques Lacan in twentieth-century psychoanalysis. Frederic Jameson offers a profound exploration of the meaning of Lacan's concept of the Imaginary – the logic of formation of the subject as a potential 'I' during the mirror stage – when he writes:

Whatever else the mirror stage is, indeed, for Lacan it marks a fundamental gap between the subject and its own self or imago which can never be bridged: 'The important point is that this form [of the subjection the mirror stage] fixed the instance of the ego, well before any social determination *in a line of fiction* which is forever irreducible for the individual himself – or rather which will rejoin the subject's evolution in asymptotic fashion only, whatever the favorable outcome of those dialectical syntheses by which as an ego he must resolve his discordance with his own reality.' In our present context we will want to retain the words 'dans une ligne de fiction/in the line of the fictional' which underscores the psychic function of narrative and fantasy in the attempts of the subject to reintegrate his or her alienated image.[16]

I shall offer a further elaboration of the Lacanian Imaginary later in this chapter. Jameson's commentary highlights the first important element: the function of narrative and fantasy as formative structures in the production of a subject whose sense of self involves aligning him/herself with an image encountered on the screen of culture. Thus I want to argue that Cavani strategically uses flashbacks to what might, on one level, be read as merely falling through time to the historical past. But they are not. Marked by their filming and framing, we, spectators lured into our own imaginary relations to the screen, are being taken into imaginary scenarios around which the key characters were psychically formed not as infants but in a remaking created in the exceptional conditions of 'play', sadism, and power that were released in 'the concentrationary universe'.

Scene II: the camp cabaret scene

The cover of Kriss Ravetto's study of the aesthetic politics of postwar Italian cinema, including Cavani and Pasolini, *The Unmaking of Fascist Aesthetics* bears the close-up of Charlotte Rampling in a famous scene from *The Night Porter* that has become the icon for the film, used on its publicity poster.[17] Dressed in partial SS uniform that only involves the peaked cap and trousers with braces, supplemented by the long black gloves of Hollywood glamour icons such as Rita Hayworth in *Gilda* (Charles Vidor, 1946) and nothing else, Rampling, with hair shorn and her natural skinniness heightened by lighting, plays the very young concentration camp prisoner performing a raunchy but perverse rendition of the cabaret song 'Wenn ich mir was wünschen dürfte' by Friedrich Holländer, a

Jewish composer of a popular song made famous by Marlene Dietrich, a known anti-Nazi, in the 1931 film *Der Mann, der seinen Mörder sucht* (5.9). The song is a sad tale about being trapped in the desire for sadness. I would like to be able to play, but readers can listen to, a recording of Marlene Dietrich's version online and compare it with Rampling's non-German speaking version.

Man hat uns nicht gefragt, als wir noch kein Gesicht
Ob wir leben wollten oder lieber nicht
Jetzt gehe ich allein, durch eine große Stadt,
Und ich weiß nicht, ob sie mich lieb hat
Ich schaue in die Stuben durch Tür und Fensterglas,
Und ich warte und ich warte auf etwas

Wenn ich mir was wünschen dürfte
Käm ich in Verlegenheit,
Was ich mir denn wünschen sollte,
Eine schlimme oder gute Zeit

Wenn ich mir was wünschen dürfte
Möchte ich etwas glücklich sein
Denn wenn ich gar zu glücklich wär'
Hätt' ich Heimweh nach dem Traurigsein.

No one had asked us, when we were still faceless
whether we'd like to live or rather not
Now I'm wandering around alone in a large city,
and I don't know if she cares for me
I'm looking into living rooms through doors and windows,
and I'm waiting and waiting for something

If I could wish for something
I'd feel awkward
What should I wish for,
a bad or a good time

If I could wish for something
I'd want to be only a bit happy
because if I were too happy
I'd long for being sad

5.9–5.13 *The Night Porter* (Cavani, 1974): (5.9) Lucia sings in the camp cabaret – the iconic image; (5.10) Max tells the Countess of 'the Biblical scene' in the camp; (5.11) Max's memory: Lucia ends her song... *Trauerigsein*; (5.12) Max's memory: Lucia anticipates her gift; (5.13) Max's memory: Lucia recoils with the decapitated head exposed between Lucia and Max.

This song gains much from its complex referentiality to a prewar, pre-fascist German culture of cabarets and cinema replaying the cabaret culture through stars such as Dietrich whose persona from *The Blue Angel*, the film that made her a star, is also being 'quoted', with a difference. This 'history' is cited by the re-creation in the camp of such a site of normal social and sexual exchange, rendered abnormal by the exceptionality of the location: the camp itself with its forced performance by anonymous masked musicians and prisoner-prostitutes dressed with clown collars. The song acquires overlays of meaning, irony rather than parody, by being chosen as the vocal score of this scene in Cavani's film, cinematically staging and filming and editing the imagined restaging within a camp by SS officers of a modernist, urban and leftist culture that their own Nazi regime denounced as degenerate.

The scene in which this performance occurs is furthermore a complex one because it is not a narrative scene. It is flashback focalized by Max who narrates it. The scene occurs quite late in the film. It is not one of the shards of returning memory that, early in the film, disrupts the everyday present of the protagonists hotel porter Max and glamorous wife Lucia, reminding them and us of Max playing the camp doctor and Lucia his teenage victim in a mythical camp environment. I stress mythical because there is no intent to recreate documentary truth or historical veracity. The scenario is formally distilled as emblematic of 'the concentrationary universe'.

The scene in question is precipitated when a disturbed, and indeed perturbed Max, who has made love to Lucia in her hotel room, moving from rapish violence to passion, confesses to the long-term hotel resident and fellow Nazi, Countess Elsa, played by Isa Miranda, not only that he has found his 'little girl' again, but also that he *loves* her (5.10). She asks him to explain the meaning of this double event. Grandiosely, he tells her 'It is a biblical story.' Thus the scene becomes the animation of his at first deliciously recalled memory. It has, therefore, a completely different status from any previous intrusion of the past into the present time of the film. Previously, those intrusions have been located in the reveries of Max or Lucia prompted by their unexpected re-encounter in the Vienna hotel lobby. Such memory-scenes have left the audience in no doubt about the sadistic abuse of power by Max over the 'selected' teenage daughter of a socialist whose ethnicity or religion is left unclear.

Max tells the countess his biblical story. This too is confusing. Max will say this twice, once to introduce the narrative recall of the scene and once after its telling to frame its imaginative meaning for him. In between we have been taken back through his memory to watch, with his eyes, Lucia dance in a mock re-creation of a Weimar cabaret scene. The attendees are SS officers but they are arrayed in somewhat unnatural and formal poses, all in full uniform in a scene that is stilled, stilted and estranging with musicians in white masks, a few women in clown costumes and exaggerated make-up, reminiscent of New Objectivity images of Weimar Berlin's prostitutional night-life. These prisoners would be forced prostitutes because they are clearly better fed than the emaciated inmates amongst whom Lucia is normally confined in abject filth and deprivation.

Their presence is an indicator of an arena of the concentrationary that is known but little discussed because it challenges a certain sanctification of survival. In some of the earliest novels to disclose the horrors of the concentrationary universe, written from 1945 onwards, Yehiel De-nur, writing under the nom de plume *Ka-Tsetnik 135633* (which stands for a prisoner of a KZ, namely a *Konzentrationslager*), brutally exposed sexual services of both boys and girls as forced or elective conditions of survival in the camps. Writing of these troubling fictions, Iris Milner argues against the critics of De-nur that *Ka-Tsetnik 135633*'s novels do not blur the distinction between perpetrator and victim, thus making the latter complicit in what Primo Levi named 'the grey zone' of ethical ambiguity that some embraced in order to survive, but rather he showed them as 'two poles in an unbroken spectrum of dehumanization'. She then states that

> what emerges from *Ka-Tsetnik 135633*'s novels is a profound understanding of what may be regarded as the basic principle of this dehumanization: the systematic distortion of the victims' most fundamental psychological make-up, to the extent of completely destroying their human competence for engaging compassionately with their fellow human beings.[18]

Ka-Tsetnik 135633 refuses the redemption offered by writers who stress the persistence of a human spirit in extremity in order to make vivid the workings of 'absolute power' that destroyed solidarity amongst the victims and perversely bound those 'selected' for special operations, such as sexual services, to their tormentors. In a more recent Israeli film set in the immediate post-war period, *Eretz Hadasha/Newland*, (Oma Ben-Dor Niv, 1994), a woman camp survivor in a displaced persons' camp in the newly formed State of Israel horrifically burns off her tattoo with an iron because she cannot bear the judgemental gaze of the young Israeli Sabras who assume that any woman who survived did so as a camp prostitute.[19]

To return now to the scene, Lucia's dance is cinematically intertextual. Bogarde and Rampling had worked together in Luchino Visconti's *The Damned* (1969), a film with a radically different tenor from Cavani's finely tuned irrealism. In *The Damned*, the murderous paedophile played by Helmut Berger travesties Marlene Dietrich's cabaret performance from *The Blue Angel*. All the accoutrements of Dietrich's relatively tame costuming in the original black and white film are refashioned as the kitsch fetishism, that, in the new discourse on Nazism that emerged in the 1960s, charges the insignia of Nazism to create what Sontag would condemn as 'fascinating fascism'.[20] Alternating between his SS uniform and his transgendering drag, Visconti's Martin displaces any real investigation of fascism onto a certain style within a highly saturated film styling. By contrast to this intensification of fascination and fetishism, Cavani films Lucia's dance in muted colour, deanimated stillness apart from her movement. The song ends with her 'fall' into a deathly immobility on the word *Traurigsein* / 'being sad'. (5.11) The whole scene is deadly and there is no escape from the disjuncture of uniformed men, masked performers, and this androgynously thin but exposed female victim, impersonating both a historical figure from German cinema and its recent, politically troubling, neo-Romantic cinematic re-quotation by Cavani's older contemporary, Visconti.

After a pause the scene shifts to Lucia sitting, capless and anticipatory, at a table with Max who has hitherto been shown standing apart from the performance, surveying the scene; for whom it unfolded as if he had moved from the moment of telling to the moment of watching, being both inside and outside the scene. Its dreamlike quality also alerts us to its function as a remembered phantasy, not a slippage back into the piercing shards of reality puncturing the present as in previous returns to the camp scenes. A soldier brings to the table a box. Max is smirking in anticipation like a little child hardly able to contain excitement at the joke. The cover is lifted as Lucia looks on expectantly, (5.12) only to reveal, but in a very reserved and non-horrific presentation, the severed head of a man from which Lucia recoils (5.13). Its meaning only becomes clear with Max's later narrative in the present to the Countess. It is the head of Johann, a prisoner who was harassing Lucia. It is this confrontation that brings to Max's mind the biblical story of Salomé.

Thus in retrospect the dance becomes the condition demanded by the desiring king and the prize the severed head, throwing the whole weight of 'guilt' onto Lucia/Salomé as femme fatale, implicated powerlessly in a scenario that is elevated by cultural association only in *afterwardness*: Laplanche's translation of Freud's key concept of *Nachträglichkeit*.[21] The silliness or even childishness of Max, playing at being doctor – one of the classic childhood games that allows access to a pre-genital sexuality – playing out roles of power and domination in the space of limitless freedom that was the concentrationary where 'everything is possible', where those in uniform have the absolute power of life and death, is exposed to Lucia's horrified response. She has been shown being slowly drawn into the games by his manipulation and indeed this scene is the culmination of the transition from innocent teenager to recreated girl-child in her white socks, party dress and hair ribbon via shorn, starved and brutalized concentrationee to this self-parodying sexualized yet androgynous performer. Her response to the severed head registers shock even within the dreamy narrative that Max so evidently enjoys in the retelling; her shocked response disturbs that narrative, marking a space of revulsion for the spectator, interrupting the self-congratulatory mode of Max and his fellow Nazis in the present who disingenuously seek absolution from guilt simply by ensuring that there survives no evidence, documentary or living, of the crimes they committed in the camps. (Earlier in the film Max has callously murdered another survivor and potential witness on a fishing trip.) It is clear from the build-up of the present-day narrative preparing for the mock trial of Max and the flashbacks that Lucia is now at risk of such summary execution. This scene in the Countess's bedroom thus restages, for the spectator, the past Max is seeking to protect, but also its radical disturbance by the discovery, in the present, of another emotion, love, for the woman the girl-child has become. He wants no longer to seal and freeze the past, but live its effects, in a different form.

Cinematically Cavani's scene of the 'Salomé' dance is, therefore, complex in its plays with temporalities and positionalities. There is clearly an ethics being established within the sequence that uses the severed head as a kind of absolute marker for the guilt of the entire SS crew. This is done without any imaging of atrocity, any feeding of the viewer's sadistic imagination such as horror films provide. There is no gore, no blood but the stark visual confrontation with a banal (thoughtless and indifferent) perversity that now has no bounds and yet has imaginative precedents in the Bible story upon which this depleted and disgusting novelty idly draws. (In the film the other Nazis complain that Max always had imagination, a capacity that becomes his undoing since, freed from the imaginary stasis and repetition, he can imagine a future.) Through

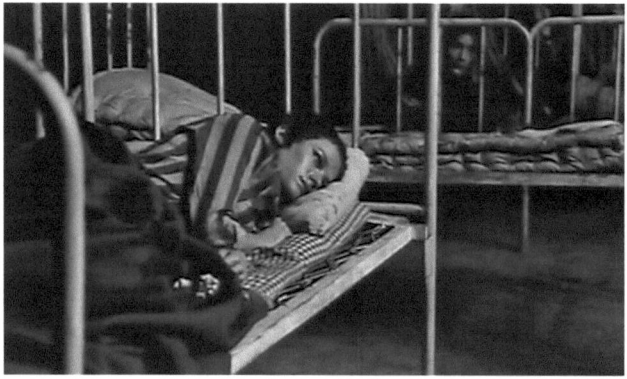

5.14 *The Night Porter* (Cavani, 1974): At the Opera: Max's flashback to the camp – Sexual initiation into sadomasochism: Lucia in the camp watching.

this interweaving of flashback, memory and narrative scenes, the film has tracked the Nazis – who are not ex-Nazis, not de-Nazified in any way – preparing the mock trial of Max to bring him to an 'exoneration' of any remaining guilt, induced not by the memory of what he/they had done but by the anxiety of knowing there may be evidence that might bring him/them still to face the law.

The scene thus functions as the signifier of a double transition. The first is the transformation or rather sexualization of the 'little girl' where abusive paedophilia on his part is matched by a disarmingly subtle representation of her initiation into a prostitutional sexuality in which sadomasochism will play a part because the whole scene is a form of role-playing (5.14–5.15).

The second is that the memory of this scene marks the transition or rather the moment of recognition within Max that the initial stage of sadistic perversity provided by the camp environment gradually gave way to an unacknowledged tenderness that effectively unmanned, or even, we might say, de-Nazified him. Hence the playing out of the scene in the Countess's bedroom, she a maternal figure now, involves Bogarde playing Max in ways that completely breach his former self-possession: uniformed, contained, hidden in the darkness of the night and in self-effacing service as a humble night porter. He kneels at her table,

5.15 *The Night Porter* (Cavani, 1974): At the Opera: Max's flashback to the camp – Sexual initiation into sadomasochism: Max chooses Lucia for his sex 'play'.

becomes florid in gestures, expressive, animated, impassioned, hysterical. He has moved from enjoying the memory of his Herod/Salomé moment. He now declares that he loves the little girl and thus does not want to 'erase' her.

Cavani uses the cinematic device of the flashback, which normally functions to insert an unseen but necessary element of the past into the plot, in order to stage a highly invested memory. The past shown in the flashback moves from the order of history into the order of phantasy. In the past (the camp-cabaret) the role-play was, however, for real: the game is horrifically interrupted for both Lucia and the audience by the *realization* – the making real – of the biblical fiction of the decapitation of a man named John/Johann. In the context of the film, therefore, the retelling, with all its anguished and delicious enjoyment on Max's part, functions almost psychoanalytically. The scene is repeated. As in the analytical space, it is told to another, but with a displacement. The film analytically restages the phantasy world in such a way that Max discovers that the concentrationary game of absolute power produced an investment in a person, Lucia, not merely a dressed-up doll, a toy over which the concentrationary universe gave him the right of life or death, on a whim.

It becomes vital, therefore, not to misread this scene as endorsing or exploiting the terms of the phantasies that it was permitted to act out for real in 'the concentrationary universe'. The concentrationary imaginary comes into play precisely when such confusion or repetition occurs. Countering the very imaginary it must reveal, *The Night Porter* outlines that imaginary precisely by staging its phantasy in a scene of telling that embeds flashbacks inside the narrative presented by Max to the Countess. It is here that Cavani offers much more than a critique: she fashions a cinematic form that enables us to glimpse the ways in which events beyond the limit not only touched, claimed and deformed their perpetrators and victims, but stored up unpredictable, delayed effects that were the very opposite. In this cinematic work of afterwardness, the film makes visible the interruption of the event's psychic effects that give rise to a political reflection on the event's imaginary power.

Nazi kitsch

The image of Charlotte Rampling with her black sheathed hands covering her naked breasts and sporting the SS cap has been extracted from the complex cinematic emplotment I have just described to function as the emblem of the film and hence to tip the film into the nouveau, revived semi-porno-kitsch of post-war aestheticizing of Nazism, and notably the SS uniform, that unexpectedly emerged in the 1960s and 1970s. So we need now to make more sense of the potential slippage between Nazi kitsch and a film that stages and undoes the concentrationary imaginary (5.9).

In her study of Italian cinema, *The Unmaking of Fascist Aesthetics*, Kriss Ravetto takes us one stage further. Analysing a critical body of Italian films whose focus is on the fascism of perpetration, Ravetto makes the telling point that the 'return' of Nazism as image or as an aesthetic paradoxically endows what we know to have been a deeply puritanical and de-eroticized historical reality with an eroticism, which is often furthermore homoerotic, which it did not itself elaborate. Ravetto also, therefore, sees a reanimation via these ostensibly 'historical' films of pre-existing tropes and discourses, which circle around the tropes of gender, purity and impurity. These invade the Nazi skeleton with their anxious enfleshments. She writes:

The fascist deviant represented in the films examined in this book functions as public spectacle while marking a return to the language of purity. In other words, the representation of the *impure* (deviant) is connected to violence performed by the language of purity. Narratives and analytical models from which post-war artists, filmmakers, historians, and theorists construct their own narrative and ideological interpretations reveal de facto encoding of historical events to satisfy present symbolic roles. These symbols (good, evil, pure, impure, etc.) organize the singularity or specificity of a historical event, yet they install that event in a transhistorical model (a moral trying to be a phenomenological model), and to that degree reconstitute a transcendent model.[22]

Ravetto seeks to undo the historical retrospect that simply inverts the historical binary opposition in which, for the Nazis, Jews were absolute evil, so that, in the aftermath, that opposition is simply turned upside down: Nazis now represent pure evil and Jews absolute victimhood. In French and Italian situations, the opposition takes a different form that exonerates as good the generalized resistance to Nazism in both societies as opposed to purely bad: French collaborators or Italian fascists. Following this logic the present instances of tyrants and oppressors and any victims of oppression and tyranny are sucked back into a pre-existing historical modelling, making the dictatorial Saddam Husseins of this world and the victimized Palestinians, for instance, play out the Manichean roles from the older scripts.

Ravetto wishes to expose, by close readings of different aesthetic-cinematic strategies, modes of resistance to fascism that might refuse this tendency. Neorealism, however, returns us to tragedy while what she names the neo-decadent (she has Visconti in mind) 'explodes bourgeois moral models by examining post-war fascination with sexualization and eroticization of fascism and Nazism, that is popular culture's rendering of fascism and Nazism as sublime'. But the films amongst which she places *The Night Porter* are neither tragic nor sublime. Such films 'expose various fascistic economies that extend beyond historical fascism – reaching into the discourses of victimization, gender difference, capitalism and bourgeois moralism'.[23] Pier Paolo Pasolini, Lina Wertmüller and Liliana Cavani 'disrupt both the feminizing and moralizing method of historicizing fascism, as well as the reliance on binary models to ensure the separation between purity and radical evil'.[24]

Ravetto considers the films as intelligent and thoughtful responses to the student movements of the 1960s and to their failures. Refusing nihilism, these movements sought to reinvent the critical position from which to move beyond a fetishization of fascism in the figures of Mussolini or Hitler so as to disclose 'the inextricable connections of bourgeois morality, technological modernization, and capitalist socioeconomic structures plugged into fascist regimes'. Their mode of resistance involves refusing disengagement from the implicating past, refusing the disassociations that arise from the binary model and the application of past models to cover over the present with similar absolutes of good and evil. If fascism is what Deleuze and Guattari name a 'desiring' but also a 'war machine', the question arises how to 'disarm fascism and salvage desire' (a process of becoming other or different). The films of Pasolini, Wertmüller and Cavani 'scandalize all ideological determinations they see as conforming to the model of purification'. Thus Ravetto brilliantly concludes that 'they problematize intersecting discourses of Nazism and sexuality by returning to the discourse of intimacy – an imposed intimacy on the victimizer'.[25] Cavani differs from Pasolini here because she dares to explore how the issues of seduction – seducing and seduced – lead to becoming other. Thus Ravetto places these films in a tradition of radical thinking in opposition to those readings that denounce the discomfort of their projects as merely pornographic or depraved or complicit with the pornography that in fact they politically expose.

In the interplay of the characters Lucia and Max, initially in their first encounter and, more significantly, in their re-encounter in the present of the film, Vienna 1957, Cavani addresses an element of the gendered imaginary that cultural theorist Klaus Theweleit so forcefully exposed in his study of the fantasies of fascist men that found an echo in European culture's mainstream from the later nineteenth century. That element concerns not only the threat to masculinity posed by women's sexuality, giving rise to the image of the Red Woman who must be destroyed, but also the threat of sexuality itself. Theweleit argues that sexuality was perceived as 'a feminine disease that weakens and afflicts the pure masculine body'.[26] Thus the 'tired metaphors of sexual difference' are undermined but without offering any redemptive or cathartic process of cleansing – the like of which the Nazi group seek to perform upon themselves.

Thus we have the ending that forces upon us the recognition of the deep fascism and bad faith of historical retrospect and contemporary bourgeois order. Max and Lucia are effectively re-imprisoned, starved and summarily killed as they walk the streets in a knowing recreation of the order of the camp itself: imprisonment, starvation and arbitrary execution. As the discomforting figures of desire created out of the ruins of a catastrophic history that could not let them go once they met again, they cannot be allowed to live either by the still-fascist Nazi group or, in a deeper sense, by post-war culture itself. There is no place for what they now represent: neither redemption nor a happy ending but a radical understanding of what love might be when it is not the alibi of the bourgeois patriarchal order – the order that is specifically represented, aestheticized and visualized in the extracts from Mozart's heteronormative and conservative opera *The Magic Flute*: a scene of which is the focus of my final analysis. It is also the scenario staged very early on in the film when Max and Lucia have not yet spoken to each other. In order to grasp the cinematic work Cavani's film performs to expose and transform, we need firstly to explore in detail how Cavani uses space as a signifying device in her cinema.

Interlude on space

The Night Porter makes urban space strange, alien and dangerous. Cavani also places most of the action in interiors, which become allegories of each other. So by contrast to the rare escapes into the city and environs of Vienna, the interior scenes play out in cloistered spaces of a hotel lobby, a series of bedrooms and a worker's miserable apartment. Running through these spaces that oscillate between elaborate and stagey or bleak and basic is a sense of unsettling irreality. Cavani says in an interview with Claire Clouzot:

> Beginning with *The Night Porter*, the true facts, and the actors within the scenes, are not realities. My point of view is beyond time, beyond realism. The atmosphere of the place, a room, and a road is transformed. My desire is to interpret them into a space of fantasy. They are mood provoking. In order to achieve this, I break the rules of cinematography; for example, I place lights to imply windows where there are none. This strategy evokes places

beyond phenomenological reality, which make up my own reality, as dreams.[27]

The space of the hotel lobby, boardroom, or bedroom is very different from those strange and irreal spaces that break into this banal everyday world of Vienna: the camp scenes. Filmed altogether at the beginning of the shoot in an abandoned building full of cracked tiles and desolation, they are not intended as historical reconstructions such as we find in Gilles Pontecorvo's 1958 fiction film *Kapò*, of which Cavani must have been aware.[28] As a practitioner of the neorealism of which Ravetto speaks, Pontecorvo reconstructed a camp on a former site in Yugoslavia, causing the local residents considerable anxiety about the return of the Germans. *Kapò* involves a young Jewish French girl who survives being gassed with her parents because she wanders into the hospital and is given a recently dead prisoner's non-Jewish identity. Becoming a camp prostitute serving the German officers further helps her. She rises to become a Kapo and behaves with typical brutality to her fellow inmates until she meets a Soviet prisoner of war with whom she falls in love. As a contaminated figure she cannot survive the film. She is redeemed, however, by giving her life for the others when an uprising is planned. She turns off the electrification of the fence. The others escape and she dies a pathetic death in the arms of her former German lover, reclaiming her Jewish identity with her last breath. This is surely what Cavani and indeed Ravetto would name a redemptive film whose setting tries hard to recreate the concentrationary universe and only succeeds in making a costume drama war film the backdrop for both the punishing of female sexuality and a woman's purification by death.

Emplotted through claustrophobic interiors and desolate exteriors that are estranged by her lighting and cinematography in early morning and evening, Cavani's cinematic universe refuses to emblematize the concentrationary. Instead it infects the characters who interiorize its logic wherever they exist. The isolated extremity of the camp – removed precisely because it flashes up into the film as almost hallucinatory memory in flashback – exacerbates and plays out the inherent totalitarianism of systems in which the strong treat the weak as slaves and objects. Cavani's treatment of her characters and their settings does not allow this to occur as an invisible norm. Her cinematography disturbs it by a complex play of denied sexualities, dependencies, longings, which Max and Lucia violently and bodily act out to explode from the cloying silence and silencing that sustain the oppressive order, an order which ultimately they cannot defeat so that their sexual encounters revert to the enclosed space of their second re-imprisonment in Max's apartment where they seek to escape the Nazi group that is starving them out. The otherness of the past when Max's sadistic play prematurely and perversely sexualized a young woman in the context of a SS-run camp is first glimpsed as unwanted flashbacks. But then the conditions of their second meeting and discovery of a bond of a form of love that is anything but romantic – it completely redefines the nature of their sex – tragically leads to the recreation of *campness*. Renouncing language, and as Kaja Silverman states, 'immersing themselves in the sensory and affective intensity of their shared past', they relive their imprisonment in shifting roles, undergoing house arrest and gradual starvation against which the sole remaining act of agency is to return to the scene of the crime, in masquerade, and solicit death as a willed act of solidarity with both their bond forged in terror and their transformation of its contingency into a present intensity and a human intimacy that does not alienate itself in voyeuristic sex (the dance scene) or falsify itself in romantic delusion (her post-war marriage).[29]

Writing at the highpoint of feminist film theory in 1988, Kaja Silverman offers a reading of Cavani's feminist authorship (not her intentions) by tracing the signature tendencies that traverse the body of Cavani's cinematic work. Stressing the obliqueness of Cavani's feminist inscriptions through predominant interest in masculine characters, Silverman identifies in Cavani's oeuvre the recurring trope of young men who 'renounce power and privilege and sever their relation to the phallus'.[30] She adds:

> It is a striking fact that the male characters who dominate Cavani's films retreat from power rather than accede to it; they entertain a highly problematic relation to discourse; and they interact with women in ways which defy the usual heterosexual conventions. Indeed these figures exist on the margins or at the limits of their cultures.[31]

In her study of *The Night Porter*, however, Marguerite Waller takes a daring turn to link the feminism recognized in this film with its deeper understanding of the link between the hatred of women and the abjection of the Jew in the culture that generated the Holocaust. Misogyny and anti-Semitism are discovered to have subterranean and symbolic links that then demand that the study of the Holocaust and its representations be opened up to gender and feminist analysis. Waller reminds us of the rejection of the film by leading Holocaust survivors and writers like Primo Levi for 'muddying our understanding of "the truth" with ... sexual allegories of concentration camp power relations'.[32] Levi saw only a confusing of victims and perpetrators, allowing the grey zone to engulf the whole history. Waller asserts that films such as *The Night Porter* and *Seven Beauties* do not attempt 'the kind of mimetic or documentary representation of what happened favoured by Levi, Bettelheim or Lanzmann' and that they 'approach the question of what happened, how it happened, why it happened and what would have to change for it not to happen again through *non-Jewish* principal characters, unrealistic mise-en-scène and plotting, and not coincidentally, exhaustive explorations of what might seem a peripheral issue of the constructedness of gender and sexualities'. The point is to show that fascism 'cannot be subverted from within the moral and ethical categories through which the world has come to know it historically'.[33]

Waller also suggests that Cavani's cinema is destabilizing precisely of the ordering of vision and sexual difference feminist theory so brilliantly revealed as a predominant, if never secure, structuring of the cinematic imaginary. Thus Max and Lucia are neither stable within the diegesis, nor is the spectator able to take up, via their apparent gendering, the neutral or mastering position that would consolidate the subject-viewer in relation to phallocentrism. On the one hand, Rampling's performance as Lucia steadfastly refuses to suffer sufficiently to allocate her a proper position as used object. On the other, her performance troubles the viewer by its indeterminacy between fear and admission into the realm of sadomasochistic pleasure games. It makes viewing difficult not because of what is actually being done and shown, but because it is not clear what is happening in scenarios that should, according to the semantic and scopic economy of phallocentric cinema, be clearly voyeuristic and hence sadistic. Even in the scenes of the medical-sexual invasions of Lucia's body – never fully shown but intimated through attention to the subjectivities, and as, importantly, the gestures and affectivities of perpetrator and victim – it is clear that Max's former power and distance signified by being shown behind the camera, the prosthesis of distancing and objectifying vision is being eroded. Max is shown succumbing to an intimacy that the tight camera framing serves to accentuate, making the viewer experience an increasing closeness between subject positions that initially are posed as radical opposites. The undoing of both Max and Lucia began in the heart of the darkness.

Once again, I would like to stress that Cavani's artful and cinematically calculated construction of space and her plotting of the spectator's relation to cinematic space are where the double work of the film – the production of a concentrationary imaginary and its critical undoing – occurs.

Scene III: *The Magic Flute*

Waller offers a close cinematic and musical reading of an early scene at the Vienna Opera when Max, full of dread and anger at the reappearance of Lucia, takes a seat in a row behind Lucia while her American husband conducts Mozart's *The Magic Flute*. Waller draws our attention to the way in which the music and libretto, which speaks about the ideals of heterosexual marriage in an opera where Pamina will be subjected to attempted rape and then married off by Zarastro, is laid over and renders continuous the flashback scenes in the irreal concentration camp hospital that are inserted into the space of the opera house. Waller concludes:

> If the Viennese opera house and the concentration camp are seen as reverse images of each other, then it becomes more difficult to oppose Lucia's husband to Max. Lucia's husband is, in his own way, reproducing and naturalizing the white or Aryan male subject position that Nazism, the epitome of the patriarchal repression of women and 'non-Aryans', tried to solidify to an absurd extent. The sexuality and organization of power that we see in the camp are, in a fundamental sense, continuous with what we see in the eighteenth century opera as well as in the post-war culture for which the opera remains a significant ruling class ritual.[34]

Waller makes us watch Cavani's direction of the camera moving in and around this setting, cutting and zooming, focusing here and there, ending on the empty seat that Max suddenly vacates, leaving Lucia exposed in her anxiously resurfacing and increasing longing. This sequence begins with Lucia at the opera becoming aware of Max's late entry to sit a few rows behind her (5.16–5.18) we become meshed in Max's flashback of a scene in the camp where a male prisoner is being raped by an officer while Lucia lies on her bed and watches before being 'chosen' by Max in his white coat (5.14–15). Moving back from Max to Lucia, we see her growing tension. She wrings her hands (5.20), a sight that dissolves into her bound hands in the camp (5.21), where she is approached by Max who introduces his fingers, pointed like a gun, preparatory for his penis, into her mouth (5.22). The movement between Lucia and Max is also a movement intercutting then and now, past and present, sutured by the continuity of the soundtrack of Mozart's opera. We are watching his relishing of the memories of his power over this woman. We are witnessing her anguished descent back into that sphere of abjection. We are also made spectators of a screen on which these two 'scenes' are technologically intercut as the cinematic means of signifying the continuity between them and the restaging of the terrifying game of perpetrator and victim. But do we fully know their meaning? What is the meaning of their pleasure and anguish?

Waller then reminds us of the extended meanings of what Cavani has done cinematically with the unsettling of positions. It is this uncertainty and overlaying that enable the revelation not of direct continuity but of a more terrible affinity that is part of the world and our subjectivities:

> Representations, in the sense that one position or effect can stand for another (whereby for example Lucia could stand for women, who could stand for victims, who could stand for Jews) would require the inert, monocular vision enforced by binary logic that produces a kind of 'truth' in which people and events appear to stay put.... In Cavani's film positionality is relative and cannot be fixed or 'clarified'. The camera's restless comparison of every position with every other is amongst the film's most powerful and disturbing strategies. These comparisons do *not* serve to minimize the horrors of the Holocaust; on the contrary, they keep them relevant. They signify the Holocaust not as the unthinkable Other, but as one distinctly possible effect of the misogynist signifying situations through which we, who share this history and culture, are ourselves articulated.[35] (Author's emphasis)

5.16–5.22 *The Night Porter* (Cavani, 1974): At the opera: (5.16) Lucia at the Opera; (5.17) Lucia becomes aware of Max and turns; (5.18) Max stares at Lucia intently; (5.19) Max looks on; (5.20) Lucia rings her hands in anguish; (5.21) Lucia's hands are bound in the camp; (5.22) Max's flashback: Max puts his fingers into Lucia's mouth.

Conclusion

In his book *Reflections of Nazism: An Essay on Kitsch and Death*, first published in 1982, Holocaust historian Saul Friedländer contemplated a surprising cultural turn. In 1945, 'Nazism was the damned part of Western Civilization, the symbol of evil. Everything the Nazis had done was condemned, whatever they touched defiled'. Friedländer notes, 'by the end of the Sixties, however, the Nazi image had begun to change'. He identified also 'an aesthetic re-elaboration that goes beyond ideology' into a psychological dimension sustained by what he names 'a structure of fantasms'.[36]

Friedländer uses the resurfacing of fantasmatic Nazism to investigate its foundations and its continuing function:

> Nazism has disappeared, but the obsession it represents for the contemporary imagination – as well as the birth of a new discourse that ceaselessly elaborates and reinterprets it – necessarily confronts us with this ultimate question: Is such attention fixed on the past only a gratuitous reverie, the attraction of spectacle, exorcism, or the result of a need to understand; or is it, again and still, an expression of profound fears and, on the part of some, *mute yearnings as well*?[37] (my emphasis)

Noting a rash of movies that unexpectedly return to a fascination with aspects of Nazism as distinct from memorialization of the genocidal Holocaust, Friedländer is not intending morally to condemn the trend, but to analyse its significance in terms of a different kind of unfinished business that operates on another register. So often 'dressed up' in clothing and identities associated with Nazism, hence leading us to focus on their relation to a fascist imaginary being given a new lease of visual life, these 'mute yearnings' call for a different order of analysis (psychoanalytical) and a different order of critical exposure and displacement (aesthetic). That combination of psychoanalytical and aesthetic is the site for an exploration of the concentrationary imaginary through cinema, the imaginary apparatus. Cinema can be, however, reworked as a critical tool for making visible the concentrationary by showing it as a locus, a scene, a set of relations, and a space of enactments that marked its unequal participants.

Referring to Hans-Jürgen Syberberg's *Hitler: A Film from Germany* (1977), Friedländer writes: 'Attention has gradually shifted from the revocation of Nazism as such, from the horror and the pain – even if muted and transformed into subdued grief and endless mediation – to voluptuous anguish and ravishing images, images one would like to see going on forever.'[38] In radical contrast to such effects, I have argued that Liliana Cavani's *The Night Porter* analytically and critically works against the grain of a seeping reclamation of Nazism as style and depoliticized visual pleasure in order for us to see beyond aestheticizing recyclings.

Cavani's cinema blasphemously refuses both the redemption through the sanctification of suffering and the elegiac and even fascinated spectacularization of Nazism's emblems and aesthetic. In muted colours, difficult camera positions, destabilized sexual and gendered identities and sometimes illegible expressions in response to troubling fields of interlaced violence and eroticism, *The Night Porter* demands of the viewer consideration of the difficult legacy of what took place in the camps which imprinted psychic effects that contain personally unsettling ambiguities that no existing ethical or political discourse touches.[39]

Beyond recognizing the deeper structures of phantasy and imagery into which the concentration camp scenario fed and from which it drew, Cavani focuses on the historical effect of the camp on the subjectivities it forged precisely through the combination of absolute power and certain conditions of unbridled intimacy between captors and captured. These theatres of torture left marks on/in the participants. Cavani's film asks us to imagine the latent potential of such lived scenarios, not only to disfigure their subjects forever frozen in their horrific postures, but to become sites of real resistance to the unexamined fascism that not only persists in real, unpunished Nazis, but in the continuities between its order and that which is the bourgeois, capitalist heteronormative order of the post-war everyday.

A text that belongs alongside the revolt of a new generation in the 1970s in Italy and Germany against their nations' unexpunged fascist pasts, *The Night Porter* articulates a discourse on misogyny, homophobia and anti-Semitism through the ever more intense examination of the bearers of a past: Max and Lucia who, unexpectedly, in their re-encounter as subjects trapped by what happened, become agents of its transfiguration. Yet, in the end, for the same political reasons, the film had to show their deaths. It had to end with the violence and intolerance that will be shown to be still active now. Max and Lucia had to be killed outside the camp, on the streets of post-war, liberated Vienna: Freud's infamous home town that at once stands for Mozart and Freud, but also for Hitler and Eichmann, and a present that requires vigilance of its still pervasive concentrationary Imaginary through the critical use of the imaginary signifier: cinema.

Cinema is about spaces, gazes, and the sequencing of scenarios invented and screened for its spectators, who are moved through time and space phantasmatically by camera and narrative. The concentrationary Imaginary emerges from *The Night Porter* as itself a kind of horrific enactment of the cinematic, made real, but also unreal since it was a release into the phantasy world of the imaginary. Having precedents prior to this unique laboratory of experimentation in power, life and death, the concentrationary persists as a form of Imaginary, a complex texture of many strands. The visual signs of Nazism are the most visible; but the structure of the concentrationary universe created under Nazism requires attention to phantasms and mute yearnings, to psychic effects unacknowledged and even unknowable to political and historical discourse alone. The intersection of the concentrationary and the Imaginary is a speculative hypothesis, not a given analytical category into which a film may be inserted. I have traced Cavani's research, by means of filmmaking, into the evidence provided by the camp survivor/witnesses to the continuing hold of a place/space. By positing a place for the concentrationary in the Imaginary/cultural imaginary through her cinematic fiction, Cavani also delineated a delayed, afterwardly – *nachträgliche* – psychological 'escape' through what Max and Lucia tried to create. That their attempt to escape and change failed is how the film refuses redemption. Instead it bears witness, as it must politically, to the persistence of the concentrationary Imaginary through the starkness of the film's ending. This film thus refuses redemption from history: the lovers die at the hands of the fascist group. This film, nonetheless, offers some elements of transformation. Meeting again, Lucia and Max are drawn back together to rework abusive sadomasochism into an equally passionate reciprocal love. Nonetheless, the film becomes blasphemous by playing out that transformation, in the presence of those who violently resist any such radical change. It is also blasphemous because the fact that this 'contaminated' couple perform such transformation challenges comfortable ideologies and norms. The film refuses the post-war lie that the past is over, and that history can be confined to a boundaried time, that people survived and moved on. The event reclaims its subjects, and those subjected to it, variously. In the unexpected re-encounter, another writing of this past is allowed, by this film, to be possible, while at the same time, the forces working against such acknowledgement and transformation have to win to make the point about the lethal force of unworked pasts.

What happened is not merely written in bodily and psychic scars on the victims, or even on the perpetrators' deformed psyches. In the form of the band of former SS men trying to efface the evidence of their crime and its witnesses, and in the intersection with the representative of art/civilization – the opera conductor and Mozart's troubling opera itself – the concentrationary is shown to be part of structural forms in which the other has no value as a person. By staging the concentrationary logic that 'everything is possible' and the human *qua* human is superfluous through sexuality rather than horrific affliction and death, *The Night Porter* risked radical misunderstanding as Nazi porn. At the same time, it achieved an equally radical intervention into the very culture that mindlessly allowed itself to be re-enchanted by the superficial style of a reclaimed Nazi kitsch aesthetic. Politically feminist and anti-fascist, *The Night Porter* performs a cinematic resistance to the concentrationary logic that infuses the post-war cinematic imaginary in general, which, at certain moments, even dares to dress itself up in historical clothing, all the better to elude the political and psychoanalytical exposure that *The Night Porter* thoughtfully sought to demand, cinematically.

PART 3

CAMP

6

SEEP AND CREEP
The Concentrationary Imaginary in Martin Scorsese's *Shutter Island* (2010)

Benjamin Hannavy Cousen

The ordering of the image

In the film *Shutter Island*, directed by Martin Scorsese in 2010, explicit and self-regarding (as opposed to self-aware, hence critically conscious) references and depictions of the German concentration camp of Dachau occlude the historical signification of 'Dachau' in favour of the film's fetishized fictional narrative and psycho-thriller plot.[1] In the following analysis of *Shutter Island*, I shall deploy a theoretical apparatus specifically developed in order to discern a concentrationary imaginary in cinema of which the occlusion I have pointed to in *Shutter Island* is symptomatic.

On the basis of my research into a range of post-war British, European and American films, I propose three registers by which a film, either in its totality or in certain sequences, becomes the bearer of, or is constituted by, *concentrationary imaginaries*. The three 'orders' of the image are the *citational*, the *indexical* and the *amnesiac*. Each provides material evidence of the presence of concentrationary imaginaries within films while maintaining a complex relationship with the others so that this specification of each order must be understood as hermeneutic rather than structural. Thus the 'orders' of the image which I will elaborate below, and which are detectable and definable, are, however, constantly overlapping; an *amnesiac* component may, for example, be present in an image that I speak of as primarily *citational* or *indexical* and an image may consist of a combination of permutations.

In *Shutter Island*, the invocation of 'Dachau' is an example of the *amnesiac* concentrationary image. In the introduction to this volume the psychoanalytical 'Imaginary' order theorized by Jacques Lacan and its relation to film studies and the concentrationary has been discussed. Some aspects of this understanding of the Imaginary are retained here. For the purposes of the initial creation of the taxonomy of the images, however, another sense of the imaginary is to be brought to the fore. In this particular understanding, film itself becomes what we might call an 'imaginarium' (after, for example, *The Imaginarium of Doctor Parnassus* (Terry Gilliam, 2009)), by which film is to be understood as a repository of imaginary elements which can be seen, analysed and, to some extent, categorized. This less specific understanding of 'imaginary' allows us to make an initial approach towards categorizing images under the hypothesis of an existing concentrationary element within them. In addition, I use the terms 'seep' and 'creep' to explore the different ways in which the three orders of the imaginary image come to inhabit or inflect a film.

The first order of concentrationary image, the *citational*, has a constant connection with the visual representation of the concentrationary universe on its surface.[2] It retains this connection even when the new purpose to which it is being put is disconnected from this origin and fails to acknowledge it. This type of image is created through the recycling of certain other images, often derived from 'liberation footage' made at the end of World War II or other primary documentation discovered during the Allied advance. Some images – such as barbed wire, cattle trucks, emaciated prisoners in striped uniforms, corpses and so on – have become, through repeated exposure, a kind of shorthand for the concentrationary experience. They get recycled as tropes for the concentrationary even while being often mistaken for an image of the extermination process that left almost no visual record.

The *citational image* raises questions about the nature of witnessing in that it relies on an existing archive of image material that is often unquestioningly and unthinkingly deployed as a pre-digested signifier of the concentrationary/exterminatory universe. The *citational image* often produces a feeling of authenticity because the archival claims to be evidence, ignoring the fact that the images that are its provenance arise from singular moments. These moments were often captured at the point of the Allies' liberation of the German concentration camps, and, as such, do not necessarily truly witness the concentrationary universe or concentrationary society, as it was lived by its inmates and which was unseen by those partial witnesses such as the 'liberators'. The *citational image* is evident when the archive of concentrationary images (including written witness accounts) is treated as a 'resource bank' for cultural production; the *citational image* does not necessarily use the actual material of the archive but can echo it and draw from it as if inspired by it. Images are deployed for use in areas beyond their original situation. In the spirit of what Pollock and Silverman have named 'concentrationary memory' – which is a form of politico-cultural vigilance as to the potential dissemination of concentrationary forms beyond the historical confines of the actual camps – analysis must ask the question of why and with what effects the cited material is being used.[3]

The *indexical image* posits that what emerges or is presented as an image is merely the surface of the underlying conditions that produce it. Unlike the *citational image* which operates to a certain extent on a surface level between a known image and the new image, the *indexical image* is a manifestation of the embedded relationship between cultural production and the society from which this emerges. This also posits a kind of unconsciousness in the production of the image. The concentrationary image exists as the visible surface of a concentrationary structure/society and as the manifestation of a dominant imaginary; it 'appears' as concentrationary because society is itself concentrationary. Whether or not the depicted society is concentrationary because a dominant 'imaginary' preceded it and thereby created it is a different question. Since the uncovering of the underlying infrastructure is involved here, it may be that this type of concentrationary image does not consist of the obviously visible tropes that constitute the *citational image*. Vigilant critical intervention can work to uncover the possibilities that are indexed and thereby breathe new life into areas of cultural production where critical discourse has previously been foreclosed. Diagnosis of the *indexical image* often contains a certain irony; like photography, cinema has an inherent 'indexicality' of the 'thisness' of its object[4] but the *indexical image* is often of something other than the concentrationary. The task of concentrationary memory is to show that it is possible that the 'thisness' of the image ('this is a factory', for example) is a concentrationary 'thisness', hitherto undiagnosed or *seen* as such. It is important to recognize that such an investigation does not create immediate or simplistic comparatives; a factory is not a camp, but something about it and/or its representation may be haunted by the concentrationary.

The third order of the concentrationary image can be closely allied to the first two but differs by a small, perhaps immeasurable, factor of amnesia. This type of image is indicative of an imaginary that acknowledges (imagines) 'everything is possible' (the phrase is Rousset's shattering definition of the horror of the concentrationary universe repeated and taken up by Hannah Arendt to define total domination), but has forgotten that it is the horror of the camps that has made everything possible. Thus, the image is produced by a certain logic and under principles that, in the sphere of cultural production, have fundamental affinities with the logic and principles of those who created the conditions and priorities of the camp, albeit in the imagination and not as acted out policy. The 'philosophical' logic and assumptions of Josef Mengele are often *repeated* in this type of image, even when it seems as if they are being addressed. The *amnesiac image* goes beyond the *indexical image* in that it occurs in a realm of pure cinematic production where the special *effect* trumps any genuine *affect* and society is not so much reflected as erased and produced again in the ideological terms of cinematic frisson. The *amnesiac image* is not necessarily an absence (although it can be); instead a referential (*citational/indexical*) image may be presented but it becomes also amnesiac when it is stripped of its full resonance. Having defined three image modes I want, however, to stress that these categories are tools to aid analysis. They cannot be understood as rigid principles governing any one image. An *amnesiac* element is almost always present within the citation and index.

Concentrationary seep and concentrationary creep

I have extended this initial taxonomy of the image with a proposal about the modes of dissemination and effect of the images. Concentrationary seep and concentrationary creep are terminologies that I have developed to describe the mechanisms by which 'the concentrationary universe' is transmitted and extended into areas beyond its own geographical borders and historical formation. The terms are to be used in conjunction with the three orders of the image so that the arrival and appearance of the different images can be understood; they may have seeped or crept into a film. These mechanisms are not exclusive to either film or society but are common to both. To start with, it can be broadly stated that 'seeping' is a passive principle which acts by a process which might be described as 'osmotic' whereas 'creep' indicates a more active principle.

'Seeping' may seem to have an inevitable logic to it. In political terms, its insidiousness is not unrelated to the Hitlerian imperialist logic of the claim for 'Lebensraum'; that is, a political expansionism. In another sense, however, it relates to the retrospective discovery of the spread of a hidden disease whose progress was undetected through its unnoticed dissemination by contagion. Finally, at the level of personal or even cultural awareness of changing conditions, seep evokes the famous anecdote of a frog in boiling water. A frog placed in cold water that is then gradually heated, does not notice the increase in temperature around it until it has become fatally hot and the creature is boiled to death. In the same way, concentrationary seep means that the conditions of existence within which a people or a society are couched (and this is inextricable at times from what is called 'the society' itself), become incrementally suffused with the conditions of the concentrationary, perhaps also to a point where it is too late to turn the tide (without revolution or violent resistance).

In a lecture delivered at the University of Leeds, Samuel Weber summarizes Italian philosopher Giorgio Agamben's structural argument about the camps in the following way. The camps are, according to Weber, 'the provision of a durable institution through which the State of Exception could become the rule'.[5] Picking up on the suggestion by Pollock and Silverman that an unrecognized 'concentrationary imaginary' might be *seeping* into culture, which was the initial provocation for a conference to which he was invited in 2011, Samuel Weber embraces the idea of 'seepage', but cautiously. He challenges any face-value acceptance of the notion by which, through employing words such as 'seepage', critical analysis inevitably reinforces the same logic which places such 'institutions' at some distance: 'such an inside-outside dichotomy which could be taken to inform notions such as seepage might itself be part of the problem to be analysed'.[6] On one level, this statement seems to be redundant in that the premise of this argument is that which appeared to be locked inside another universe (for example, the concentrationary which we here note can be categorized as an institution), escapes the perimeters of institutions and enters the wider world. Nearly all movies based around institutions of any sort exhibit, at some level of their narrative interest, the potential of escaping and thus taking up a position outside of that institution. Weber's comment warns us about our use of language in forming this critical discourse – that it should never be seduced into accepting its own critical logic of 'inside and outside' and in resting on terms that have a concrete appearance but which, in reality, describe amorphous territories and blurred edges. Perhaps we could then propose that the predominant mechanism by which a *concentrationary imaginary* pervades non-institutional sites such as culture as a whole, or cinema in particular, is by means of a seepage of concentrationary elements. [Seepage causes an internalization by these cultural or cinematic forms of those 'un-thought' elements through which the concentrationary effect gets its existence and foothold, by which, in turn, it functions as an internal logic of the work.]

Concentrationary 'creep' may, however, be closer to the linguistic truth of the matter in that, just as the 'state of exception' violates its original purpose and boundaries to 'become the rule', 'creep' indicates a similar 'extension' of an originary remit. Here, I am working closely with the carefully mapped out writing of Agamben who notes both this 'overspill' phenomenon and its ironic outcome: 'When life and politics – originally divided, and linked together by means of the no-man's land of the state of exception that is inhabited by bare life – begin to become one, all life becomes sacred and all politics becomes the exception.'[7] Agamben's point as to where this leads in terms of the concentrationary is clear: 'The camp – as the pure, absolute, and impassable political space (insofar as it is founded solely on the state of exception) – will appear as the hidden paradigm of the political space of modernity, whose metamorphoses and disguises we will have to learn to recognise.'[8]

The idea of agency implied by the verb/noun 'creep' also makes it more difficult for the question of responsibility to be avoided. The aptness of the term 'creep', then, becomes apparent when we look at the origins of the term 'mission creep' from which I borrow the notion:

> Originating in Somalia in 1993, the modern term 'mission creep' became part of official U.S. Army vocabulary a decade later. Field Manual 3-07, *Stability Operations and Support Operations* (February 2003) acknowledges two types of mission creep. The first occurs when 'the unit receives shifting guidance or a change in mission

for which the unit is not properly configured or resourced.' The second occurs 'when a unit attempts to do more than is allowed in the current mandate and mission.'[9]

Mission creep is directly connected to a spread of a network of militarized spaces around the globe. US bases, such as that at Menwith Hill in North Yorkshire, are spaces where sovereignty (of the 'host' nation) is suspended. The American policy of 'creeping' over the surface of the globe through such spatial installations is discussed in an article entitled 'America's Global Military Presence: Mission Creep', where the specific manifestation in Africa is described:

> In Africa, where the military is establishing a new command called AFRICOM, the Pentagon is busy planting lily pads, officially 'Cooperative Security Locations.' US troops can use these low-key outposts to stash weapons and supplies, and to train local forces. In a crisis, boom! They can convert to a real wartime base.[10]

Coded use of language ('lily pads', 'cooperative security locations') indicates an attempt to obscure the potentiality that is embedded in these creeping spaces of exception. I want to make an imaginative leap from the reality of mission creep that is happening on the Earth today and the practice of 'concentrationary creep' that enables us to identify hitherto unnamed tendencies within cultural production that are related to the political ground of the extension of the states of exception while working on and through the cinematic imaginary. If the contemporary political, globalized, militarized situation can be characterized in this way with pockets of exception primed to burst through their boundaries, the visions presented by filmmakers may also, with more or less responsibility and ethical/aesthetic integrity, act in the same way.

I argue, therefore, that concentrationary *seep* and *creep* are ways in which the concentrationary universe 'haunts' other universes that we may have been seduced into thinking were inviolable or uncontaminated by its spectre. The boundaries of the concentrationary universe (a radical space set apart), and the 'normal' universe (the everyday), are seen to be, to some extent, illusory since they have always been porous.[11] This may be the greatest irony of the recycled image of the concentration camp in the common imagination (no doubt to the political advantage of those who maintain power through such concentration) in that the image of the concentrationary is linked to barriers, fences and separations. In fact, it may be truer to say that, rather than 'beginning' to haunt beyond its own space, the concentrationary is always already beyond any confines. This then makes sense of the proposition that certain images and ways of imagining make reference to, and are imbued by, the concentrationary universe without this being the intention of the production of the image.

Using the mirror of what Pollock and Silverman are naming concentrationary memory and its vigilance – in the sense of an opposition to the concentrationary – I aim to shine a light on social anxieties and cultural structures as they are represented in film and which can be revealed through an analysis of the seep and creep of a concentrationary imaginary. The film in question is *Shutter Island* in which the concentrationary effect exceeds the reference to 'Dachau' with which I began.

Synopsis of *Shutter Island*

In 1954, Federal Agent Teddy Daniels (Leonardo DiCaprio), a veteran of the Allied liberation of Dachau, and his new partner, Chuck (Mark Ruffalo), travel to Shutter Island, the site of a secure psychiatric unit for the criminally insane. They are investigating the impossible and mysterious disappearance of one of the prisoners, Rachel Solando, who was guilty of killing her three children. The two agents get stranded on the island when it is hit by a freak hurricane. Meanwhile, Daniels seems to uncover a conspiracy of sanctioned human experimentation and he fears he will never be allowed to leave the island. He reveals to Chuck that he had arranged to be put onto this assignment because he knew that Andrew Laeddis, an arsonist who killed Daniels's wife Dolores, was imprisoned on the island, probably in the sinister Ward C. Chuck disappears and Daniels is told that Chuck had never existed and that he (Daniels) arrived on the island alone. Eventually, after many sinister episodes and attempts at breaking mysterious codes and layers of conspiracy, the story unfolds with a final twist. It turns out that Daniels was in fact a patient on the island and all that had happened in the film was part of an elaborate attempt at narrative therapy whereby Dr Cawley (Ben Kingsley) allowed Daniels to 'act out' his habitual fantasy. Daniels is in fact Andrew Laeddis, who killed his wife after she had murdered their three children. Daniels appears to submit to the lobotomizing procedure that, as an extremely dangerous patient, he was sentenced to undergo if Cawley's experiment did not work. The ending is ambiguous because it is not clear whether Daniels is still fantasizing or whether he is submitting with a clear mind. The narrative of this psychological thriller allows the filmmaker to utilize many flashback and hallucinatory effects.

Trauma, creep, seep and amnesia

A full exploration of theories of trauma is not the remit of this chapter. Nevertheless, certain aspects of trauma are relevant for the current argument. Insofar as trauma has become a theme of current analyses of aesthetic representation, it is often paradoxically signified by images which are themselves already pre-digested signifiers of an 'already known' shock to the system. Of course, such substitution of an image of an atrocious or traumatic event fundamentally ignores the 'unknowable' character of trauma – precisely what bypasses both cognition and fantasy – and replaces its void with something, the sole *raison d'être* of which, from the point of view of the creators of the film, the art or whatever, is precisely that it *will be recognized by the viewers for its traumatic referent*. Similar, or even the same, chains of mis- and re-signification can sometimes operate as a swirling *concentrationary imaginary* when images are severed from their provenance and historical moment. In certain cases, the images, which stand in for a traumatic event, are used in a sophisticated manner. Unlike the (in many ways illuminating) naivety of the ruptures in which something of the concentrationary breaks through in some less 'self knowing' films (my example would be *Pink Floyd: The Wall* (Sir Alan Parker, 1982) which I have discussed in another volume in this series), such films are aware of the theoretical discourses they rely upon and utilize.[12] This use of theoretical discourse is again the key to my argument that amnesia is the dominant form of the concentrationary image in *Shutter Island* since the very act of proclaiming a 'visibility' and a 'knowability' in this way – the referencing of a famous camp by means of recycling famous images of its gate or of the atrocity of the frozen bodies in the railcars filmed by George Stevens and photographed by many others – in fact, produces an occlusion. Far from becoming illuminating, the evocation of the image becomes an amnesiac image. Thus, in *Shutter Island* and its 'unfaithful' representation of Dachau, we learn nothing about Dachau. Instead we are provided with an 'idea' represented by a name and an iconic image of Dachau that furthers the film for the film's own sake. Not only is the historical specificity of Dachau overlaid, but the affect of history is manipulated in relation to the film's current narrative. Occlusion and amnesia are not total. They operate on different levels and upon a scale of references wherein an image is used to trigger associations other than those by which the image was originally generated. [This represents an incidence of concentrationary creep, its hallmark being the extension of an original's remit with the loss of the referent.] The *amnesiac image* also possesses qualities similar to those 'materials of memory' outlined by Crownshaw in his summary of the theories of Ann Rigney:

> The materials of memory must be subject to a continual symbolic investment for them to retain their memorative value, and their form may not always be appropriate to the events remembered or how they should be remembered, potentially leading to their modification, convergence with other materials and media of memory, or de-selection in favour of alternatives from the archive of latent cultural objects awaiting significant and symbolically invested circulation.[13]

There are several elements in this quotation which are relevant to the operation of the amnesiac image and which seem to pitch 'cultural memory' against 'concentrationary memory'. Cultural memory, in the way it is described in Crownshaw's sentence, is contained in 'materials' (in this case, images or a stock of images) that are, in turn, reliant on a symbolic investment. But this investment has the potential to become misplaced and appropriated to the inappropriate. These materials are also at risk of being 'de-selected' and such de-selection has a relation to the idea of 'narrative fetishism'. I shall discuss all of these theories and elements and the way in which they relate to the idea of an 'amnesiac concentrationary image' in the context of a reading of *Shutter Island*.

Before turning to the filmic text, however, it will be helpful to see it as existing, as a cultural product, in a space that, in terms of theory, can be read equally in differing ways. The oscillation between memory, forgetting and amnesia needs to be looked at in more detail. In the article to which Crownshaw makes reference above, Rigney rightly talks of memory as being the 'product of representations' and is hence always 'vicarious'.[14] She goes on to suggest that there is a scarcity about culture in relation to the total that could *possibly* be said or produced. This creates an interesting nexus with regard to the way in which cultural production can be part of a plethora of on-going production that takes one far away from the originary 'event' and thus might be seen to be on the side of misappropriation, occlusion and forgetting. On the other hand, the production of cultural forms in response to (or *inspired by*) an event, can be read as the ability to engender an ever-expanding life and proliferation of memory. I have argued elsewhere in an exploration of Picasso's painting *Guernica*, that cultural memory can be conceived as the surplus of an event.[15] In such a reading, the afterlives and re-appropriations of a work such as *Guernica* work in the opposite way to a plenitude and scarcity model. The work spreads into the future from its originary event in the manner of a kind of 'active haunting'. There is a certain idealism in this reading but it should be posited against models which negatively privilege the embodiment of forgetting in all that is produced.

Shutter Island operates on a teleological level and, like all films that rely heavily upon a narrative disclosure or twist in the denouement, the second time of watching is a completely different experience from the first. In fact, a second viewing is almost necessary so that the significance of what we see and now know can be appreciated. For example, the apparently innocuous initial comment Chuck makes to Daniels about his seasickness – 'doesn't exactly square with Teddy Daniels, the man, the legend, I'll give you that' – becomes freighted with significance. Almost every subsequent utterance, glance or gesture is charged with further interest on a second viewing. It is only then that we see the fragility of the fantasy as both 'sides' attempt to maintain it. In the film there are at least seven 'flashback' scenes in which Teddy Daniels 'remembers' the liberation of Dachau (depending on whether one distinguishes between the same recollection interrupted by a brief shot) (6.1) These are seemingly triggered by various Proustian instances, such as Brahms playing on the gramophone. On the surface, they take on the characteristics of an originary 'trauma' in the narrative of the film.[16]

This apparently initial 'traumatic' moment is treated, however, precisely as a trope of trauma – it is posited as a knowable *beginning* in the metanarrative of the film, a moment which is preceded by nothing and which purportedly carries an explanatory power with regard to the rest of the narrative. It is also utilized in the manner of an archive, with a built-in retrieval system, and becomes, as Crownshaw says in the quotation above, part of the 'archive of latent cultural objects awaiting significant and symbolically invested circulation'. In this instance, the

6.1   *Shutter Island* (Scorsese, 2011): Flashback of Dachau using the *Arbeit Macht Frei* Gate from Auschwitz.

liberation of Dachau and a recycling of *citational* images becomes the part of the archive that has been selected for its use in the service of the various narratives that 'sit on top' of it. This is a variation of narrative fetishism, a phenomenon described by Eric Santner as 'the construction or deployment of a narrative consciously or unconsciously designed to expunge the traces of the trauma or loss that called that narrative into being in the first place'.[17] Santner opposes narrative fetishism to the 'symbolic behaviour' that is the Freudian 'work of mourning'.[18] Indeed, the plot of *Shutter Island* revolves around the stories and narratives that Teddy Daniels has concocted and lives by and which occlude for him the traumatic 'truth' that his wife drowned their babies and he subsequently shot her. The liberation of Dachau is thereby positioned as the original trauma that caused 'Teddy'/Andrew to become a heavy drinker, distanced from his wife and her needs. It is thereby posited as the place and moment which makes him culpable.

The liberation of Dachau occurred (or began) on 29 April 1945 when troops of the 3rd Battalion, 157th Infantry Regiment of the US Thunderbird Division entered the camp and discovered the atrocious conditions, the piles of corpses and the emaciated survivors (those who were not amongst the 10,000 prisoners forcibly evacuated on 26 April). The camp, located 10 miles northwest of Munich, was the first established under National Socialist rule in 1933 as a camp for political prisoners.[19] From this point until its liberation the camp grew vastly in size and the constitution of its inmates, with the installation of 150 subsidiary camps in 1942. By 1944 there were more than 63,000 prisoners in Dachau, living and dying in conditions of severe malnutrition and a typhus epidemic.[20]

It is difficult to be entirely sure of the exact nature of the filmic evidence of the liberation of Dachau and its subsequent relationship with the *citational* images in *Shutter Island*. The photographer Lee Miller was there on 30 April and George Stevens also recorded the camp at the beginning of May. Some film from 27 April shows American troops moving through woods and this is not dissimilar to the depiction of Daniels's unit in *Shutter Island*, except that it is neither snowing nor dark in this footage.[21] In the film *D-Day to Berlin*, consisting of Stevens's footage, the Dachau material (about four minutes in total) is introduced in the narration when 'Stevens' unit received orders to march south through Germany to Bavaria', but it is not specified exactly when the film was taken. Certainly Stevens seems to have arrived in Dachau not before the evening of the official day of liberation.[22] This footage, along with that which forms part of the film *Memory of the Camps*, is clearly influential on the representations of Daniels's memory.[23] Open cattle trucks have piles of bodies spilling out of them and piles of bodies also have snow on them. This fact is corroborated in other photographic sources.[24] It is not certain, however, that it was snowing on 29 April, nor that the severe ice that locks in the bodies in *Shutter Island*, was actually present. Of course, this could be seen as the representation of a memory and, therefore, subject to construction and unintended imaginative embellishment. Further slippages happen in Scorsese's reconstruction: the '*Arbeit Macht Frei*' wrought metal gateway of Daniels's Dachau and the gateway itself, is from Auschwitz I rather than Dachau (more iconographic for the film's audience?)[25] (6.1 and 6.2).

A recurring theme of Daniels's memory is that of the emaciated, drawn inmates looking out through the barbed wire (6.3). This clearly recalls a famous photograph taken by Margaret Bourke-White. Bourke-White's image was in fact taken at Buchenwald (a corresponding shot was not taken by Miller). Stevens's Dachau footage, which contains the same elements (prisoners gathered behind the wire), shows joyful and laughing survivors (6.4). There is, thus, an imbrication of images, historical specificity and the representation of memory. In itself this shows the (amnesiac) slippages that can occur with the *citational* image

6.2 *Arbeit Macht Frei* Gate at Dachau concentration camp, photograph (Arbeit Macht Frei Dachau 8235).

and how a certain amount of internal seepage can occur with the use of the archive.

Shutter Island is a cultural product and becomes itself, as a text, the site of a kind of metanarrative fetishism. In order to produce a cinematic effect, to affect the viewer, the narrative of the liberation of Dachau, signified by a recycling of images already in existence, is treated as a known,

6.3 *Shutter Island* (Scorsese, 2011): Flashbacks of prisoners at Dachau camp.

6.4 Margaret Bourke-White, *Survivors at Buchenwald, April 1945* (Getty Images).

pre-digested signifier of the traumatic. Teddy Daniels's memories are not only fictions within the film but they serve as a greater fiction on the meta-level of the film's consumption. Dachau is a convenience upon which the story of greater ideological effect is superimposed. This story is that of murderousness harboured within the great and perfect ideal of the American family (in this case, as in most, a family constituted by singularly beautiful elements). That the traumatic experience of being exposed to Dachau is shown to be the cause of this shocking rupture is a further displacement that again operates at the level of the seeing subject. Daniels/Laeddis has seen what we as spectators also apparently see and he later superimposes his family into Dachau and all this places more layers between the focus of the film and any experience *of* Dachau (as an internee for example). Daniels/Laeddis hallucinates and in his hallucinations his own children are amongst the dead frozen in ice at Dachau. This is a literal blurring and embellishment of the two narratives, which in itself indicates the ideological parcelling out of history and psychic events into narrative forms.[26] It could be argued that such scenes indicate the film's awareness of the problems of a lack of working through, and they may be true to the manifestation and structures of post-traumatic hallucinatory experiences (there is not necessarily an ethical problem with embellishment of such a memory in this sense). It is, however, the very fact that the film refers self-consciously to theories of trauma that engenders a very deep problem.[27] This problem leads us back to narrative fetishism once again – although here the narrative that is presented contains the traumatic event as a blatant part of the very surface by which it now presents itself. It is as if the event had been fully and satisfactorily worked through and can now be treated as a source of renewable material for fresh narratives. Renewable and recyclable, Dachau hits two marketable buzzwords for a commodity. Dachau itself is, however, occluded and excluded from the scene by means of its very 'inclusion' as image for the trope of explanatory trauma. In this schema there is the illusion that there is no longer any real event somewhere in history that needs working through or mourning – all that is left is the conflict of the representations of ideologies (the film industry as a competitive conflict of representations) and the production of affects (with a market and a box office in mind). As Godard says, looking directly at the camera in part 1B of *Histoire(s) du Cinéma*, 'It boils down to entertainment. It can't be explained otherwise.'[28]

It is interesting to view the treatment of the representation of the scenes of the liberation of Dachau in *Shutter Island* in the light of what Gillian Rose calls 'Holocaust Piety', which requires a distinction between the 'representation of fascism' and the 'fascism of representation'.[29] The 'representation of fascism'

> leaves the identity of the voyeur intact, at a remove from the grievous events which she observes. Her self-defences remain untouched, while she may feel *exultant revulsion* or *infinite pity* for those whose fate is displayed.[30]

The 'fascism of representation' is thus defined:

> beyond the limit of voyeurism, [it] provokes the grief of encountering the violence normally legitimised by individual moral will, with which we defend our own particular interests, and see only the

egoism of the other – these may be the interests of disinterested service, race, gender, religion, class. This grief expresses the crisis of the dissolution of particular identity and the vision of the universal. Across the unprotected exposure of our singularity, of our otherness to ourselves, the 'we', which we otherwise so partially and carelessly assume.[31]

Holocaust piety occurs with the conflation or misrecognition of the intimacy between, the two. In many ways *Shutter Island* sidesteps the problematic that Rose posits. There is, however, all the more reason to question the film because of this. Scorsese *represents* the liberation of Dachau as a subjectively embedded memory flashback or a dream that is pertinent to the specific individual phenomenological state of Teddy Daniels/Andrew Laeddis, thus releasing the treatment of a historical image from the primary injunction to be 'authentic'.

Scorsese stays well within the 'limits of representation' as there is no attempt to represent the 'unwitnessed' events of the Holocaust or areas for which documentary evidence does not provide 'inspiration'. On the other hand, through choosing the *concentrationary* topic of Dachau as the trope which stands in for an original trauma (Dachau itself becoming the amnesiac image of the invisible exterminatory), Scorsese's film touches on the very heart of what concerns Rose and presents its own unanswered questions. It is not the dreamlike, 'inaccurate' representation of the camp that is the problem. Rose's complex argument about the nature of representation and its inherent relationship with fascism is clear from the outset that representation is necessary for its inherently human (and thereby 'flawed') nature which provides (when approached by a sufficiently critical and open mind) a mirror by which its own flaws can be made visible: 'Only the persistence of always fallible and contestable representation opens the possibility for our acknowledgement of mutual implication in the fascism of our cultural rites and rituals.'[32] The necessity of contestability is demonstrated here and the notion of a *concentrationary imaginary* is a tool for use in the field of contestability. Without the cultural production itself (*Shutter Island*) the readability and visibility of what such films emerge from and reflect (society) is impossible to attain. It is for this reason that films cannot be dismissed out of hand for what they represent. Instead, we might begin to see the *concentrationary imaginary* as existing at a step beyond the representative directness of *Schindler's List*

(Spielberg, 1993) (which carried its own pedagogical agenda). Here it is as if the lessons have been entirely absorbed and there is no longer a question in the air to be dealt with. Rose positions the viewer of film (in a gesture related to the Lacanian model) as the 'ultimate predator',[33] distanced and able to sympathize safely or [identify and sentimentalize] in a detached manner with characters, situations or narrative elements.

In *Shutter Island* the spectator is left in an even safer place regarding the concentrationary scenes presented. The complacency revolves around the amnesiac and deadened images of Dachau, which are distanced in affect and in the narrative trajectory under several layers of fetishized narrative. The meta-position of the spectator is simply one who knows Dachau as a stand-in for trauma; it is beyond complacency even the first time around but the teleological knowledge of a second viewing, when one knows the 'secret', rewards the viewer with an even greater self-congratulatory sense. The film operates from *within* a pre-processed, overarching *concentrationary imaginary* that assumes the pre-digested understanding of the history it touches on for its own ends. In other words, the silent osmotic process of concentrationary seep has begun to saturate the conditions and attitudes from which this film emerges. The self-reflexivity that is in evidence (even if it does not reflect to the greatest degree or depth possible – there is no reflection, for example on the manner or ethics of the use of trauma theory as an aesthetic tool) does show that the film is not produced in a totally saturated imaginary. What we might regard as an element of the concentrationary has, however, crept past some major blindspots in this self-reflexivity in the form of a certain type of thought*lessness*.

All of this is ambiguous territory in the sense that one does not want to prescribe a certain manner of representation and there is no reason for a film about individual trauma not to be made. There is a tiny moment in *Shutter Island*, however, which can be read in terms which bring us back to the ethical dilemmas at the heart of the arguments of Gillian Rose, Bryan Cheyette and Jean-François Lyotard, and, indeed, to the debate between Godard and Lanzmann (highlighted by Libby Saxton and focusing on the potentially hypothetical 'missing reel').[34] In her extremely perspicacious commentary on the mechanisms of cinematic identification around which she builds her argument, Rose draws our attention to a particular moment in *Schindler's List* which, for her, has the characteristics of a 'point of no return':

6.5 *Schindler's List* (Spielberg, 1993): Auschwitz-Birkenau shower scene.

After the scene of the excursion to Auschwitz, the film is degraded: the salvific waters which issue from the shower heads, as Bryan Cheyette points out, cause a crisis in the viewer who is suspended from the limit of the decency of witness. I would suggest that, from that point, there is no decent position: water not gas – to show that death agonies would exceed the limits of permissible representation; but water not gas induces the regressive identification ('philosophic innocence'?) with the few women who are saved.[35]

The device of a very similar identification is 'played with' 93.5 minutes into *Shutter Island* when the camera (and thereby the subject-position of the spectator) looks straight up into a showerhead which immediately emits water (6.4). Daniels/Laeddis is having a shower and, at this point, the politics of identification are manipulated to great effect by the filmmakers. A momentary shock occurs at this moment that hardly exists in the temporal sense. As spectators, we are caught for a split second beneath the showerhead before it emits water. It is not enough time to think (there is no lingering of the camera to force one to *think* about what one is seeing) but it is a perfectly calculated piece of editing designed to induce a frisson of shock. And this shock, I will argue, is unethically related to the 'crisis point' in *Schindler's List* (6.5).

It is necessary to wonder what is going on with this image and the sequence of which it is a part in the light of the concept of the amnesiac image. I suggest that, in the context of a film which already contains a

6.6 *Shutter Island* (Scorsese, 2011): Shower.

direct 'concentrationary' theme, also references other movies throughout (particularly Miloš Foreman's *One Flew Over the Cuckoo's Nest*, 1975) and, given when it occurs within the plot line, this momentary image of the shower cannot but contain within it the image of the 'salvific' waters of *Schindler's List*. This brings with it a series of ethical problems related to the *concentrationary imaginary* and the amnesiac image in particular. The shower is shown within the institutional context that we have previously been led to believe that Daniels/Laeddis is on the verge of exposing. His experiences have been shown, however, in a more and more hallucinatory manner. Daniels/Laeddis is beginning to be stripped of his sure identity and our sure identification with him. Doubt has been cast as to whether he did indeed have a partner with him on the island. The identification of the spectator is still solicited by the filmmakers for Daniels/Laeddis and the *politics/manipulation* of identification mean that the spectator is likely to believe that the *institution/system* is trying to hoodwink the individual. The film is very clever in its construction, however, and with the cut to the showerhead we are left with the stripping away of sure identity within a hostile, confusing, possibly deceptive institutional environment. Since something of the concentrationary universe has been suggested to the spectator through flashbacks, the moment the shower comes on is laden with an allusive tension to the dark core of that universe.[36]

Not only does Scorsese present an unjustifiable allusion to an un-witnessed event, but this allusion is in fact not directed to the event but to an already dubious representation in the history of cinema – the shower scene in *Schindler's List*, a moment that, for Rose, possesses a 'regressive' quality. Furthermore, it is the simplicity of analogy to which Scorsese appeals and this analogy is merely a surface that relies upon a series of semi-conscious associations; the relief felt by the spectator is a relief on behalf of Daniels/Laeddis with whom we desire to sympathize (and in fact this desire is never fully quenched, his 'terrible crime' is always ringed around with an air of justification). This image of the showerhead, followed by the 'healthy' cleansed naked body of Daniels/Laeddis, is possessed of the qualities of the amnesiac image which precisely forgets what it contains and where it comes from merely in order to produce pure affect. In the worst possible sense of a postmodern valorization of the notion of 'play', Scorsese does not wrestle with any ethical position, even to the degree, we must presume, that Spielberg did.[37] Instead, the film uses the device of an overlay of referential narrative layers that, however sophisticated they might be (and indeed this sophistication is part of the problem), avoid or occlude the ethical issue at the centre of what they show.

If we suggest that the glut of referential imagery and the surfeit of potential chains of meaning invoked by this shower sequence are examples of the *concentrationary imaginary*, it goes to show the amnesia of the images that can accompany their deployment. The showerhead is an overdetermined image that relies upon a particular identification on the part of the spectator. Concomitant with the politics of identification (with the supreme predator) discussed by Rose, the narrative relies on the spectator being able to identify the reference that is being made (even if this is on a 'subliminal' level). The reference 'forgets' the gas chambers in the death camps which have never been filmed and of which there is no true witness but 'remembers' a film that is itself compromised by showing this very moment. Thus, the substitution is complete in a suturing of forgetfulness where the 'affect' of something horrible is produced – the signifier reigns. In *Shutter Island* the shock is produced by the concentrationary not because of what the concentrationary image 'means' in and of itself but because the concentrationary is a signifier of something shocking – in fact just shock itself.

It should be acknowledged that, in using the example above which brings into play the idea of the 'missing reel/real', there is a risk that we are ourselves conflating the 'concentrationary' and the 'exterminatory'. It is, however, part of the nature of the amnesiac image to conflate the two – concentrationary seep is not a nuanced process and the exterminatory which occurred within the larger frame of the concentrationary is not distinguished in the popular cinematic cultural productions which contain the amnesiac image. I am not discussing the exterminatory image in order to compound this non-distinction but, hopefully, to make various things visible so that distinctions can then be made. It is an irony of the concept of haunting that, although it relies itself on an ability to eliminate boundaries (the idea of a ghost being able to pass through walls), it does so often with the aim of eventual clarification and laying the ghost to rest: 'Nothing could be worse, for the work of mourning, than confusion or doubt: one *has to know* who is buried where – and *it is necessary* (to know – to make certain) that, in what remains of him, *he remain there*. Let him stay there and move no more!'[38]

This statement contains an acknowledgement that such closure is unattainable in the world. It is particularly unattainable in the sphere of studying the concentrationary, which has (unlike the carceral) no correlation with any form or structure of justice (even a form of justice or law that is *produced* from an unjust basis, thus resulting in unfair convictions). The images of the camps, journalistic photographs, 'liberation' footage, and the scraps of 'evidence' become elements that can be re-circulated and, as such, are ghostly, haunting elements. A 'Huyssenian' gap or fissure appears which is the gap wherein *representation* occurs in the form of cultural production; representation is the stuff of life. We should not be too hasty in condemning cultural products in this sense; rather, we should look at the nature of the constructions that are made from the materials. This, in a quite simple and perhaps banal sense, brings the haunting capacity of the element from the past (sometimes stored in an archival form) right up to the here and now (the point of production and the point of reception of the 'new' film, work of art and so on): 'The more memory we store on our data banks, the more the past is sucked into the orbit of the present, ready to be called up on screen.'[39]

As Huyssen also states: 'The past is not simply there in memory, but it must be articulated to become memory.'[40] In the quest for concentrationary memory – a vigilant and anxious act of resistance to concentrationary seep and creep – the manner of such articulations must be taken as they appear; popular culture cannot be prescribed but only observed and re-articulated to identify the operations of a *concentrationary imaginary* and the nature of both the amnesia and occlusion which this effects.

The re-articulation provides new 'joints' for the time that is 'out of joint' and it allows in the ghost and the Memory. Thus, even *Shutter Island*,with its flaws and its amnesia, can be a bearer of some memory; the restlessness of the concentrationary injustice (in fact, the lack of the notion of justice) inhabits and haunts the most occluding of narratively fetishized images and productions.

7

HANEKE AND THE CAMPS

Max Silverman

The image and the camp

In his famous article, written in 1992, on Gillo Pontecorvo's film *Kapò* (1960) about the concentration camps, the French art and film critic Serge Daney criticizes Pontecorvo's aestheticization of death in a particular tracking shot in the film.[1] Despite admitting to never having himself seen *Kapò*, Daney is inspired to write about it because of an earlier condemnation of the film by the director Jacques Rivette in a brief article published in *Cahiers du cinéma* in 1961 entitled 'De l'abjection' ('On abjection').[2] Daney takes up Rivette's critique by suggesting that the tracking shot, which ends up with a close-up image of an internee, played by the actress Emmanuelle Riva, electrified on the barbed wire of the camp, was a step too far for

> inconsiderately abolishing a distance [Pontecorvo] should have 'kept'. The tracking shot was immoral for the simple reason that it was putting us – him filmmaker and me spectator – in a place where we did not belong.[3]

As a counter to this 'step too far', Daney, like Rivette, posits Alain Resnais's film about the camps, *Night and Fog* (*Nuit et brouillard*), which appeared four years before Pontecorvo's film, in 1955. According to Daney, the major difference between Resnais's treatment of the image and that of Pontecorvo is that Resnais puts a 'stop' on the image and, in that crucial moment, avoids the aestheticization of horror, thus respecting Adorno's injunction about art after Auschwitz. In Rivette's words, *Kapò* allows us to become 'accustomed to the horror, which little by little is accepted by morality, and will quickly become part of the mental landscape of modern man', yet 'you cannot accustom yourself to *Night and Fog*'.[4]

Daney's essay is both a celebration of the ability of cinema to warn us of the persistence of horror in these post-war years and, in the second part of the essay, a lament on the demise of cinema in the decades following, overtaken by television and the endless manipulation of images for entertainment and profit. As Daney says:

> [T]he stop on the image has ceased to operate; the banality of evil can launch new, electronic images ... The images are no longer on the side of the dialectical truth of 'seeing' and 'showing'; they have entirely shifted to the side of promotion and advertising, the side of power.[5]

Daney bemoans the aestheticization and banalization of structures of inhumanity through the endless repetition of gestures of inhumanity that have inured us to the menace of real horror. In other words, what Daney movingly describes as the necessary stop on the image to allow for seeing beyond the surface and the reading of a complex history has been overtaken by the impulse behind Pontecorvo's tracking shot to fix the image within a banalized and commodified aesthetic.

The idea of a concentrationary imaginary that has been assimilated unknowingly into popular culture, that Griselda Pollock and I are attempting to articulate in this book, has close links with the arguments made by Rivette and Daney on the distinction between *Night and Fog* and *Kapò*: the horror to which we cannot accustom ourselves in *Night and Fog* and that *Kapò* aestheticizes has, as Rivette says, 'quickly become part of the mental landscape of modern man'. Daney suggests that this marks the evolution of cinema in the post-war period: the conditions under which Resnais (and his collaborators Jean Cayrol, Hans Eisler and Chris Marker) were operating in 1955 are radically different from those today, thus altering the parameters for any critical intervention into the field of representing horror. The spectacularization and commercialization of extreme violence through new digital technologies of image fabrication and transmission have blurred the frontiers between real violence and entertainment and reshaped our imaginary of violence.

Daney is certainly not alone in viewing the image in contemporary culture in such bleak terms, as the work of Jean Baudrillard, Paul Virilio, Bernard Stiegler and many others clearly demonstrates. Though not specifically about the role of the image today, Giorgio Agamben's post-Foucauldian thesis on the camp as the new *nomos* of the modern similarly engages with forms of dehumanization today which have become assimilated into the familiar landscape of everyday life. Agamben suggests that attention to the juridico-political structures of the camp rather than to the historical events which took place in concentration camps 'will lead us to regard the camp not as a historical fact and an anomaly belonging to the past (even if still verifiable) but in some way as the hidden matrix and *nomos* of the political space in which we are still living'.[6] If Daney sees the persistence of evil in new digitalized images today, Agamben seeks to open up the everyday to the persistence of camp life. In this sense, they describe two linked but different ways in which the presence of horror is embedded in everyday structures today: for Agamben, the camp as 'the new *nomos* of the modern' defines a new political ethos, while for Daney, the electronic image as the contemporary vehicle for the banality of evil defines a new cultural imaginary.

In this chapter I will discuss two films by the Austrian director Michael Haneke – *Funny Games* (1997, remade in Hollywood in 2007) and *Das weiße Band – Eine deutsche Kindergeschichte* (*The White Ribbon*) (2009). Haneke's films, in general, constitute a serious reflection on the relations between violence, politics and the image today, while simultaneously running the risk of reinforcing the very links that the films are, ostensibly, challenging. My discussion of *Funny Games* and *The White Ribbon* will suggest that, by reinvesting the image with a complex history in relation to extreme violence, Haneke responds to the twin concerns expressed by Daney and Agamben and counters Daney's bleak assessment of the demise of cinema in an age of new technologies of the image.

Exposing violence: *Funny Games* and *The White Ribbon*

The storyline of *Funny Games* is fairly simple: a bourgeois couple, Anna and Georg Schober, their son (also Georg) and their dog arrive at their lakeside holiday home and are then subjected to a series of sadistic games by two young men, Peter and Paul (who also refer to each other in the film as cartoon characters Beavis and Butthead and Tom and Jerry). The games format is introduced in the opening scene, however, before we meet Peter and Paul: driving to their holiday home, Anna and Georg are guessing titles and composers of pieces of classical music. Their game includes the familiar catchphrases 'my turn now', 'no peeping', 'I give up. What is it?', '3–2 to me', and so on. Paul's later questions to camera as he proposes that the couple bet on the timing of their own death – 'What do you think? Can they win? You're on their side aren't you? Who will you bet on?', 'As they say on TV, "Place your bets"' – are, similarly, clichés from popular reality and game shows, except now the banal expressions have been detached from the family entertainment of the original game and inserted into a gruesome scene of sadism and cruelty. This slippage means that the games format acquires an uncanny character, part familiar and domesticated routine, part accompaniment to torture. The games are 'funny' in the ambiguous sense of being light-hearted and 'just for fun', on the one hand, and strange and sinister on the other. Like the disturbing juxtaposition in the opening scene of the sublime voices in pieces by Tebaldi and Handel and John Zorn's screeching saxophone on the chaotic track 'Bonehead' (played by his avant-garde fusion band 'Naked City'), the demarcation lines between order and disorder, and horror and the everyday are breached and discrete spaces are made to overlap uncomfortably.[7]

This unsettling combination of games routine and the torture chamber or concentration camp is central to the film's structure. Paul plays 'hot and cold' to lead Anna to the family's dog which Paul has bludgeoned to death; the game 'kitten in the bag' consists of placing a cushion cover over the son's head whilst his mother is forced to strip (7.1); 'hide and seek' is the structure underpinning young Georg's attempt to escape from captivity and Paul's search for him in the neighbour's house; 'eeny, meeny, miny, mo' will decide who, of Anna and Georg, will die first; and the proceedings in general are regulated by the bet proposed by Paul that the family will be dead in twelve hours. There are powerful echoes here of the influential post-war analysis of the 'concentrationary universe' by the French camp survivor David Rousset, in which the horrific acts of the SS are carried out in the form of games and sport:

> The regime of camps like Neue-Bremm, near Sarrebruck,... is typified by two basic directions: no work, but rather, 'sports'; and

7.1 *Funny Games* (Michael Haneke, 2007): Sitting room as torture chamber.

a minimum of food... One of the games consists of making the prisoners dress and undress several times a day at top speed and to the tune of the blackjack. Another is to make them run in and out of the barracks while two SS men stand at the door with rubber bludgeons to beat them over the head. In the little rectangular cement courtyard, there are all sorts of sports. (La structure des camps comme Neue-Bremm, près de Sarrebrück... est commandée par deux orientations fondamentales: pas de travail, du 'sport', une dérision de nourriture... Un des jeux consiste à faire habiller et dévêtir les détenus plusieurs fois par jour très vite et à la matraque; aussi à les faire sortir et entrer dans le *Block* en courant, tandis que, à la porte, deux S.S. assomment les Häftlinge à coups de *Gummi*. Dans la petite cour rectangulaire et bétonnée, le sport consiste en tout.)[8]

Funny Games adopts a similar Kafka-esque slippage between camp brutality and the games format. The difference is that Rousset describes horror in the form of the everyday while Haneke transforms the everyday into horror. Could it be that games are privileged cultural vehicles for the extreme violence of the camps and, as such, the domesticated containers of a concentrationary imaginary?

7.2 *Funny Games* (Michael Haneke, 2007): Camp gates.

In *Funny Games*, the conversion of the games format into a system of violence is paralleled by an overlaying of a camp iconography on the familiar setting of the holiday home. The gates to the house begin to resemble the gates to a concentration camp (especially when the young Georg tries to climb the gate in the dark in his unsuccessful attempt to escape) (7.2); the play of light and dark on the façade of the house at night, and the oblique camera angle from which it is shot, transform the familiar features of the home into a place of menace; and the contents of the domestic, bourgeois interior, TV and remote control, golf clubs, kitchen knives and so on, are converted into objects of extreme violence so that the humdrum sitting room becomes a torture chamber. The norm and the extreme are drawn together uncannily so that the 'funny games' slide uncomfortably between entertainment and horror.[9]

Critics of the film have, in general, referred to the way in which Haneke disturbs our culture of violence for entertainment by making it leap out of the virtual world of the TV set and mainstream Hollywood cinema screen and inhabit the 'real' world of the bourgeois sitting room. (The shooting of the couple's son Georg, indexed by the blood dripping down the screen of the television set, is a graphic example of this exposure of the real violence contained in the banal TV image.) Haneke himself has said that his main aim in the film was to critique the violence on our screens that we consume on a daily basis for entertainment, and that his reason for remaking the film, shot for shot, in Hollywood, ten years after its release in Germany, was because the original version did not reach its main target audience (that is, the American public) for whom it was originally intended.[10] This understanding of the film could also be applied to other Haneke films, like *Caché* (2005) for example, in which the gated world and smooth screens of bourgeois space are shown to hide violence, trauma and death.[11] However, I believe we need to be more precise about the links Haneke creates between bourgeois space, the popular games format and violence in *Funny Games*. Agamben's thesis on the camp here becomes a useful conceptual model for understanding. It is not simply that bourgeois space hides a world of violence (despite Agamben's description of the camp as 'the hidden matrix' of modern life); that space is actually part of the new locus for camp life. Agamben's argument rests on the idea, first, that what starts out as a state of exception, in which the rule of law is temporarily suspended, actually becomes the norm and, second, that what is defined as the exception is not, strictly speaking, outside the norm anyway but profoundly articulated with it, as the one can only define itself in relation to the other. Agamben's approach thus deconstructs the binary opposition of outside/inside the law to create a far more fluid version of the juridico-political structures of the camp. The camp is no longer that which defines a specific, identifiable and compartmentalized space in which, in Rousset's words subsequently adopted by Hannah Arendt in *The Origins of Totalitarianism* 'everything is possible'[12] (just as, for Foucault, disciplinary power in modern society is not simply confined to penal institutions), but any space in which human beings are subject to the unregulated bio-political power of the state. In his book *The Remnants of Auschwitz*, Agamben suggests that the real scandal of the famous football match played between SS guards and members of the *Sonderkommando* at Auschwitz is not simply the 'grey zone' of complicity which it establishes between victims and perpetrators (which Primo Levi talks about in *The Drowned and the Saved*), but the way in which the illusion of normality hiding real horror persists in different forms today. Agamben says the following:

> I ... view this match, this moment of normalcy, as the true horror of the camp. For we can perhaps think that the massacres are over – even if here and there they are repeated, not so far away from us.

But that match is never over; it continues as if uninterrupted. It is the perfect and eternal cipher of the 'gray zone', which knows no time and is in every place. Hence the anguish and shame of the survivors... But also hence our shame, the shame of those who did not know the camps, and yet, without knowing how, are spectators of that match, which repeats itself in every match in our stadiums, in every television broadcast, in the normalcy of everyday life. If we do not succeed in understanding that match, in stopping it, there will never be hope.[13]

If a simple football match can be the site of horror, this should act as a warning to us all of the presence of horror in the most unlikely of places.

There is a similar logic at work in *Funny Games* except that the football match at Auschwitz has become the bourgeois, domestic space. Haneke blurs the opposition between outside and inside the law by transforming the domestic space, and the banal format of the game or reality show, into the sadistic space of the torture chamber or concentration camp in which 'normal' social rules and ethics have been waived. He demonstrates that the structures of inhumanity – a world without law and ethics – do not inhabit a separate world but are deeply embedded in the structures of contemporary popular culture, and within the legal and ethical framework of modern democratic societies.[14] But it is the accompanying internalization of a new cultural imaginary, by which concentrationary structures have become normalized, which blinds us to the true nature of this political reality. The family's inability to understand the 'logic' at play here (at one stage Georg shouts 'You want our money? Help yourselves and get out', as if Peter and Paul's games could be neatly fitted into the legal categories of 'breaking and entering' and 'theft') is due to their blind attachment (and our own) to 'normal' conventions which fail imaginatively to perceive the presence of a camp 'logic' within the logic of bourgeois law and popular culture. The everyday reality show for popular entertainment, in which the fate of individuals (punishment, eviction and so on) is in the hands of the viewers (that is, our hands), is shown to share the structures of the camp. Paul's questions and winks to camera encouraging us to place our bets and show our allegiances are simple variations of the banal Big Brother catchphrase 'you decide' by which we are interactively implicated in the fate of others. And although we empathize with the victims (as Paul recognizes), we nevertheless willingly cast our vote as perpetrators for their eviction and demise on a daily basis. What, then, has happened to the domesticated space that we thought we were inhabiting when we sit down to watch a game or reality show (or, indeed, go to the cinema for entertainment) and the ethical norms of empathizing with the victim that we thought we shared? Haneke not only forces us to witness the real violence that is hidden by contemporary popular culture; we are also made to confront the possibility that that culture (our culture) is late capitalism's version of camp life and, what is more, that it is pleasurable as we consume it avidly on a daily basis. Agamben's depiction of the variety of spaces that the camp may inhabit in modern society allows us to understand more fully the logic of Haneke's transformation of bourgeois space:

> If the essence of the camp consists in the materialization of the state of exception and in the subsequent creation of a space in which bare life and the juridical rule enter into a threshold of indistinction, then we must admit that we find ourselves virtually in the presence of a camp every time such a structure is created, independent of the kinds of crime that are committed there and whatever its denomination and specific topography.[15]

By 'bringing home' (so to speak) the complicity between domestic and camp space, and the norm and the state of exception, Haneke demonstrates that today's camp structures are inside the citadel. Yet, by showing how this is dependent on the easy consumption of images in domestic space, he also challenges the ideological power of the image itself to transmit evil in banal form.

Although *The White Ribbon* takes us back to a small village in pre-First World War Germany, in which a series of sadistic acts seems to be perpetrated by the village children, it nevertheless presents, like *Funny Games*, an uncanny blurring of horror and the everyday and a complicity between a camp culture and 'normal' society. Haneke once again demonstrates how violence, cruelty and torture are not only compatible with strict moral and religious codes but are part of the same fabric. What is particularly striking in both films is the way in which exposure to the inner logic of cruelty inherent in 'normal' life shocks its representatives when they are its victims. In *Funny Games*, for example, although the world of senseless punishment and gratuitous violence is part of the very culture consumed by the bourgeois family, it is simply not recognized as such (in fact, not recognized as anything to do with their normal world) when they are confronted with it in their own home. Similarly, in *The White Ribbon*, all the upholders of order and purity in the village – the pastor, the doctor, the baron, the baron's steward and even the school-teacher (as I shall discuss shortly) – are shocked and disturbed when their own everyday cruelty is reciprocated by the children of the village.[16] Yet, if the recognition of their complicity with violence is denied the guardians of order, that recognition is nevertheless made visible to the viewers of both films, and, indeed, our own complicity with the violence of our culture.

Complicity is achieved in *The White Ribbon* through the drawing together of opposites. The sadistic acts of torture carried out on Sigi and Karli, the sons of the baron and the midwife respectively, can only be reconciled with the pure and innocent faces of the other children of the village if we cease to see purity and cruelty in discrete terms: the country idyll, in which the two sons of the baron's steward and Sigi are lying on the river bank shaping and playing whistles (the pan-pipes to accompany the pastoral scene), suddenly becomes a scene of attempted murder when one of the brothers throws Sigi into the river; the measured tone of the doctor belies his sadism as he pronounces the cruellest of words to the midwife (his mistress); the brutal torture of Karli, in which he is almost blinded, is followed by the concern of the children enquiring about his condition. When the pastor gives his two eldest children, Klara and Martin, ten lashes of the cane for having stayed out and lying about their whereabouts, and then forces them to wear the white ribbon for their sins, the camera remains outside the room where the beating takes place while we hear the cries from within, thus transforming the bland and puritanical interior of the pastor's house into a torture chamber.[17]

Haneke achieves this blurring of opposites by showing how the surface image is an illusion hiding a complex layering of practice. Hence, the image in which the pastor's children are seen looking out of the window at the fire blazing outside, with the reflection of the fire in the window, as if engulfing their innocent faces in a hellish furnace (7.3), or that of the 'innocent' gaze of the doctor's young son looking into the room in which his father is sexually abusing Anni, his daughter, become the composite images of choice for Haneke, as they achieve, within a single frame, the superimposition of 'differences' (like a collage) so much a

7.3   *The White Ribbon* (Michael Haneke, 2009): Innocence and hell.

part of his politico-aesthetic practice. Once this way of reading the image is established, we cannot see the innocent faces of the children (or the bland interior of the pastor's house) without also seeing the invisible but present 'other' face of evil. Even the purest of gestures – for example, the gift of the caged bird that the pastor's youngest son offers his father – cannot simply be taken at face value, as we are led to doubt the truth of the visible. It is through the lens of the unreliability of the visible image that we should read (or understand) the account of the events in the village by the school-teacher; if the image can lie, then so can the word. The device of the unreliable narrator (and hence the unreliability of memory, as the teacher/narrator reflects on events from his past) complements the ambivalence of the image. Is the teacher himself not complicit in the children's violent acts that he describes? After all, he is, arguably, more directly involved than the other figures of authority in the village in impressing on the young the values of civilization as he is their teacher. When he denounces the children to the pastor, should we not question his own role (as well as that of all the other adults) in the cruel acts that he exposes? Is his courtship of the young governess Eva in their garden of Eden quite as pure as he describes it as the serpent has already penetrated paradise?[18]

The illusion of surfaces would suggest that 'purity' is not a 'pure' term and that the white ribbon always contains traces of darkness, even though

7.4 *The White Ribbon* (Michael Haneke, 2009): Even a peaceful countryside...

they are not immediately visible. Haneke uses the classic modernist device of exposing 'the illusion of the image as offering a "window on the world"' as a means of reintroducing into the frame civilization's discontents (habitually denied by the self and projected onto the other).[19] Images of the peaceful countryside around the village – vast open skies and cornfields blowing gently in the wind – bring to mind the opening words of Jean Cayrol's haunting commentary in *Night and Fog*: 'Even a peaceful countryside... can lead to a concentration camp' ['Même un paysage tranquille... peut mener à un camp de concentration'] (7.4). Like Resnais, Haneke draws horror into the most becalmed of sites.

The image and history

Towards the end of *The White Ribbon*, the voice-over of the narrator (himself an ambivalent presence, as I have suggested) announcing the outbreak of the First World War (the grand conflagration that was to give the lie to the march towards the light and progress of the Enlightenment project) accompanies an image in which the baronial hall in light can be seen through a dark archway, not only literally and metaphorically playing with light and dark but also resembling an eye or an aperture. The final image in the film of the congregation in church assembling to the angelic sound of the choir in the gallery above, directed by the teacher/narrator, is like the final bow by the cast at a theatre, or a coming-together for a photograph. Both these sequences are indicative of Haneke's method for staging history within the image: they are a complex montage in which multiple meanings are condensed into a single image, a *mise-en-abyme*, or miniature, of the film as a whole.

In *Funny Games* and *The White Ribbon* Haneke thus disturbs the surface image by transforming it into a site of overlapping and interconnecting pieces which never coalesce to form a completed puzzle. As I suggest above, this is both an aesthetic and political strategy.

The superimposition of different frames of reference (the games format and the camp in *Funny Games*, the authoritarian order of traditional society and the disorder of random cruelty in *The White Ribbon*) is a poetic condensation of elements to open up the moment to a complex history. Haneke's images are a spatialization of history, converting the linearity of chronological time and the discrete nature of different spaces into a new paradigmatic and palimpsestic spatio-temporal configuration. These images resemble the Benjaminian 'image' or 'constellation' in which history can be perceived in the moment and depth invades the surface.[20] It is this structure which provides a response to Daney's questions about the ability of the cinema today to respond to history and the Agambenian proposition of the normalization of the camp.

If Haneke's approach to the image is to transform it into a site of overlapping contexts, especially drawing together horror and the everyday, then it clearly presents a challenge to our understanding of good and evil as binary opposites. Haneke's cinema points up the illusion of divorcing civilization from barbarity and invites us, instead, to see them as inextricably related. He places us in the realm of those critiques of modernity by Adorno, Arendt, Fanon, Christopher Browning, Zygmunt Bauman and others which understand instances of extreme violence in modern history – for example, the Holocaust and colonialism – as profoundly articulated with the Enlightenment project and the Western invention of Man rather than as aberrations from it. Arendt's use of the expression 'the banality of evil' to describe Adolf Eichmann's role in the Final Solution, to which Daney consciously refers in his article on the tracking shot in *Kapò*, could also be used to describe Haneke's cinema.

Haneke's politico-aesthetic model therefore puts the particular into contact with the wider structures of the modern world to penetrate the new ideological masquerade of camp structures. Indeed, Haneke often suggests that his films should not only be seen as relating to specific times and places but in more general terms. *The White Ribbon* opens with the teacher/narrator explaining that the strange events that he is about to recount 'could perhaps clarify certain things that happened in this country'. The clear implication of this statement is that the behaviour of the village children on the eve of the First World War can tell us something about the violence of the adults that they would become in the following decades. Yet this interpretation is itself too limited, for, as Haneke has himself said of *The White Ribbon*,

> it isn't a film about Germany specifically. I am just using Germany as a model to be able to talk about radicalism in general... I don't think it is right to push the film away from you and say that it is only about Germany. It is the nature of a particular situation which could exist in any country or culture.[21]

Elsewhere Haneke has said '[t]he film uses the example of German fascism to talk about the mental preconditions for every type of terrorism, whether it comes from the right or the left, and whether it's politically or religiously motivated.'[22] This is not simply a question of using the particular to talk about the universal; Haneke's aesthetic practice, as I have defined it here, reshapes the relationship between the particular and the universal so that they, too, have to be reformulated in a non-dichotomous way. By blurring the contours of horror and the everyday, one time and other times, one space and other spaces, he shows us the intersections and similarities between 'opposites' without collapsing these into a homogeneous whole. Agamben's notion of the presence of camp structures in different spaces is, similarly, an understanding of the tension between similarity and difference. His thesis emerges, in part, from the critiques of the concentrationary universe proposed by Rousset and Arendt (and which underpin the making of Resnais's *Night and Fog*) that warn us of the continued presence of the radical potential of 'total domination' in the aftermath of the war. It does not imply that all life is camp life; but it does jolt us into an awareness of the hidden presence of camp structures in 'normal' life whose phenomenal form can appear under different guises. The mistake would, therefore, be to confuse an understanding of the concentrationary universe (of which, as Arendt said, '[the] camps are the true central institution of totalitarian organizational power')[23] with the Holocaust, which is (in the way we have come to understand the term since the 1970s) the specifically targeted genocide of a particular racialized group (the Jews). The concentrationary and the exterminatory programmes clearly overlap but also need to be distinguished if we are to understand the continued presence of a systematic attack on the notion of what is a human being (that is, all human beings), a programme which was introduced in its most egregious form in the concentration camps but which cannot be contained in that singular instance. This is not to universalize the Holocaust and efface the singularity of the attempted genocide of the Jews (a critique that has been made of *Night and Fog* and, indeed, any attempt to relate the Holocaust to other moments of extreme violence); it is, rather, to suggest that Agamben's return to the theories elaborated by Rousset and Arendt on the concentrationary universe and 'total domination' reminds us of a juridico-political assault on the human, and a need to see through its ruses, that persists in different sites today and affects us all.[24]

Haneke's relational politico-aesthetic approach to film, exemplified in *Funny Games* and *The White Ribbon*, can perhaps be more clearly understood, then, within a concentrationary or camp logic rather than through the lens of the Holocaust, which specifies the singularity of the event. These films show how the image can carry the concentrationary disease unleashed on the post-war world but, when transformed into a site of intersections between different times and places, can also show (self-reflexively) how the most banal of scenes is haunted by a dark presence of unimaginable cruelty. They reinvest the image with imagination; it is only by going beyond the visible that we can perceive the connections between one thing and another. These reflexions return us to Daney's concern that the cinema no longer has the ability to break through the accumulated layers of entertainment images to put a stop on the image (with all that that entails) in the manner of *Night and Fog*. In the immediate aftermath of the war, Rousset, Arendt, Cayrol and Resnais were acutely aware of the difficulty of exposing the persistence of horror in everyday life. It could be said that that task is greater still today, as the capacity of the image to efface a sense of history has been extended in an age of new technologies and globalized commodity capitalism. Daney recognizes that, in this climate, 'the banality of evil can launch new, electronic images'. Yet Haneke's politico-aesthetic strategy could be seen as a challenge to the way evil is hidden in those new images today.

His way of defamiliarizing the everyday to show how camp structures have been normalized and become an integral part of our cultural imaginary is one possible indication that cinema can still stage the tension between the visible and the invisible, and the moment and history, in ways that disturb the Matrix-like cocoon of late capitalist culture, and can still warn us in the new millennium, as *Night and Fog* did in the aftermath of the war, of the continued presence of structures that we thought were buried in the past.

8

SPEC(TAC)ULARIZING 'CAMPNESS'
Nikita and *La Femme Nikita* the Series

Brenda Hollweg

> What is at stake is not the end of a human life but the human condition itself, as incarnated in the singularity of vulnerable bodies.
> Adriana Cavarero, *Horrorism: Naming Contemporary Violence*[1]

Revisiting *Nikita* with/through/after *La Femme Nikita*
Some films have the potential to linger on – in our personal archive of stories and characters but also within the wider popular imagination. *Nikita* (1990), an action-thriller by French director Luc Besson, belongs to this group of films. It tells the story of a female drug-addict who kills a policeman and is sentenced to life imprisonment. But instead of serving her time in prison, the eponymous Nikita is made the offer to work for The Centre, a clandestine government organization whose remit it is to eliminate political personages, apparently without any legal restraints. Under the pressure of her circumstances, the young woman agrees and her previous life officially ends: Nikita is declared dead and her funeral staged by The Centre. Over a period of three years, she is trained to become an assassin and kill enemies of the state on call-off order. Nikita's code name is 'Josephine', and she becomes involved in a series of dangerous missions, of which the last one – a complex piece of counter-espionage – goes horribly wrong. But she manages to escape and 'disappears', without papers and identity, into the dark unknown.

Besson was known to me from two of his earlier productions, *Le Dernier Combat* (1983) and *Subway* (1985), and in various ways *Nikita* echoed elements of his previous work: a dystopian world controlled by weapons, technology and an invasive system of surveillance; strange and unfamiliar places where his rebel-heroes and heroines seek refuge; a stylish, neo-noir 'look' deployed to glamourize scenarios of violence, cruelty and human suffering. The latter, in particular, impacted negatively on my viewing experience at the time, and despite my short-lived fascination with the leading actress – the beautifully androgynous Anne Parillaud – I could not share the euphoria with which many young viewers in France received *Nikita*. 'When Besson went on tour with this film,' Susan Hayward relates in her close reading of the film, 'young people applauded him vigorously, young women talked of crying at Nikita's story and others spoke of how the film made them feel good because someone was talking about their issues.'[2] One such socio-political issue was the high rate of youth unemployment during the late 1980s and early 1990s that coincided with the period of the film's production and release. A general feeling of disaffection and a sense of disenfranchisement, Hayward argues, left French youths vulnerable and eager to seek out products of popular culture which triggered identification processes with fragile yet resilient protagonists, who asserted themselves *vis-à-vis* an all-powerful state in a series of violent acts.[3]

Revisiting *Nikita* in the 2010s, I am less provoked by Besson's use of cruelty and terror than two decades earlier, which is likely to be due to my increased familiarity with scenarios of violence on the large as well as the small screen. Such scenarios include several reincarnations of Besson's Nikita material: *Nikita* has been remade into new feature films and adapted twice for television. Cinematic features are the American *The Assassin/Point of No Return* (John Badham, 1993) and the Hong Kong productions *Black Cat* (*Hei Mao*, Stephen Shin, 1991), set in the USA, and its sequel by the same director, *Black Cat 2* (*Hei mao zhi ci sha Ye Li Qin*, 1997), which chooses post-communist Russia as its prime location. Their post-Cold War stories make way for new materializations in the 2000s, triggered by events like 9/11 and 7/7, the 'War on Terror' and 'counterterrorist' emergency laws and provisions in liberal democracies. In the 2010 television adaptation *Nikita* (Warner Brothers Television), a newly cast Nikita (Maggie Q), who had previously escaped what is now termed Division, returns to take revenge on her former oppressors and destroy the covertly operating organization. Like Besson's original, these later productions draw on generic conventions of secret agent films, political (conspiracy) thrillers, Cold War or anti-terrorist drama and narratives centring on fugitive or maverick mercenary characters. They also refer back to British and US television productions of the 1960s and 1970s, among them, most prominently, the 1967–68 British TV programme *The Prisoner* (ITC Entertainment), which was remade into a shorter US mini-series in 2009. Here, too, an uninvolved character is abducted and brought to the Village, a surreal place marked by totalitarian structures, from which he (who is later renamed Number Six) repeatedly attempts to escape.

My renewed interest in the Nikita narrative can be attributed, however, to the other, perhaps internationally most acclaimed, adaptation of the original storyline: the television series *La Femme Nikita*, co-produced by Canadian Fireworks and US Warner Brothers Television and broadcast by USA Networks in North America from 1997 to 2000. The series was also televised in Germany, France, Italy, Portugal, Spain, Poland and the Czech Republic. In 2001, a shorter fifth season was aired in America, due to a passionately fought campaign by the series' large fan community.[4] This translation of the Nikita material from film to television led to a significant shift in the series' main objective: no longer predominantly a narrative about a youth who resists an oppressive state system, *La Femme Nikita* focuses on the totalitarian logic and structures of Section One, the American version of Besson's The Centre. This qualitative shift is important,[5] but it was only recently that research on audiovisual imaginaries of violence, undertaken by Griselda Pollock and Max Silverman in the context of a critical reappraisal of Alain Resnais's *Night and Fog* (1955),[6] suggested to me a new reading of the Nikita scenarios with reference to the analytical category of the *concentrationary*.

Pollock and Silverman locate the politico-aesthetic roots of the concentrationary in the work of French writer David Rousset who was a political deportee in the German concentration camp Buchenwald and a witness to the conditions of the camp, which included prolonged and systematic deprivation, wasting, exposure to ('medical') experiments and progressive breaking of the will to live.[7] Rousset's notion of a *concentrationary universe* (*l'Univers concentrationnaire*), they write, invokes a political system of terror whose aim was to demolish the social humanity of all its actual and potential victims within and beyond the actual sites. Enclosed within the camp, the concentrationees experience its brute violence and pain directly in their bodies. They directly witness the terrifying novelty where 'everything is possible'. As the laboratory of limitless possibility the camp functions, paradoxically, as the heart of the totalitarian society that creates it at once a 'world apart', utterly other to the everyday world beyond its barbed wire enclosures and as an emblem of total domination infected and destroying all political life in the apparently 'normal' world around it.[8]

Rousset understood that such a system of violence and terror is not reducible to a singular 'moment of extreme atrocity', but marked by 'the inception and initiating actualization of a new political possibility in modern political life of a form of terror that, as a result of this realized experiment under the Third Reich, will always be with us now that it has been unleashed on the world'.[9] Pollock's and Silverman's explorations of Rousset's work (and the conclusions they draw from it) can be closely related to Giorgio Agamben's notion of the camp as 'the pure, absolute, and impassable biopolitical space . . . insofar as it is founded solely on the state of exception'.[10] The camp is the result of 'an inner solidarity between democracy and totalitarianism',[11] he writes in *Homo Sacer: Sovereign Power and Bare Life* (1995), and as such also 'the hidden paradigm of the political space of modernity, whose metamorphoses and disguises we will have to learn to recognise'.[12]

In his 1989 study *Modernity and the Holocaust*, Zygmunt Bauman cautions us, however, not to embrace too eagerly the camp as a trope for modernity:

> If everything we know is like Auschwitz, then one can live with Auschwitz, and in many a case live reasonably well. If the principles that ruled over life and death of Auschwitz inmates were like those that rule our own, then what has all the outcry and lamentation been about?[13]

I agree with Bauman that it is mandatory to attend to the 'uniqueness' of the historical event, to its social, political or cultural specificity.[14]

But, at the same time, we must continue to pay close attention to elements of a fascist legacy that are located in products of the popular imagination in an unconscious or politically unprocessed form. My mode of thinking here draws on a psychoanalytically informed understanding of culture that is seen in homology to Sigmund Freud's concept of the 'unconscious mind', a locus of implicit knowledge and a repertory of forgotten memories, repressed feelings, anxieties and desires, which may or may not become accessible to consciousness at a later point in time.[15] But when they resurface – as, for Freud, is the case in dreams as well as in slips of the tongue or jokes – these unconscious processes typically emerge from areas that may initially be seen as distinct from the original event. Freud's interpretations of such slippages are based on 'a mode of thinking which may be capable of an awareness of the differences between things, but is more interested in their confluences (overdetermination and condensation), and their similarities and ability to replace each other (displacement)'.[16] Drawing on the writings of Agamben, Bauman, Hannah Arendt and Adriana Cavarero, among others, I want to recuperate this mode of thinking for my own explorations of the *concentrationary imaginary* in *Nikita* and *La Femme Nikita*.

The relationship these two productions have to the camp or notion of 'campness' is not one of simple or literal audiovisual transcription; it is oblique. Events 'become identified with certain icons that evoke aspects of the concentrationary without aiming at all to represent the concentrationary'.[17] In other words, it is not the Nazi concentration camp and its historically, geopolitically or culturally specific conditions that these two products of popular culture (aim to) re-present; rather, the camp is deployed – in a more or less unconscious way – as a resource for the staging of a larger narrative about the inscription of totalitarian structures and logics in Western democracies. Elements of the concentrationary which become visible on the surface level – in the dialogue or *mise-en-scène* – are both a symptom of and a vehicle for such deployment. The state-sanctioned criminality of Besson's action-thriller, for instance, hints at actual events that took place in France in the 1980s.[18] In *La Femme Nikita*, which was conceptualized and realized in a different socio-political climate, namely that of North America in the 1990s, an increase in new forms of East European war crimes, Islamist extremism and corresponding counterterrorist activities function as a general historical reference point for many episodes.

Apart from these references, however, both productions make use of the idea that a secret organization with links to the CIA operates in a 'world apart' from the constitutional apparatus of Western democracies and is empowered, without political and legal restraints, to do things that it would not be able to do otherwise. Its operative conditions, I argue here, are analogous to those of the concentrationary universe with its totalitarian and dehumanizing structures inscribed in juridical law. Due to this corresponding relationship, other elements of plot, character development or setting acquire concentrationary meaning. Bearing this analogy in mind, Besson's The Centre functions as a metonym for state-sanctioned terrorism in France, but also refers to forms of counterterrorism (with their potential for human rights violations) which are practised in precisely those 'societies who imagine themselves the very opposite of the totalitarian',[19] including the USA, Canada, the United Kingdom and Germany.[20] Similarly, in *La Femme Nikita* the fictional world of Section One with its sinister performance indicators and corporate dictates of efficiency mimics the ideal workplace imagined by the New Economy and, in a more or less cynical way, conforms to the juridico-political structures and operative conditions that once allowed the concentration camp to become a real possibility.

It often requires, however, the active work of memory and concentrationary memory, in particular, for certain scenarios to become recognizable or readable as concentrationary. Traces of the concentrationary can emerge as unconscious or politically unprocessed citations from the visual archive of the camp. From 1945, the concentrationary universe has been made accessible in mediated form, through an archive of photographs, illustrations, documentary footage, verbal and written witness accounts from the Nazi period and liberation. Over the last 60 and more years, this archive has been reused innumerable times in film, literature, drama and other popular forms – to the effect that certain images or narrative elements now stand in for the camp and its complex historical reality. As icons of 'campness' they condense many 'unspeakable' and 'unimaginable' experiences 'into an eloquent form whose simplicity and directness makes it ideal for duplication and repetition. And its very simplicity helps it condense multiple narratives into a single *gestalt*'.[21] It is this reproduced and redeployed visual and narrative archive of the camp that popular culture tends to work with. Obviously, such use raises questions about cultural memory and the role these popular productions play therein. Through the iconic image or other more subtle elements in the narrative, dialogue or score, the popular – concentrationary – imaginary retains a connection to historical reality, even if the scenario in which these elements unfold their novel potentiality is disconnected from or fails to acknowledge the original source.[22] Representation is here understood to be the effect of a multi-layered and multi-directional process of different forms of conscious and unconscious audiovisual re-imaginations to which the concentrationary imaginary contributes.

The camp often functions as an (unconscious) imaginative source for the *mise-en-scène* and the construction of various action scenes. My explorations of Besson's *Nikita* highlight the ways in which the concentrationary haunts the central character (her appearance and development) on the image level of the film as well as through the plot which positions her both as collaborator and victim of The Centre's totalitarian regime. These scenarios also play on our own pre-articulate anxieties and desires which the cinematic apparatus is able to transform – through point-of-view shots, editing, camera angles, etc. – 'into an audiovisual form that is then shared and rendered accessible externally to an audience'.[23] The cinematic/televisual screen functions as a 'transitional space' which moves its viewers unconsciously – similar to the projective techniques deployed in relations with others – and helps them to mediate a sense of self, both individually and on a group scale.[24]

Logics of 'disappearance', desire to reconnect with a feminine space: *Nikita*

It should not surprise us . . . that *Nikita* . . . has elements of the Bond type of spy thriller – a spectacular disregard for human life being one of the key links here.[25]

In her rereading of *Nikita* as a neo-baroque symphony, Hayward distances herself from previous analyses of the film as noir-pastiche and instead stresses the important part surveillance plays in Besson's film in disciplining the (female) body.[26] My own reading of *Nikita* builds on this argument, but takes it further. I follow Hayward in her use of Foucault's notion of bio-power as an 'invasive and effective form of social control',[27] but disagree with her in terms of the extent to which she credits Nikita with agency based on her non-compliance. In my view, Hayward does

8.1   George Stevens, *A Cattle Truck with Corpses at Dachau Concentration Camp, 2 May 1945*. George Stevens Collection, Library of Congress, Washington DC.

not take into account the utterly dehumanizing quality of the totalitarian world/system that sets out, from the beginning, to destroy individuality, spontaneity and uniqueness and to which Nikita is exposed throughout the film. The following three scenes are particularly expressive of the concentrationary imaginary and show how Nikita's identity/subjectivity slowly but surely disintegrates.

After her arrest and life sentence, Nikita is given a dose of tranquillizers and transferred to The Centre or, more precisely, to a white and sparsely furnished room that resembles a prison cell, already reflecting her isolated and imprisoned existence. She is visited several times by Bob (Tchéky Karyo), who recruits her and observes her training as a sleeper agent. When Bob enters the cell we see Nikita slouching on the bed with drooping shoulders and a tired, defiant face. In one scene, her naked legs and feet, which are those of a fragile human being, barely touch the floor. A low-angle shot of her legs, taken from behind and underneath the bed, disrupts the narrative continuity and is reminiscent of images from the camp's visual archive in which the limbs of deportees spill out of train compartments or dangle over the edges, once these trains were

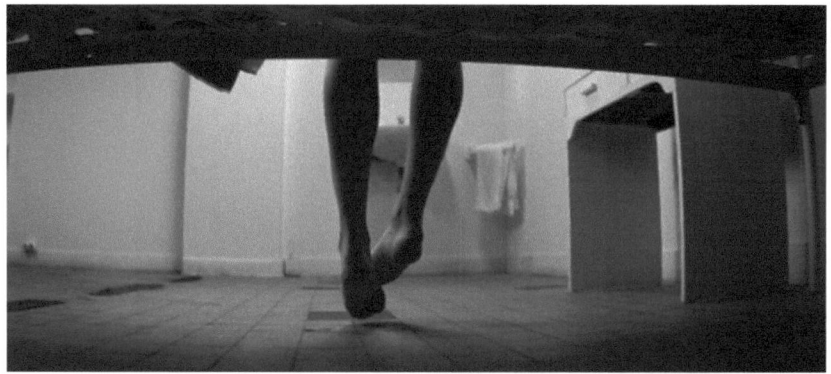

8.2 *Nikita* (Luc Besson, 1990): First day at The Centre, medium-long shot of Nikita's (Anne Parillaud) legs.

stopped and opened on the premises. This visual citation is the first one that suggests Nikita's subjectivity as a potential 'concentrationee' (8.2).

The *mise-en-scène* of her cell confirms this association, even though it foregrounds a particular actualization of the camp's conditions. The functional space with its sparsely decorated interior mimics in an uncanny way a typical Kapo room, known from archival footage of the camp.[28] (8.3–8.4) Kapos or 'prisoner functionaries' (*Funktionshäftlinge*) were an integral part of the camp's hierarchical structure; although they were concentrationees themselves and could fall prey to the deadly and arbitrary machinery of the camp, they were also known for their brutality towards fellow camp inmates. A number of Kapos had criminal convictions or were recruited from violent gangs; within the camp system they had certain privileges such as extra rations and a room of their own, provided they performed their duties to the satisfaction of the SS guards.[29] Nikita, likewise, is introduced as a member of a youth gang and a drug junkie who kills a policeman in cold blood. In subsequent scenes, at court and in police custody, she is established as impulsive, full of rage and prone to violent reactions. Her disposition makes Nikita interesting for Bob, who desires to harness her aggression and make use of it by rigorously turning her into an executioner of The Centre's violent aims, who has no choice but to comply.[30]

I am not suggesting here that Nikita *literally* represents a Kapo; rather, her relation to this historical figure needs to be understood in Jacques

8.3 *Night and Fog* (*Nuit et Brouillard*, Alain Resnais, 1955): A typical Kapo room at the camp.

Rancière's sense of mimesis as 'a way of making resemblances function within a set of relations between ways of making, modes of speech, forms of visibility and protocols of intelligibility'.[31] Elements of 'Kapo-ness' are inscribed in the imaginative space her character occupies in the film as indices of a larger logic of oppression and cruelty. But Nikita's relationship to violence is an ambivalent one: 'at first, she owns it, but subsequently it owns her'.[32] Her position is as precarious as that of the Kapo: she shares

8.4 *Nikita* (Luc Besson, 1990): Nikita's recruitment room at The Centre.

the moral dilemma and her life hangs by a silken thread: 'I can't stand you. I'd have let you die. So toe the line. You won't be warned. Clear?', the administrative head of The Centre, an Oedipal Father and voice of the 'Law', scolds her. Nikita has yet to prove her use value for The Centre, but even after she has become a fully fledged sleeper agent, she can be physically killed any time and, according to the concentrationary logic, no sacrifice is made.

The restaurant and kitchen sequence in *Nikita*, which entails one of the most memorable action scenes of the film, takes this logic and gradual suppression of Nikita's humanity further. It is Nikita's twenty-third birthday, and she has been invited by Bob to celebrate the evening at the elegant Parisian restaurant Le Train Bleu. Before they order, she is given what looks, at first, like a birthday present. In the box, however, she finds the deadly weapon that Bob will order her to use within less than a minute from her initial discovery. This cinematic moment actualizes the concentrationary through what might be regarded as a secondary citation. Its intertext is Liliana Cavani's *Night Porter* (*Il Portiere di Notte*, 1974), a film that focuses on the sadomasochistic relationship between a former SS Officer, Maximilian Theo Aldorfer (Dirk Bogarde), and his (possibly Jewish) ex-concentrationee lover Lucia Atherton (Charlotte Rampling).[33] In an equally memorable encounter between the two at a nightclub table, Max presents Lucia with a gift that contains the head of a fellow camp inmate. Although Cavani, unlike Besson, is interested in the sadomasochistic desire that connects these two people on a personal level, both productions foreground a moment of utter helplessness and emotional pain on the part of the female characters, which comes with the realization that their life is at the hands of an all-powerful (male) other whose control cannot be broken. Through the skilful acting of Rampling and Parillaud this moment of totalitarian terror is made palpable.

Outlawed in her own country, Nikita's juridical person has already ceased to exist: she is forced to live 'in a twilight of favour [sic] and misfortune'.[34] In the table scene at Le Train Bleu her new function as de-individualized killing machine for The Centre comes to the fore. Completely separated from communal life her actions lack moral meaning: Nikita kills her target in the busy restaurant, as she has been ordered, and then attempts to escape back to The Centre from the victim's armed bodyguards. In her short black dress, high heels and evening make-up, she embodies the 'macha killerette' or 'killer-*femme*', an ambiguous post-feminist icon she has been described to represent in this film.[35]

But this impression is deceptive, as is the whole set-up at the restaurant, because it endows her with too much agency. Although a low-angle camera initially contributes to the fetishization of the qualities of an action heroine (assertiveness, bravery, a quick eye, physical strength), the camera at other moments invites the viewer to empathize with Nikita's mental and emotional state of being, which is one of belittlement and humiliation. Her subjectivity as a human being made up of feelings, a moral conscience and the ability to empathize is constantly at risk being destroyed by the totalitarian system. Medium to close-up shots of Nikita's face amplify the emotional destabilization she experiences at the table and also later, when she discovers that the bathroom window – through which she expects to make a quick and safe exit – has been intentionally bricked up. This significant detail of the *mise-en-scène* adds further urgency and thus narrative interest to Nikita's escape, but it also metonymically points to her overall condition of entrapment and her victimization by the larger terror of her role within the organization. This time, Nikita gets away by sliding down the kitchen's waste chute, just before a fire blast caused by an exploding hand grenade can reach her. She comes out alive from her 'baptism of fire' and trial run as an assassin, because she manages to play the system rather than being destroyed by it. The cinematic tropes of casually taking and risking lives and converting 'ordinary' settings into sites of shootings, bombings and (near-)incineration, however, both follow and underpin the essentially dehumanizing logic that Nikita is exposed to. These plot elements, as well as the action heroine's narrow escape from death, have been staged in many action films and endless variations before. But the spectacular way in which the vulnerable body of a woman becomes human waste in a container placed underneath the chute is characteristic of the concentrationary imaginary of Besson's film.

Once more, during Nikita's final mission, elements of the concentrationary emerge from the *mise-en-scène*. 'Josephine'/Nikita and a fellow agent are given orders firstly to drug the representative of an unspecified country and later to enter his embassy in disguise to photograph secret documents from his office. But things already spiral out of control while they are still with the (drugged) ambassador at an art dealer's apartment. The Centre sends in Victor, a seasoned and desensitized assassin, to 'clean up' after Nikita. Upon arrival, Victor shoots two bodyguards and, grabbing each man by his feet, drags the bodies across the apartment floor to dump them into the bathtub. Once this has been achieved,

8.5 'Disposal: two former guards placing corpses in a mass grave'. *The Liberation of Bergen-Belsen Concentration Camp, April 1945* (BU 4031). War Office Second World War Official Collection No. 5 Army and Photographic Unit, Sgt. H. Sykes. Courtesy of the Imperial War Museum.

he starts pouring hydrochloric acid over their bodies to destroy all evidence, which causes the two men – who are still alive – to react to his treatment with mute convulsions. While the bathtub occupies the foreground, Nikita and her fellow agent (now dressed up as the ambassador) are positioned further in the back. Medium-long shots of their stunned faces and gestures of helplessness, taken from a slightly low angle, make the horrifying quality of the bathroom scene tangible to us and reflect our own spontaneous reaction to the depicted violence. We find here a culmination of the noir-specific uncanny: a rapid change from the mundane to the sinister, from a scene of domestic ordinariness to one of human atrocity. But such is the concentrationary logic expressed in this scenario, in which a room with shower sprinklers for hygienic purposes always threatens to be a visual metonymy for the extermination of human life (8.5–8.8). The just as efficient as contemptuous way The

8.6–8.8   *Nikita* (Luc Besson, 1990): Disposal of human bodies after failed mission.

8.9 *Night and Fog* (*Nuit et Brouillard*, Alain Resnais, 1955): The survivors look on.

Centre gets rid of people here brings up uncomfortable associations with a mode of human disposal once practised at European concentration and extermination camps during the Second World War: while the corpses of human beings were thrown into open mass graves, those who were still alive looked on (8.9 and 8.10).

8.10 *Nikita* (Luc Besson, 1990): Dead bodies in the bathtub, the agents look on.

8.11 John Heartfield, *As in the Middle Ages... /... so in the Third Reich* [*Wie im Mittelalter... /... so im Dritten Reich*] 1934, photo-lithograph, 1957. Courtesy of Gallery of Modern Art, Queensland and DACS.

In the same scene, one of the dying bodyguards lifts up his arm and hand in a gesture that denotes human vulnerability and submission but also bears traces of his final struggle for survival. In the twentieth century, this iconic posture has been taken up as a political signifier of human suffering in different contexts, including John Heartfield's anti-Nazi photomontage *As in the Middle Ages... /... so in the Third Reich* [*Wie im Mittelalter... /... so im Dritten Reich*] (1934; 8.11), in which a Nazi victim is broken on the swastika, and in the memorable tracking shot of Gillo Pontecorvo's film *Kapò* (1960). The figure of the bodyguard in Besson's film is not a representation of a camp inmate, but his protruding arm gestures towards the same thanato-political logic and destructive qualities of the fascist regime that are expressed in Heartfield's montage and lead Terese (Emanuelle Riva), a starving inmate, to kill herself in the camp's electrified wire fence in Pontecorvo's film (8.12).[36]

Only seconds later, Nikita's fellow agent is also shot by Victor, and she has a nervous breakdown; we see her sliding down – once more – into a foetal position, as if self-soothing and shielding herself from the potentially traumatic experience. By means of staging these acts of ego defence, Besson allows the violence of the system to come into visibility, while Nikita's exposure to it is equally stressed. Throughout the film, we see her seek comfort and relief in behaviour typically associated

8.12 *Kapò* (Gilles Pontecorvo, 1958): Last gesture of human vulnerability.

with children, including holding on to a toy rabbit, nibbling or biting her thumb, throwing herself into the arms of her boyfriend Marco, or jumping excitedly up and down on an armchair. Nikita can be likened here to a feral child-woman who resists the disciplinary control imposed by the bio-power of The Centre; her gestures express joy, happiness and temporary freedom from the *Kadavergehorsam* or blind 'obedience of corpses'[37] demanded of her. Or, in more psychodynamic terms, her pre-verbal, pre-oedipal state of being, which is one of anarchy, excess and *jouissance*, has a disruptive quality and makes strong inroads into the Symbolic. In post-Lacanian, poststructuralist feminist theory (Cixous, Kristeva, Irigaray) the pre-oedipal or Imaginary is fashioned as a feminine space marked by playfulness and plenitude around the mother's body: a space of jubilation and celebration, but not necessarily amenable of encoding or decoding reality. Nikita's quirky habits speak of her desire to reconnect with this pre-oedipal feminine space – the space of the m/other/breast – in the traumatic absence of a real mother, an absence that is revealed shortly before she is given the dose of tranquillizers instead of the lethal injection and we hear her cry out for her mother in desperation. These scenes also, however, bear traces of her still existing and resisting individuality and spontaneity, i.e. her essential humanity that has not been destroyed by the repressive and totalitarian regime of The Centre/state/camp – yet.

The film's ending is inconclusive and leaves the viewer with feelings of ambivalence. Does Nikita's 'disappearance' without papers and identity – her 'occupying a space of absence and therefore, arguably, of non-being'[38] – constitute, as Hayward suggests, an escape from the concentrationary abyss? Does she 'get away with it'[39] and thus assert herself outside the system that co-opted her? Or does her leaving connote an unconscious wish for self-annihilation? Is her act a form of 'resistance', echoing the last sovereign decision of Pontecorvo's concentrationee, even if this means killing oneself in the electrified fence, or does her final move simply follow the destructive totalitarian logic? I am tempted to read the film's ending, despite its ambiguities, as a grim comment on existing concentrationary logics that cut people short of their lively presence and unique potential. In *Nikita*, human beings – already declared 'dead' and reduced to disposable functionaries – also 'disappear' into 'night and fog'; other prospects lie outside of the film's imaginary.

In Besson's *Nikita* latent concentrationary content of popular imaginaries of violence becomes manifest, belatedly and perhaps repeatedly, in/through citations from the archive that haunt the film as ghosts of the past. Elements of the concentrationary inscribed in this film also become visible when they are being resisted – through the choice of visual tropes and performative acts and gestures. Our conventional ways of seeing are stalled, the flow of narrative is ruptured, things start to drift and meaning becomes dislocated – a space for critical reflection is opened up. As a 'figuration of the uncanny' (Spivak) the concentrationary also potentially becomes a figure of thinking, allowing us to engage in a reading/viewing process that, ideally, can also be likened to a 'working-through' process in the sense of a re-consideration of the central signifiers in question (Badmington).[40]

More problematic are scenarios that do not even obliquely draw attention to the fact that the conditions of their diegetic worlds are the same that once constituted the real camp and its fatal logic of unlimited possibility, including the destruction of the human(e). *La Femme Nikita* can serve as a case in point. In the televisual adaptation, the concentrationary imaginary can be traced, once again, in/through visual citations. The bleak factory halls, abandoned petrochemical plants or old warehouses to which field operatives are sent to meet and/or kill their adversaries are not only examples of the 'compromised landscapes of noir effect',[41] but also correspond in various ways to the topography of the camp. My objective now is, however, to explore the normalized camp-like structures and totalitarian conditions that determine the imaginative space of Section One.

The 'state of exception' and the *homines sacri* of *La Femme Nikita*

In some ways, the show stopped being Nikita and ... started being Section One.[42]

Section One is *La Femme Nikita*'s covertly operating anti-terrorist organization, located underground, somewhere in the West.[43] Like Besson's The Centre, it is not a conventional workplace but a paradoxical 'post-mortem' space for convicted criminals, murderers and terrorists, whose death has been purposefully staged to render the agents as nonexistent. Like Besson's leading character, the televisual Nikita (Peta Wilson) comes to Section One as a homeless young woman who has been sentenced to life imprisonment. In line with the common North American narrative cliché of the wrongly accused, however, she has not killed but has been framed for murder. Once in Section One, she is subjected to an affect-stifling discipline and paramilitary training that aims to transform human beings into 'docile bodies' (Foucault) or 'operatives' of a totalitarian system. Under the guidance of lead operative Michael Samuelle (Roy Dupuis), a leaner version of Besson's Bob and her later on-and-off lover, she acts as an unwilling but increasingly efficient agent. (8.13) Nikita's status in the organization remains volatile, and she repeatedly attempts to escape. Notably, however, the series ends with her in post as the new head of Section One, reflecting a Gramscian logic of power that is 'consolidated through an incessant process of movement, negotiation, and cooptation, which also insures its radical vulnerability to resistance'.[44]

Section One is overseen by Oversight and Centre, two equally covert organizations, but apart from these added layers of quality assurance, it operates entirely outside the law, the nation-state and any supra-national entity and without directive from an elected government, a ministry or accountable representative.[45] For its manhunts, infiltrations, kidnappings, break-ins, thefts, ad-hoc executions and bombings, Section

8.13 *La Femme Nikita* (TV series, Canadian Fireworks/Warner Brothers, 1997–2000): Peta Wilson as 'Nikita'.

One freely accesses sensitive data repositories through intrusive interception technology. Ultra-dangerous missions are generated by crises over the development and use of super-weapons, nuclear and other technological threats, insurgency and ethnic cleansing, terrorism, assassinations, organized crime and diffuse forms of sociopathy. Terrorist groups such as Red Cell, The Legion or Freedom League serve as 'all-purpose figure[s] of the Other, a perfect projection screen for dark, all-too-imaginable paranoid fantasies'.[46] The death of uninvolved people, a frequent side-effect of Section One's missions, is registered as 'acceptable collateral' and justified in the name of higher ends: the prevention of terrorism, coups d'état, war and humanitarian crises.[47] Although concrete historical events, sites or figures are rarely mentioned,[48] Section One's alleged role as global arbitrator, enforcer and 'peace keeper' alludes to US

8.14 *La Femme Nikita* (TV series, Canadian Fireworks/Warner Brothers, 1997–2000): Operations (Eugene Robert Glazer) overlooks Section One from The Perch.

involvement and interests and NATO peacekeeping missions in Bosnia or Yugoslavia in the late 1990s. But apart from these general references to ethnic conflicts and terrorist threats on a global scale, Section One is removed from society[49] and functions in a world in which imaginaries of violence are unleashed, totalitarian structures prevail and human beings can be killed and disposed of without impunity – not only outside, but also inside the organization.

In corresponding analogy to the camp Section One is characterized by a rigorous system of surveillance, intimidation and total control, as well as the excruciating demands it makes on its labour force. Operations (Eugene Robert Glazer), the strategic head of the organization, overlooks in-house activities from The Perch, a panoptic command tower that can be darkened to allow for unhindered observation. (8.14) The central work space where most of the activities take place, as well as the surrounding areas, are riddled with CCTV cameras and microphones; digital files are kept of all staff and are constantly filtered, analysed and reviewed for performance enhancement. Stacy Takacs astutely captures *La Femme Nikita*'s allegorical take on the inhumanity of post-industrial labour and management culture with its 'desocializing effects' and power structure that 'is deterritorialized and dispersed but omnipresent'.[50] Section One staff are on call around the clock; private homes are equipped with advanced surveillance technology, and some workers, like computer specialist Seymour Birkhoff (Matthew Ferguson), even live permanently on the premises.

As 'cyborgs'[51] or 'symbiotic creature[s] in which biology and technology intimately interact',[52] operatives experience the totalitarian regime of Section One directly in their body. Field operatives carry special gadgets with them and an invisible tracking device has been implanted under their skin without their knowledge, while in-house personnel are able to command and direct them on their missions via a sophisticated satellite navigation system. Operatives are upgraded versions of Besson's killing machine; their hybrid character invites us to engage 'with the "transhumanising" aspects of new media, the life sciences, and the various bio-, nano-, cogno- and info-technologies that look to reshape the reach and the nature of the human'.[53] Through 'mind control' or 'behaviour adjustment', the organization makes sure that operatives adhere to the rules and perform accordingly.[54] If they, however, become dysfunctional, volatile, weak, disloyal or emotionally attached to another person, they are put 'in abeyance', a disciplinary stage which means they await being sent on missions with a low P.O.S. ('probability of survival') or on 'suicide missions'. Such missions follow a 'calculating-instrumental rationality, which makes the bodies of the "actors" an organic component of the technological device of destruction',[55] as well as self-destruction.[56]

In the late 1950s, German Jewish philosopher and journalist Günther Anders identified at the root of Western capitalism, technological advancement and the desire to construct the nuclear bomb an unconscious operative condition that treats human beings as 'expendable', while the survival and future existence of the technical construction is insured. Western democratic societies, he argues in *Die Antiquiertheit des Menschen* take great care to keep this political unconscious a secret – but it is an *Überlebenslüge* (lie of survival) of the Ego, as the reality of the bomb makes this inhuman logic visible in a spectacular way.[57] Correspondingly, (most) operatives in *La Femme Nikita* are reduced to their depersonalized function while the technological and bureaucratic regime of the organization remains sacrosanct. Coerced by Section One into an existence apart from conventional life, operatives resemble Agamben's *homines sacri*, i.e. those who are deprived of association, rights

8.15 *La Femme Nikita* (TV series, Canadian Fireworks/Warner Brothers, 1997–2000): Torture in the White Room.

and liberty and thus a 'good' or 'qualified' life; most characters in this series are reduced to 'bare life'.[58] Section operatives, in particular, lead a 'bestialized' existence;[59] they have no agency or 'free will', as Michael reminds Nikita in Season One, Episode Ten ('Choice'), and most of them can be disposed of at any time.[60]

While Operations executes his terror regime as *Lagerführer* from The Perch, second-in-command Madeline – the organization's psychological profiler and chief interrogator – rules over the 'White' and 'Gambit' rooms, two aseptic torture chambers, in which enemy agents (and, occasionally, 'abeyance' operatives) are fastened to a metal chair for 'debriefing' under threat of mutilation or electric shocks (8.15).[61] In a psychodynamic reading of the programme Madeline represents the omnipotent Mother (complementing Operations as Father/Law): she is a symbol of male castration anxiety and object of a fetishizing gaze, but also in possession of the phallus. Her power is not so much expressed through the infliction of physical pain as through her ability to totally organize, calculate and control the effect she has on others, including the audience. Alberta Watson's performance as the sadistic female torturer plays on unconscious sexual fantasies of domination and submission, aggression and surrender, first conditioned in early infancy. Such fantasies, as Susan

Sontag points out in her 1974 essay 'Fascinating Fascism', are typically called upon in a fascist aesthetics, which is an idealized form of erotics 'based on the containment of vital forces; movements are confined, held tight, held in'.[62] This argument can be further traced in Madeline's cool and detached personality and her passionate care for orchids – symbols of (feminine) elegance and the exotic, but also of control and perfection.

Operations and Madeline oversee a world that is marked by cruel, gender-specific hierarchies and the total absence of empathy. From Season Two, Episode Four ('Approaching Zero'), the production design of the series changes: there are no warm tones or decor any more, to make Section look colder, meaner and leaner. 'It became the ultimate oppressive atmosphere', executive consultant and co-writer Surnow commented on this change: 'What we really all fell in love with, and I think our fans did too, is just how cold Section is.'[63] This is also reflected in the techno-bureaucratic language that is spoken at Section One: killings become 'cancellations' and love or empathy a 'personal component'.[64] Feelings that operatives may have for one another are typically denied or held in, unless they are induced by Section One (through drugs or technological priming) to aid a mission or serve the organization's strategic interests. Michael's 'one-night stand' with Nikita at her apartment (Season One, Episode Eight: 'Escape') is later disclosed to be a 'big manipulation' to prevent her escape from Section One.[65] Playing with the audience's desire for romance, Nikita and Michael are allowed to come physically close only when their act/ing is framed as professional operation (at least this is true for the first part of the series). In Season One, Episode Six ('Love'), Nikita performs a striptease for Michael in order to capture a voyeuristic on-screen villain who watches the duo via a CCTV camera. Her short haircut, black leather lingerie and cap in the style of an SS officer hat function as a hybrid intertextual reference to Liliana Cavani's *Night Porter* (1974). Her erotic performance cites Lucia's dance for Max (and other Nazi personnel) at the nightclub, while simultaneously hailing the off-screen viewer to partake in the same voyeurism and thus the spectacle of a fascist aesthetics.

Likewise, the relationship Operations and Madeline have throughout the television series is marked by coercion, mutual intimidation and struggles over power. Madeline, who, in a feminist reading, represents the powerful executive woman of the 1990s, is also shown to be the victim of sexual assault and humiliation, even the possibility of rape is hinted at; Operations ab/uses his position as head of Section One to satisfy his sexual needs, test Madeline's loyalty to the organization and keep its male-dominated hierarchy intact.[66] With the same ruthlessness, however, Madeline aligns herself with Section One's policy and practice or, figuratively, corporate power.[67] Under her (and Operations') regiment human beings can be tortured and, if no longer useful or posing a risk, 'cancelled'. The latter stands for disappearance into 'containment' (an on-site isolation unit) and execution, followed by the erasure of any personal data.[68] Except for Nikita, hardly any character in the series questions this practice, and very rarely is anyone's absence mourned. The minimalist mode of killing – pushing buttons on a computer – and subsequent obliteration are reminiscent of the bureaucratic regulation and extermination of concentrationees by the Nazis for the purpose of maximum efficiency. It follows the same instrumental rationality that is highlighted when the decision to execute an enemy agent or 'cancel' an operative is suddenly reversed or putative rules ignored, because Section has a 'working relationship' with this terrorist/criminal[69] or detects a new use value in an operative.[70]

If operatives (or captives) are 'cancelled' or killed, no sacrifice is made as they no longer have a 'life worth valuing and preserving, a life that qualifies for recognition'.[71] This violence, the 'unsanctionable killing', Agamben argues in *Homo Sacer*, 'opens a sphere of human action that is neither the sphere of *sacrum facere* nor that of profane action . . . [It] is that of the sovereign decision, which suspends law in the state of exception and thus implicates bare life within it.'[72] The 'state of exception', he elaborates further, originated from the modernist-revolutionary tradition, not the absolute one and insofar as it 'is not a special kind of law (like the law of war)' but 'a suspension of the juridical law, it defines law's threshold or limit concept'.[73] In *La Femme Nikita*, Section One's extraordinary power to do 'the most vile, despicable things' in the name of good and 'get away with it', as Surnow describes Section One's exceptional yet unquestioned inhumanity,[74] which is directed towards its own members as well as anybody else, echoes this 'paradox of sovereignty' that Agamben sees expressed in the state of exception.[75]

'In its cynical account of American intelligence agencies', Rosie White argues, '*La Femme Nikita* is post-Watergate and pre-9/11.'[76] In an uncannily prescient way, the series also familiarizes its audiences with imaginaries of violence that are distinctly *post*-9/11. Significantly, both the torture and the killing/'disappearance' of human bodies do not happen 'elsewhere' but on the premises: on homeland territory. In this regard, *La Femme Nikita* not only set the imaginative ground for *24* (Fox Networks) – the US prime time crime drama that was also co-written by Surnow (with Robert Cochran) and premiered in 2001, shortly after the attacks on New York's World Trade Center – but also anticipated a wider public debate in the USA following news about human rights violations, including torture, rape and homicide of prisoners held in Abu Ghraib, Baghdad's central prison, in 2003.[77] At the time, the US government was publicly known as the supporter of a continent-wide network of intelligence operatives, secret prisons and 'enhanced interrogation techniques' elsewhere, particularly in Latin America where hundreds of people had been imprisoned without trial, tortured and 'disappeared' since the collapse of the Soviet Union in 1991. The fact that in both productions a form of 'homebound torture' takes centre stage, however, alerted audiences to the possibility that this form of 'interrogation technique' was not merely 'a practice of medieval lords, fascists, totalitarian communists, and shadowy, repressive dictators in remote national capitals' but must be reckoned with 'as a practice of modern, liberal, democratic societies'.[78]

Does a world that follows the operative conditions of a state of exception (which were also those of the concentration camp) to do things it could not do otherwise offer any possibilities of resistance – and if so, in which ways are they imagined in *La Femme Nikita*? In an arc across several episodes, Michael chases after Salla Vacek (Hrant Alianak), an elusive high-ranking criminal. To gain his trust, he infiltrates his family, even marries his daughter Elena (Samia Shoaib), a wealthy and intelligent young woman, and has a son with her. Sequences of Michael with his family show him, who usually embodies Section's affect-less rationality, as a warm and caring family man.[79] The mission comes to a successful end, Vacek is killed and Michael's death in the 'other' world is fabricated. He returns to Section One and learns from Madeline that his wife and son are unharmed and will receive 'the full [care] package'. Over the following months, however, he develops a schizoid personality disorder and becomes inefficient as an operative, which nearly causes his 'cancellation'.[80] Michael is haunted by the humanity of his own double and by the superimposition of an alternative reality onto the concentrationary world to which the former is usually subordinated. Although the series is mostly marked by moral amnesia, this rare presence of both spheres positions the audience 'in-between' and opens up a temporary space for critical reflection.

Likewise, Nikita's resistance functions as a critical counterpoint to the dehumanizing logic of the camp: 'You're a good operative, Nikita. Don't let your humanity get in the way', Madeline reprimands her, when Nikita attempts to save an 'abeyance' operative from dying.[81] Although Nikita's choices are limited,[82] her character retains a residue of individuality, spontaneity and uniqueness. She refuses to be the object of Section's surveillance policy at home,[83] and she repeatedly attempts to subvert Section discipline and her pre-determined role of a 'docile body' or law-abiding operative/killing machine. She takes issue with the killing of civilians and the destructive bio-power of the organization: 'Section let those people get slaughtered. Who are these butchers we're working for, Michael?'[84] Nikita reflects about her 'action as a political being, whose own life and thinking is bound up with the life and thinking of others'.[85] She acts as the 'moral conscience' of the series; through her, a discourse on humanity – its possibilities and limits – is maintained, which is related to questions raised by a number of violent/self-destructive acts that are either committed *by* women – several central female characters commit suicide – or *to* women in form of off-screen executions.[86] The latter scenarios draw attention to the 'social vulnerability of our bodies – as a site of desire and physical vulnerability, as a site of a publicity at once assertive and exposed'[87] and ask: 'Who counts as human? Whose lives count as lives? What *makes for a grievable life?*'[88]

Generally speaking, however, reflective moments are short and soon become schematic; their main function is to create suspense and sustain interest in the female protagonist and her relationships. As the series progresses, the concentrationary becomes ever more hermetic: violations of trust, scenarios of denigration, mind modifications, real and mock 'cancellations' abound. Nikita's moral dilemmas – should she leave a failing operative behind or save him from death,[89] should she risk evacuating a young woman and her child or accept their deaths as collateral'? – are further aggravated by guilt, when she realizes that her interventions have driven the individual saved into worse or extended conditions of suffering. The many narrative twists and turns – a typical feature of long-running TV programmes – also make it increasingly difficult to distinguish between an act of humanity and the execution of just another order woven into the fabric of a counterterrorist plot concocted by Section One.

White reads Section One's 'scant regard for the lives of its operatives, together with its disregard of their human rights ... [as] a scathing critique of both the espionage bureaucracy and the powers that support it'.[90] I agree with White on the critical *potential* that such scenarios have in aiming to alert viewers to the disciplinary power and bio-politics of the totalitarian (also in liberal democracies); I also side with Takacs's critique of *La Femme Nikita* as an allegory of 'the New Economy and its Empire of control'.[91] 'The appeal of such genres, as Fredric Jameson has shown, ... lies in their formal and stylistic arrangement, which unconsciously registers "the political content of daily life".'[92] Section One's workplace scenarios, in which formal labour relations have been suspended, brings up associative material around the current neo-liberalist economic and political climate, in which corresponding totalitarian logics are noticeable in the way labour is subjected to inhumane practices such as contract maximization, continuous assessment and performance monitoring, as well as other more subtle forms of managerial 'fascism'.[93]

The central cynicism of *La Femme Nikita* to which White refers in her analysis, however, is at risk of losing its transgressive power when scenarios of violence, cruelty and torture become a regular feature of media consumption that fosters a particular viewing experience – one in which 'the special *effect* trumps any genuine *affect* and [our own] society is not so much reflected as erased and produced again in the ideological terms of cinematic frisson'.[94] As a product of US/Canadian prime time television, *La Femme Nikita* displays a high level of aesthetic creativity and technical mastery, comparable to that of commercials and music videos. Like these media products, *La Femme Nikita* aims for a synthesis of music, fashion design and plot. Its seductive score with a hybrid melange of psychedelic rock and electronica, trance and *Sade*-an jazz[95] – music associated with nightclubs and psycho-stimulants, but also with festivals that emphasize love, peace and respect – is able to transform political and personal violence and aggression into a hyper-stylish, ecstatic spectacle: operatives become 'smooth operators'. On a diegetic level, characters are constantly exposed to traumatizing experiences, and they also employ a terminology that is reminiscent of the euphemistic language of destruction once used by the Nazis. But it is due to this refined video clip aesthetic in combination with the multiple close-ups and slow motion sequences as vehicles for the inscription of romance and desire, as well as the perfect bodies of a glamorous cast in haute-couture outfits and stylish sets,[96] that viewers are pulled into the narrative again and again, deriving pleasure in fascist ideology inscribed in this series.

This pull is difficult to resist: *La Femme Nikita* both reflects and encourages an attitude of 'cynical chic' towards totalitarian logics that accounts for the thrill that audiences experience when viewing this series and for the obsessive relationship that large fan communities develop with certain elements, engaging their fantasy beyond the screen reality. A significant number of *LFN* fan sites imitate the language and logic of Section in reviews, summaries and glossaries. These sites provide readers with music lists, interviews by the production team and background information and gossip on the cast. Pieces of set design are displayed as memorabilia and the 'Torture Twins' (Madeline's two assistants in the 'White' and 'Gambit' rooms) are chosen as a challenge for fan fiction.

In *Moral Blindness: The Loss of Sensitivity in Liquid Modernity*, Bauman and Leonidas Donskis see social life in liquid modernity increasingly become *adiaphorized*, i.e. exempt from moral obligations and evaluations.[97] Can *La Femme Nikita*'s casual embrace of atrocious and dehumanizing scenarios (and the pleasure in watching them) be read as a symptom of a growing indifference and insensitivity towards the suffering of others? I wonder how much our own 'moral blindness' or 'numbness' is reflected in an episode of the series in which Nikita finds out that Jenna Vogler (Gina Torres), a black lesbian terrorist, is a human carrier of a bomb.[98] After being tortured, Jenna is given the choice to work as a new operative or die in 'containment'; she opts for death. In the next scene, Operations and Michael congratulate Nikita on her successful mission; then a bomb can be heard to explode off-screen and Jenna's destruction is left to the audience's imagination. Suicidal resistance in the context of terrorism is, as Gayatri Chakravorty Spivak writes, 'a message inscribed on the body when no other means will get through. It is both execution and mourning, for both self and other. For you die with me for the same cause, no matter which side you are on.'[99] But the collective notion of Jenna's suicide is thwarted here, as her body has already been moved to 'containment'. There are, it seems, no redeeming or phantasmatic moments of intersubjective relationality left in the camp/Section; what such scenarios speak to is the same politically unprocessed logic that

Anders understood to be at the heart of humankind's desire to build the bomb and that suggests the essential superfluity of the human/e.

Notably, Surnow – at the time a strong supporter of George W. Bush – commented on this scene: 'These are one of my favorite moments in the show,' he said, 'when it seems like horrible things are happening and people are moving on as if nothing is going on'.[100] He could not have better expressed 'the word-and-thought defying *banality of evil*' that allowed fascism to become 'ordinary'.[101] 'We live in a reality of possibilities, not one of dilemmas', Bauman and Donskis write in their introduction to *Moral Blindness*.[102] The global popularity of the Nikita narratives gives good reason to believe that concentrationary imaginaries – which also always include imaginaries of adiaphora [Gr. indifferent things] – are a widespread, perhaps global, phenomenon of our time.

NOTES

Series Preface

1. David Rousset, *L'univers concentrationnaire* [1946] (Paris: Hachette, 2008), 181; translation as *The Other Kingdom*, trans. Ramon Guthrie (New York: Reynal & Hitchcock, 1947), 168–9:

   > The concentrationary universe shrivels away within itself. It still lives on in the world like a dead planet laden with corpses. Normal men do not know that everything is possible. Even if evidence forces their intelligences to admit it, their muscles do not believe it. The concentrationees do know it … The decomposition of a society and all of the classes of that society, in the fetid stench of destroyed social values, they came to know at first hand, an immediate reality like an ominous planet threatening the entire planet in which all men must share. The evil far outweighs any military triumphs. It is the gangrene of a whole economic and social system. Its contamination spreads far beyond the ruin of cities.

   In 1951, Hannah Arendt wrote, 'The concentration and extermination camps of totalitarian regimes serve as the laboratories in which the fundamental belief of totalitarianism that everything is possible [Rousset's phrase] is being verified' Hannah Arendt, *The Origins of Totalitarianism* [1951] (New York: Harcourt, Brace, Jovanovich, 1996), 565.

2. Griselda Pollock and Max Silverman (eds), *Concentrationary Cinema: Aesthetics as Political Resistance in Alain Resnais's Night and Fog* (New York: Berghahn, 2014).
3. Hannah Arendt, 'The Concentration Camps', *Partisan Review* 10:7 (1948), 761.
4. David Runciman, 'Is This How Democracy Ends?', *London Review of Books* 38:23 (1 December, 2016), 1 of 5, https://www.lrb.co.uk/v38/n23/david-runciman/is-this-how-democracy-ends.
5. Runciman, 'Is This How Democracy Ends?', 5 of 5.
6. Steven Levitsky and Daniel Ziblatt, *How Democracies Die* (New York: Crown, 2018).
7. Levitsky and Ziblatt, *How Democracies Die*, 9–10.

Introduction

1. J. Lacan (Paris), 'The Looking Glass Phase', *International Journal of Psychoanalysis* 18/1 (1937), p. 78. On this absence see Jane Gallop 'Where to Begin?', in Jane Gallop, *Reading Lacan* (Ithaca: Cornell University Press, 1985), pp. 74–92.

2 Jacques Lacan, 'Le Stade du miroir comme formateur de la fonction du Je: telle qu'elle nous est révélée dans l'expérience psychanalytique', *Revue française de psychanalyse* 4 (1949), pp. 449–55. For an account of the various forms of this paper and our knowledge of the earliest presentations based on notes taken by the psychoanalyst Françoise Dolto at an earlier presentation in Paris, see Élisabeth Roudinescu, 'The Mirror Stage: An Obliterated Archive', in Jean-Michel Rabaté, *The Cambridge Companion to Lacan* (Cambridge: Cambridge University Press, 2003), pp. 25–34. See her long chapter, 'Marienbad', in *Jacques Lacan*, trans. Barbara Bray (New York: Columbia University Press, 1997 and Cambridge: Polity Press, 1997), pp. 107–20.

3 Jacques Lacan, 'The Mirror Phase as Formative of the Function of the "I" in Psychoanalytic Experience', *Ecrits: A Selection*, trans. Alan Sheridan (London: Tavistock Publications, 1977), pp. 1–7, p. 6. It was also printed as 'The Mirror-phase as Formative of the Function of the I: 1949', *New Left Review* 51 (1968), pp. 71–7.

4 Lacan: 'Le Stade du miroir comme formateur de la fonction du Je: telle qu'elle nous est révélée dans l'expérience psychanalytique', *Revue française de psychanalyse* 4 (1949), p. 454.

5 Lacan: 'The Mirror Phase', p. 7: note 4.

6 In her short return to Lacan, whose biography she had written in 1993, Élisabeth Roudinescu argues that 'He was the only psychoanalytical thinker to consider the legacy of Auschwitz in a Freudian fashion, mobilizing Greek tragedy as well as the writings of Marquis de Sade to evoke its horror'. Élisabeth Roudinescu, *Lacan: In Spite of Everything*, trans. Gregory Elliott (London: Verso, 2014), pp. 7–8.

7 David Rousset, *L'Univers concentrationnaire* (Paris: Editions de Pavois, 1946; reprinted Paris: Hachette/Pluriel, 2008). The English versions appeared as David Rousset, *The Other Kingdom*, trans. Ramon Guthrie (New York: Reynal and Hitchcock, 1947) and *A World Apart*, trans. Y. Moyse and R. Senhouse (London: Secker & Warburg, 1951). The phrase occurs on p. 181 in the French edition (2008) and p. 168 in the English edition (1947).

8 Griselda Pollock and Max Silverman (eds), *Concentrationary Cinema: Aesthetics as Resistance in Alain Resnais's Night and Fog* (London and New York: Berghan, 2011); Griselda Pollock and Max Silverman (eds), *Concentrationary Memories: Totalitarian Terror and Cultural Resistance* (London: I.B.Tauris, 2013).

9 I shall italicize concentrationary or imaginary to stress which element is the focus of analysis in each section. The capitalized 'Imaginary' refers specifically to Lacan's psychological register, whereas 'imaginary' is the more general term.

10 Benjamin Hannavy Cousen, *The Seeping and Creeping of Haunted Memory: Tracing the Concentrationary in Post-war Cinema* (unpublished PhD thesis, University of Leeds, 2011).
11 Fredric Jameson, *The Political Unconscious: Narrative as a Socially Symbolic Act* (Ithaca: Cornell University Press, 1982).
12 Susan Sontag, 'Fascinating Fascism', *New York Review of Books*, 6 February 1975. It was a review of Leni Riefenstahl's *The Last of the Nuba* and Jack Pia's *SS Regalia*. Reprinted in Susan Sontag, *Under the Sign of Saturn* (London: Writers and Readers Collective, 1980), pp. 73–108.
13 Hannah Arendt, *The Origins of Totalitarianism* [1951] (New York: Harcourt Inc., 1976), p. 438.
14 Arendt: *The Origins of Totalitarianism*, p. 438.
15 Giorgio Agamben, 'The Camp as "Nomos" of the Modern', *Homo Sacer: Sovereign Power and Bare Life* [1995], trans. Daniel Heller-Roazen (Stanford: Stanford University Press, 1998), p. 166.
16 Wolfgang Sofsky, *The Order of Terror: The Concentration Camp* [1993], trans. William Templer (Princeton: Princeton University Press, 1997), p. 13.
17 Sofsky: *The Order of Terror*, p.13.
18 Sofsky: *The Order of Terror*, p. 14.
19 Sofsky: *The Order of Terror*, p. 281.
20 Paul Virilio, *Bunker Archeology* (Princeton: Princeton Architectural Press, 1994; new edition 2009) and *War and Cinema: The Logics of Perception* (London: Verso, 2009).
21 The Holocaust is now used to include a general sense of 'Nazi atrocities' or what happened during 'the War' to religious minorities, gay and lesbian men and women, physically and mentally disabled Germans, criminals and those whom the Nazis defined as social deviants.
22 The first and a rare report on a death camp occurs in a powerful essay by Jewish Soviet writer Vassily Grossman, an embedded reporter with the Red Army. In 'The Hell of Treblinka', written in September 1944, Grossman writes of the discovery of the erased remains of Treblinka II (the killing site) and the investigation into its operations from bystanders and the few survivors of the revolt of the Sonderkommando that brought the camp to an end. The essay is translated in Vassily Grossman, *The Road: Stories, Journalism and Essays*, edited by Robert Chandler and Yury Bit-Yunan, trans. Robert and Elizabeth Chandler and Olga Mukovnikova (New York: NYRB, 2010), pp. 116–62.
23 Operation Reinhard built camps at Bełżec, Sobibor and Treblinka (Chełmno was already in operation as of 7 December 1941) that operated between 1942 and 1943. Auschwitz II-Birkenau was built in summer 1942 as an extension to a concentration and prisoner of war camp, Auschwitz I, which

also became a major site of mass murder between 1942 and 1944. Majdanek also performed this function within its larger concentrationary activity. There were also two extermination camps in Serbia.

24 In the immediate aftermath of World War II, the specificity of the fate of Jewish and Romany Europeans as victims of racialized genocidal persecution was downplayed or even masked by being assimilated to the general condemnation of 'Nazi atrocities' that were reported in the Western media by journalists and photographers travelling with the liberating Allied armies as they moved eastwards to Berlin. The lineaments and specific modes of mourning and commemoration of the fate of Jewish and to a much lesser extent the Romany peoples of Europe have emerged slowly into popular cultural memory. The genocide and racial persecution were, of course, urgently witnessed by its survivors immediately and in many languages, but without full cultural acknowledgement. For a study that contests the historical narrative of delayed registration of the genocide, see David Cesarani and Eric Sundquist (eds), *After the Holocaust: Challenging the Myth of Silence* (London: Routledge, 2012); Alan Rosen, *The Wonder of their Voices: The 1946 Holocaust Interviews of David Boder* (Oxford: Oxford University Press, 2010).

25 In addition to Operation Reinhard, we must also recall the mass killing fields of Belarus, Lithuania, Latvia and Ukraine during Operation Barbarossa initiated 22 June 1941 as the invasion of the Soviet Union. Special units, *Einsatzgruppen* (Mobile Killing Units) followed the German armies and murdered, mostly by shooting, later by gas vans, the large Jewish and smaller Roma populations of these areas. Yitzhak Arad, Shmuel Krakowski, Shmuel Spector and Stella Schossberger. *The Einsatzgruppen Reports: Selections from the Dispatches of the Nazi Death Squads' Campaign against the Jews, July 1941–January 1943* (New York: Holocaust Library, 1989); Ronald Headland, *Messages of Murder: A Study of the Reports of the Einsatzgruppen of the Security Police and the Security Service, 1941–1943* (Rutherford, NJ: Fairleigh Dickinson University Press, 1992).

26 One of the major debates in this area concerns the representability of the mass murder, and the status of four photographs taken by a Sonderkommando team in Auschwitz-Birkenau in August 1944 that appear to be the only directly witnessed images of a mass gassing and subsequent burning of the bodies. See Georges Didi-Huberman, *Images in Spite of All: Four Photographs from Auschwitz*, trans. Shane B. Lillis (Chicago: University of Chicago Press, 2012) and Nicholas Chare and Dominic Williams, *The Scrolls of Auschwitz* (London and New York: Berghahn, 2015).

27 Bergen-Belsen was a peculiar place. Initially founded as the prisoner of war camp, Stalag XI-C, it underwent many changes of name and purpose before

becoming a concentration camp, KZ (*Konzentrationslager*), under SS control in 1943 when Himmler sent there selected high-profile Dutch-Jewish hostages who, being too visible to destroy, were being held as potential exchanges for German prisoners of war overseas. The population of the camp included as its main occupants 50,000 Soviet prisoners, of whom 37,000 perished from the abominable conditions. Around 8,000 women (Jewish and non-Jewish) were sent from Auschwitz in mid-1944, while it also became a camp for the sick from other camps in the concentration system that spread across Germany. In December 1944, there were only 15,000 inmates whose number forced movements of concentrationees from the East swelled as the Russians advanced through Poland arriving at Auschwitz in January 1945. Some of these were indeed Jewish. Anna and Margot Frank were among them. There were no gas chambers functioning as a systematic death factory. Overcrowding, radical undernourishment and unfettered disease produced an accelerating death rate in the first months of 1945.

28 On 7 December 1971 Hitler signed the *Nacht und Nebel* directive targeting all political resisters in domestic and occupied areas. Two months later Field Marshal Wilhelm Keitel extended it to all prisoners taken by the German army and security forces still alive after eight days in custody. Taking the term from Wagner's opera *Rheingold*, the punishment was to be 'disappeared' without trace, the prisoner knowing no one could trace him or her, the families losing the prisoner to an abyss of untraceability. Unmarked graves further compounded this grave breach of the Hague Convention. Leaving offender and relatives both ignorant of the fate was considered a necessary deterrent beyond penal servitude or hard labour. This further illustrates the function of such orders to terrorize entire populations by what was done to those taken to its multitude of camps.

29 For an account of her argument and a critique of it from a different conception of the political, see Andrew Schaap, 'Enacting the right to have rights: Jacques Rancière's critique of Hannah Arendt', *European Journal of Political Theory* 10/1 (2011), pp. 22–45.

30 Dana Villa, 'Genealogies of Total Domination: Arendt, Adorno and Auschwitz', *New German Critique* 100 (Winter 2007), p. 2.

31 Villa: 'Genealogies of Total Domination', p. 45.

32 Villa: 'Genealogies of Total Domination', p. 45.

33 For a discussion of the effects of deterritorialized globalizing capitalism on the safety and humanity of unprotected peoples, see Zygmunt Bauman, *Wasted Lives: Modernity and its Outcasts* (Cambridge: Polity Press, 2003).

34 The concentrationary manifests itself in movements in which the plurality of humanity is to be erased in the name of a single unifying belief system or pseudopolitical order, what Hannah Arendt named pan-movements.

Religion as much as race or political doctrine can function as this false unifying factor in which ultimately everyone becomes superfluous or dispensable as a human subject.

35 Saul Friedländer, *Reflets du Nazisme* (Paris: Editions du Seuil, 1982); *Reflections of Nazism: An Essay on Kitsch and Death*, trans. Thomas Weyr (New York: Harper & Row, 1984). I shall cite from the 1993 revised edition.
36 Friedländer: *Reflections of Nazism* (1993), p. 12.
37 Friedländer: *Reflections of Nazism* (1993), p. 15.
38 Friedländer: *Reflections of Nazism* (1993), p. 18.
39 Friedländer: *Reflections of Nazism* (1993), p. 18.
40 Friedländer: *Reflections of Nazism* (1993), p. 18.
41 Friedländer: *Reflections of Nazism*, (1993), p. 27.
42 Friedländer: *Reflections of Nazism* (1993), p. 134.
43 Friedländer: *Reflections of Nazism* (1993), pp. 134–5.
44 Friedländer: *Reflections of Nazism* (1993), p. 136.
45 Sontag: 'Fascinating Fascism' (1980), p. 90
46 Sontag: 'Fascinating Fascism' (1980), p. 91.
47 David Scroggy (ed.), *Blade Runner Sketchbook* (San Diego: Blue Dolphin Enterprises 1982); Danny Peary, *Cult Movies 3* (New York: Vermillion, 1988); James McDonald, *Fantasy and the Cinema* (London: BFI, 1989); Judith B. Kerman (ed.), *Retrofitting Blade Runner: Issues in Ridley Scott's Blade Runner and Philip K. Dick's Do Androids Dream of Electric Sheep?* (Bowling Green, Ohio: Bowling Green University Popular Press, 1991); Paul Sammon, *Future Noir: The Making of Blade Runner* (New York: Orion, 1996); Scott Bukatman, *Blade Runner* (London: BFI 1998).
48 Fredric Jameson, 'Postmodernism, Or The Cultural Logic of Late Capitalism', *New Left Review* 146 (July–August 1984), pp. 53–92.
49 Donna Haraway, 'A Cyborg Manifesto Science, Technology, and Socialist-feminism in the Late Twentieth Century', in *Simians, Cyborgs and Women: the Reinvention of Nature* (London and New York: Routledge, 1991), pp. 149–81.
50 Kaja Silverman, 'Back to the Future', *Camera Obscura* 9/3 (1991), p. 115.
51 *Blade Runner: Five Disk Collector's Edition* (Warner Brothers, 2007), Disk 4: *Inception:* Philip K. Dick: The Blade Runner Interviews.
52 On the role of language in creating and sustaining the delusions of the Third Reich, see Victor Klemperer, *The Language of the Third Reich: A Philologist's Notebook*, trans. Martin Brady (London: Bloomsbury Academic, 2006).
53 I could do similar kinds of readings for other science fiction films from *Star Wars* to *Lord of the Rings*: largely drawing your attention to the manner in which the cinematic telling of these tales, notably *Lord of the Rings*, cannot but imagine visually the fictive battles of the future or Middle Earth in the costume of fascist aesthetic representations and representations of fascist

regimes. What is particularly significant for me in *Star Wars* is not the premise of a world domination seeking to maintain domination for its own sake and at all costs harrying its potential resistance to destruction, but that the forces leading and defending this world are a) militarized and b) faceless: the darkest of which is the metallically, plastically shielded and electronically enhanced Darth Vader who, like the Wizard of Oz, is an amplified man beneath his black cape and clearly resonant black helmet and face mask.

54 This line of research leads us to studies such as *Male Fantasies* by Klaus Theweleit, who read the diaries and letters of the paramilitary and military men who became members of the SA and the SS in order to identify the tropes of anxious fear about purity and survival in the face of monstrous others and the gross caricaturing of that which is imagined as other, notably the red woman, against whom fantasies of bloody destruction are commonly expressed. Klaus Theweleit, *Male Fantasies, Vol. 1: Women, Floods, Bodies, Histories*, trans. Chris Turner and Stephen Conway (Minneapolis: University of Minnesota Press, 1987).

55 Fredric Jameson, 'Imaginary and Symbolic in Lacan: Marxism, Psychoanalytical Criticism and the Problem of the Subject', *Yale French Studies* 55/56 (1977), pp. 338–95, p. 353.

56 Christian Metz, *Psychoanalysis and Cinema: The Imaginary Signifier* [1977] trans. Celia Britton et al. (Basingstoke: Macmillan, 1982).

57 Jameson: 'Imaginary and Symbolic in Lacan', p. 357.

58 Arendt: *The Origins of Totalitarianism*, pp. 445–56.

Chapter 1: Framing Horror

1 Don DeLillo, 'In the Ruins of the Future', *The Guardian Online*, 22 December 2001 (first published in *Harper's Magazine*, December 2001), http://www.theguardian.com/books/2001/dec/22/fiction.dondelillo (accessed 2 March 2011).

2 'A Dialogue with Jacques Derrida', in *Philosophy in a Time of Terror: Dialogues with Jürgen Habermas and Jacques Derrida: Interviewed by Giovanna Borradori* (Chicago: The University of Chicago Press, 2003), p. 94.

3 Adriana Cavarero, *Horrorism: Naming Contemporary Violence*, trans William McCuaig (New York: Columbia University Press 2009). Many of the topics mentioned in this chapter are treated at length in this book.

4 Marcello Flores, *Tutta la violenza di un secolo* (Milan: Feltrinelli, 2005), p. 68.

5 Flores: *Tutta la violenza di un secolo*, p. 12.

6 Hannah Arendt, *The Origins of Totalitarianism* (New edn. New York: Harcourt, Brace and World, 1966), p. 443.

7 Arendt: *The Origins of Totalitarianism*, pp. 458–9.

8 Arendt: *The Origins of Totalitarianism*, p. 459. Editors' note: the term *Lager*, the German term for storage space used by the SS in naming *Konzentrationslager* and *Vernichtungslager* (death camps)and used by Primo Levi in his writings, is the customary term in Italian writings on the topic. The English word 'camp' has been substituted in some cases but *Lager* is retained in this chapter in accordance with the author's original text.
9 Hannah Arendt, 'Mankind and Terror', in *Essays in Understanding, 1930–1954*, edited by Jerome Kohn (New York: Harcourt, Brace and Co., 1994), p. 297.
10 Arendt: *The Origins of Totalitarianism*, p. 440.
11 Arendt, *The Origins of Totalitarianism*, p. viii from the preface to the first edition, dated 1950.
12 Arendt: *The Origins of Totalitarianism*, p. 440.
13 Arendt: *The Origins of Totalitarianism*, p. 444.
14 Arendt: *The Origins of Totalitarianism*, p. 457.
15 Arendt: *The Origins of Totalitarianism*, p. 454.
16 Arendt: *The Origins of Totalitarianism*, p. 453.
17 Arendt: *The Origins of Totalitarianism*, p. 455.
18 Arendt: *The Origins of Totalitarianism*, p. 443.
19 Judith Butler, *Precarious Life* (London: Verso 2006), p. 20.
20 Primo Levi, *The Drowned and the Saved*, trans. Raymond Rosenthal (New York: Summit Books, 1988), pp. 83–4.
21 See Francesca Consolaro, 'Il "vulnerabile" come chiave del "mondo che viene": considerazioni etimologiche', *Filosofia Politica* 1 (2009), pp. 45–50.
22 Primo Levi, *Survival in Auschwitz and the Reawakening*, trans. Stuart Woolf (New York: Summit, 1986), p. 191.
23 Elsa Morante, *History: A Novel*, trans. William Weaver (London: Penguin Books 2001), p. 272.
24 Morante, *History: a novel*, p. 417.
25 Morante, *History: a novel*, p. 418.

Chapter 2: Between Realism and Fiction

1 Alfred Camus, *The Rebel* (1951) trans. Anthony Bower (London: Penguin Classics, 2001). [*L'homme révolté*: 'Il y a des crimes de passion et des crimes de logique.']
2 Alexander Pope, *An Essay on Man* [1734] (Charleston, SC: BiblioBazaar, 2008).
3 G.W.F. Hegel, *Grundlinien der Philosophie des Rechts* [1821] (Suhrkamp: Frankfurt am Main 1972), p. 11.
4 Hannah Arendt, *The Life of the Mind* (New York: Harcourt Brace Jovanovich, 1978), part I, p. 91.

5 Hannah Arendt, *On Revolution* [1963] (New York: Viking Penguin 1977), p. 56.
6 Jacques Taminiaux, *The Thracian Maid and the Professional Thinker: Arendt and Heidegger* (Albany: Suny Press, 1997), p. 161.
7 Arendt: *The Life of the Mind*, I, p. 54.
8 Arendt, *Essays in Understanding: 1930–1954*, ed. Jerome Kohn (New York: Harcourt Brace and Co, 1994), p. 319.
9 Arendt: *On Revolution*, p. 55.
10 Arendt: *The Life of the Mind*, p. 89.
11 Hannah Arendt, *On Violence* (New York: Harcourt, Brace and World, 1970).
12 Hannah Arendt, *The Origins of Totalitarianism* [1951] (New York: Harcourt Brace and Co. Harvest, 1979), p. 455.
13 Paul Ricoeur insists on the importance of the plot in 'symbolizing events', as not being a mere construction, a mere textual device devoid of legitimacy in the representation of life and reality, but a configuration able to symbolically represent what otherwise would remain unspeakable in language, namely the aporetic nature of the human experience of time: 'the speculation on time is an inconclusive rumination to which narrative activity can alone respond'. Paul Ricoeur, *Temps et Récit I* (Paris: Éditions du Seuil, 1983), p. 6, my trans.
14 Hannah Arendt, *The Human Condition* (Chicago: Chicago University Press, 1958), pp. 42–3.
15 Hannah Arendt, 'On Humanity in Dark Times: Thoughts about Lessing', in *Men in Dark Times* [1968] (New York: Harvest Books, 1995), p. 20.
16 Arendt: *On Humanity in Dark Times*, p. 21.
17 Arendt: *On Humanity in Dark Times*, p. 22.
18 Arendt: *The Origins of Totalitarianism*, p. 438.
19 Arendt: *The Origins of Totalitarianism*, p. 438.
20 Arendt: *The Origins of Totalitarianism*, p. 438.
21 Arendt: *The Origins of Totalitarianism*, p. 439.
22 Arendt: *The Origins of Totalitarianism*, p. 443.
23 Arendt: *The Origins of Totalitarianism*, p. 441.
24 Arendt: *The Origins of Totalitarianism*, p. 441.
25 Arendt: *The Origins of Totalitarianism*, p. 441.
26 Arendt: *The Origins of Totalitarianism*, p. 442.
27 Primo Levi, 'Shemà', *Collected Poems* trans. Ruth Feldman and Brian Swann (London: Faber & Faber 1992), p. 9.
28 Azar Nafisi, 'The Republic of the Imagination', *Washington Post*, 5 December 2004, http://www.washingtonpost.com/wp-dyn/articles/A30117-2004Dec2.html (accessed 3 October 2011).
29 As is the custom in Italian writing on the camps, the German term *Lager* is used throughout this chapter.

30 Hayden White, *Figural Realism: Studies in the Mimesis Effect*, (Baltimore and London: Johns Hopkins University Press, 2000), pp. 41–2.
31 Primo Levi, *I sommersi e i salvati* (Turin: Einaudi 1986). In this chapter I refer to the Italian original edition, and the translations of the passages are mine. The English edition is *The Drowned and the Saved*, trans. Raymond Rosenthal (New York: Vintage Books, 1989).
32 Hayden White, *Comparare: Considerations on a Levian Practice*, paper presented in Verona, Società Letteraria, 13 June 1997, [n.pub.], p. 6 of the manuscript.
33 My translation. Levi, *I sommersi e i salvati*: p. 6: Questo stesso libro è intriso di memoria: per di più, di una memoria lontana. Attinge dunque ad una fonte sospetta, e deve essere difeso contro se stesso. Ecco: contiene più considerazioni che ricordi, si sofferma più volentieri sullo stato di cose quale è oggi che non sulla cronaca retroattiva.
34 'Considerare' means literally to observe the stars in order to obtain a divinatory response from the sky.
35 White: *Comparare*, p. 8 of the manuscript.
36 An English edition of the memoirs of some members of the *Sonderkommando* in Auschwitz (originally in Yiddish) is out of print but available in certain libraries (contrarily to the Italian edition, *La voce dei sommersi*, Carlo Saletti ed., Venice: Marsilio, 2000, easily available): *The Scrolls of Auschwitz*, trans. Sharon Neemani (Tel Aviv: Am 'Oved, 1985). In the form of clandestine manuscripts – pieces of scrap paper, cigarette boxes – these memoirs have been found near Auschwitz many years later, and they are shocking insofar as they probably offer us the perfect testimony of which Levi speaks, namely the testimony of those who experienced the bottom of the *Lager* and did not come back. Interestingly enough these memoirs are all in the form of a literary, fictive recount. A fictive narrator is supposed to take a fictive listener to see, to witness, to experience the entire journey of the deported persons, from the ghetto evacuation to the train journey to their final destination – the camp. A literary study on these memories should be interesting and revealing with regard to the issue of a fictionalized or imaginary reconstruction of the unimaginable. On this topic see Nicholas Chare, *Auschwitz and Afterimages: Abjection, Witnessing and Representation* (London & New York: I.B.Tauris, 2011) and Nicholas Chare and Dominic Williams, *The Scrolls of Auschwitz* (London: Berghahn, 2016).
37 Levi: *I sommersi e i salvati*, pp. 3–4.
38 Giorgio Agamben, *Remnants of Auschwitz: The Witness and the Archive*, trans. Daniel Heller-Roazen (Cambridge, MA: MIT Press, 2000).
39 Luca Zevi, *Conservazione dell'avvenire* (Macerata: Quodlibet, 2011), p. 9.
40 As Akeel Bilgrami has effectively pointed out, by drawing on Gandhi's critique of the West, scientific rationality as it developed in Europe in the

seventeenth century, by way of disenchanting the world, gave rise to the horrors of modern industrial life, to destructive technological frames of mind, to rank commercialism, to the surrender of spiritual casts of mind', not to mention colonialism and racism. There was though, he affirms, an alternative and radical Enlightenment that did not accept the metaphysical background of Newtonian science, namely that the world was 'brute and disenchanted' and as such 'could not move us to any such engagement since any perception of it, given the sort of thing it was, would necessarily be a detached form of observation; and if one ever came out of this detachment, if there was ever any engagement with a world so distantly conceived, so external to our own sensibility, it could only take the form of mastery and control of something alien, with a view to satisfying the only source of value allowed by this outlook – our own utilities and gain' (398). To the alternative tradition of radical Enlightenment, critical of the predatory nature of modern rationality, belonged, not by chance I would claim, poets and writers: 'Blake, Shelley, William Morris, Whitman, Thoreau, and countless anonymous voices of the nontraditional Left, the Left of the radical Enlightenment' (p. 402). Akeel Bilgrami, 'Occidentalism, the Very Idea: An Essay on Enlightenment and Enchantment', *Critical Inquiry* 32 (2006), pp. 381–411.
41 On the link between nihilism and entertainment as it takes form in contemporary Italy under Berlusconi's rule, see C. Chiurco, ed., *Filosofia di Berlusconi. L'essere e il nulla nell'Italia contemporanea* (Verona: ombre corte, 2011).
42 The reference is to the Arab Spring of 2011.
43 Azar Nafisi, 'The Republic of the Imagination', *Washington Post*, 5 December 2004, http://www.washingtonpost.com/wp-dyn/articles/A30117-2004Dec2.html (accessed 3 October 2011).
44 Azar Nafisi, 'The Republic of the Imagination', *Washington Post*, 5 December 2004, http://www.washingtonpost.com/wp-dyn/articles/A30117-2004Dec2.html (accessed 3 October 2011).

Chapter 3: Totality, Convergence, Synchronization

1 Hannah Arendt, *The Origins of Totalitarianism* (New York: Harvest, 1973).
2 Paul Virilio, *Bunker Archeology*, trans. G. Collins (New York: Princeton Architectural Press, 1994).
3 Virilio: *Bunker Archeology*, p. 29.
4 Virilio: *Bunker Archeology*, p. 40.
5 Virilio: *Bunker Archeology*, p. 12.

6 Jean-Luc Nancy and Philippe Lacoue-Labarthe, *Le Mythe nazi* (Paris: Éditions de l'Aube, 1991); 'The Nazi Myth', trans. Brian Holmes, *Critical Inquiry*,16:2 (1990), pp. 291–312.
7 Nancy and Lacoue-Labarthe: *Le Mythe nazi*, p. 9; 'The Nazi Myth', p. 292.
8 David Rousset, *L'Univers concentrationnaire* (Paris: Minuit, 1965), pp. 186–7.
9 Arendt, *The Origins of Totalitarianism*, p. 459.
10 Nancy and Lacoue-Labarthe: *Le Mythe nazi*, p. 23; 'The Nazi Myth', p. 294.
11 Nancy and Lacoue-Labarthe: *Le Mythe nazi*, p. 71; 'The Nazi Myth', p. 312.
12 Nancy and Lacoue-Labarthe: *Le Mythe nazi*, p. 25; 'The Nazi Myth', p. 295.
13 Nancy and Lacoue-Labarthe: *Le Mythe nazi*, p. 71; 'The Nazi Myth', p. 312.
14 See for example, Philippe Lacoue-Labarthe 'La Fable (philosophie et littérature)', *Poétique*, no. 1 (1970), pp. 51–63 and *Le Sujet de la philosophie* (Paris: Aubier-Flammarion, 1979). See also, Jean-Luc Nancy, *Ego Sum* (Paris: Flammarion, 1979).
15 Virilio: *Bunker Archeology*, p. 29.
16 Virilio: *Bunker Archeology*, pp. 46–7.
17 Paul Virilio, *Défense Populaire et luttes écologiques* (Paris: Galilée, 1978), p. 68; *Popular Defense and Ecological Struggles*, trans. Mark Polizzotti (New York: Semiotext(e), 1990), p. 70.
18 Virilio: *Défense Populaire et luttes écologiques*, p. 62; *Popular Defense and Ecological Struggles*, p. 64.
19 Paul Virilio, *L'Insécurité du territoire* (Paris: Stock, 1976 [Paris: Galilée, 1993]), p. 283.
20 Virilio: *L'Insécurité du territoire*, p. 283.
21 Virilio: *L'Insécurité du territoire*, p. 283.
22 Paul Virilio and Philippe Petit, *Cybermonde ou la politique du pire* (Paris: Éditions Textuel, 1996), pp. 84–85; *Politics of the Very Worst*, trans. Michael Cavaliere (New York: Semiotext(e), 1999), p. 87.
23 Paul Virilio, *Ville Panique: Ailleurs commence ici* (Paris: Galilée, 2003), p. 48; *City of Panic*, trans. Julie Rose (New York: Bloomsbury, 2007).
24 Bernard Stiegler, *La Technique et le temps 3. Le Temps du cinéma et la question du mal-être* (Paris: Galilée, 2001), p. 19.
25 Stiegler: *La Technique et le temps* 3, pp. 19–20; *Technics and Time 3*, trans. Stephen Barker (Stanford: Stanford University Press 2011), p. 3.
26 Stiegler: *La Technique et le temps* 3, pp. 187–8; *Technics and Time 3*, p. 124.
27 Stiegler: *La Technique et le temps* 3, p. 157; *Technics and Time 3*, p. 101.
28 For a recent extended polemic against contemporary discourses which align innovations in information technology with processes of democratic emancipation see Evgeny Morozov, *The Net Delusion: How Not to Change the World* (London: Allen Lane, 2011).

29 Jean-Luc Nancy, *La Communauté désœuvrée* (Paris: Christian Bourgois, 1990), p. 36.
30 Virilio: *Bunker Archeology*, p. 29.
31 Nancy and Lacoue-Labarthe: *Le Mythe nazi*, p. 71; 'The Nazi Myth', p. 312.

Chapter 4: Wrap Me Up in Sadist Knots

1 For a discussion of sadism see for example Max Horkheimer and Theodor Adorno, 'Juliette or Enlightenment and Morality', in *The Dialectic of Enlightenment*, trans. John Cumming (New York: Continuum, 1996); Pierre Klossowski, *Sade My Neighbour*, trans. Alphonso Lingis (London: Quartet Books Limited, 1992); in addition to these scholars, but only indirectly addressing the issue of sadism, is Jacques Lacan, 'Kant avec Sade', published in *October* 51 (Winter 1989), pp. 55–104; which has been subsequently 're-read' by Slavoj Žižek in two essays, 'Much Ado about a Thing', *For They Know Not What They Do: Enjoyment as a Political Factor* (London: Verso, 1991), pp. 229–77 and 'Kant with (or against) Sade', in Elizabeth and Edmond Wright (eds), *The Žižek Reader* (Oxford: Blackwell, 1999), pp. 283–301. Žižek re-contextualizes Lacan's work in productive framework relative to the materialization of sadism, and even begins 'Kant with (or against) Sade' by referencing the similarities between Horkheimer and Adorno's perspective to Pier Paolo Pasolini's 1975 film *Salò, or the 120 Days of Sodom*.
2 Marquis de Sade, *Justine, Philosophy in the Bedroom and Other Writings* (London: Arrow Books, 1991), p. 332.
3 Žižek: 'Kant with (or against) Sade', p. 285.
4 Žižek: 'Kant with (or against) Sade', p. 287.
5 Žižek: 'Kant with (or against) Sade', p. 287. Also see Horkheimer and Adorno: *Dialectic of Enlightenment*, p. 88.
6 Alexandra Przyrembel, 'Transfixed by an Image: Ilse Koch, the "Kommandeuse of Buchenwald,"' trans. Pamela Selwyn, *German History* 19/3 (October 2001), p. 369. Przyrembel's thorough scholarship reveals a complex picture of the infamous Ilse Koch; the infamy of this sadistic couple even caught the attention of the Nazis: 'Ilse Koch lived with her husband and their children, who were born at Buchenwald, in Haus Buchenwald on the concentration camp grounds from October 1937 until her arrest in August 1943 as part of the corruption proceedings initiated against her husband by the SS. Koch, who had already been transferred to the concentration and extermination camp of Majdanek/Lublin in the winter of 1941 and ultimately had to accept several demotions, was sentenced to death by the SS and shot at Buchenwald concentration camp in April 1945. Ilse Koch was acquitted. After being recognized by a former Buchenwald inmate in the summer of

1945 in Ludwigsburg, where she and her children were living with her sister-in-law, Ilse Koch spent the rest of her life in various prisons and clinics until hanging herself in September 1967 in Aichach prison' (Przyrembel, 'Transfixed by an Image', p. 377). As Przyrembel observes, little is truly known of Ilse Koch because she didn't serve in any official capacity, and thus there are no records or documents to account for her actions during the war. There are however numerous witnesses who testified to her cruelty.

7 Przyrembel notes: 'During his interrogation in December 1949 Werner B., who had spent four years at Buchenwald as a so-called action inmate, described his work as a technician in the pathology lab from December 1939 to the summer of 1942. He reported not only having prepared several shrunken heads himself but also that he had participated in the dissection of tattooed bodies. According to his own account he had been "entrusted" with both the preservation of skins and the production of the legendary lamp-shade about which there was so much talk after 1945. One of the SS doctors had set him the task of "covering a round, not very large wire frame with tattooed skin... This lamp did not, however, have a base of human bone, but rather a wooden one... As to the later fate of this lamp, I recall that Dr Müller [one of the SS doctors] took it with him out of the camp when it was finished." Shortly thereafter the lamp reappeared in the pathology lab and the individual pieces of skin were placed in a portfolio, but the base was left "in some corner or other." None of the inmates questioned could confirm that Ilse Koch had known of the tattoos and their use'. Przyrembel: 'Transfixed by an Image', pp. 383–4.

8 Made on a shoestring budget, and shot in only nine days, the film was put into development following the box-office success of *Love Camp 7* (Lee Frost, 1969) another film of the Naziploitation genre; the so-called 'Sultan of Sleaze', David F. Friedman, produced both films. The success of *Ilsa: She Wolf of the SS*, and its subsequent cult status, led to a number of other films that used the Nazi concentration camp as a plot device for salacious and sadistic spectacles. Despite the fact that the title character is killed in the first film – such a trivial detail hardly matters in the exploitation genre – in quick succession three sequels to the first *Ilsa* film were released: Don Edmonds's 1976 film *Ilsa, Harem Keeper of the Oil Sheiks*, and one year later *Ilsa, the Tigress of Siberia* directed by Jean LaFleur, and finally the 1977 unauthorized film *Ilsa, the Wicked Warden* directed by Spanish director Jesus Franco.

9 Survivor Jolana Roth recounts seeing female SS guards at Auschwitz, noting that you never saw many, 'But the ones you did see – they were worse than the men. I will never forget the one who would stand at the peephole of the gas chamber just because she wanted to'. Jolana Roth cited in Claudia

Koonz, *Mothers in the Fatherland: Women, the Family, and Nazi Politics* (New York: St Martin's Press, 1987), pp. 404–5.

10 Marc Lanval cited in Elizabeth D. Heineman, 'Sexuality and Nazism: The Doubly Unspeakable?', *Journal of the History of Sexuality* 11: 1/2 (January/April 2002), p. 63. Originally published in Marc Lanval, 'Ilse Koch – Sex Terrorist', *Sexology* 19/1 (1951), pp. 30–6.

11 Barbara Creed, *The Monstrous Feminine: Film, Feminine and Psychoanalysis* (London and New York: Routledge, 1993).

12 Lynn Rapaport arrives at a similar conclusion: 'Is this masculine anxiety part of a whole backlash in the 1960s and 1970s in popular culture against the women's movement and women reaching positions of power? Why is the Holocaust being eroticized and gendered? In the film there is a mirroring of two conflicts – the Nazis against the prisoners, and women torturing men. These male anxieties are being exaggerated by fantastical instances of female violence. It is the female guards who throughout the film beat or torture male and female prisoners. Ilsa, the main character and movie monster, symbolizes generic evil, Nazism, horror, perverse sexuality, and social malaise. The Holocaust is not just being sexualized, but it is also being gendered – a woman in power is evil, a Nazi, a feminazi.' Lynn Rapaport, 'Holocaust Pornography: Profaning the Sacred in Ilsa: *She-Wolf of the SS*', *Shofar: An Interdisciplinary Journal of Jewish Studies* 22/1 (Fall 2003), p. 63.

13 This rhetorical strategy is part of a renewed interest in Holocaust scholarship, generations removed from the event, to locate affinities in representing the catastrophic, or traumatic experience (e.g., the post-colonial experience). This is evident in, for example, the seminar series *Research Project Concentrationary Memories* at the University of Leeds, organized by Griselda Pollock and Max Silverman. See for example Max Silverman's work, 'Interconnected Histories: Holocaust and Empire in the Cultural Imaginary', where he writes regarding this new trend in research: 'It is ... an attempt to unearth an overlapping vocabulary, lexicon, imagery, aesthetic and, ultimately, history, shared by representations of colonialism and the Holocaust' Max Silverman, 'Interconnected Histories: Holocaust and Empire in the Cultural Imaginary', *French Studies* 62/4 (October 2008), p. 420. Routinely film critics characterize Torture Porn films as sadistic; Brian Price, for instance, observes, 'Above all else, [Michael] Haneke's work is violent. It would be quite simple to describe Haneke as an immoral sadist who relishes in the desecration of the body as a form of entertainment' Brian Price, 'Pain and the Limits of Representation', *Framework: The Journal of Cinema and Media* vol. 47/2 (Fall 2006), p. 22. David Edelstein's review of Michael Haneke's 2007 film *Funny Games* also observes that, 'it's difficult to grapple with serious themes when

what comes through most vividly is the director's sadism' David Edelstein, 'Audience is Loser in Haneke's Unfunny "Games"', *Fresh Air*, 14 March 2008, http://www.npr.org/templates/story/story.php?storyId=88230619 (accessed 5 April 2011). *Funny Games* is a re-make of Haneke's own film, by the same name, made ten years earlier in 1997. Anthony Lane in the *New Yorker* review of the more recent American film describes the viewing experience as akin to 'shackled prisoners trudging back to the rack and the thumbscrews...' Anthony Lane, 'Recurring Nightmare', *The New Yorker* 17 March 2008, http://www.newyorker.com/arts/critics/cinema/2008/03/17/080317crci_cinema_lane (accessed 5 April 2011).

14 Gabrielle Murray similarly observes: 'We never know who Jigsaw, our serial killing psychopath is, but there are many cases of mistaken identity as victims are pitted against each other. The film's concerns are universal ones. What will you do to survive? Would you take another's life to save your own, to save your family? These films are full of existential anxiety about how we live our lives.' Gabrielle Murray, '*Hostel II*: Representations of the Body in Pain and the Cinema Experience in Torture-Porn', *Jump Cut* 50 (Spring 2008), http://www.ejumpcut.org/archive/jc50.2008/TortureHostel2/text.html (accessed 5 April 2011).

15 In Szabó's film *Sunshine* it is interesting to note that Ralph Fiennes plays three characters – successive generations of the Sonnenschein family – as if to atone for his role in *Schindler's List* (Fiennes plays Amon Goeth). Characteristic of Szabó's films, *Sunshine* follows the Sonnenscheins, a Hungarian Jewish family, through Hungary's tumultuous modern history.

16 In a discussion between Paul A. Taylor and Srecko Horvat, the former suggests that *Hostel* is in effect a return of the repressed, insofar as Eastern Europe – in the Western (European) imagination – is the site of the unconscious, of trauma and the 'primal' underbelly of European thinking: 'A propos of this, it would be interesting to hear Žižek's analysis of Eli Roth's recent film, *Hostel*, based as it is upon a sickeningly dark reversal of the usual US exploitation of people from less developed economies. Perhaps, to some extent, Žižek and others are the intellectual versions of *Hostel*'s malevolent surgeons? They use an obscene supplement to dismember US-centric attitudes.' Paul A. Taylor, interview by Srecko Horvat, *International Journal of Žižek Studies* 1/0 (2007), p. 5.

17 Kim Newman, 'Torture Garden', *Sight & Sound* 16/6 (June 2006), p. 30.

18 In the first film it's $5,000 for a Russian, $10,000 for a European, and $25,000 for an American, in the second film, *Hostel: Part II*, victims are auctioned off to the highest bidder.

19 In Eli Roth's 2007 film *Hostel: Part II* Whitney pleads, 'What did I do wrong?'

20 http://www.imdb.com/character/ch0101641/ (accessed 8 February 2010).
21 In Elaine Scarry's seminal book on torture, *The Body in Pain*, she discusses this precise issue: 'The room, both in its structure and its content, is converted into a weapon, deconverted, undone. Made to participate in the annihilation of the prisoners, made to demonstrate that everything is a weapon, the objects themselves, and with them the fact of civilization, are annihilated: there is no wall, no window, no door, no bathtub, no refrigerator, no chair, no bed.' Rather there are only objects that have the potential to execute pain. Elaine Scarry, *The Body in Pain: The Making and Unmaking of the World* (New York: Oxford University Press, 1985), p. 41.
22 Scarry: *The Body in Pain*, p. 41.
23 Szell too has real-life counterparts, as Scarry notes, 'Reports of torture from prisoners in the Philippines include references to "unwanted dental work." ... In Brazil, there were forms of torture called "the mad dentist" and "the operating table."' The topsy-turvy world where medicine is employed for the purposes of torture was the *modus operandi* of the concentration camp. '[I]t is in the nature of torture that the two ubiquitously present [institutions] should be medicine and law, health and justice, for they are the institutional elaborations of body and state. These two were also the institutions most consistently inverted in the concentration camps, though they were slightly differently defined in accordance with Germany's position as a modern, industrialized mass society: the "body" occurring not in medicine but in its variant, the scientific laboratory; the "state" occurring not in the process of law, the trial, but in the process of production, the factory'. Scarry: *The Body in Pain*, p. 42.
24 Julia Kristeva, *Powers of Horror: An Essay on Abjection*, trans. Leon S. Roudiez (New York: Columbia University Press, 1982), p. 21.
25 David Rousset, *L'Univers concentrationnaire* (Paris: Editions de Pavois, 1946; reprinted Paris: Hachette/Pluriel, 2008). The English versions appeared as David Rousset, *The Other Kingdom*, trans. Ramon Guthrie (New York: Reynal and Hitchcock, 1947) and *A World Apart*, trans. Y. Moyse and R. Senhouse (London: Secker & Warburg, 1951). The phrase occurs on p. 181 in the French edition (2008) and p. 168 in the English edition (1947).
26 Edelstein: 'Audience is Loser in Haneke's Unfunny "Games"'.
27 Silverman: 'Interconnected Histories', p. 427, n. 29.
28 Haneke explains that at the age of 20 he saw *Salò* for the first time, 'I was completely destroyed. I was sick, destabilized for two weeks.' Anthony Lane, 'Happy Haneke', *The New Yorker* 5 October 2009, p. 65.
29 See *Reassemblage: From the Firelight to the Screen* (T. Minh-ha Trinh, 1983).
30 Lane: 'Happy Haneke', p. 66.

31 Lane: 'Happy Haneke', p. 66.
32 Lane: 'Happy Haneke', p. 67.
33 Michael Haneke comments on the representation of fascists: 'Usually in cinema a fascist is a fascist and remains so. It's much more realistic to take this fascist, Jean, who behaves like a pig, and give him moments where he expresses his humanity. It doesn't justify him and I'm not suggesting we forgive his sins. But even an asshole can commit occasional acts that are good or compassionate. I think it would have been more of a cliché if it had been one of the others who saved the boy.' Michael Haneke, interview by Nick James, *Sight & Sound* 13/10 October 2003, p. 18. If *Marathon Man* is a predecessor for the Torture Porn genre, perhaps it is also informative in its depiction of the Nazi; for as Sheryl Gross argues the film is neither black or white, but filled with grey. In describing its antagonist, Gross says, 'Incredible as it may seem to those who like their villains two-dimensional, especially if they happen to be Nazis, the audience often responds with a nervous giggle, or even a smattering of applause, when Szell, like Babe, escapes in a Checker cab.' Sheryl W. Gross, 'Guilt and Innocence in *Marathon Man*', *Literature Film Quarterly* 8/1 (1980), p. 64. One would imagine that we should view Quentin Tarantino's character Col. Hans Landa in *Inglourious Basterds* (2009), in the same light.

Chapter 5: Redemption or Transformation

1 For a discussion of David Rousset's concept of 'the concentrationary universe' see Introduction.
2 Griselda Pollock and Max Silverman (eds), *Concentrationary Cinema: The Aesthetics of Resistance in Alain Resnais's Night and Fog* (London: Berghan, 2011 and 2013); Griselda Pollock and Max Silverman (eds), *Concentrationary Memories: Totalitarian Terror and Cultural Resistance* (London: I.B.Tauris, 2014).
3 Griselda Pollock, 'Death in the Image: The Responsibility of Aesthetics in *Night and Fog* and *Kapò*', in Pollock and Silverman (eds.), *Concentrationary Cinema*, pp. 258–302.
4 Teresa de Lauretis, 'Cavani's *Night Porter*: A Woman's Film?', *Film Quarterly* 30/2 (1976/77), pp. 35–38; Chiara Bassi, 'Fathers and Daughters in the Camp: *The Night Porter* by Liliana Cavani', in Laura Benedetti, Julia L. Hairston and Sylvia M. Ross (eds), *Gendered Contexts: New Perspectives on Italian Cultural Studies*, (New York: Peter Lang, 1996), pp. 165–75; Kaja Silverman, *The Acoustic Mirror: The Female Voice in Psychoanalysis and Cinema* (Bloomington: Indiana University Press, 1988), pp. 218–33; Marguerite Waller, 'Signifying the Holocaust: Liliana Cavani's *Il Portiere di Notte*', in Laura Pietropaolo

and Ada Testaferri (eds), *Feminisms in the Cinema* (Bloomington: Indiana University Press, 1995), pp. 206–19.
5   Jane Caplan and Nikolaus Wachsmann (eds), *Concentration Camps in Nazi Germany: The New Histories* (London: Routledge, 2009). Hannah Arendt, *The Origins of Totalitarianism* (New York: Harcourt Brace, 1951).
6   The four camps of Operation Reinhard, situated in Poland, were Sobibór, Treblinka, Bełżec and Chełmno, operating between late 1941 and 1943. Madjanek also had an exterminatory extension.
7   Roger Ebert, *Chicago Sun-Times*, 10 February 1975; Susan Sontag, 'Fascinating Fascism', *New York Review of Books*, 6 February 1975. It was a review of Leni Riefenstahl's *The Last of the Nuba* and Jack Pia's *SS Regalia*. Reprinted in Susan Sontag, *Under the Sign of Saturn* (London: Writers and Readers Collective, 1980), pp. 73–108. See also Daniel H. Magilow, Elizabeth Iridges and Kirstin T. Vander Lugt (eds), *Nazisploitation! The Nazi Image in Low-Brow Cinema and Culture* (London: Continuum, 2011).
8   'Thesis I. Ideology represents the imaginary relationship of individuals to their real conditions of existence.' Louis Althusser, 'Ideology and Ideological State Apparatuses: Notes Towards an Investigation', *Lenin and Philosophy and Other Essays* trans. Ben Brewster (London: Monthly Review Press, 1971), p. 153.
9   Primo Levi, *The Drowned and the Saved*, trans. Raymond Rosenthal (New York: Vintage Books, 1989), pp. 36–69.
10 Christian Metz, *Psychoanalysis and Cinema: The Imaginary Signifier*, trans. Celia Britton, Annwyl Williams, Ben Brewster and Alfred Guzzetti (Basingstoke: Macmillan, 1982).
11 Roger Ebert, *Chicago Sun-Times*, 10 February 1975, http://rogerebert.suntimes.com/apps/pbcs.dll/article?AID=/19750210/REVIEWS/502100301/1023 (accessed 10 November 2012).
12 Annette Insdorf, 'The Night Porter', http://www.criterion.com/current/posts/66 (accessed 10 December 2012).
13 De Lauretis: 'Cavani's *Night Porter*: A Woman's Film?'
14 Charlotte Delbo, *Auschwitz and After I: None of Us Will Return* trans. Rosette C. Lamont (New Haven: Yale University Press, 1985).
15 Giorgio Agamben, 'The Camp as "Nomos" of the Modern', *Homo Sacer: Sovereign Power and Bare Life*, trans. Daniel Heller-Roazan (California: Stanford University Press, 1998), pp. 166–80.
16 Fredric Jameson, 'Imaginary and Symbolic in Lacan: Marxism, Psychoanalytic Criticism, and the Problem of the Subject', *Yale French Studies* 55/56 (1977), p. 353.
17 Kris Ravetto, *The Unmaking of Fascist Aesthetics* (Minneapolis: University of Minnesota Press, 2001).

18 Iris Milner, 'The "Gray Zone" Revisited: The Concentrationary Universe in Ka. Tzetnik's Literary Testimony', *Jewish Social Studies* 14/2 (2008), pp. 113–205.
19 For more detailed studies of this area, see Sonia Hedgepeth and Rochelle Saidel (eds), *Sexual Violence against Jewish Women during the Holocaust* (Boston: Brandeis University Press, 2010).
20 Susan Sontag, 'Fascinating Fascism', *New York Review of Books*, 6 February 1975. It was a review of Leni Riefenstahl's *The Last of the Nuba* and Jack Pia's *SS Regalia*. Reprinted in Susan Sontag, *Under the Sign of Saturn* (London: Writers and Readers Collective, 1980), pp. 73–108.
21 Jean Laplanche, 'Notes on Afterwardness', *Essays on Otherness* edited by John Fletcher (London: Routledge, 1999), pp. 260–65. Freud's concept of retroaction in psychic temporality and causation, *Nachträglichkeit* has been translated as 'deferred action' in English or 'après coup' in French. The idea is that the traces or memories of events that happen early acquire not only meaning but psychic effects when they encounter new experiences or are retriggered at a later stage in psychic development. This is a crucial concept for understanding the structure of delay and the non-linear form of time in the psyche.
22 Ravetto: *The Unmaking of Fascist Aesthetics*, p. 6.
23 Ravetto: *The Unmaking of Fascist Aesthetics*, p. 12.
24 Ravetto: *The Unmaking of Fascist Aesthetics*, p. 14.
25 Ravetto: *The Unmaking of Fascist Aesthetics*, p. 15.
26 Ravetto: *The Unmaking of Fascist Aesthetics*, p. 18.
27 Cited in Gaetana Marone, *The Gaze and the Labyrinth: The Cinema of Liliana Cavani* (Princeton: Princeton University Press, 2000), pp. 82–8.
28 For a reading of this film see Pollock, 'Death in the Image', pp. 258–302.
29 Kaja Silverman, *The Acoustic Mirror: The Female Voice in Psychoanalysis and Cinema* (Bloomington: Indiana University Press, 1988), pp. 223–4.
30 Silverman: *The Acoustic Mirror*, p. 219.
31 Silverman: *The Acoustic Mirror*, p. 220.
32 Waller: 'Signifying the Holocaust', p. 261.
33 Waller: 'Signifying the Holocaust', p. 262.
34 Waller: 'Signifying the Holocaust', p. 268.
35 Waller: 'Signifying the Holocaust', p. 269. For Waller, as for so many writers, all of Nazism, fascism, the SS, concentration camps and genocide collapse into the collective noun, the Holocaust. Max Silverman and I have, however, been seeking to reactivate the concept of the concentrationary, forged in immediate political analysis of and resistance to what the political deportees to German concentration camps such as Buchenwald and Mauthausen had

experienced as a novel anti-political laboratory of total terror, in order to allow analytical space between what is obscured by this enfolding. We need to acknowledge that the Holocaust as a concept emerged to delineate, against the backdrop of a post-war tendency to generalize everything as 'Nazi atrocities', the specificity of the racially targeted genocide of Jewish and Romani Europeans. Having been asserted, the term now is used in such a way as to confuse co-emerging and interconnected but significantly different systems and sites of concentrationary terror and genocidal horror. Returning to a focus on the concentrationary is not a displacement of the necessary focus on racist violence; it is a supplementation of the continuous work of analysis of the meaning for the present of the totalitarian experiments of the twentieth century that were never confined to Germany's barbed wire enclosures.

36 Saul Friedländer, *Reflections of Nazism: An Essay on Kitsch and Death*, trans. Thomas Weyr (Bloomington: Indiana University Press, 1993), p. 15.
37 Friedländer: *Reflections of Nazism*, p. 19.
38 Friedländer: *Reflections of Nazism*, p. 21.
39 We might recall perhaps the shocking ending of the novel *Fatelessness* [*Sorstalanság*] (1975) by Hungarian author Imre Kertesz. György Köves, estranged and alone in a Budapest that knows nothing of his experiences, yearns for the camp again as the place where alone he had experienced happiness. In his memoir of his experiences in Gandersheim and Dachau, *The Human Race* (1947), French political deportee Robert Antelme too writes of certain joyful moments experienced during his ordeal – created of course by absolute and momentary contrast to the grinding reality of pain. Robert Antelme, *The Human Race* [*L'Espèce Humaine*] trans. Jeffrey Haight and Annie Mahler (Chicago: Marlboro Press, 1998).

Chapter 6: Seep and Creep

1 I shall more fully explain the distinction between these two modes, self-regarding and self-aware, in the course of the text as they represent specific orientations of the image towards the concentrationary that need fuller elaboration.
2 The term 'concentrationary universe' is taken from the original formulation by French political deportee, concentration camp survivor and writer David Rousset who published an anatomy of the world of the concentration camp in 1946 as *L'univers concentrationnaire* (Paris Editions de Pavois, 1946). See also Griselda Pollock and Max Silverman, *Concentrationary Memories: Totalitarian Terror and Cultural Resistance* (London: I.B. Tauris, 2013) for a full exploration of the meaning and usefulness of this concept of the camp

and its relation to Hannah Arendt's subsequent study of the concentration camps as the laboratory of totalitarian domination in which humanity is rendered superfluous. Hannah Arendt, *The Origins of Totalitarianism* (New York: Harcourt Brace 1951).

3 Griselda Pollock and Max Silverman (eds), *Concentrationary Memories: Totalitarian Terror and Cultural Resistance* (London: I.B. Tauris, 2013).

4 See Mary Ann Doane, *The Emergence of Cinematic Time* (Cambridge, MA, and London: Harvard University Press, 2002), p. 10. Doane's text provides a comprehensive exploration of the indexical nature of the cinematic image through the theories of Charles Peirce.

5 Samuel Weber, 'Concentration and Isolation', http://www.leeds.ac.uk/cath/Recordings/samuel-weber.html (accessed 5 August 2011).

6 Weber, 'Concentration and Isolation', http://www.leeds.ac.uk/cath/Recordings/samuel-weber.html (accessed 5 August 2011).

7 Giorgio Agamben, *Homo Sacer: Sovereign Power and Bare Life*, trans Daniel Heller-Roazen (Stanford: Stanford University Press, 1989), p. 148.

8 Agamben: *Homo Sacer*, p. 123.

9 Charles E. White, 'Mission Creep During the Lewis and Clark Expedition', http://www.history.army.mil/LC/The%20Mission/mission_creep.htm (accessed 12 May 2011). In relation to this, it is worth noting that Weber, the author of a book subtitled 'On the Militarization of Thinking', also reminds us of the primary association of the term 'concentration camp' with the military and fields of conflict (although in an investigation of the *concentrationary imaginary* this is an association which may also become unhinged): 'The first thing that strikes anyone reviewing this history is that the term arose in connection with military conflicts, a characteristic that it was to retain until the present.' It is clearly in societies which are impinged upon by a military, conflictual situation that the state of exception makes the concentrationary universe an acceptable *institution* (in that it is instituted in a moment in time as well as being a structural institution). Weber, 'Concentration and Isolation', http://www.leeds.ac.uk/cath/Recordings/samuel-weber.html (accessed 5 August 2011).

10 Michael Mechanic, 'America's Global Military Presence: Mission Creep', http://www.globalresearch.ca/index.php?context= va&aid= 10011 (accessed 23 September 2011).

11 Max Silverman, 'Horror and the Everyday in Post-Holocaust France: *Nuit et Brouillard* and Concentrationary Art', *French Cultural Studies* 17/1 (2006), pp. 5–18.

12 Benjamin Hannavy Cousen, 'Isn't this Where . . . ? Projections on Pink Floyd *The Wall*: Tracing the Concentrationary Image', in Griselda Pollock and Max Silverman, *Concentrationary Memories* (London: I.B.Tauris, 2013), pp. 203–22.

13 Richard Crownshaw, *Afterlife of Holocaust Memory in Contemporary Literature and Culture* (Basingstoke: Palgrave Macmillan, 2010), p. 3.
14 Ann Rigney, 'Plenitude, Scarcity and the Circulation of Cultural Memory', *Journal of European Studies* 35/8 (2000), 11–28, p. 15.
15 Benjamin Hannavy Cousen, 'Memory, Power and Place, Where is *Guernica?*', *Journal of Romance Studies* 9/2 (2009), pp. 47–64.
16 The inevitable teleological framework for watching the film after the first time means that one could see these Proustian triggers as deliberately engineered within the diegesis of the narrative by the therapeutic 'game' that is apparently being 'acted out' in order to 'work through' the case of Teddy Daniels.
17 Eric Santner, 'History Beyond the Pleasure Principle', in Saul Friedländer (ed.) *Probing the Limits of Representation: Nazism and the Final Solution* (Cambridge, MA: Harvard University Press, 1992), p. 144.
18 Santner: 'History Beyond the Pleasure Principle', p. 144.
19 http://www.ushmm.org/wlc/en/article.php?ModuleId=10005214 (accessed 5 September 2013] and http://www.kz-gedenkstaette-dachau.de/1945.html (accessed 5 September 2013).
20 http://www.kz-gedenkstaette-dachau.de/1945.html (accessed 5 September 2013).
21 http://resources.ushmm.org/film/display/detail.php?file_num=6 (accessed 5 September 2013).
22 See William Kirchner, 'Conversation with George Stevens', in Paul Cronin (ed.), *George Stevens: Interviews* (Jackson: University Press of Mississippi, 2004), pp. 18–23.
23 'Frontline: *Memory of the Camps*', http://www.pbs.org/wgbh/pages/frontline/camp/view/#lower (accessed 15 August 2011).
24 For example, Colonel Alexander Zabin photographed snow on the bodies of SS guards on 1 May, http://digitalassets.ushmm.org/photoarchives/detail.aspx?id=1144535 (accessed 5 September 2013).
25 The Jourhaus gateway at Dachau to the prisoners' compound does bear this inscription in a modernist insertion at the centre of the iron gates under a heavy stone archway.
26 Santner also remarks that 'Historians, after all, strive for intellectual and not psychic mastery of events' ('History Beyond the Pleasure Principle', p. 145). Cinema gives the illusion that psychic events have been and are being mastered by the filmmaker and by the spectator. The fact that the affected spectator believes he or she 'understands' what is going on psychologically also relies upon the illusion that the 'history' upon which this understanding is based (in this case the end of World War II and the liberation of the

camps) is also understood. In fact, it is as likely as not founded upon further cinematic constructions and glib, half-grasped comprehensions of history whereby history is merely only ever a trope upon which and from which to unleash affect (for box office gain).

27 This self-awareness is made explicit 95 minutes into the film when the German doctor Dr Naehring is attacked by Daniels and the following dialogue takes place whilst Naehring is pinned to the wall: Naehring: 'Forgive me, what doesn't provoke you? Remarks? Words?'
Daniels: 'Nazis.'
Naehring: 'Well that too, and of course memories, dreams. Did you know that the word trauma comes from the Greek for wound hmm? And what is the German word for dream? *Traum*. Ein traum...wounds can create monsters and you are wounded, Marshal and wouldn't you agree, when you see a monster, you must stop it?' Daniels: 'Yes I agree.'

At this point Daniels injects the doctor with a sedative. Once again a historical perspective, in which Daniels's interjection 'Nazi' which is conflated with the figure of Naehring (not least because of his profession and, in the non-teleological mind of the first-time viewer, in agreement with a certain typecast demeanour), becomes immediately subsumed by, or, rather, is only allowed to briefly emerge from, the very personal psychological wounds and dreams suffered by Daniels and the unfolding and 'explanation' of which the film is heading towards as the denouement approaches.

28 This remark occurs at around 10 mins 15 seconds into Part 1B of *Histoire(s) du Cinéma*. The idea of the commodification of the memory and the imagery of the concentration camps or the Holocaust is illustrated in an ironic fashion by the actress Kate Winslet. In an episode of the sitcom *Extras* Winslet plays herself as an actress playing a nun in a Nazi occupied country. The humour is based on her portrayal of herself as a callous and greedy actress: 'I don't think we need another film about the Holocaust do we, it's like, how many have there been? Yeah we get it, it was grim, move on. No I'm doing it because I've noticed that if you do a film about the Holocaust, you are guaranteed an Oscar' (*Extras* Series 1, Episode 3, August 2005). In 2009, Winslet won an Oscar for her portrayal of Hanna Schmitz in the film *The Reader*, itself based upon Bernard Schlink's 1995 novel. The story of *The Reader* has been read in terms of a perpetrator narrative (see for example Crownshaw, *The Afterlife of Holocaust Memory*, pp. 145–69). However, in terms of the theme of the amnesiac image under discussion here, a similar 'narrative fetishism' occurs as we have discussed in *Shutter Island*. A concentrationary, or Holocaust, narrative is used as a 'raft' upon which to float the petty story of Michael Berg, whose memories from the

beginning are seen to be triggered by the ordinary elements of everyday life and which are presented at a level of a kind of Mills and Boon romance. In fact, at the moment when the student Berg turns around from visiting Hanna in prison, the film has a similar degraded effect, as will be discussed shortly with reference to *Schindler's List*. From this point, the dilemma of the individual character and the fictional story of reading will occlude the actuality of concentrationary memories which become once again vehicles of affect. Similarly, Michael's visit to the concentration camp is positioned impossibly in the middle of the trial, and follows a kind of 'tourist trail' entirely modelled on the tracking shots and the structure of Alain Resnais's *Night and Fog* (1955). In *The Reader* this sequence is presented as an already incorporated, well known narrative (barbed wire–bunks–corridor–gas-chamber–crematoria) that it is a summation of sealed thought; a master-narrative delivered to the spectator as a short-hand capsule of information which enables the rest of the film to progress. Thought is not induced or provoked in any way and the earnest intent of *The Reader* makes such gestures less forgivable than those of *Shutter Island*.
29 Gillian Rose, 'Beginnings of the Day: Fascism and Representation', in *Mourning Becomes the Law* (Cambridge: Cambridge University Press, 1996), p. 41.
30 Rose: 'Beginnings of the Day: Fascism and Representation', p. 54.
31 Rose: 'Beginnings of the Day: Fascism and Representation', pp. 54–5.
32 Rose: 'Beginnings of the Day: Fascism and Representation', p. 41.
33 Rose: 'Beginnings of the Day: Fascism and Representation', p. 48.
34 Saxton describes the opposing stances of the two directors vis-à-vis 'representation and representability' and she suggests that a hypothetical reel of film 'lie[s] at the heart of the directors' dispute: a piece of footage shot by the Nazis depicting a gas chamber in action', Libby Saxton, *Haunted Images: Film, Ethics, Testimony and the Holocaust* (New York: Columbia University Press, 2008), p. 20.
35 Rose: 'Beginnings of the Day: Fascism and Representation', p. 47.
36 It should be pointed out that the association of the showerhead that emits water and the actual entry point of gas into a gas chamber is powerful and associative but not necessarily accurate. The showerheads were disguises; they were not the way that gas got into the space (although we are not able to be sure what this space was actually like). The association is so strong, though, that Rose can justifiably make her argument and Spielberg (and then Scorsese) can make the showerhead the unjustifiable locus of terror. The association is made specific, indeed, in the editorial construction of *Memory of the Camps* where, in the Dachau section, a 'bathhouse' is shown and revealed as a gas chamber by a close-up of a showerhead and then a cut to a canister

of Zyklon B on the ground. It would be interesting to trace the provenance of these close-up shots.
37 The intensity of the close-ups of the showerhead and water are dissipated to a longish shot of Daniels/Laeddis. The fact that he is naked, however, means that the tension is not entirely dissipated, nor is the allusion to the *Schindler's List* sequence. In fact, according to Saxton, this moment is 'A recurrent and harrowing motif in Holocaust films'; we see Daniels/Laeddis from a voyeuristic position: 'the spyhole or small window that was set in the [gas] chamber doors for observation purposes... this motif calls the viewer's look into question, foregrounding the non-reciprocal structure of the confrontation between the inviolable body of the viewer and the vulnerable bodies viewed' (Saxton, *Haunted Images*, p. 21). This is a very clever manoeuvre in terms of the diegetic structure of the film – Scorsese firstly makes us identify with Daniels/Laeddis but then situates us in a position of superiority and distance from him and his naked vulnerability. It is a subliminal clue that Daniels may not be exactly who he is and someone with whom we should identify.
38 Jacques Derrida, *Specters of Marx*, trans Peggy Kamuf (New York and London: Routledge, 1994), p. 9 (emphasis in original).
39 Andreas Huyssen, *Twilight Memories: Marking Time in a Culture of Amnesia* (London and New York: Routledge, 1995), p. 253.
40 Huyssen: *Twilight Memories*, p. 3.

Chapter 7: Haneke and the Camps

1 An earlier version of this chapter first appeared under the same title in Axel Bangert, Robert S.C. Gordon and Libby Saxton (eds), *Holocaust Intersections: Genocide and Visual Culture at the New Millennium* (London: Legenda, 2013), pp. 84–96. I wish to thank the publisher for permission to reproduce parts of that essay.
2 Serge Daney, 'The Tracking Shot in *Kapò*', *Senses of Cinema*, 30 (January–March 2004), www.sensesofcinema.com/2004/feature-articles/Kapò_daney/ (accessed 23 August 2011; first published in *Trafic*, no 4, P.O.L. Editions, 1992; trans. Laurent Kretzschmar); Jacques Rivette, 'On Abjection', translated by David Phelps with the assistance of Jeremi Szaniawski, www.dvdbeaver.com/rivette/OK/abjection.html (accessed 24 October 2011: first published as 'De l'abjection', *Cahiers du cinéma*, no. 120, juin 1961, pp. 54–5). For a discussion of Rivette, Daney and Pontecorvo in relation to Resnais's *Night and Fog*, see Griselda Pollock, 'Death in the Image: The Responsibility of Aesthetics in Resnais's *Night and Fog* (1955) and *Kapò* (1959)', in Griselda Pollock and Max Silverman (eds), *Concentrationary Cinema:*

Aesthetics as Resistance in Alain Resnais's Night and Fog (London: Berghahn Books, 2011), pp. 258–302.
3 Daney: 'The Tracking Shot in *Kapò*'.
4 Rivette: 'On Abjection'.
5 Daney: 'The Tracking Shot in *Kapò*'.
6 Giorgio Agamben, *Homo Sacer: Sovereign Power and Bare Life* [1995] (Stanford: Stanford University Press, 1998), p. 166.
7 As Catherine Wheatley observes, 'what initially appears as unthreatening and knowable soon transforms into something strange and unsettling', *Michael Haneke's Cinema: The Ethics of the Image* (New York and Oxford: Berghahn, 2009), p. 79. Should we be shocked, though, by this sudden descent from the sublime to Hell, given what we know about the orchestras formed by inmates in a number of the concentration camps?
8 David Rousset, *L'Univers concentrationnaire* [1946] (Paris: Editions de Minuit, 1965), pp. 54–5; *The Other Kingdom*, trans. by Ramon Guthrie (New York: Reynal and Hitchcock, 1947), pp. 58–9. For other examples of connections between sport and the concentrationary universe in French literature, see Georges Perec, *W ou le souvenir d'enfance* (Paris: Denoel, 1975) and Philippe Grimbert, *Le Secret* (Paris: Grasset, 2004).
9 For a discussion of Freud's concept of the uncanny ('Das Unheimliche') in relation to Haneke's treatment of domestic space, see David Sorfa, 'Uneasy Domesticity in the Films of Michael Haneke', *Studies in European Cinema* 3/2 (2006), pp. 93–104.
10 See for example 'Michael Haneke: Interview', *Time Out*, www.timeout.com/film/features/show-feature/3658/Michael_Haneke-interview.html (accessed 24 October 2011).
11 For further discussion of the relationship between bourgeois culture and hidden violence in Haneke's *Caché*, see my articles 'The Empire Looks Back', *Screen*, 48/2 (2007), pp. 245–49 and 'The Violence of the Cut: Michael Haneke's *Caché* and Cultural Memory', *French Cultural Studies*, 21/1 (2010), pp. 57–65.
12 Rousset: *L'Univers concentrationnaire*, p. 181.
13 Giorgio Agamben, *Remnants of Auschwitz: The Witness and the Archive* [1998], trans. Daniel Heller-Roazen (New York: Zone Books, 1999), p. 26. I am grateful to Griselda Pollock for these insights.
14 In relation to his film *Children of Men*, the Mexican film director Alfonso Cuaron says the following of extreme violence today: 'Many of the stories of the future involve something like "Big Brother", but I think that's a 20th century view of tyranny. The tyranny happening now is taking new disguises – the tyranny of the twenty-first century is called "democracy".' Cited in Slavoj Žižek, *Violence* (London: Profile Books), p. 24.

15 Agamben: *Homo Sacer*, p. 174.
16 A similar process is at work in *Caché* as the return of the violence of their own culture (if not by a child, at least through naive and child-like drawings) is simply not understood by Georges and Anne (the later incarnations of Georg and Anna of *Funny Games*).
17 The word 'torture' is explicitly mentioned when the baron addresses the congregation in church following the brutal treatment inflicted on his son: 'At first I thought my child had been tortured by those who cut off my cabbages to get even.' By connecting this act with the earlier 'accident' involving the doctor, the baron implies that torture is endemic and that responsibility and guilt are collective rather than simply individual acts. (The mutual suspicion and denunciations in the film and the filming in black and white are reminiscent of Henri-Georges Clouzot's 1943 war-time allegory *Le Corbeau* (*The Raven*).)
18 The narrator does, of course, give us a clue at the very beginning of his story as to his uncertainty about the accuracy of all the details: 'I don't know if the story I want to tell you is entirely true. Some of it I only know from hearsay. After so many years, a lot of it is still obscure, and many questions remain unanswered.' This opening statement is made against a black screen; the first image only emerges gradually out of darkness. The play of light and dark (literally and metaphorically) is thus established early on to warn us of claims to truth and objectivity. In an interview which accompanies the DVD of the film, Haneke explained his intentions in the following way: 'I am trying to point out to the viewer that the film is an interpretation, it is an artefact of someone's memory and someone saying that this is "how it might have been". What I want to do is to counter this lie and false realism which claims that we know how things were. No one can know this.'
19 Wheatley: *Michael Haneke's Cinema*, p. 92. For discussions of Haneke's aesthetic of staging off-screen space, see Libby Saxton, 'Secrets and Revelations: Off-screen Space in Michael Haneke's *Caché* (2005)', *Studies in French Cinema* 7/1 (2007), pp. 5–17, and Michael Cowan 'Between the Street and the Apartment: Disturbing the Space of Fortress Europe in Michael Haneke', *Studies in European Cinema* 5/2 (2008), pp. 117–29.
20 Walter Benjamin, *The Arcades Project* (Cambridge, MA: Belknap Press of Harvard University Press, 1999), p. 416.
21 Interview with Haneke that accompanies the DVD of *The White Ribbon* (2009).
22 'Every Film Rapes the Viewer', *Spiegel* interview with director Michael Haneke, *Spiegel Online International*, 21 Oct. 2009, www.spiegel/de/inter

national/spiegel/0,1518,656419,00.html (accessed 17 August 2011). As Rousset says at the end of his essay on the camps:

> it would be easy to show that the most characteristic traits of both the SS mentality and the social conditions which gave rise to the Third Reich are to be found in many sectors of world society... It would be blindness – and criminal blindness, at that – to believe that, by reason of any difference of national temperament, it would be impossible for any other country to try a similar experiment. Germany interpreted with an originality in keeping with her history, the crisis that led her to the *concentrationary* universe. But the existence and the mechanism of that crisis were inherent in the economic and social foundations of capitalism and imperialism. Under a new guise, similar effects may reappear tomorrow. There remains therefore a very specific war to be waged. [... il serait facile de montrer que les traits les plus caractéristiques et de la mentalité S.S. et de soubassements sociaux se retrouvent dans bien d'autres secteurs de la société mondiale... Ce serait une duperie, et criminelle, que de prétendre qu'il est impossible aux autres peuples de faire une expérience analogue pour des raisons d'opposition de nature. L'Allemagne a interprété avec l'originalité propre à son histoire la crise qui l'a conduite à l'univers concentrationnaire. Mais l'existence et le mécanisme de cette crise tiennent aux fondements économiques et sociaux du capitalisme et de l'impérialisme. Sous une figuration nouvelle, des effets analogues peuvent demain encore apparaître. Il s'agit, en conséquence, d'une bataille très précise à mener] (*L'Univers concentrationnaire*, pp. 186–87; *The Other Kingdom*, p. 173).

23 Hannah Arendt, *The Origins of Totalitarianism* [1951] (New York: Schocken Books, 2004), p. 566.
24 For further discussion of the distinction between the concentrationary and exterminatory programmes, see Sylvie Lindeperg and Annette Wieviorka, *Univers concentrationnaire et génocide: voir, savoir, comprendre* (Paris: Mille et une nuits/Arthème Fayard, 2008), and my co-written essays with Griselda Pollock, 'Introduction: Concentrationary Cinema', in Griselda Pollock and Max Silverman (eds), *Concentrationary Cinema: Aesthetics as Political Resistance in Alain Resnais's Night and Fog*, (New York and Oxford: Berghahn, 2011), pp. 1–54 and 'The Politics of Memory: From Concentrationary Memory to Concentrationary Memories', in Griselda Pollock and Max Silverman (eds), *Concentrationary Memories: Totalitarian Terror and Cultural Resistance* (New York and London: I.B.Tauris, 2013), pp. 1–28.

Chapter 8: Spec(tac)ularizing 'Campness'

1 Adriana Cavarero, *Horrorism: Naming Contemporary Violence* [2007], trans. William McCuaig (New York: Columbia University Press, 2009), p. 8.
2 Susan Hayward, *Nikita* [1990, Luc Besson] (London and New York: I.B.Tauris, 2010), p. 11.
3 Hayward: *Nikita*, pp. 9–11.

4 During the 'Save LFN' campaign, 25,000 letters were written, online petitions formed and an advertisement printed in *The Hollywood Reporter*, which requested that USA Networks and Warner Brothers reconsider the cancellation. See the message board 'The LFN Haven' (http://save lfn69411.yuku.com/) and Rachel Stein's blog, 'Gone too soon – *La Femme Nikita*: Can't keep a good assassin down', 29 January 2010, http://www.televisionwithoutpity.com/brilliantbutcancelled/2010/01/la-femme-nikita-do-we-still-wa.php (both accessed 3 July 2014).

5 See also the title of Christopher Heyn's production study *Inside Section One: Creating and Producing TV's* La Femme Nikita (Los Angeles: POV Press, 2006).

6 Griselda Pollock and Max Silverman (eds), *Concentrationary Cinema: Aesthetics as Political Resistance in Alain Resnais's Night and Fog* (New York and Oxford: Berghahn, 2011).

7 In *Between Camps: Nations, Cultures and the Allure of Race* [2000] (London: Routledge, 2004), Paul Gilroy differentiates between the 'concentration' and 'extermination' camp: 'Let me be absolutely clear: the death factory is not itself a camp – its inmates are unlikely to be alive long enough for camp rules to be engaged. But camps gain something from their proximity to the death factory and other places of organized mass killing' (p. 88).

8 Pollock and Silverman: *Concentrationary Cinema*, p. 18.

9 Pollock and Silverman: *Concentrationary Cinema*, p. 18.

10 Giorgio Agamben, *Homo Sacer: Sovereign Power and Bare Life* [1995], trans. Daniel Heller Roazen (Stanford, CA: Stanford California Press, 1998), p. 123.

11 Agamben: *Homo Sacer*, p. 10.

12 Agamben: *Homo Sacer*, p. 123.

13 Zygmunt Bauman, *Modernity and the Holocaust* (Cambridge: Polity, 1989), p. 87.

14 Janet Wolff's intervention is illuminating here: 'The Holocaust is exceptional in its extremity and its scale. It is not unique, in the sense that there have been other historical events with which it shares some characteristics (systematic murder on the basis of ethnicity, for example), though it is unique in the sense that any event is unique – historically and geographically specific, larger or smaller than similar events, affecting this population rather than that, and so on.' In 'Memento Mori: Atrocity and Aesthetics', in Shelley Horstein and Florence Jacobowitz (eds), *Image and Remembrance: Representation and the Holocaust* (Bloomington and Indianapolis: Indiana University Press, 2003), pp. 153–74; here p. 156.

15 See Sigmund Freud, *The Psychopathology of Everyday Day Life* [1901], trans. Alan Tyson, ed. James Strachey (with Angela Richards and Alan Tyson) (Harmondsworth: Penguin, 1975); *The Interpretation of Dreams* [1900], trans.

James Strachey, ed. James Strachey (with Alan Tyson and Angela Richards) (Harmondsworth: Penguin Books, 1976).

16 Gary Gillard, 'Supertext and the Mind-Culture System: Freud, Lévi-Strauss, Bateson' (unpublished PhD thesis, Murdoch University, 1994), http://www.garrygillard.net/writing/supertext/ch3.html (accessed 3 July 2014).

17 Griselda Pollock, 'Concentrationary Memories and the Politics of Representation', Imperial War Museum, London, 2 June 2010; available as podcast, http://backdoorbroadcasting.net/2010/06/concentrationary-memories-and-the-politics-of-representation/, here 00:54:12 (accessed 3 July 2014).

18 See Jeremy Shapiro and Benedicte Suzan, 'The French Experience of Counter-terrorism', *Survival* 25/1 (Spring 2003), pp. 67–98.

19 Pollock: 'Concentrationary Memories', 00:52:04.

20 See 'No Questions Asked', a report on cooperation between the French, German and UK governments and intelligence services in countries that routinely use torture (New York: Human Rights Watch, 2010), http://www.hrw.org/node/91221 (accessed 3 July 2014); see also Darius M. Rejali, *Torture and Democracy* (Princeton and Oxford: Princeton University Press, 2007).

21 W.J.T. Mitchell, 'The Unspeakable and the Unimaginable: Word and Image in a Time of Terror', *ELH* 72/2 (Summer 2005), p. 305.

22 Benjamin Hannavy Cousen, *The Seeping and Creeping of Haunted Memory: Tracing the Concentrationary in Post-war Cinema* (unpublished PhD thesis, University of Leeds, 2011), p. 28.

23 Claire Pajaczkowska, 'The Emotional Work of Cinema', Everyman Cinema, London, 9 May 2009, available as podcast, http://www.miwnet.org/Website/audio-items/the-emotional-work-of-cinema-round-table/, here: 0:26:20 (accessed 3 July 2014).

24 Nicola Diamond, 'The Emotional Work of Cinema', Everyman Cinema, London, 9 May 2009, available as podcast, http://www.miwnet.org/Website/audio-items/the-emotional-work-of-cinema-round-table/, starting at: 0:42:10 (accessed 3 July 2014).

25 Hayward: *Nikita*, p. 87.

26 Hayward: *Nikita*, pp. 126–7.

27 Hayward: *Nikita*, p. 58.

28 I am referring here, in particular, to documentary footage of a Kapo room included in Alain Resnais's *Night and Fog*.

29 For two case studies see René Wolf, 'Judgement in the Grey Zone: The Third Auschwitz (Kapo) Trial in Frankfurt 1968', *Journal of Genocide Research* 9/4 (2007), pp. 617–35.

30 Nikita's role as a marionette of this regime is also expressed in the half-parodic ballet dance she performs at the training centre. Her clown-esque movements and the classic music score also point to the two connected dance scenes of the male concentrationee (Amedeo Amodio) in Liliana Cavani's *Night Porter*.
31 Jacques Rancière, *The Future of the Image* [2007] (London: Verso, 2009), p. 73.
32 Hayward: *Nikita*, p. 8.
33 See Chapter 5 for another reading of this film.
34 Hannah Arendt, *The Origins of Totalitarianism* [1948] (New York: Schocken Books, 2004), p. 810.
35 Hilary Ann Radner, 'Nikita: Consumer Culture's Killer Instinct and the Imperial Imperative', in Susan Hayward and Phil Powrie (eds), *The Films of Luc Besson: Master of Spectacle* (Manchester: Manchester University Press, 2006), pp. 135–46; here p. 140.
36 For a critical reading of Pontecorvo's film, see Griselda Pollock, 'Death in the Image: The Responsibility of Aesthetics in *Night and Fog* (1955) and *Kapò* (1959)', in Pollock and Silverman (eds), *Concentrationary Cinema*, pp. 258–301.
37 Hannah Arendt, *Eichmann in Jerusalem: A Report on the Banality of Evil* [1963] (New York/Toronto/London: Penguin, 2006), p. 135.
38 Hayward: *Nikita*, p. 76.
39 Hayward: *Nikita*, pp. 84, 127.
40 Gayatri Chakravorty Spivak, *Death of a Discipline* (New York: Columbia University Press, 2003), p. 76; Neil Badmington, 'Theorizing Posthumanism', *Cultural Critique* 53 (Winter 2003), pp. 19–21.
41 Stacy Takacs, 'Speculations on a New Economy: *La Femme Nikita*, the Series', *Cultural Critique* 61 (Autumn 2005), p. 157.
42 Joel Surnow quoted in Ted Edwards, *La Femme Nikita X-posed: The Biography of Peta Wilson and Her On-screen Character of* La Femme Nikita (Roseville, CA: Prima, 1998), p. 68; Cited in Edward Gross, La Femme Nikita Episode Guide, Retrovision # 6 (1999), http://lfnforever.tripod.com/id10.htm (accessed 3 July 2013).
43 Although shot in Toronto, the series avoids recognizable locations. It makes reference to mission destinations (Prague, Belgrade, Liberia, Asia, Europe etc.), but does not situate Section in a specific place or national context.
44 Takacs: 'Speculations on a New Economy', p. 175.
45 Season One, Episode Nine ('Gray') entails a 'rare suggestion that Section One works in cooperation with local authorities (a theme that will be further developed in Episode 19 ('Voices')', Dawn Connolly, *La Femme Peta: The Unofficial Story of the Woman Behind Nikita* (Toronto: ECW, 2000), p. 113; see also http://lfnforever.tripod.com/id110.htm (accessed 3 July 2014).

46 Mitchell: 'The Unspeakable and the Unimaginable', p. 301.
47 See Season Three, Episode Two ('Someone Else's Shadow') and Season Two, Episode 22 ('End Game').
48 An exception to this rule is a reference to the Iraqi dictator Saddam Hussein in Episode 22 of Season Two ('End Game', 1998). A rare politicized discourse on Section One's or, figuratively speaking, the USA's role in global power struggles is raised.
49 See Madeline's comment to Nikita in Season One, Episode Ten ('Choice'): 'The world outside these walls is an illusion, it's not really there for us, we're ghosts.'
50 Takacs, 'Speculations on a New Economy', p. 152; see also pp. 167–68.
51 Donna J. Haraway, *Simians, Cyborgs and Women: The Reinvention of Nature* (New York: Routledge, and London: Free Association Books, 1991).
52 Giuseppe O. Longo, 'Body and Technology: Continuity or Discontinuity?', in Leopoldina Fortunati, James E. Katz and Raimonda Riccini (eds), *Mediating the Human Body: Communication, Technology and Fashion*, (Mahwah, NJ: Lawrence Erlbaum), p. 23.
53 Ivan Callus and Stefan Herbrechter, 'Introduction: Posthumanist Subjectivities, or, Coming After the Subject . . . ', *Subjectivity* 5 (2012), p. 250.
54 See Season Three, Episode 22 ('Borrowed Time').
55 Angelo Bolaffi and Giacomo Marramao, *Frammento e Sistema* (Rome: Donzelli, 2001), p. 166; cited in Cavarero, *Horrorism*, p. 77.
56 See, for example, a self-induced heart attack as part of a mission in Season One, Episode Eleven ('Rescue').
57 Günther Anders, *Die Antiquiertheit des Menschen: Über die Zerstörung des Lebens im Zeitalter der Dritten Industriellen Revolution*, Volume Two [1980] (München: C. H. Beck, 2002), p. 281. Anders argues that the nuclear bomb declares 'unser Gemachtes, die opera creata, als überlebenswerter, als *ontologisch wichtiger denn uns Macher*, die creatores' (p. 281).
58 Agamben: *Homo Sacer*, pp. 71–4.
59 The phrase 'bestialization of man' refers us back to Michel Foucault and his idea of 'docile bodies' as the effect of disciplinary bio-powers; see Agamben: *Homo Sacer*, p. 3.
60 See also Madeline's comment to Nikita in Season One, Episode Eight ('Grey'): 'The relationship you have with us is the only real relationship you'll ever have.'
61 Season One, Episode 14 ('Gambit'); at the beginning of the episode Madeline is seen practising her art of torture/killing in virtual reality.
62 Susan Sontag, 'Fascinating Fascism' [1974], *Under the Sign of Saturn* (New York: Farrar, Straus, Giroux, 1980), p. 93.

63 Cited in Gross, *La Femme Nikita Episode Guide*, http://lfnforever.tripod.com/id190.htm (accessed 3 July 2014).
64 See particularly Season Three, Episode 18 ('Third Party Ripoff'). For a discussion of language use in the Third Reich see Henry Friedlander, 'The Manipulation of Language', in Henry Friedlander and Sybil Milton (eds), *The Holocaust: Ideology, Bureaucracy, and Genocide* (Millwood, NY: Kraus International, 1980), pp. 103–13, and John Wesley Young, 'From LTI to LQI: Victor Klemperer on Totalitarian Language', *German Studies Review* 28/1 (2005), pp. 45–64.
65 See also Season Two, Episode Ten ('First Mission') in which Operations orders Michael to 'crush' Nikita's feelings.
66 See Season Three, Episode 14 ('Hand to Hand').
67 In Season Two, Episode 22 ('End Game'), Adrian (Sîan Phillips), the organization's original mastermind, blames Madeline for 'sleeping with every young stud', i.e. new male operative, in Section One.
68 See Season One, Episode Seven ('Treason') or Season Two, Episode Five ('New Regime').
69 See Season One, Episode Eleven ('Rescue').
70 See Season One, Episode Six ('Love') or Season Three, Episode One ('Looking for Michael').
71 Judith Butler, 'Violence, Mourning, Politics', in Jennifer Harding and E. Deirdre Pribram (eds), *Emotions: A Cultural Studies Reader* (Abingdon and New York: Routledge, 2009) p. 394.
72 Agamben: *Homo Sacer*, pp. 82–3.
73 Giorgio Agamben, *State of Exception* [2003], trans. Kevin Attell (Chicago: University of Chicago Press, 2005), p. 4.
74 Cited in Gross: *La Femme Nikita Episode Guide*, http://lfnforever.tripod.com/id190.htm (accessed 3 July 2014).
75 Agamben: *Homo Sacer*, pp. 15–210.
76 Rosie White, *Violent Femmes: Women as Spies in Popular Culture* (New York: Routledge, 2007), p. 122.
77 For detailed insights into this debate, see Karen J. Greenberg, *The Torture Debate in America* (Cambridge: Cambridge University Press, 2007); on questions of morality and torture, see also Yuval Ginbar, *Why Not Torture Terrorists? Moral, Practical and Legal Aspects of the 'Ticking Bomb' Justification for Torture* (Oxford: Oxford University Press, 2008); James E. White (ed.), *Contemporary Moral Problems: War, Terrorism, and Torture*, 3rd edn (Belmont, CA: Thomson Wadsworth, 2009).
78 Greg A. Mullins, 'Atrocity, Literature, Criticism', *American Literary History* 23/1 (Spring 2011), p. 217.

79 See Season Three, Episode One – Three ('Looking for Michael', 'Someone Else's Shadow', 'Opening Night Jitters').
80 See Season Three, Episode Four ('Gates of Hell').
81 See Season One, Episode Seven ('Treason').
82 'Nikita wants to resist, but in order to stay alive, she has no choice but to comply with their plans.' (USA Network description of first episode, Cited in Mary Margoulick, 'Frustrating Female Heroism: Mixed Messages in Xena, Nikita and Buffy', *Journal of Popular Culture* 39/5 (2006), pp. 729–54.
83 See Season One, Episode Eight ('Escape').
84 See Season One, Episode Six ('Love') and Season Two, Episode 22 ('End Game').
85 Judith Butler, 'Hannah Arendt's challenge to Adolf Eichmann', *The Guardian Online*, 29 August 2011, http://www.guardian.co.uk/commentisfree/2011/aug/29/hannah-arendt-adolf-eichmann-banality-of-evil (accessed 3 July 2014).
86 Jenna Vogler's bomb explodes; Adrian is executed off-screen in an act that connotes matricide; Simone (Mung-Ling Tsui), Michael's ex-colleague and partner, commits suicide; Madeline also takes her life later in the series; Belinda (Jill Dyck), the fiancée of Section's weapon specialist Walter (Don Francks) is cancelled.
87 Butler: 'Violence, Mourning, Politics', p. 387.
88 Butler: 'Violence, Mourning, Politics', p. 387.
89 This conflict is central to Season One, Episode 22 ('Mercy').
90 White: *Violent Femmes*, p. 122.
91 Takacs: 'Speculations on a New Economy', p. 166.
92 Fredric Jameson, 'Class and Allegory in Contemporary Mass Culture: *Dog Day Afternoon* as Political Film', *Screen Education* 30 (Spring 1979), pp. 75–92; Cited in Takacs: 'Speculations on a New Economy', p. 156.
93 For the thought-defying structures of the contemporary university system see Griselda Pollock, 'Saying No! Profligacy Versus Austerity, or Metaphor Against Model in Justifying the Arts and Humanities in the Contemporary University', *Journal of European Popular Culture* 3/1 (2012), pp. 87–104.
94 Hannavy Cousen: 'The Seeping and Creeping of Haunted Memory', p. 210.
95 An original soundtrack album for the series was released in 1998 and includes, among others, electronic music by Enigma, Depeche Mode, alternative/electronic rock by Curve and jazz and soul samples by DJ Krush.
96 Charlene Tung highlights Nikita's role as 'fashion diva' that allows the series' producers to create an environment directed at the female consumer; 'Embodying an Image: Gender, Race and Sexuality in *La Femme Nikita*', in

Sherrie A. Inness (ed.), *Action Chicks: New Images of Tough Women in Popular Culture* (London: Palgrave, 2004), p. 97. Radner observes that 'the television show served as vehicle for Costume National, a European Italian-based designer shoes and clothing line' ('*Nikita*', p. 138).

97 See Zygmunt Bauman and Leonidas Donskis, *Moral Blindness: The Loss of Sensitivity in Liquid Modernity* (Cambridge: Polity Press, 2013), pp. 9, 15.
98 See Season Two, Episode Nine ('Open Heart').
99 Cited in Cavarero: *Horrorism*, p. 56 (with further footnote).
100 Cited in Gross: La Femme Nikita Episode Guide, http://lfnforever.tripod.com/id195.htm (accessed 3 July 2014).
101 Arendt: *Eichmann in Jerusalem*, p. 252.
102 Bauman and Donskis: *Moral Blindness*, p. 5.

BIBLIOGRAPHY

Adorno, Theodor and Horkheimer, Max. *The Dialectic of Enlightenment*, trans. John Cumming (New York: Continuum, 1996).

Agamben, Giorgio. 'The Camp as "Nomos" of the Modern', *Homo Sacer: Sovereign Power and Bare Life*, trans. Daniel Heller-Roazan (California: Stanford University Press, 1998), pp. 166–80.

—— *Homo Sacer: Sovereign Power and Bare Life* [1995], trans. Daniel Heller-Roazen (Stanford: Stanford University Press, 1998).

—— *Remnants of Auschwitz: The Witness and the Archive*, trans. Daniel Heller-Roazen (Cambridge, MA: MIT Press, 2000).

—— *State of Exception* [2003], trans. Kevin Attell (Chicago: University of Chicago Press, 2005).

Althusser, Louis. 'Ideology and Ideological State Apparatuses: Notes Towards an Investigation', *Lenin and Philosophy and Other Essays*, trans. Ben Brewster (London: Monthly Review Press, 1971), pp. 121–76.

Anders, Günther. *Die Antiquiertheit des Menschen: Über die Zerstörung des Lebens im Zeitalter der Dritten Industriellen Revolution*, Volume Two [1980] (München: C.H. Beck, 2002).

Antelme, Robert. *The Human Race [L'Espèce Humaine]* trans. Jeffrey Haight and Annie Mahler (Chicago: Marlboro Press, 1998).

Arad, Yitzhak, Krakowski, Shmuel, Spector, Shmuel and Schossberger, Stella. *The Einsatzgruppen Reports: Selections from the Dispatches of the Nazi Death Squads' Campaign against the Jews, July 1941–January 1943* (New York: Holocaust Library, 1989).

Arendt, Hannah. *Eichmann in Jerusalem: A Report on the Banality of Evil* [1963] (New York/Toronto/London: Penguin, 2006).

—— *Essays in Understanding: 1930–1954*, edited by Jerome Kohn (New York: Harcourt, Brace and Co., 1994).

―――― *The Human Condition* (Chicago: Chicago University Press, 1958).
―――― *The Life of the Mind* (New York: Harcourt Brace Jovanovich, 1978).
―――― 'Mankind and Terror', in *Essays in Understanding, 1930–1954*, edited by Jerome Kohn (New York: Harcourt, Brace and Co., 1994).
―――― 'On Humanity in Dark Times. Thoughts about Lessing', in *Men in Dark Times* [1968] (New York: Harvest Books, 1995), pp. 3–32.
―――― *On Revolution* [1963] (New York: Viking Penguin, 1977).
―――― *On Violence* (New York: Harcourt, Brace and World, 1970).
―――― *The Origins of Totalitarianism* [1951] (New York: Harcourt Brace and Co., 1976) (New York: Schocken Books, 2004).
Badmington, Neil. 'Theorizing Posthumanism', *Cultural Critique* 53 (Winter 2003), pp. 10–27.
Bassi, Chiara. 'Fathers and Daughters in the Camp: *The Night Porter* by Liliana Cavani', in Laura Benedetti, Julia L. Hairston and Sylvia M. Ross (eds), *Gendered Contexts: New Perspectives on Italian Cultural Studies* (New York: Peter Lang, 1996), pp. 165–75.
Bauman, Zygmunt. *Modernity and the Holocaust* (Cambridge: Polity, 1989).
―――― *Wasted Lives: Modernity and its Outcasts* (Cambridge: Polity Press, 2003).
Bauman, Zygmunt and Donskis, Leonidas. *Moral Blindness: The Loss of Sensitivity in Liquid Modernity* (Cambridge: Polity Press, 2013).
Bilgrami, Akeel. 'Occidentalism, the Very Idea: An Essay on Enlightenment and Enchantment', *Critical Inquiry* 32 (2006), pp. 381–411.
Bukatman, Scott. *Blade Runner* (London: BFI 1998).
Butler, Judith. 'Hannah Arendt's Challenge to Adolf Eichmann', *The Guardian Online*, 29 August 2011, http://www.guardian.co.uk/commentisfree/2011/aug/29/hannah-arendt-adolf-eichmann-banality-of-evil (accessed 3 July 2014).
―――― *Precarious Life* (London: Verso 2006).
―――― 'Violence, Mourning, Politics', in Jennifer Harding and E. Deirdre Pribram (eds), *Emotions: A Cultural Studies Reader* (Abingdon/New York: Routledge, 2009) pp. 387–402.
Callus, Ivan and Herbrechter, Stefan. 'Introduction: Posthumanist Subjectivities, or, Coming After the Subject...', *Subjectivity* 5 (2012), pp. 241–64.
Camus, Alfred. *The Rebel* (1951) trans. Anthony Bower (London: Penguin Classics, 2001).

Caplan, Jane and Wachsmann, Nikolaus (eds). *Concentration Camps in Nazi Germany: The New Histories* (London: Routledge, 2009).

Cavarero, Adriana. *Horrorism: Naming Contemporary Violence* [2007], trans. William McCuaig (New York: Columbia University Press, 2009).

Cesarani, David and Sundquist, Eric (eds). *After the Holocaust: Challenging the Myth of Silence* (London: Routledge, 2012).

Chare, Nicholas. *Auschwitz and Afterimages: Abjection, Witnessing and Representation* (London and New York: I.B.Tauris, 2011).

Chare, Nicholas and Williams, Dominic. *The Scrolls of Auschwitz* (London: Berghan 2015).

Chiurco, C. (ed.). *Filosofia di Berlusconi. L'essere e il nulla nell'Italia contemporanea* (Verona: ombre corte, 2011).

Connolly, Dawn. *La Femme Peta: The Unofficial Story of the Woman Behind Nikita* (Toronto: ECW, 2000), see also http://lfnforever.tripod.com/id110.htm (accessed 3 July 2014).

Consolaro, Francesca. 'Il "vulnerabile" come chiave del "mondo che viene": considerazioni etimologiche', *Filosofia Politica* 1 (2009), pp. 45–50.

Creed, Barbara. *The Monstrous Feminine: Film, Feminine and Psychoanalysis* (London and New York: Routledge, 1993).

Crownshaw, Richard. *Afterlife of Holocaust Memory in Contemporary Literature and Culture* (Basingstoke: Palgrave Macmillan, 2010).

Daney, Serge. 'The Tracking Shot in *Kapò*', *Senses of Cinema* 30 (January–March 2004), www.sensesofcinema.com/2004/feature-articles/Kapò_daney/ (accessed 23 August 2011; first published in *Trafic*, no 4, P.O.L. Editions, 1992; trans. Laurent Kretzschmar).

de Lauretis, Teresa. 'Cavani's *Night Porter*: A Woman's Film?', *Film Quarterly* 30/2 (1976/77), pp. 35–8.

De Sade, Marquis. *Justine, Philosophy in the Bedroom and Other Writings* (London: Arrow Books, 1991).

Delbo, Charlotte. *Auschwitz and After I: None of Us Will Return* trans. Rosette C. Lamont (New Haven: Yale University Press, 1985).

DeLillo, Don. 'In the Ruins of the Future', The *Guardian*, 22 December 2001 (first published in *Harper's Magazine*, December 2001), http://www.theguardian.com/books/2001/dec/22/fiction.dondelillo (accessed 2 March 2011).

Derrida, Jacques. 'A dialogue with Jacques Derrida', in *Philosophy in a Time of Terror: Dialogues with Jürgen Habermas and Jacques Derrida: Interviewed* by Giovanna Borradori (Chicago: The University of Chicago Press, 2003).

―――― *Specters of Marx*, trans. Peggy Kamuf (New York and London: Routledge, 1994).

Didi-Huberman, Georges. *Images in Spite of All: Four Photographs from Auschwitz*, trans. Shane B. Lillis (Chicago: University of Chicago Press, 2012).

Doane, Mary Ann. *The Emergence of Cinematic Time* (Cambridge, MA and London: Harvard University Press, 2002).

Edelstein, David. 'Audience is Loser in Haneke's Unfunny "Games"', *Fresh Air*, 14 March 2008, http://www.npr.org/templates/story/story.php?storyId=88230619 (accessed 5 April 2011).

Edwards, Ted. *La Femme Nikita X-posed: The Biography of Peta Wilson and Her On-screen Character of* La Femme Nikita (Roseville, CA: Prima, 1998), p. 68. Cited in Edward Gross, La Femme Nikita Episode Guide, Retrovision # 6 (1999), http://lfnforever.tripod.com/id10.htm (accessed 3 July 2013).

Egbert, Roger. *Chicago Sun-Times*, 10 February 1975 http://rogerebert.suntimes.com/apps/pbcs.dll/article?AID=/19750210/REVIEWS/502100301/1023 (accessed 10 November 2012).

Flores, Marcello. *Tutta la violenza di un secolo* (Milan: Feltrinelli, 2005).

Fogu, Claudio. *The Historic Imaginary: Politics of History in Fascist Italy* (Toronto: University of Toronto Press, 2003).

Freud, Sigmund. *The Interpretation of Dreams* [1900], trans. James Strachey, ed. James Strachey (with Alan Tyson and Angela Richards) (Harmondsworth: Penguin Books, 1976).

―――― *The Psychopathology of Everyday Day Life* [1901], trans. Alan Tyson, ed. James Strachey (with Angela Richards and Alan Tyson) (Harmondsworth: Penguin, 1975).

Friedlander, Henry. 'The Manipulation of Language', in Henry Friedlander and Sybil Milton (eds), *The Holocaust: Ideology, Bureaucracy, and Genocide* (Millwood, NY: Kraus International, 1980), pp. 103–13.

Friedländer, Saul. *Reflections of Nazism: An Essay on Kitsch and Death*, trans. Thomas Weyr (New York: Harper & Row, 1984).

―――― *Reflets du Nazisme* (Paris: Editions du Seuil, 1982).

Gallop, Jane. 'Where to Begin?', *Reading Lacan* (Ithaca: Cornell University Press, 1985), pp. 74–92.

Gillard, Gary. 'Supertext and the Mind-Culture System: Freud, Lévi-Strauss, Bateson' (unpublished PhD thesis, Murdoch University, 1994), http://www.garrygillard.net/writing/supertext/ch3.html (accessed 3 July 2014).

Gilroy, Paul. *Between Camps: Nations, Cultures and the Allure of Race* [2000] (London: Routledge, 2004).

Ginbar, Yuval. *Why Not Torture Terrorists? Moral, Practical and Legal Aspects of the 'Ticking Bomb' Justification for Torture* (Oxford: Oxford University Press, 2008).

Greenberg, Karen J. *The Torture Debate in America* (Cambridge: Cambridge University Press, 2007).

Gross, Sheryl W. 'Guilt and Innocence in *Marathon Man*', *Literature Film Quarterly* 8/1 (1980), pp. 52–68.

Grossman, Vassily. *The Road: Stories, Journalism and Essays*, edited by Robert Chandler and Yury Bit-Yunan, trans. Robert and Elizabeth Chandler and Olga Mukovnikova (New York: NYRB, 2010).

Haneke, Michael. 'Michael Haneke: Interview', *Time Out*, www.timeout.com/film/features/show-feature/3658/Michael_Haneke-interview.html (accessed 24 October 2011).

Hannavy Cousen, Benjamin. 'ISN'T THIS WHERE...? Projections on *Pink Floyd The Wall*: Tracing the Concentrationary Image', in Griselda Pollock and Max Silverman (eds), *Concentrationary Memories: Totalitarian Terror and Cultural Resistance* (London: I.B.Tauris, 2013), pp. 203–22.

―――― 'Memory, Power and Place, Where is *Guernica?*', *Journal of Romance Studies* 9/2 (2009), pp. 47–64.

―――― 'The Seeping and Creeping of Haunted Memory: Tracing the Concentrationary in Post-war Cinema' (unpublished PhD thesis, University of Leeds, 2011).

Haraway, Donna. 'A Cyborg Manifesto: Science, Technology, and Socialist-feminism in the Late Twentieth Century', in *Simians, Cyborgs and Women: the Reinvention of Nature* (New York: Routledge, and London: Free Association Books, 1991), pp. 149–81.

―――― *Simians, Cyborgs and Women: The Reinvention of Nature* (New York: Routledge, and London: Free Association Books, 1991).

Hayward, Susan. *Nikita* [1990, Luc Besson] (London and New York: I.B.Tauris, 2010).

Headland, Ronald. *Messages of Murder: A Study of the Reports of the Einsatzgruppen of the Security Police and the Security Service, 1941–1943* (Rutherford, NJ: Fairleigh Dickinson University Press, 1992).

Hedgepeth, Sonia and Saidel, Rochelle (eds). *Sexual Violence against Jewish Women during the Holocaust* (Boston: Brandeis University Press, 2010).

Hegel, G.W.F. *Grundlinien der Philosophie des Rechts* [1821] (Suhrkamp: Frankfurt am Main 1972).

Heineman, Elizabeth D. 'Sexuality and Nazism: The Doubly Unspeakable?', *Journal of the History of Sexuality* 11: 1/2 (January/April 2002), pp. 22–66.

Heyn, Christopher. *Inside Section One: Creating and Producing TV's* La Femme Nikita (Los Angeles: POV Press, 2006).

Horvat, Srecko. 'Interview with Paul A Taylor', *International Journal of Žižek Studies* 1/0 (2007), n.p.

Huyssen, Andreas. *Twilight Memories: Marking Time in a Culture of Amnesia* (London and New York: Routledge, 1995).

Insdorf, Annette. 'The Night Porter', http://www.criterion.com/current/posts/66 (accessed 10 November 2012).

Jameson, Fredric. 'Class and Allegory in Contemporary Mass Culture: *Dog Day Afternoon* as Political Film', *Screen Education* 30 (Spring 1979), pp. 75–92.

—— 'Imaginary and Symbolic in Lacan: Marxism, Psychoanalytical Criticism and the Problem of the Subject', *Yale French Studies* 55/56 (1977), pp. 383–95.

—— *The Political Unconscious: Narrative as a Socially Symbolic Act* (Ithaca: Cornell University Press, 1982.

—— 'Postmodernism, Or The Cultural Logic of Late Capitalism', *New Left Review* 146 (July–August 1984), pp. 53–92.

Kerman, Judith B. (ed.). *Retrofitting Blade Runner: Issues in Ridley Scott's* Blade Runner *and Philip K. Dick's* Do Androids Dream of Electric Sheep? (Bowling Green, Ohio: Bowling Green University Popular Press, 1991).

Kertesz, Imre. *Fatelessness [Sorstalanság]* trans. Tom Wilkinson (New York: Vintage, 1975).

Kirchner, William. 'Conversation with George Stevens', in Paul Cronin (ed.), *George Stevens: Interviews* (Jackson: University Press of Mississippi, 2004), pp. 18–23.

Klemperer, Victor. *The Language of the Third Reich: A Philologist's Notebook* trans. Martin Brady (London: Bloomsbury Academic, 2006).

Klossowski, Pierre. *Sade My Neighbour* trans. Alphonso Lingis (London: Quartet Books Limited, 1992).

Koonz, Claudia. *Mothers in the Fatherland: Women, the Family, and Nazi Politics* (New York: St Martin's Press, 1987).

Kristeva, Julia. *Powers of Horror: An Essay on Abjection*, trans. Leon S. Roudiez (New York: Columbia University Press, 1982).

La Caze, Marguerite. *The Analytic Imaginary* (Ithaca: Cornell University Press, 2002).

Lacan, Jacques. 'Kant avec Sade', *October* 51 (Winter 1989), pp. 55–104.

——— 'The Looking Glass Phase', *International Journal of Psychoanalysis* XVIII, no. 1 (1937).

——— 'The Mirror Phase as Formative of the Function of the "I" in Psychonanalytic Experience', *Ecrits: A Selection*, trans. Alan Sheridan (London: Tavistock Publications, 1977), pp. 1–7.

——— 'The Mirror-phase as Formative of the Function of the I: 1949', *New Left Review* 51(1968), pp. 71–7.

——— 'Le Stade du miroir comme formateur de la fonction du Je: telle qu'elle nous est révélée dans l'expérience psychanalytique', *Revue française de psychanalyse* 4 (October 1949), pp. 449–55.

Lacoue-Labarthe, Philippe. 'La Fable (philosophie et littérature)', *Poétique* 1 (1970), pp. 51–63.

Lacoue-Labarthe, Philippe and Nancy, Jean-Luc. *Le Mythe nazi* (Paris: Éditions de l'Aube, 1991).

——— 'The Nazi Myth', trans. Brian Holmes, *Critical Inquiry* 16:2 (1990), pp. 291–312.

——— *Le Sujet de la philosophie* (Paris: Aubier-Flammarion).

Lane, Anthony. 'Recurring Nightmare', *The New Yorker* 17 March 2008, http://www.newyorker.com/arts/critics/cinema/2008/03/17/080317crci_cinema_lane (accessed 5 April 2011).

——— 'Happy Haneke', *The New Yorker* 5 October 2009, pp. 6–67.

Lanval, Marc. 'Ilse Koch – Sex Terrorist', *Sexology* 19/1 (1951), pp. 30–6.

Laplanche, Jean. 'Notes on Afterwardness', *Essays on Otherness* edited by John Fletcher (London: Routledge, 1999), pp. 260–5.

Levi, Primo. *The Drowned and the Saved*, trans. Raymond Rosenthal (New York: Summit Books, 1988).

——— *I sommersi e i salvati* (Turin: Einaudi 1986).

―――― *Survival in Auschwitz and the Reawakening*, trans. Stuart Woolf (New York: Summit 1986).

Lindeperg, Sylvie and Wieviorka, Annette. *Univers concentrationnaire et génocide: voir, savoir, comprendre* (Paris: Mille et une nuits/Arthème Fayard, 2008).

Longo, Giuseppe O. 'Body and Technology: Continuity or Discontinuity?', in Leopoldina Fortunati, James E. Katz and Raimonda Riccini (eds), *Mediating the Human Body: Communication, Technology and Fashion* (Mahwah, NJ: Lawrence Erlbaum), pp. 23–30.

McDonald, James. *Fantasy and the Cinema* (London: BFI, 1989).

Magilow, Daniel H., Iridges, Elizabeth and Vander Lugt, Kirstin T. (eds). *Nazisploitation! The Nazi Image in Low-Brow Cinema and Culture* (London: Continuum, 2011).

Margoulick, Mary. 'Frustrating Female Heroism: Mixed Messages in Xena, Nikita and Buffy', *Journal of Popular Culture* 39/5 (2006), pp. 729–54.

Mark, Bernard (ed.). *The Scrolls of Auschwitz*, trans. Sharon Neemani (Tel Aviv: Am 'Oved, 1985).

Marone, Gaetana. *The Gaze and the Labyrinth: The Cinema of Liliana Cavani* (Princeton: Princeton University Press, 2000).

Mechanic, Michael. 'America's Global Military Presence: Mission Creep', http://www.globalresearch.ca/index.php?context=va&aid=10011 (accessed 23 September 2011).

Metz, Christian. *Psychoanalysis and Cinema: The Imaginary Signifier*, trans. Celia Britton, Annwyl Williams, Bew Brewster and Alfred Guzzetti (Basingstoke: Macmillan, 1982).

Milner, Iris. 'The "Gray Zone" Revisited: The Concentrationary Universe in Ka. Tzetnik's Literary Testimony', *Jewish Social Studies* 14/2 (2008), pp. 113–205.

Mitchell, W.J.T. 'The Unspeakable and the Unimaginable: Word and Image in a Time of Terror', *ELH* 72/2 (Summer 2005), pp. 291–308.

Morante, Elsa. *History: a novel*, trans. William Weaver (London: Penguin Books 2001).

Morozov, Evgeny. *The Net Delusion: How Not to Change the World* (London: Allen Lane, 2011).

Mullins, Greg A. 'Atrocity, Literature, Criticism', *American Literary History* 23/1 (Spring 2011), pp. 217–27.

Murray, Gabrielle. '*Hostel II*: Representations of the Body in Pain and the Cinema Experience in Torture-Porn', *Jump Cut* 50 (Spring 2008) http://www.ejumpcut.org/archive/jc50.2008/TortureHostel2/text.html (accessed 5 April 2011).

Nafisi, Azar. 'The Republic of the Imagination', *Washington Post*, 5 December 2004, http://www.washingtonpost.com/wp-dyn/articles/A30117-2004Dec2.html (accessed 3 October 2011).

Nancy, Jean-Luc. *La Communauté désœuvrée* (Paris: Christian Bourgois, 1990).

—— *Ego Sum* (Paris: Flammarion, 1979).

Newman, Kim. 'Torture Garden', *Sight & Sound* 16/6 (June 2006), pp. 28–31.

Pajaczkowska, Claire. 'The Emotional Work of Cinema', Everyman Cinema, London, 9 May 2009, available as podcast: http://www.miwnet.org/Website/audio-items/the-emotional-work-of-cinema-roundtable/, here: 0:26:20 (accessed 3 July 2014).

Peary, Danny. *Cult Movies 3* (New York: Vermillion, 1988).

Pollock, Griselda and Silverman, Max (eds). *Concentrationary Memories: Aesthetics as Resistance in Alain Resnais's Night and Fog* (London and New York: Berghan, 2011).

—— *Concentrationary Memories: Totalitarian Terror and Cultural Resistance* (London: I.B.Tauris, 2013).

Pollock, Griselda and Silverman, Max. 'The Politics of Memory: From Concentrationary Memory to Concentrationary Memories', in Griselda Pollock and Max Silverman (eds), *Concentrationary Memories: Totalitarian Terror and Cultural Resistance* (New York and London: I.B. Tauris, 2013), pp. 1–28.

Pollock, Griselda. 'Concentrationary Memories and the Politics of Representation', Imperial War Museum, London, 2 June 2010, available as podcast: http://backdoorbroadcasting.net/2010/06/concentrationary-memories-and-the-politics-of-representation/, here 00:54:12 (accessed 3 July 2014).

—— 'Death in the Image; The Responsibility of Aesthetics in *Night and Fog* (1955) and *Kapò* (1959)', in Pollock and Silverman (eds), *Concentrationary Cinema: The Aesthetics of Resistance in Alain Resnais's Night and Fog* (London: Berghan, 2011 and 2013), pp. 258–302.

—— 'Saying No! Profligacy Versus Austerity, or Metaphor Against Model in Justifying the Arts and Humanities in the Contemporary

University', *Journal of European Popular Culture* 3/1 (2012), pp. 87–104.
Pope, Alexender. *An Essay on Man* [1734] (Charleston, SC: BiblioBazaar, 2008).
Price, Brian. 'Pain and the Limits of Representation', *Framework: The Journal Of Cinema And Media* 47/2 (Fall 2006), pp. 22–9.
Przyrembel, Alexandra. 'Transfixed by an Image: Ilse Koch, the "Kommandeuse of Buchenwald,"' trans. Pamela Selwyn, *German History* 19/3 (October 2001), pp. 369–99.
Radner, Hilary Ann. 'Nikita: Consumer Culture's Killer Instinct and the Imperial Imperative', in Susan Hayward and Phil Powrie (eds), *The Films of Luc Besson: Master of Spectacle* (Manchester: Manchester University Press, 2006), pp. 135–46.
Rancière, Jacques. *The Future of the Image* [2007] (London: Verso, 2009).
Rapaport, Lynn. 'Holocaust Pornography: Profaning the Sacred in Ilsa: She-Wolf of the SS', *Shofar: An Interdisciplinary Journal of Jewish Studies* 22/1 (Fall 2003), pp. 104–15.
Ravetto, Kris. *The Unmaking of Fascist Aesthetics* (Minneapolis: University of Minnesota Press, 2001).
Rejali, Darius M. *Torture and Democracy* (Princeton and Oxford: Princeton University Press, 2007).
Ricoeur, Paul. *Temps et Récit I* (Paris: Éditions du Seuil, 1983).
——— 'Imagination in Discourse and in Action' in *From Text to Action: Essays in Hermeneutics II*, trans. Kathleen Blamey and John B. Thompson (Evanston, IL: Northwestern University Press, 1991), pp. 168–87.
Rigney, Ann. 'Plenitude, Scarcity and the Circulation of Cultural Memory', *Journal of European Studies* 35/8(2000), pp. 11–28.
Rivette, Jacques. 'On Abjection', translated by David Phelps with the assistance of Jeremi Szaniawski, www.dvdbeaver.com/rivette/OK/abjection.html (accessed, 24 October 2011: first published as 'De l'abjection', *Cahiers du cinéma* 120, juin 1961, pp. 54–5).
Rose, Gillian. 'Beginnings of the Day: Fascism and Representation', in *Mourning Becomes the Law* (Cambridge: Cambridge University Press, 1996), pp. 41–62.
Rosen, Alan. *The Wonder of their Voices: The 1946 Holocaust Interviews of David Boder* (Oxford: Oxford University Press, 2010).
Roudinescu, Élisabeth. *Jacques Lacan*, trans. Barbara Bray (New York: Columbia University Press, 1997 and Cambridge: Polity Press, 1997).

―― *Lacan: In Spite of Everything*, trans. Gregory Elliott, 2014).
―― 'The Mirror Stage: An Obliterated Archive', in Jean-Michel Rabaté, *The Cambridge Companion to Lacan* (Cambridge: Cambridge University Press, 2003), pp. 25–34.
Rousset, David. *L'Univers concentrationnaire* (Paris: Editions de Pavois, 1946; reprinted Paris: Hachette/Pluriel, 2008).
―― *The Other Kingdom*, trans. Ramon Guthrie (New York: Reynal and Hitchcock, 1947).
―― *A World Apart*, trans. Y. Moyse and R. Senhouse (London: Secker & Warburg, 1951).
Saletti, Carlo (ed.). *La voce dei sommersi* (Venice: Marsilio, 2000).
Sammon, Paul. *Future Noir: The Making of Blade Runner* (New York: Orion, 1996).
Santner, Eric. 'History Beyond the Pleasure Principle', in Saul Friedländer (ed.), *Probing the Limits of Representation: Nazism and the Final Solution* (Cambridge, MA: Harvard University Press, 1992), pp. 143–54.
Sartre, Jean-Paul. *L'Imaginaire: psychologie phénoménologique de l'imagination* (Paris: Gallimard, 1940).
―― *The Imaginary: A Phenomenological Psychology of the Imagination*, trans. Jonathan Webber (New York and London: Routledge, 2004).
Saxton, Libby. *Haunted Images: Film, Ethics, Testimony and the Holocaust* (New York: Columbia University Press, 2008).
Scarry, Elaine. *The Body in Pain: The Making And Unmaking of the World* (New York: Oxford University Press, 1985).
Schaap, Andrew. 'Enacting the Right to Have Rights: Jacques Rancière's Critique of Hannah Arendt', *European Journal of Political Theory* 10/1 (2011), pp. 22–45.
Scott, Ridley. *Blade Runner: Five Disk Collector's Edition* (Warner Brothers, 2007).
Scroggy, David (ed.). *Blade Runner Sketchbook* (San Diego: Blue Dolphin Enterprises 1982).
Shapiro, Jeremy and Suzan, Benedicte. 'The French Experience of Counter-terrorism', *Survival* 25/1 (Spring 2003), pp. 67–98.
Silverman, Kaja. *The Acoustic Mirror: The Female Voice in Psychoanalysis and Cinema* (Bloomington: Indiana University Press, 1988).
―― 'Back to the Future', *Camera Obscura* 9/3 (1991), pp. 108–32.
Silverman, Max. 'The Empire Looks Back', *Screen* 48/2 (2007), pp. 245–49.

―――― 'Interconnected Histories: Holocaust and Empire in the Cultural Imaginary', *French Studies* 62/4 (October 2008), pp. 417–28.

―――― 'The Violence of the Cut: Michael Haneke's *Caché* and Cultural Memory', *French Cultural Studies* 21/1 (2010), pp. 57–65.

Sofsky, Wolfgang. *The Order of Terror: The Concentration Camp* [1993], trans. William Templer (Princeton: Princeton University Press, 1997).

Sontag, Susan. 'Fascinating Fascism', *New York Review of Books*, 6 February 1975; reprinted *Under the Sign of Saturn* (London: Writers and Readers Collective, 1980), pp. 73–108.

Sorfa, David. 'Uneasy Domesticity in the Films of Michael Haneke', *Studies in European Cinema* 3/2 (2006), pp. 93–104.

Spivak, Gayatri Chakravorty. *Death of a Discipline* (New York: Columbia University Press, 2003).

Stiegler, Bernard. *La Technique et le temps 3. Le Temps du cinéma et la question du mal-être* (Paris, Galilée, 2001).

Takacs, Stacy. 'Speculations on a New Economy: *La Femme Nikita*, the Series', *Cultural Critique* 61 (Autumn 2005), pp. 148–85.

Taminiaux, Jacques. *The Thracian Maid and the Professional Thinker. Arendt and Heidegger* (Albany: Suny Press, 1997).

Theweleit, Klaus. *Male Fantasies, Vol. 1: Women, Floods, Bodies, Histories*, trans. Chris Turner and Stephen Conway (Minneapolis: University of Minnesota Press, 1987).

Tung, Charlene. 'Embodying an Image: Gender, Race and Sexuality in *La Femme Nikita*', in Sherrie A. Inness (ed.), *Action Chicks: New Images of Tough Women in Popular Culture* (London: Palgrave, 2004), pp. 95–118.

Villa, Dana. 'Genealogies of Total Domination: Arendt, Adorno and Auschwitz', *New German Critique* 100 (Winter 2007), pp. 1–45.

Virilio, Paul and Petit Philippe. *Cybermonde ou la politique du pire* (Paris: Éditions Textuel, 1996).

Virilio, Paul. *Bunker Archeology*, trans. G. Collins (New York: Princeton Architectural Press, 1994; new edition 2009).

―――― *Défense Populaire et luttes écologiques* (Paris: Galilée, 1978).

―――― *L'Insécurité du territoire* (Paris: Stock, 1976 [Galilée, 1993]).

―――― *Ville Panique. Ailleurs commence ici* (Paris: Galilée, 2003).

―――― *War and Cinema: The Logics of Perception* (London: Verso, 2009).

Waller, Marguerite. 'Signifying the Holocaust: Liliana Cavani's *Il Portiere di Notte*', in Laura Pietropaolo and Ada Testaferri (eds), *Feminisms in the Cinema* (Bloomington: Indiana University Press, 1995), pp. 206–19.

Weber, Samuel. 'Concentration and Isolation', http://www.leeds.ac.uk/cath/Recordings/samuel-weber.html (accessed 5 August 2011).

Wheatley, Catherine. *Michael Haneke's Cinema: The Ethics of the Image* (New York and Oxford: Berghahn, 2009).

White, Charles E. 'Mission Creep During the Lewis and Clark Expedition', http://www.history.army.mil/LC/The%20Mission/mission_creep.htm (accessed 12 May 2011).

White, Hayden. *Comparare: Considerations on a Levian Practice*, paper presented in Verona, Società Letteraria, 13 June 1997.

—— *Figural Realism: Studies in the Mimesis Effect* (Baltimore and London: Johns Hopkins University Press, 2000).

White, James E. (ed.). *Contemporary Moral Problems: War, Terrorism, and Torture*, 3rd edn (Belmont, CA: Thomson Wadsworth, 2009).

White, Rosie. *Violent Femmes: Women as Spies in Popular Culture* (New York: Routledge, 2007).

Wolf, René. 'Judgement in the Grey Zone: The Third Auschwitz (Kapo) Trial in Frankfurt 1968', *Journal of Genocide Research* 9/4 (2007), pp. 617–35.

Wolff, Janet. 'Memento Mori: Atrocity and Aesthetics', in Shelley Horstein and Florence Jacobowitz (eds), *Image and Remembrance: Representation and the Holocaust* (Bloomington and Indianapolis: Indiana University Press, 2003), pp. 153–74.

Young, John Wesley. 'From LTI to LQI: Victor Klemperer on Totalitarian Language', *German Studies Review* 28/1 (2005), pp. 45–64.

Zevi, Luca. *Conservazione dell'avvenire* (Macerata: Quodlibet, 2011).

Žižek, Slavoj. 'Kant with (or against) Sade', in Elizabeth and Edmond Wright (eds), *The Žižek Reader* (Oxford: Blackwell, 1999), pp. 283–301.

—— 'Much Ado about a Thing', *For They Know Not What They Do: Enjoyment as a Political Factor* (London: Verso, 1991), pp. 229–77.

—— *Violence* (London: Profile Books, 2008).

FILMOGRAPHY

Caché (*Hidden*) (Michael Haneke, 2005)
Cannibal Holocaust (Ruggero Deodato,1980)
Le Corbeau (*The Raven*) (Henri-Georges Clouzot, 1943)
Funny Games (Michael Haneke, 1997)
Funny Games (remake) (Michael Haneke, 2007)
The Gestapo's Last Orgy (Cesare Canevari, 1977)
Hostel (Eli Roth, 2005)
Hostel: Part II (Eli Roth, 2007)
Ilsa: She Wolf of the SS (Don Edmonds, 1975)
Kapò (Gillo Pontecorvo 1960)
Marathon Man (John Schlesinger, 1976)
The Night Porter (Liliana Cavani, 1974)
Nuit et brouillard (*Night and Fog*) (Alain Resnais, 1955)
Rome, Open City (Roberto Rossellini, 1945)
Salò (Pier Paolo Pasolini, 1975)
Saw (James Wan, 2004)
Saw II (Darren Lynn Bousman, 2005)
Saw III (Darren Lynn Bousman, 2006)
Shutter Island (Martin Scorsese, 2010)
Das weiße Band: Eine deutsche Kindergeschichte (*The White Ribbon*) (Michael Haneke, 2009).

CONTRIBUTORS

Adriana Cavarero is Professor of Political Philosophy at the University of Verona. She has also held visiting appointments at the University of California, Berkeley and Santa Barbara and at New York University and Harvard. She is the author of *In Spite of Plato* (1995), *Relating Narratives* (2000), *Stately Bodies* (2002), *For More than One Voice* (2005) and *Horrorism: Naming Contemporary Violence* (2008). She extends political philosophy with the feminist study of narration, voice and contemporary violence.

Olivia Guaraldo received a doctoral degree in Political Science from the University of Jyväskylä, Finland, and began researching and teaching at the University of Verona, Italy, where she is currently Associate Professor in Political Philosophy. Her publications include *Storylines: Narrative, History and Politics from an Arendtian Perspective* (2001); *Politica e racconto: Trame arendtiane della modernità* (2003); *Comunità e vulnerabilità: Per una critica politica della violenza* (2012); 'To the Narrative Turn and Back: The Political Impact of Storytelling in Feminism' in Hyvarinen, Havatara, Hydén (eds), *The Travelling Concepts of Narrative* (2013).

Benjamin Hannavy Cousen is a cultural analyst who completed a doctoral thesis at the University of Leeds as part of the AHRC-funded research project on *Concentrationary Memories: the Politics of Representation*. The thesis is titled: *The Seeping and Creeping of Haunted Memory: Tracing the Concentrationary in Post War Cinema*. He is interested in cultural memory as it is transmitted through all areas of visual culture and previous publications include an article on Picasso titled 'Memory, Power and Place: Where is Guernica?', *Journal of Romance Studies* 9/2 (2009), pp. 47–64.

Brenda Hollweg is currently Research Fellow in the School of Fine Art, History of Art and Cultural Studies at the University of Leeds. A specialist in American literature and a scholar of the essay as literary and expanded cultural form, she is also a filmmaker. She has worked on a major research collaboration on the aesthetic and affective dimensions of democratic participation (*The Road to Voting*) and has published on contemporary documentary and the video essay. Her most recent publications include: 'How Voting Happens: Video-essayistic Practice as Object-oriented Fabulation', *Journal of Media Practice* 15/2 (2014), pp. 157–75 and 'Political Sensibilities, Affect and the Performative Space of Voting', *Contemporary Theatre Review* 25/2 (2015), pp. 177–89.

Ian James is Reader in Modern French Literature and Thought Department of French at the University of Cambridge. He specializes in twentieth-century and contemporary French literature and philosophy. He is the author of *Pierre Klossowski: The Persistence of a Name* (2000), *The Fragmentary Demand: An Introduction to the Philosophy of Jean-Luc Nancy* (2006), *Paul Virilio* (2007) and *The New French Philosophy* (2012). He is also co-editor of *Whispers of the Flesh: Essays in Memory of Pierre Klossowski* (*Diacritics*, Spring 2005) and *Exposures: Critical Essays on Jean-Luc Nancy* (*Oxford Literary Review* 27, 2005). He is currently developing a collaborative project that will examine the role played by science and technology in recent and contemporary French thought and culture.

Aaron Kerner is Associate Professor of Film at San Francisco State University. Kerner has taught in the SFSU Cinema Department since 2003; prior to this he was a lecturer in the History of Art and Visual Culture Department at UC Santa Cruz. He was the recipient of, among other things, an NEA grant for his exhibition *Reconstructing Memories* (2006). In 2011 he published *Film and the Holocaust* – an extensive survey of narrative, documentary and experimental representations of the Holocaust. He is currently working on a range of subjects in and around the concept of ugliness and disgust (e.g., Torture Porn, Butoh and cinema).

Griselda Pollock is Professor of Social and Critical Histories of Art and Director of the Centre for Cultural Analysis, Theory and History at the University of Leeds. Known for her major feminist interventions in cultural theory and visual analysis and work on trauma, aesthetics and psychoanalysis she has written extensively in cultural studies and art history. Major recent publications include *Encounters in the Virtual Feminist Museum: Time, Space and the Archive* (2007), *Digital and Other Virtualities: Renegotiating the Image* (2010, with Anthony Bryant), *Bracha L Ettinger: Art as Compassion* (2011, edited with Catherine de Zegher), *After-affect / After-image: Trauma and Aesthetic Transformation*, (2013) *Concentrationary Cinema: Aesthetics as Resistance in Alain Resnais's Night and Fog* (2011 with Max Silverman) which won the Kraszna-Krausz Award for Best Book on the Moving Image 2011. Forthcoming are *From Trauma to Cultural Memory: Representation and the Holocaust* and *The Nameless Artist in the Theatre of Memory: Life, Death, Love and Loss in Charlotte Salomon's* Leben? Oder Theater? (1941–42).

Max Silverman is Professor of Modern French Studies at the University of Leeds. His most recent work is on post-Holocaust culture, colonial and postcolonial theory and cultures, and questions of memory, race and violence. He has just completed a book on connections between the Holocaust and colonialism in the French and Francophone cultural imaginary entitled *Palimpsestic Memory: The Holocaust and Colonialism in French and Francophone Fiction and Film* (2013). His co-edited book with Griselda Pollock *Concentrationary Cinema: Aesthetics as Political Resistance in Alain Resnais's 'Night and Fog'* was published in 2011 and won the Kraszna-Krausz Award for Best Book on the Moving Image 2011.

INDEX

Figures in italics indicate captions.

7/7 bombings (London, 7 July 2005) 204
9/11 attacks (2001) 49, 204
   and *La Femme Nikita* 228
   Ground Zero 47
   inadequate political vocabulary 47–48
   post 9/11 era 10–18, 109, 115, 118
   Twin Towers collapse, World Trade Center, New York 47, 48, 52, 228
   unilateral violence on defenceless people 48
   violent aftermath of 48, 52, 55
24 (crime drama) 228
Abu Ghraib prison, Baghdad, Iraq 109, 118, 228
adiaphora, imaginaries of 232
Adorno, Theodor xvi, 16, 188, 199
aesthetics
   critical use of 125
   fascist 23, 226
   and Nazism 124
   political xiii, xv, xvi, xix, 122–123
   of resistance 125, 127
Afghanistan 49, 78
AFRICOM 169
Agamben, Giorgio xvi, 7–8, 75, 137, 167, 168, 189, 193, 195, 199, 200, 201, 207
   Homo Sacer: Sovereign Power and Bare Life 206, 227
   operatives in *La Femme Nikita* resemble *homines sacri* 224–225
   The Remnants of Auschwitz 193–194
aggressivity 35, 36
Alianak, Hrant 228
alienation 33, 36, 37
'America's Global Military Presence: Mission Creep' (Michael Mechanic) 169
amnesia 19, 118, 130, 166, 172, 184, 185
   moral 229
Anders, Günther 231–232
   Die Antiquiertheit des Menschen 224
animals
   animal/machine opposition 24–25
   empathy for 25
   human/animal distinction 24
anti-Semitism 65, 66, 84, 85, 153, 158

Apartheid 17
Arab revolts 78
Arendt, Hannah xiv, xvi, 15–16, 18, 31, 74, 76, 78, 81, 166, 199, 200–201, 207
   analysis of evil xiii
   Arendtian notion of politics 64
   the game and the dream 39
   on the Hegelian notion of history 62–63
   the human condition 16, 19, 40, 52, 64
   the human as a creation of the political 16, 17
   human *qua* human rendered superfluous xvii–xviii, 5
   observes horror of the camps from refugee perspective 70–71
   the political and the historical 61–62
   on reports from the camps 68–69
   the role of imagination 69–70
   and storytelling 63, 64, 65
   and total terror 50, 51
   totalitarian ideology 84–85
   Eichmann in Jerusalem: an Essay on the Banality of Evil 27–28, 199
   The Human Condition 16, 41, 64–65
   On Humanity in Dark Times 66
   The Origins of Totalitarianism xiii–xiv, 6–7, 16, 50, 67–68, 83, 84, 95, 126, 193
   On Violence 16, 63–64
Aristotle 63
Armenian deportees 49
Aryan peoples 86
   the Aryan male subject position 154
   Jews seen as an obstructive anti-race 18
   and Mengele's medical experiments 103
   national fiction of the unified Aryan people 34
   and the Subject-State 85
Assassin, The/Point of No Return (film) 4, 204
asylum seekers 78
Auschwitz-Birkenau extermination and labour camp, Poland xiii, 10, 48, 52, 70, 71, 75, 188
   '*Arbeit Macht Frei*' gateway *174*, 175
   Bauman on 206
   football match 193–194
   gas chambers 126

Auschwitz-Birkenau extermination and labour camp, Poland (*cont.*)
  Jewish prisoners selected for concentration camps 126
  and Kantian formalist ethics 100
  Mengele's medical experiments 101
  racialized mass murder of European Jewry 10
  and *Schindler's List* 181, *181*
  Sonderkommando 110, 193
automatism 90

Badham, John 4, 204
Badminton, Neil 220
Bagram Air Base detention facility, Afghanistan 118
Baudrillard, Jean 189
Bauman, Zygmunt 199
  Modernity and the Holocaust 206
Bauman, Zygmunt and Donskis, Leonidas: *Moral Blindness: The Loss of Sensitivity in Liquid Modernity* 231, 232
Bellow, Saul 78
Bełżec extermination camp, Poland 10
Ben-Dor Niv, Oma 142
Benjamin, Walter 199
Bergen-Belsen concentration camp, near Hanover, Germany
  circulated images not representations of genocide 13–14
  liberation of 10, 11–12, 13, *215*
  unburied corpses in 28
Berger, Helmut 143
Berlin, Germany
  Olympic Games (1936) 1
  prostitutional night-life in Weimar Berlin 141
Berlusconi, Silvio 77
Besson, Luc 204
  see also Nikita
Bettelheim, Bruno 153
Big Brother (reality show) 194
bio-power 209, 219, 229
Black Cat (*Hei Mao*) (film) 204
Black Cat 2 (*Hei mao zhi ci sha Ye Li Qin*) (film) 204
Blade Runner (film) 24–31
Blue Angel, The (film) 140, 143
Bogarde, Dirk 122, *123*, 124, 142, 145, 213
Bolshevism, and erosion of the political 17
bombing
  aerial 87
  intelligent bombs 53–54
  London (7 July 2005) 204
  Madrid train (2004) 52–53
  napalm 49
  saturation 88
  suicide 54
Bosnia, NATO peacekeeping mission in 223
bourgeois
  law 194
  moralism 148, 149
  order 22, 136, 150, 158
  space 193, 194, 195
bourgeoisie, the, and human superfluity 18
Bourke-White, Margaret 175, *177*
Bousman, Darren Lynn 108
Boy in the Striped Pyjamas (film) 32

Boyne, John 32
Britain: occupation of Vienna 127
Browning, Christopher 199
Buchenwald concentration camp, Germany
  Bourke-White's photograph 175, *177*
  Ilse Koch's brutality 101–102
  liberation of 102
  Rousset as a survivor xiii, 3, 205
Bullock, Alan: *Hitler: A Study in Tyranny* 27
Bush, George W. 232
Butler, Judith: *Precarious Life* 53, 55

Caché (Hidden) (film) 116, 193
Cahiers du cinéma 187
Cambodian killing fields 49
camp space 195
Camus, Albert 78
  The Rebel 59
Canadian Fireworks 205
Canevari, Cesare 102
Cannibal Holocaust (film) 111
capitalism 18, 84, 85, 136, 148, 195, 201, 224
Cavani, Liliana *see Night Porter, The*
Cavarero, Adriana 28, 40–41, 207
  Horrorism: Naming Contemporary Violence 203
Cayrol, Jean xiii–xvi, xviii, 188, 198, 201
  Jean Cayrol: Œvre lazaréenne xviii–xix
  Lazare parmi nous xviii
  'Pour un romanesque lazaréen' (reprinted as 'De la vie à la mort') xviii
  'Les Rêves lazaréens' xviii
Céline, Louis-Ferdinand 65
Channel 4 television 12
Chelmno extermination camp, Poland 10
Chesterton, G.K. 65
Cheyette, Bryan 180, 181
chronopolitics 90
CIA (Central Intelligence Agency) 208
cinema
  Cavani breaks the rules 150–151
  critiquing imaginary relations to screen and image 125
  demise of 188
  fascist 1
  flashback technique 102, 122, 134, 138, 141, 144–147, *145*, *146*, 151, 152, 154, 155, *156*, 171, 173, *174*, *176*, 179, 182
  the Imaginary and the Symbolic in 36–37
  the imaginary signifier 127, 135, 159
  Italian 138, 147
  loss of critical potential 42, 43
  as a machine of the Imaginary 31, 38
  making visible the concentrationary 157
  the paradox of 'the imaginary signifier' 35
  passive viewing 38
  phallocentric 153
  rhetoric of 129
  semiotically produced meanings 35
  spectacle 35–36
Cixous, Hélène 219
Clouzot, Claire 150
Cochran, Robert 228
Cold War 95, 205
colonialism xv, 18, 24, 26, 116, 199

INDEX

communism 17
  Stalinist 67
concentration camps
  compared with death camps 14
  concentrationary origins xvii, 6, 30
  concentrationary system developed and run by SS 14, 15, 126, 134
  death toll in German camps 10
  experiment of total domination 6–7, 9, 40
  Final Solution not represented by 13–14
  human disposal *215*, 217
  iconic signifier of Nazi atrocity and its racialized genocide 11
  images of opened camps xiii, 10, 11–12, 13, 164
  juridico-political structure 7–8, 189, 193, 208
  Kapos (*Funktionshäftlinge*) 211
  the 'living dead' 15, 51–52, 69
  logic of 3, 134, 135, 137
  network in Germany 10, 11, 126, 127, 132
  as the new *nomos* of the modern 7, 137, 189
  perpetrators' behaviour on and off duty 39
  population of 10, 126
  prisoner life in 14–15
  prostitution in 141–142, 151
  reality in 73–74, 75
  reports from 68–69
  and space-time 14–15, 18, 40
  a system of terror 8, 12
  totalitarianism xvi
concentrationariness xviii
concentrationary
  beyond any confines 170
  continued presence of xix
  destruction of democracy 18–19
  and the exterminatory 14
  a feature of Stalin's Soviet Union 17
  and its founding imaginary 33
  four aspects of xv
  historical origins xvii, 6
  and the Imaginary 36
  logic of 17, 18
  normalizes war as the permanent condition 19
  not confined to the Third Reich 17
  persistence of 43, 127
  politico-aesthetic roots of 205
  in popular culture 39
  potential dissemination into popular culture 11
  resisting its seepage and normalization 19
  and total domination xiv, xv, 9
concentrationary art
  Cayrol's term xiii, xv, xviii, xix
  and normalization of the concentrationary universe xix
Concentrationary Art xiii, xviii
Concentrationary Cinema 125
'concentrationary disease' (*la peste concentrationnaire*) xv
concentrationary exterminatory complex 17, 29
Concentrationary Imaginaries xiii, xvi–xviii
concentrationary imaginary 2
  defined 31
  distorts responses to death and dying 6
  and the fascist imaginary 20–21
  Hannavy Cousen's work on 5–6
  identifiable primarily in the negative 5
  and popular culture xv, xvii–xviii, 30, 31, 124
  reinforced by the 'imperative of the Now' 76
  stock of images 32
  theorizing 137–138
  and Torture Porn 108
  and totalitarian mentality xv
concentrationary Imaginary 33, 38, 39–40, 159
concentrationary logic 42, 160, 213, 215, 220
Concentrationary Memories xiii, xv–xvi, 125
Concentrationary Memories and the Politics of Representation project xiii, 3–4
concentrationary memory xv, xvi, 127, 129, 130, 165, 170, 172, 184, 208
concentrationary social nexus 2, 5, 30
concentrationary system 23
  Arendt's retrospective analysis 15
  developed by the SS 14
  locations of 14
  Nazi-created 17
concentrationary universe
  accessibility in mediated form 208
  in *Blade Runner* 24–31
  boundaries of 169
  and the citational image 164
  continued threat of xv, xvi
  created under Nazism 159
  critiques of 200
  culturally analysed 127
  dehumanization in 137
  dying days of (1945) 13
  and images/ways of imagining 170
  and Levi's *The Drowned and the Saved* 71
  logic of 5
  in *The Night Porter* 124
  normalization of xix
  novels disclose horrors of 142
  a novelty of twentieth-century politics 127
  operative conditions 208
  political lessons of 19
  potential seepage into the cultural imaginary xvii, 5
  Rousset's term xiii, xv, 3, 84, 166, 205–206
  the time-space of death in life 14–20
  unimaginable character of 74
  vigilance of its ruses xix
  where 'everything is possible' 3, 5
  the work of survivor/witness to 41
concentrationnaire 2, 3–4
Conrad, Joseph 65
consciousness
  facts as products of consciousness 61
  and the mind's thinking process 63
  mobilizing 60
  of the other 3
  pure 2
  subjective 91
  synchronized 89, 93
  tempral flux of 93
convergence 42, 81, 87, 89–90, 91, 95–96
'Cooperative Security Locations' (lily pads) 169
counterterrorism 208
'counterterrorist' emergency laws 204
Coventry 49
Creed, Barbara 106

creep *see* seep and creep
Crownshaw, Richard 172, 173
cruelty 38, 42, 43, 102, 117, 190, 195, 196, 199, 201, 204, 212, 230
cultural identity 15
cultural imaginary 20
  and the banality of evil 189
  and camp structures 43, 202
  and the cinematic culture of spectacular violence 23
  the concentrationary in 7, 14, 19, 159
  and the Final Solution 11
  internalization of 194
  of modernity 24
  potential seepage of the concentrationary universe into xvii, 5
cultural resistance xvii
culture
  bourgeois 125
  cabaret 140
  capitalist 202
  cinematic xvii, 23
  contemporary 75–76, 189
  endemic fascism of post-war European culture 125, 131
  Homeric 77
  management 223
  militarization of 9
  Nazi kitsch in 131
  patriarchal 104, 106
  political culture of democracy 90
  popular *see* popular culture
  role of the Imaginary in 35
  Western 86, 87
Current TV 76
cyborgs 24, 25, 224

D-Day to Berlin (film) 175
Dachau concentration camp, Germany 3, 132
  Arbeit Macht Frei Gate 176
  building of 10, 174–175
  filmic evidence of the liberation 175
  liberation of 42, 174–179
  location 174
  and *Shutter Island* 163, 171, 175
Damned, The (film) 142–143
Daney, Serge 187, 188, 189, 199, 201
Darfur, Sudan 78
De-Lillo, Don 47
de-synchronization 42, 96
death
  aestheticization of 187
  culture of 22
  dehumanization of 30
  the extra-legal right to determine life and death 26–27
  glamourized by fascism 23
  and kitsch 21
death camps *see* extermination camps
defamiliarization xix
dehumanization 136, 142, 189, 210
  logic 6, 214, 229
  systematic 137
  vision of a desocialized world 7

Delbo, Charlotte 137
Deleuze, Gilles 149
democracy
  comfortable assurance in 86, 95
  destruction by the concentrationary 18–19
  the dream of 31
  inscription of totalitarian structures and logics in 207
  liberal 41, 94, 204, 228, 230
  political culture of 90
  threatened 42
  Western 207, 208, 224
Deodato, Ruggero 111
Dernier Combat, Le (film) 204
Derrida, Jacques 54
Descartes, René 60
DiCaprio, Leonardo 170
Dick, Philip K. 27–30
  Do Androids Dream of Electric Sheep? 27
  Man in the High Castle 27
Dietrich, Marlene 139, 140, 143
differentiation 93
dis-identification 36
disabled, the 10
'disappeared', the 15, 18, 228
disease
  the concentrationary disease xv, 201
  deaths 11, 13
  untreated 13, 17
divergence 42, 96
domestic space 194, 195
Donskis, Leonidas 231, 232
Dresden, Germany 49
Dupuis, Roy 221

East European war crimes 207
economy
  home 16
  instrumentalized 23
  New Economy 208, 230
  the realism of 76
  the rule of the 17
Edelstein, David: 'Now Playing at Your Local Multiplex: Torture Porn' 106
Edmonds, Don 103, 104, 106
ego, the 33, 34, 35, 36, 38, 138, 218, 224
  dyadic Imaginary ego (self/other) 37
  ego ideal 37
Eichmann, Adolf 128, 159, 199
Eichmann Trial (1961) 27
Eisler, Hanns xiv, 188
Elite Hunting (film) 109
empathy 25, 28, 29, 118, 194, 195, 214, 226
Enlightenment 24, 59, 100, 198, 199
enslavement 18, 23, 27, 100
Eretz Hadasha/Newland (film) 142
eroticism 147, 158
'everything is possible' 3, 5, 7, 18, 38, 51, 114, 130, 137, 144, 160, 166, 193, 206
evil
  absolute 50, 148
  Arendt's analysis of xiii, 40
  banality of 188, 189, 195, 199, 201, 232
  good versus evil 115

Ilsa as the epitome of evil 106
persistence of 189
radical 149
of totalitarianism xvi
Existentialism 2
exploitation film genre 101, 103
extermination camps
 death inflicted within hours of arrival 15
 destruction of (1943) 10
 experiment of total domination 6–7
 human disposal 217
 industrialized nature of the extermination process 101
 invisibility of 13, 14, 164, 182
 racialized mass murder 10, 136
 and *Saw II* 108
 short-lived death factories in Poland 10, 11, 126
 and space-time 14, 15

Fanon, Frantz 199
fascism 17, 20
 endemic fascism of post-war European culture 125, 131
 eroticization of 148
 'fascinating fascism' xvii, 6, 143
 fascist aesthetics 23
 fascist secret societies 42
 fetishization of 149
 German 84, 85, 200
 historicizing 149
 ideal of physical courage and victory of the strong over the weak 22–23
 imagery of 125, 126
 and the nature of representation 179
 Nazi 23, 126
 relationship with the bourgeois order and capitalism 136
 of representation 178–179
 representation of 178
 resistance to 148
 sexualization of 130, 148
 a unified Aryan people 34
 well-springs of 84
fascist cinema 1
fascist imaginary 21, 124, 125, 127, 131, 157
Father, the authority of 36, 37
female gaze, perversion of the 103–104
feminine space 219
feminism
 and the cyborg 25
 feminist film critics 125
 feminist film theory 104
 feminist theory 153, 219
 and *The Night Porter* 42, 152–153, 160
Femme Nikita, La (television series) 4
 and American intelligence agencies 208, 227
 central cynicism of 227, 230
 change in focus of 43, 205
 the concentrationary becomes ever more hermetic 229
 the concentrationary imaginary in visual citations 220–221
 conceptualized and realized in North America 207
 'cynical chic' 231
 large fan community 205, 231
 music in 230
 operatives in 220, 221, 224–230
 The Perch 223, *223*, 225
 post-9/11 imaginaries of violence 227–228
 Section One 205, 208, 221–228, *223*, 230
 terminology 230
 violence, cruelty and affectless killing as entertainment 43
 see also Nikita
Ferguson, Matthew 224
fetishism
 kitsch 143
 metanarrative 176
 narrative 172, 174
fetishizing gaze 225
fiction
 and Arendt 65, 66
 imaginative potentialities of 79
 and Levi 71, 73, 74
 literary 56, 66, 71
 storytelling 41
film noir 43
Final Solution
 Eichmann's role 199
 not represented by concentration camps 13–14
 proposed mass destruction of European Jews 10
Ford, Harrison 24
Foreman, Miloš 182
Fortress Europe 88
Foucauld, Charles de 189, 193, 209, 221
Fox Networks 228
France
 Nazi occupation of 3
 occupation of Vienna 127
Frankenstein 22
freedom
 economic 96
 human 62
 public 16
French Revolution 100
Freud, Sigmund 159
 Nachträglichkeit 143
 stages of psychic development 33
 the 'unconscious mind' 207
 'work of mourning' 174
Freudian phase 1
Friedländer, Saul: *Reflets du nazisme (Reflections of Nazism: An Essay on Kitsch and Death)* 20–22, 30, 157–158
functional integration 92–93, 94
Funny Games (film) 43, 115–118, 189–196, *191*, *192*
 complicity with violence 195–196
 deciding the fate of individuals 194–195
 domestic space transformed into sadistic space 194
 and game culture 43, 116, 190–193, 199
 Haneke aims to critique screen violence 192–193
 Kafka-esque slippage between camp brutality and the games format 191
 made in German, then remade in English 43, 115–116, 193
 synopsis 116, 189–190
future noir 24

game shows 190, 194, 195
gender difference 148
genocide 48
  Armenian 54
  and destruction of the political 7
  at the heart of Nazism's atrocities xiv
  industrial 2, 11
  racialized xiv, 9–12, 14
German dream 82–83, 87, 88, 89, 95
Germanic peoples 86
Germany, network of concentration camps in 10, 11, 126, 127, 132
Gestapo's Last Orgy, The (film) 102–103
Gilda (film) 138
Gilliam, Terry 164
Glazer, Eugene Robert 223, *223*
Godard, Jean-Luc 178, 180
good
  good versus evil 115, 118, 149
  good/bad 36
Gramsci, Antonio 221
grey zone 54, 74, 134, 142, 153, 193, 194
Grey Zone, The (film) 110
Guantánamo Bay prison, Cuba 109, 118
Guaraldo, Olivia 41, 42, 56
Guardian, the 47
Guattari, Félix 149
Guernica, Spain 49
guilt 116, 128, 130, 136, 143, 144, 145, 229
gulags xvi, xvii, 6, 14, 49

Hamburg, Germany 49
Handel, George Frideric 190
Haneke, Michael 43, 119
  gamesmanship motif 116
  and Pasolini's *Salò* 118
  politico-aesthetic approach to film 43, 197, 199, 201
  sadomasochistic themes 115
  work deals with the existence of violence in the world 115
  see also Caché; Funny Games; The White Ribbon
Hannavy Cousen, Benjamin 4, 5–6, 42
Haraway, Donna 24–25
Ha'Shoah (the destruction) 11
Hauer, Rutger 26
Hayward, Susan 204, 209–210, 220
Hayworth, Rita 138
Heartfield, John: *As in the Middle Ages. . . / . . . so in the Third Reich (Wie im Mittelalter. . . / . . . so im Dritten Reich)* 218, *218*
Hegel, Georg Wilhelm Friedrich
  and history 41, 60, 61, 62–63
  and politics 60
  and rationality 60
  and reality 60
  and Reason 60
  and thinking 60, 61, 62
  Versöhnung 62
  Phenomenology of Spirit 62
Hegelian theories of history 41, 61
Herman, Mark 32
Hiroshima, Japan 49, 54
Histoire(s) du Cinéma (film) 178

historiography xiv, 62, 64, 71–72, 73
history
  cinematic 110
  elimination of decadent classes 67
  fictionalization of 73
  and Hegel 41, 60, 61, 62–63
  notion of history as a process 63
  philosophy of 61, 62, 63, 64, 67
  the Real defined as 37, 39
  spatialization of 199
  supra-political force of 18
  totalizing theory of (Communism) 41, 67
Hitler, Adolf 128, 149, 159
  ambition for Jewish Europe 27
  defeat of his fascist regime 126
  and Riefenstahl 22
Holländer, Friedrich: 'Wenn ich mir was wünschen dürfte' 138–140, *140*, 143
Hollweg, Brenda 4, 43
Holocaust 199
  commemoration xiv
  defined 17, 201
  films 115, 118, 119
  historiography xiv l
  iconography of 116
  images used from German concentration camps 10
  memorialization of 157
  and *The Night Porter* 135–136, 155
  style of writing on 71
  term covers every terror and horror of the Third Reich 9–10
  testimonial works on xv
  and Torture Porn 106, 107, 108, 115, 118
  an umbrella concept 136
'Holocaust Piety' 178, 179
homoeroticism 147
homogenization 81, 83, 87, 89, 90, 91, 93, 94, 96
homophobia 158
Horkheimer, Max 16
horror
  aestheticization of 188
  derivation of the word 50
  and the everyday 189, 190, 191, 195, 199, 200
  Medusa as classical icon of horror 54
  persistence of 188, 201
  poetizing 71
  prevails over terror 50
  real 193
horror film genre 101, 108
horrorism 40–41, 48, 50, 52, 53, 55
Hostel (film) 109–110, 111, 113, *114*, 115
Hostel: Part II (film) 110, 111
human condition 41, 52, 64, 203
  and Arendt 16, 19, 40, 52, 64
  assault on 7, 40
  a constitutive and shared human condition 53
  vulnerability 50, 53, 54
human rights violations 208, 228
humanity
  being groomed to accept a profound compromise of the human 31
  degradation of the human as human 54
  destruction of xiv, 3, 14, 15, 16, 126, 213, 219–220

discourse on 229
as expendable 17, 224
human/animal distinction 24
human/machine distinction 24
juridico-political assault on the human 201
'natural' development of 67
political 16, 17
secret experimentation on bodies 19
social 206
structures of 194
superfluous xvii–xviii, 5, 16, 18, 23, 50, 51, 52, 67, 68, 78, 232
violence against the helpless 40–41, 48, 49–50
Hurbinek 56
Huyssen, Andreas 184
hyperterrorism 47

identification xvii, 26, 32, 33
  and cinema 36
  distorting 11
  process of 34
  and rejection 35, 36
  specular xviii
  structures 23–24
  taking on/taking in 35
identity
  cultural 15
  disintegration of 210
  Jewish 151
  structure of 8
  sure 182
Ilsa: She Wolf of the SS (film) 103–105, *104*
imagery
  associations of 20
  of the concentration camp 99
  etymological 56
  fascist 124, 125, 126
  of Nazism 125
  referential 183
images
  of abject suffering 14
  amnesiac 6, 163–164, 166, 171–172, 175, 179–184
  the banality of evil and electronic images 188, 201
  citational 6, 163–166, 174, 175
  and the concentrationary universe 10, 32
  digitalized 189
  fascist 124
  indexical 6, 163, 164, 166
  lack of images of death camps 13, 14
  mythic signifiers 31
  narratively fetishized 185
  of opened concentration camps xiii, 10, 11–12, 13
  power of 20, 195
  repertoire of xvii
  and a second coming of Nazism 21
  and the totalitarian mind-set xvii
imaginarium 33, 164
Imaginarium of Doctor Parnassus, The (film) 164
imaginary
  cinematic 153, 160, 169
  concentrationary *see* concentrationary imaginary
  cultural *see* cultural imaginary
  fascist 124, 125, 127, 131, 157
  as a feminine space 219

gendered 149
  use of the term in the cultural field xvii
  of violence 189, 220
Imaginary (Lacan concept) 2, 4, 164
  binary structure 36, 37
  cinema as a machine of 31, 38
  classic articulation of 1
  and the concentrationary 36
  defined 33
  an image-based mode 33
  the imaginary space of the Imaginary at play 39
  Jameson's exploration of 137–138
  role in culture 35
  safe from History 37
  specularity 26
  and the Symbolic 34, 37
imaginary conflation 9–14
imaginary signifier 127, 134–135, 159
imagination 30, 33
  the art of the imagination 79
  creative 41
  human need for 70
  ideological 82
  lack of 77, 78
  past and present 21
  political 64
  the republic of the imagination 79
  role of 69–70
  virtual work of the concentrationary in 6
imago 34, 35, 36, 38
imperialism xiii, 18, 65, 84, 85, 167
individuality 210, 219, 229
individuation 8, 92, 93, 94
Inglourious Basterds (film) 111
inhumanity 106, 188, 194, 223, 227
Insdorf, Annette 135–136
intelligibility 47, 48, 49, 54
International Journal of Psychoanalysis 1
International Psychoanalytical Association (IPA)
  Fourteenth International Congress (Marienbad (Mariánské Lázne), 1936) 1
  Sixteenth International Congress (Zurich, 1949)
internet, democratizing power of 94
introjection 36
Iraq 78
Irigaray, Luce 219
Islamic extremism 207
Italy
  German invasion and occupation 132
  resistance 132
Itard, Jean 24
ITC Entertainment 205

James, Ian 9, 41–42
Jameson, Fredric 6, 24, 35, 36, 37, 39, 137–138, 230
Japan 27
Jews
  and Aryans 17
  attempted annihilation of xiv, 10, 126, 201
  death statistics 49
  deaths in ghettos 11, 49
  killed during invasion of Soviet territories (1941) 10–11
  perception of 35

Jews (*cont.*)
  pogrom against German Jews (1938) 126
  power of 35
  sites of racialized mass murder of European Jewry 10
  transferred from Auschwitz to other camps 126–127
jihad terrorism 47
Jones, Ernest 1
jouissance 37, 219

Ka-Tsetnik 135633 (nom de plum of Yehiel Denur) 142
Kadavergehorsam ('obedience of corpses') 219
Kant, Immanuel 60, 100
Kapò (film) 32, 125, 151, 187, 199, 218, *219*
Kapos (*Funktionshäftlinge*) 211–212, *212*
Karas, Anton 127
Karyo, Tchéky 210
Kerner, Aaron 42
Kingsley, Ben 170
Kipling, Rudyard 65
  Jungle Book 24
kitsch
  and death 21, 30
  fascist 19
  Nazi 130, 131, 147–150, 160
Kleinian position 1
Koch, Ilse 101–102, 103, 105–106
Koch, Karl Otto 101, 102
Kosminsky, Peter: *The Promise* 12–13
Kristeva, Julia 219

Lacan, Jacques 21, 40
  concentrationary social nexus 2, 3
  formation of subjectivity 26
  model of three registers on which subjectivity operates 33
  society of total utility 17
  and 'subjective impasses' 2, 3
  'The Looking-Glass Phase' 1
  'Le Stade du miroir' ('The Mirror Phase') 1–2, 4, 33, 34, 35, 137, 138
  see also Imaginary
Lacoue-Labarthe, Philippe 41, 81, 84–87, 91, 93, 94, 95, 96
Lagers 50, 51, 52, 54, 56, 64
  conceptualizing the inexplicable nestled in horror 52
  core of the totalitarian experiment 64
  evil in 50
  experimentation of a new kind of living being 68
  Konzentrationslager (KZ) 142
  looking at the face of the Gorgon 54
  manipulation of human nature 51
  the need to convey a meaning for the *Lager* experience 75
  repression and killing of superfluous people 68
  unimaginable reality of 56, 69
Lampedusa, boat-people in 78
Lane, Anthony 118
Lang, Fritz 24
Lanzmann, Claude 10, 153, 180
Laplanche, Jean 143

Latin America
  the concentrationary in 17
  'disappeared' people in 228
Lazarean art xix
Lebensraum 88, 167
Leibniz, Gottfried Wilhelm von 59
Levi, Primo 41, 52, 56, 70, 70–75, 77
  direct experience of the concentrationary reality 71
  the grey zone 54, 74, 134, 142, 153, 193, 194
  on Hurbinek 56
  inability to be a historian 72–73
  prose style 72
  scientific background 71, 72
  uses of fiction in his literary work 71, 73, 74
  writing torn between realism and imagination 75
  I sommersi e i salvati (*The Drowned and the Saved*) 54, 71, 193
Levinas, Emmanuel 55
libertines 100, 107, 115
Lisbon earthquake (1755) 59
Łódź ghetto, Poland 74
Lord of the Rings (film) 23
Lyotard, Jean-François 180

machine
  animal/machine opposition 24–25
  culture of the machine and war 22
  economic 3
Madrid train bombings (2004) 52–53
Majdanek extermination camp, Poland 10, 126
male castration anxiety 225
malnutrition 13, 17, 175
Manichean
  features 137
  roles 148
  scenario 38
  worldview 36, 115, 118
Mann der seinen Mörder sucht, Der (film) 139
Marathon Man (film) 111–113, *114*
Marker, Chris 188
Marxism 20, 22
masculinity
  phallic 136
  and women's sexuality 149
Mauthausen-Gusen concentration camp, Austria xiv, xviii, 10
medical experimentation 101, 103, 126, 205
Medusa the Gorgon 50, 54
memory
  concentrationary xv, xvi, 127, 129, 130, 165, 170, 172, 184, 208
  cultural 14, 20, 92, 172, 173, 208–209
  Holocaust xiv
  industrialized synthesis of 92
  materials of 172
  and persistence of totalitarianism 125
  politics of cultural memory 14
  representation of 175
  unreliability of 197
Memory of the Camps (film) 175
Mengele, Josef 101, 103, 111, 113, 166
Menwith Hill, North Yorkshire 169
Metropolis (film) 24

Metz, Christian 135
Miike, Takashi 110–111
Miller, Lee 175
mirror phase (Lacan) 1–2, 4, 33, 34, 35, 137, 138
misogyny 152–153, 155, 158
misrecognition xvii, 35
mission creep 168–169
modernity 7, 22, 24
  and the camp 206
  cultural 18
  economic 18
  political 18
Monowitz-Auschwitz concentration camp, Poland 54
Morante, Elsa: *History* 56–57
Mozart, Wolfgang Amadeus 159
  The Magic Flute 122, 150, 154, 155, 160
Muriel, ou le temps d'un retour (film) xviii
Muselmann condition 15
Mussolini, Benito 126, 132, 149

'Nacht und Nebel' ('Night and Fog') 15
Nachträglichkeit 143
Nafisi, Azar 70, 78–79
Nagasaki 49, 54
Naked City 190
Nancy, Jean-Luc 41, 81, 83–84, 93–96
  The Inoperative Community 95
Nancy, Jean-Luc and Lacoue-Labarthe, Philippe:
  The Nazi Myth (originally *Le Mythe nazi*) 84–87, 91, 95
napalm bombing 49
narcissism 35, 36
nation-state xiv, 221
NATO 223
Nature
  cyclical process of 63
  extermination of unfit races 67
  supra-political force of 18
  totalizing theory of (Nazism) 41, 66
Nazi chic 135
Nazi Germany 27
  and the concentrationary disease xv
  ideological imagination of 82
  search for total domination xiv
Naziploitation 101–106
Nazism 42
  biological purity laws 67
  bureaucratic regulation and extermination of concentrationees 227
  cinematic reflections of 22
  concentrationary universe created under 159
  defeat of 130
  denial of humanity by Nazi machine 38
  diabolic intention of 69
  and erosion of the political 17
  euphemistic language of destruction 230
  fantasmatic 157
  fascism 23, 126
  and good versus evil 118
  imagery of 125
  imaginary re-appearance of Nazism 'as a free game of phantasms' 20
  indictment of 10
  inner logic of 84
  insignia of 143
  misrepresentation of concentration camp and Jewish experience 11
  mythology 86–87
  the Nazi gaze 104
  Nazi kitsch 130, 131, 147–150, 160
  Nazi porn 130
  Nazi power 21
  and *The Night Porter* 123–124
  occupation of France 3
  patriarchal repression of women and 'non-Aryans' 154
  persecution of political enemies (1933) 126
  plundering of loot collected from deportees 110
  pursuit of 'Total War' 83
  racially-targeted genocide xiv
  racism 126
  resurgence as exploitation and entertainment 42
  revocation of 158
  Riefenstahl's Nazi-commissioned films 22
  spectacularization of its emblems and aesthetic 158
  the symbol of evil 20, 157
Nelson, Tim Blake 110
neoliberal capitalism 17
neorealism 148, 151
Neue-Bremm concentration camp, near Saarbrücken, Germany 190–191
New Economy 208, 230
New Objectivity 141
New York magazine 106
Newman, Kim 109
Night and Fog (*Nuit et brouillard*) (film) 125, 200, 201, 202, 205, *212*, *217*
  Cayrol's narrated script xviii, 198
  a commemorative study of the experience of political deportation xiv 51
  'the concentrationary disease' xv
  and *Kapò* 187–188
Night Porter, The (*Il Portiere di Notte*) (film) 121 160
  Cavani's approach to the film 132, *133*, 134–135
  Cavani's purpose in the film 130
  emergence of the concentrationary Imaginary 159
  fascist or concentrationary imaginary 124–127
  final scene 121–124, *122*, *123*, 128
  focus of 213
  interlude on space 150–154
  Nazi kitsch 147–150
  political aesthetics of 122–123, 136
  reception of 135–137
  and resurgence of Nazism as exploitation and entertainment 42
  Scene II: The Camp Cabaret Scene 138–147, *140*, *145*, *146*
  Scene III: *The Magic Flute* 154–155, *156*
  theorizing a concentrationary imaginary 137–138
  Vienna, 1957 127–131, *128*
Nikita (film)
  The Centre 203, 205, 208–211, *211*, *212*, 213, 214, 215, *217*, 219, 221
  cruelty and terror in 204
  disposal of bodies 214–215, *216*, *217*, *217*
  ending of 220

Nikita (film) (*cont.*)
  French youths' identification with 204
  and Kapos in 211–212
  reincarnations of *Nikita* material 4, 43, 204–205
  restaurant and kitchen sequence 213–214
  social control in 209–210
  synopsis 203
  television adaptation (2010) 204–205
  see also La Femme Nikita
non-identification 35
Nordic peoples 86
Now, the 76, 78
Nuba people (Sudan) 22

Occupied Zones 15
Oedipal moment 36
Oedipal triad 37
oikos 16
Olympiad (film) 1
One, the
  the embodying leader 32
  the Führer 34
  ideal 35
One Flew Over the Cuckoo's Nest (film) 182
Operation Reinhard 10
other, the 33, 222
  the black 'other' 26
  and self 36, 231
  the specular other 38
otherness 37, 38, 152, 179
overwork 15, 17, 126

paedophilia 142, 145
Parillaud, Anne 204, 213
Paris, Daniele 127–128
Paris, France: reception of *The Night Porter* 135
Parker, Sir Alan 171
Pasolini, Pier Paolo 115, 118, 136, 138, 148–149
patriarchalism 131
patriarchy: the cyborg as anti-patriarchal allegy 25
Pavlov's dog 68
Pentagon, Arlington County, Virginia 169
Petit, Philippe 90
phallocentrism 153
phantasy
  in *Night Porter* 143, 146, 147, 158, 159
  omnipotent 38
  phantasy world of the imaginary 159
  polarizing 36
  psychoanalytical notion of 124
Picasso, Pablo: *Guernica* 173
Pink Floyd: The Wall (film) 171
plurality 17, 18, 19, 41, 42, 64
pogroms 48, 126
Point of No Return (aka *The Assassin*) (film) 4, 204
Pol Pot 49
Poland, death camps in 10, 126
polis 16–17, 64, 89
political, the
  anti-political project 7
  erosion of 17, 19
  the human as a creation of the political 16, 17

political aesthetics xiii, xv, xvi, xix
  of *The Night Porter* 122–123, 136
political community, destruction of 6–7
political culture 3, 90
politics
  aesthetic 138
  Arendtian notion of 64
  calculated management of 89
  of cultural memory 14
  fascist 34
  gender 4
  and Hegel 60
  of interrogative resistance to the concentrationary 29
  linguistic reaction to the 9/11 catastrophe 47–48
  neutralization of 61
  of representation 19, 39
  of total domination 14
Pollock, Griselda 114, 165, 167, 170, 188, 205–206
Pontecorvo, Gillo 220
  see also Kapò
Pope, Alexander: 'Whatever is, is right' (in *An Essay on Man*) 59–60, 61, 63, 76
popular culture
  and the concentrationary imaginary xv, xvii–xviii, 30, 31, 124, 188
  concentrationary in xvi, 39
  identification with products of 204
  Imaginary fantasies in 40
  and inhumanity 194
  the logic of 194
  potential dissemination of the concentrationary into 11
  real violence hidden by 195
  rendering of fascism and Nazism as sublime 148
  and totalitarian mentality xv
pornography
  Nazi 130
  pornographic film genre 101
power
  absolute 8, 142, 146, 158
  aspiration for 22, 29, 50
  bio-political 193
  concentrationary represents an experiment in enactment of total power 14
  in the concentrationary universe 138
  democratizing 94
  disciplinary 193, 230
  Gramscian logic of 221
  of images 20, 195
  imaginative 74
  of Jews 35
  military 83
  Nazi 21
  phallic 104
  politically ordained 19
  punitive 8
  sadistic 101, 103
  state 83, 84, 85
  terror functioning as a space-time of a new kind of power 6
  totalitarian 88, 94, 200–201
Prisoner, The (British TV programme) 205
projection 36

Proust, Marcel 65
purity 32, 147, 149, 197
    laws of biological purity 67
    of the 'race' 66

Q, Maggie (Margaret Denise Quigley) 204

racialization 32
racism xiv, 24, 26, 34, 35, 78, 134
    genocidal 126
    Nazi 126
Rampling, Charlotte 122, *123*, 124, 138, 142, 147, 153, 213
Rancière, Jacques 211–212
rapid decompression 103
rationality 60, 61, 62, 85, 224, 227, 228
    of the spirit 62
Ravensbrück concentration camp, Germany 3, 10
Ravetto, Kriss 151
    The Unmaking of Fascist Aesthetics 138, 147–149
Real, the 33, 124, 131
    defined as History 37, 39
realism
    abandoning 79
    both scientific and trivial 76–77
    governs our present 76
    and racism 78
    the reality of so-called 'realism' 76–77
    tyranny of 77–78
reality
    in the camps 73–74, 75
    concentrationary 68, 71
    current obsession for 75
    and Hegel 60
    historical 147, 209
    of the past 21
    phenomenological 151
    political 5, 20, 194
    public 16
    a radically altered xix
    and reason 60
    spectacularization of 76
    and the Symbolic 39
    theological definition of 24
    and thinking 61, 62
    of total domination xiv
    total reliance on 77
reality shows 41, 75–78, 190, 194, 195
Reason
    enlightenment insistence on its autonomy 100
    and reality 60
    the sadist as enslaved to reason 100
    Spirit of 62
Red Army 10, 127
Red Woman image 149
Reed, Carol 127
Reign of Terror 100
rejection, and identification 35, 36
religious dissidents 10
religious persecution 134
Resnais, Alain xiv, xv, xvi, xviii, 125, 187–188, 198, 200, 201, 205
Revue française de psychoanalyse 4 1
Rice Burroughs, Edgar: *Tarzan* 24

Riefenstahl, Leni 1, 22–23
rights
    deprived of 224
    disregard of human rights 230
    human rights violations 208, 228
    the right to have rights 16
    women's 105
Rigney, Ann 172
Riva, Emmanuelle 187, 218
Rivette, Jacques 188
    'De l'abjection' ('On abjection') 187
robotics 24
Roma, città aperta (*Rome, Open City*) 114, *114*
Romanies (Roma)
    attempted annihilation of xiv, 126
    deaths in ghettos 11
    killed during invasion of Soviet territories (1941) 10–11
Romanticism, and human superfluity 18
Rose, Gillian 178–181, 183
Rossellini, Roberto 114, *114*
Roth, Eli 109, 110, 111, *114*
Rousset, David xiv, 6, 69, 190–191
    and the 'concentrationary universe' xiii, xv, 166, 190, 200, 201
    'everything is possible' remark 3, 5, 114, 193
    a survivor of Buchenwald xiii, 3, 205
    L'Univers concentrationnaire 3, 84, 205–206
Ruffalo, Mark 170
Rumkowski, Chaim 74

Sade, Marquis de 100, 107
sadism 42
    clinical 116
    in the concentrationary universe 138
    defined 99–100
    fetishistic visions of 101
sadistic space 194
sadomasochism
    in Haneke's work 115
    in *The Night Porter* 145, *145*, *146*, 153, 159, 213
Salò, or the 120 Days of Sodom (film) 115, 118, 136
Salomé 143, 144, 146
Santner, Eric 174
Sartre, Jean-Paul xvi
Saw (film) 108, 109
Saw II (film) 108
Saw III (film) 108
Saxton, Libby 180
Scarry, Elaine 113
Schindler's List (film) 99, 179–181, *181*, 182, 183
Schlesinger, John 111, *114*
science fiction 5, 19, 24, 27, 30–31
Scorsese, Martin *see Shutter Island*
Scott, Ridley 24, 27, 29
seep and creep 163–185
    'creep' as an 'extension' of an originary remit 168
    'creeping' as an active principle 167
    defined 6, 166
    insidiousness of seeping 167
    mission creep 168–169
    operation of creep 42
    'seeping' as a passive principle 167
    and the three orders of the image 166

seep and creep (*cont.*)
   trauma, creep, seep and amnesia 171–185
   Weber on seepage 167–168
seepage 43, 131, 137
   between the fascist imaginary and bourgeois culture 125
   defined 130
   resisting the concentrationary's continuing seepage 19
   of a totalitarian mentality into popular culture 15
   see also seep and creep
self, the
   'image of a self' 33
   imaginary unified self 34
   negation of the human relation to the self 8
   and other 36, 231
Seven Beauties (film) 153
sexploitation films 42
sexual difference 36, 131, 149
   phallocentric ordering of 136
sexual perversity 42
sexuality 132
   feminine 104, 149, 151
   persecution for 134
   prostitutional 145
   threat of 149
sexualization 145
   of fascism 130, 148
sexually diverse people 10
Sheridan, Alan 2
Shin, Stephen 204
Shirer, William L.: *Rise and Fall of the Third Reich* 26
Shoah (film) 10
Shoaib, Samia 228
Shutter Island (film) 6, 42, 163–185
   concentrationary seep and concentrationary creep 166–170
   the ordering of the image 163–166
   shower scene in 181–182, *182*
   synopsis 170–171
Sight and Sound Top Ten Poll (2002) 118
Silverman, Kaja 26, 152
Silverman, Max 3, 42–43, 116, 165, 167, 170, 205–206
singularization 42, 93, 96
Slasher films 106, 107
slave labour camps 126, 127
Sobibor extermination camp, Poland 10
sociality
   of human life 17
   political 40
   reconfigured in the negative 8
socially undesirable people 10
society/societies
   the camp and war as matrices of post-war society xvi, 9
   capitalist 137
   civil society 72
   classless society 67
   consumer 76, 94
   democratic 194, 224, 228
   domination by utilitarian purposes 2, 17
   hyper-industrial 92–93
   modern 2, 22, 193, 195
   racist 17

socialist 137
technological 81, 94
total mobilization of 83
totalitarian 14, 17, 206
Western affluent 77
Sofsky, Wolfgang 14–15
   The Order of Terror 8–9
Sonderkommando 74, 110, 193
Sontag, Susan 131
   'fascinating fascism' xvii, 6, 143, 226
   on Riefenstahl 22–23
South Africa: Apartheid 17
Soviet Union
   collapse of 228
   the concentrationary as a feature of Stalin's Soviet Union 17
   occupation of Vienna 127
   search for total domination xiv
space-time 39
   and concentration camps 14–15, 40
   terror as a space-time of a new kind of power 6
Spielberg, Steven 99, 180, 183
Spivak, Gayatri Chakravorty 220, 231
spontaneity 7, 17, 18, 19, 41, 42, 64, 68, 210, 219, 229
SS (*Schutzstaffel*)
   abandonment of prisoners to starvation and disease 13
   concentrationary system developed and run by 14, 15, 126, 134
   extermination camp secrets preserved 13
   horrific acts in the form of games and sport 190–191
   indictment of 10
   and Kapos 211
   tattoos 110
   uniform 147
Stalingrad, Russia, German defeat in (2 February 1943) 10
Stalinism xv, 67
Star Wars (film) 23
starvation 11, 13, 15, 126
Stevens, George 171, 175
   A Cattle Truck with Corpses at Dachau Concentration Camp, 2 May 1945 210
Stiegler, Bernard 41, 81–82, 92–96, 189
storytelling
   versus the philosophy of history 63–66
   vital and political role of 41
student movements (1960s) 63, 149
Subject-State 85, 87
subjectivity xvii, 24, 90, 96
   conditioned as structure reflex reaction 91
   formation of 124
   a homogenization and monolithic becoming of 96
   and the imaginary 127
   in *Nikita* 210, 211, 214
   production of 26, 31, 33, 92, 124
   properly democratic 90
   a singular plural becoming of 96
Subway (film) 204
suicidal resistance 231
Sunshine (film) 108
super-ego 134
Surnow, Joel 226, 227, 228, 232
Survivor (reality show) 76

survivors' literature 72
swastika 84, 218
Syberberg, Hans-Jürgen: *Hitler: A Film from Germany* 158
Sykes, Sgt. H. *215*
Symbolic, the
  defined 33
  defined as Thought 37
  and the Imaginary 34, 37
  and Reality 39
  rule of Law represented by 37
  triangulated system 37
Symbolic Law 134
synchronization 42, 81, 87, 89–96
Szabó, István 108

Takacs, Stacy 223–224, 230
Taminiaux, Jacques 62
Tarantino, Quentin 111
Tebaldi, Renata 190
technophobia 24
television
  and cinema 188
  as a cinematic derivative 36
terror
  the camp as a system of terror 8, 12
  functioning as a space-time of a new kind of power 6
  horror prevails over 50
  the order of 8–9, 23
  political xiv, 50–51, 206
  reading the terror in our midst xix
  state 18
  total 50, 52, 126
  totalitarian xiv, 51, 213
terrorism 47, 208, 231
Theweleit, Klaus 149
thinking
  dialectical 60
  and Hegel 60, 61
  historical 130
  mobilizing 60
  radical 149
  and reality 61, 62
Third Man, The (film) 127
Third Reich 206
  Berlin Olympic Games 1
  bunker fortifications 82
  concentrationary not confined to 17
  fall of xv, 2, 95
  Jews seen as an anti-race 18
  racialized genocide 9
  spatial imaginary of 88
  Subject-State 87
  as a suicidal regime 95
  and the term Holocaust 9–10
  Total State 86
  totalitarian expansionism 89
thoughtlessness 19, 40, 180
time
  a boundaried time 160
  dead 42
  the tyranny of real time 90
Tocqueville, Alexis de 62
Torres, Gina 231

torture 48, 136
  of Abu Ghraib prisoners 228
  consistent 17
  'enhanced interrogation techniques' 228
  and erosion of the human condition 15
  in *La Femma Nikita* 225, *225*, 227, 228, 231
  in *Funny Games* 189, 190, *191*, 192
  German concentration camps as locations of 132
  increase in cultural representation of 38
  the sadistic space of the torture chamber 194
  in *The White Ribbon* 195, 196
Torture Porn genre 42, 100, 106–115, *114*, 118
total domination 166, 201, 206
  becoming accustomed to situations of 23
  and the concentrationary xiv, xv, 9
  and destruction of the human *qua* human 126
  evacuation of the conditions of the political 15–16
  historical and other conditions for 18
  totalitarianism 17
Total Peace 88
Total War 49, 83, 87, 88
totalitarian ideology 84–85
totalitarian logic(s) 81, 85, 95, 130, 230, 231
totalitarian militarism 9
totalitarian mind-set xvii, 5
totalitarianism xiv, xvi, 17, 20, 63, 65
  the ambition to exercise total domination 17
  deadening experiences of 63, 64
  history of 65
  inhabiting war 9
  a method of government based on 'the law of movement' 66–67
  not inevitable 18
  persistence of 125
  seepage into popular culture 15
  spectres of 75
totality 81, 82–87, 95–96
  homogenous 93
  as a hypothesis 61
  and reality 60, 70
totalization 42, 81, 87, 88, 93, 95, 96
trauma 116, 132, 134, 180
  and amnesia 130
  of the Lisbon earthquake 59
  tropes of 173, 178
  'unknowable' character of 171
Treblinka extermination camp, Poland 10
Trinh T. Minh-ha 118

unconscious
  apolitical 6
  cultural xvii
  political 6, 39, 224
'unconscious mind' 207
United States
  occupation of Vienna 127
  reception of *The Night Porter* 135
University of Leeds 167
unpredictability 62
urbanism 24
US Army 102
  Field Manual 3-07: *Stability Operations and Support Operations* 168–169
US Thunderbird Division: 3rd Battalion, 157th Infantry Regiment 174

USA Network 205

victimization 148, 214
Victor of Aveyron 24
video games 5
    and camp logic 137
    choices without consequence or responsibility 38
    as a cinematic derivative 36
    interactive viewing 38
    played precisely as a space 48
    and Torture Porn 108, 109
Vidor, Charles 138
Vienna 159
    Allied occupation of 127
    Hotel zür Oper (Hotel beside the Opera) 127, *128*
Vietnam War (1955–75) 49
Villa, Dana 16, 18
violence
    accustoming to xvii
    against the helpless 40–41, 48, 49–50
    arbitrary 17
    audiovisual imaginaries of 205
    celebrating 32
    cinematic culture of spectacular violence xvii, 5, 23
    commercialization of 188–189
    complicity with 195–196
    creative 37
    an ecstatic masculinist vision of 22
    gratuitous 195
    historical 118
    imaginary of 189
    increase in cultural representation of 38
    normalization of 43
    political presentation of xvii, 23
    popular imaginaries of 220
    real 189, 192, 195
    spectacularization of 188–189
    statistics of twentieth-century deaths in acts of mass violence 49
Virilio, Paul xvi, 9, 41, 81–82, 84, 94, 95, 96, 189
    chronopolitics 90
    and the new media 88–89
    and the polis 89
    tyranny of real time 90, 91, 92
    Bunker Archeology 82–83, 87–88, 95
    City of Panic (Ville panique) 91
    Popular Defence and Ecological Struggles 88
Visconti, Luchino 142, 143
Voltaire: *Candide* 59
voyeurism 3, 118, 178, 226
vulnerability 218
    empathy for 28
    etymology 55–56
    the human condition 50, 53, 54
    physical 229
    vulnerable civilians as defenceless victims 49

Waffen-SS 110
Waller, Marguerite 152–153, 154–155
Wan, James 108

Wansee Conference (20 January 1942) 10
war
    East European war crimes 207
    a matrix of contemporary society 9
    as the norm in medical culture 5
    normalized by the concentrationary as the permanent condition 18
    preventive 48
    Total War 83, 87, 88
    total war model 49
    totalitarianism in 9
    war crime trials 32
    War Office Second World War Official Collection No.5 Army and Photographic Unit: 'Disposal: two former guards placing corpses in a mass grave' from *The Liberation of Bergen-Belsen Concentration Camp, April 1945 215*
war on terror 48, 204
Warner Brothers 204
Warner Brothers Television 205
warrior, the 48–49, 53, 55, 56
waterboarding 118
Watson, Alberta 225
weapons of mass destruction 54
Weber, Samuel 167
Weiss, Peter 13
    Die Ästhetik des Widerstands (The Aesthetic of Resistance) 11
    Die Ermittlung (The Investigation) 11
    Der Fluchtpunkt (The Vanishing Point) 11
Wertmüller, Lina 148–149
White, Hayden 71, 72–73
White Ribbon, The (film) 43, 118, *197, 198*
    authoritarian order of traditional society in 199
    blurring of horror and the everyday 195
    complicity between a camp culture and 'normal' society 195
    complicity with violence 196
    disorder of random cruelty in 199
    the final image in the film 198–199
    Haneke on 200
    opening of 200
    the unreliable narrator 197, 198
White, Rosie 227, 230
Wilson, Peta 221, *222*
women
    fascist treatment of 22–23
    patriarchal repression of 154
Women's Liberation movement 104, 105
World War I (1914–18) 198, 200
    refugees 78
    total war model 49
World War II (1939–45) 2
    bunker fortifications 82–83, 88–89, 91, 95
    civilians as a majority of victims 49

Yugoslavia, NATO peacekeeping mission in 223

Zevi, Luca 75
Žižek, Slavoj 100
Zola, Émile 65
Zorn, John 190